PENGUIN BOOKS

OUT WEST

Born and raised in a small town in Iowa, Dayton
Duncan moved "Back East" to earn a B.A. from the
University of Pennsylvania, and then settled in New
Hampshire. He has been a reporter, humor columnist,
editorial writer, chief of staff to a governor of New
Hampshire, and deputy press secretary for a presiden-
tial campaign.

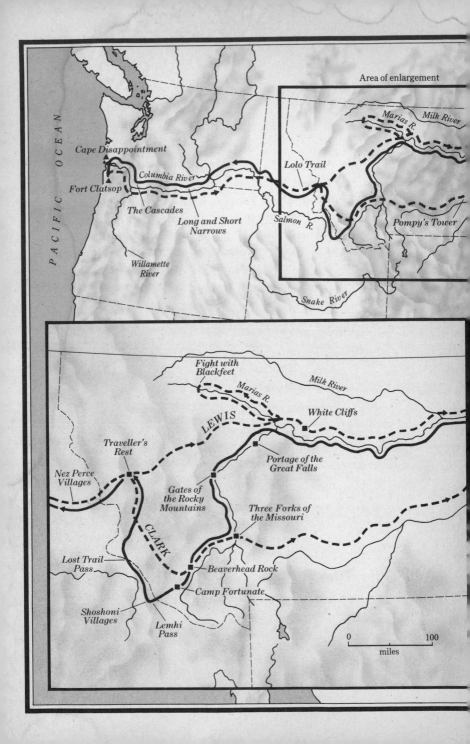

Area of enlargement

PACIFIC OCEAN

Cape Disappointment

Columbia River

Fort Clatsop

The Cascades

Long and Short
Narrows

Willamette
River

Lolo Trail

Marias R.

Milk River

Salmon R.

Pompy's Tower

Snake River

Fight with
Blackfeet

Marias R.

Milk River

White Cliffs

LEWIS

Traveller's
Rest

Portage of the
Great Falls

Nez Perce
Villages

Gates of
the Rocky
Mountains

Three Forks
of the Missouri

CLARK

Lost Trail
Pass

Beaverhead Rock

Camp Fortunate

Shoshoni
Villages

Lemhi
Pass

0   100
miles

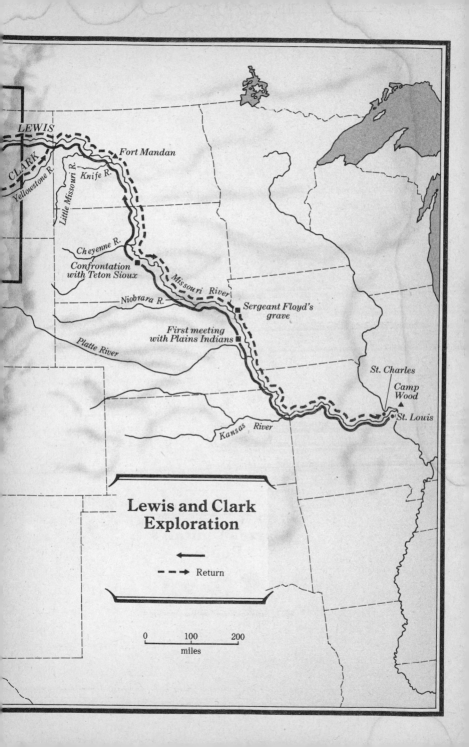

LEWIS

CLARK

Yellowstone R.

Little Missouri R.

Knife R.

Fort Mandan

Cheyenne R.

Confrontation
with Teton Sioux

Missouri River

Niobrara R.

Sergeant Floyd's
grave

First meeting
with Plains Indians

Platte River

St. Charles

Camp
Wood

St. Louis

Kansas River

Lewis and Clark
Exploration

→ Return

0   100   200
miles

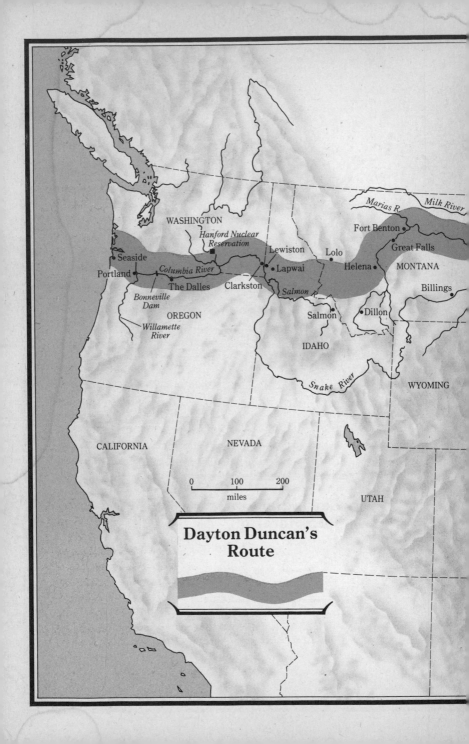

Dayton Duncan's Route

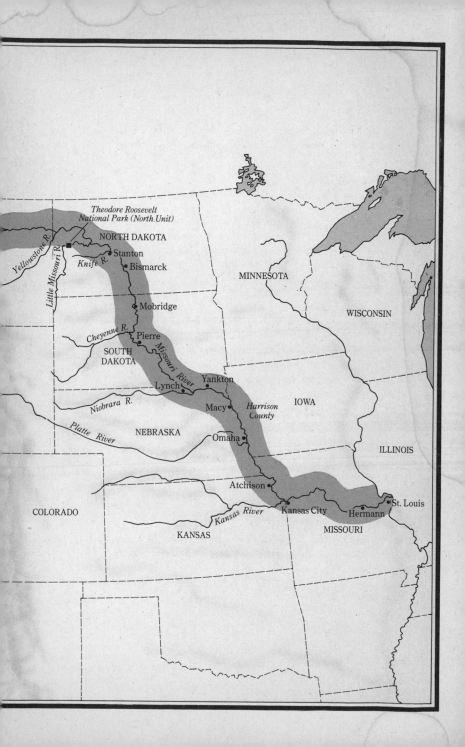

Theodore Roosevelt National Park (North Unit)

NORTH DAKOTA

Yellowstone R.

Little Missouri R.

Knife R. Stanton

Bismarck

MINNESOTA

WISCONSIN

Mobridge

Cheyenne R. Pierre

SOUTH DAKOTA

Missouri River

Yankton

Lynch

Niobrara R.

Macy *Harrison County*

IOWA

Platte River

NEBRASKA

Omaha

ILLINOIS

Atchison

Kansas River Kansas City Hermann St. Louis

COLORADO

KANSAS

MISSOURI

To my grandfather, who taught me to love and nourish the land; and to my mother and father, who taught me to dream and encouraged me to follow my dreams.

> *Honored Parence.*
> *. . . I am now on an expidition to the westward, with Capt. Lewis and Capt. Clark . . . through the interior parts of North America. We are to ascend the Missouri River with a boat as far as it is navigable and then to go by land, to the western ocean, if nothing prevents. . . . will write next winter if I have a chance.*
>
> From Sgt. John Ordway's letter to his parents
> Wood River
> April 8, 1804

———————————————————————

> *Stood alone on a mountain top starin' out at the Great Divide.*
> *I could go east, I could go west, it was all up to me to decide.*
> *Just then I saw a young hawk flyin' and my soul began to rise.*
> *And pretty soon, my heart was singin':*
>
> > *Roll, roll me away,*
> > *I'm going to roll me away tonight.*
> > *Gotta keep rollin', gotta keep ridin',*
> > *Keep searching till I find what's right.*
>
> *And as the sunset faded, I spoke to the faintest first starlight.*
> *And I said, "Next time, next time we'll get it right."*
>
> Bob Seger

> *I will go up and down the country and back and forth across the country . . . I will go out West where the States are square. I will go to Montana and the two Dakotas and the unknown places.*
>
> Thomas Wolfe

Out West

American Journey Along the Lewis and Clark Trail

Dayton Duncan

PENGUIN BOOKS

PENGUIN BOOKS
Published by the Penguin Group
Viking Penguin Inc., 40 West 23rd Street,
New York, New York 10010, U.S.A.
Penguin Books Ltd, 27 Wrights Lane, London W8 5TZ, England
Penguin Books Australia Ltd, Ringwood,
Victoria, Australia
Penguin Books Canada Limited, 2801 John Street,
Markham, Ontario, Canada L3R 1B4
Penguin Books (N.Z.) Ltd, 182–190 Wairau Road,
Auckland 10, New Zealand

Penguin Books Ltd, Registered Offices: Harmondsworth,
Middlesex, England

First published in the United States of America by
Viking Penguin Inc. 1987
Published in Penguin Books 1988

Portions of this book first appeared, in different form, in
The Boston Globe and the *Kansas City Star.*

Grateful acknowledgment is made for permission to reprint excerpts
from the following copyrighted material:
"Big City" by Merle Haggard and Dean Holloway. © 1982 Shade Tree Music,
Inc. All rights reserved. Used by permission.
"Cool Water" by Bob Nolan. Copyright © 1936 by American Music, Inc.
Copyright renewed and assigned to Unichappell Music, Inc. (Rightsong Music,
Publisher), and Elvis Presley Music. All rights administered by Unichappell
Music, Inc. International copyright secured. All rights reserved.
Used by permission.
"Roll Me Away" by Bob Seger. © Gear Publishing Co. 1982.
Of Time and the River by Thomas Wolfe. Copyright 1935 Charles Scribner's
Sons; copyright renewed © 1963 Paul Gitlin, Administrator C.T.A. Reprinted
with the permission of Charles Scribner's Sons.

Photographs by Dayton Duncan

LIBRARY OF CONGRESS CATALOGING IN PUBLICATION DATA
Duncan, Dayton.
Out West.
Reprint. Originally published: New York: Viking, 1987.
Bibliography: p.
Includes index.
1. Lewis and Clark Expedition (1804–1806)   2. Lewis, Meriwether,
1774–1809.   3. Clark, William, 1770–1838.   4. West (U.S.)—Description and
travel—1981–   .   5. Duncan, Dayton—Journeys—West (U.S.)   I. Title.
[F592.D86   1988]   917.8'042   87-25730
ISBN 0 14 00.8362 6

Printed in the United States of America by
R. R. Donnelley & Sons Company, Harrisonburg, Virginia
Set in Old Style No. 7
Maps by Paul Pugliese

Preface

My idea of a good time has always been getting in a car and driving nowhere in particular. For whatever reasons, I have defined relaxation as driving long distances; freedom is associated with a steering wheel in my hands and a new section of America somewhere out past the windshield where the yellow center line dips over the horizon.

During a two-week vacation in the summer of 1981, spent putting 5,000 miles on a new car, a friend gave me a book about the Lewis and Clark expedition. Prior to that, I had only the vaguest notions about who the two explorers were and what, exactly, they had done—something about the Louisiana Purchase, a trip west, and an Indian woman. As with so many people I have since met, reading one book led me to another, and then another. Mild interest soon became fascination. I identified myself somewhat loosely with Lewis; in our late twenties, we both served as close aides to chief executives (a president for him, a governor for me) whom we looked up to as leaders and father figures, and we both seem prone to grand theorizing over the slightest information. A further connection, twisted with its own ironies: it was Lewis's association with a winning presidential candidate that sent him out West on his historic expedition; it was my association with losing campaigns that gave me the time to follow him.

No one has ever been able to explain fully Lewis and Clark's tenacious grip on the imaginations of so many Americans. Historians have called the story of the expedition "America's odyssey" and "our national epic of exploration." Some have been drawn to the historical and scientific importance of the Voyage of Discovery; others have focused on the sheer adventure and human drama of the expedition. There is something for everyone in the story of Lewis and Clark. An anecdote related to me by John Logan Allen, author of *Passage Through the Garden,* a fine book about the expedition's impact on the American conception of geography, conveys this remarkably broad appeal. While researching his book, Allen was camped one evening in the Bitterroot Mountains of

Idaho, where the expedition nearly perished from starvation and cold, wet weather. Camping next to him was a plumber, who told Allen he spends his summer vacations visiting different sites along the Lewis and Clark trail. The two men—one with a doctorate and the other with a sixth-grade education—shared a campfire and talked late into the night about the one thing they had in common: a deep interest in the first American citizens to camp in the same spot nearly two hundred years earlier.

I traveled out and back along the route of Lewis and Clark twice—in the summer of 1983 and the summer of 1985. In addition, I spent two frigid weeks of February 1985 in northern North Dakota, where the expedition encamped during its first winter. For the purposes of this book, my experiences during the two summer trips have been merged into one narrative; the winter visit is covered in its own chapter, Winter Interlude.

Just as this book is the story of my three trips, it is also the story of three separate journeys: Lewis and Clark's in 1804–1806, mine in 1983 and 1985, and the American West's during the years in between. I do not pretend to be a historian, and this is not intended to be a history book. It is a travel book, written in the hope of conveying the same sense of adventure, wonder, and fascination I felt while retracing the footsteps of my exploring predecessors.

And yet history is an important part of the account of my travels. As footloose and unfettered as my expeditions were in terms of deciding how far to travel each day or how long to linger in one place, I had a particular route—Lewis and Clark's—to follow, and my trips had a definite purpose: to compare what they encountered so many years ago with what I saw and what I experienced. Neither journey, theirs or mine, existed in a historical vacuum. To understand either one, and to be able to place their differences in any perspective, requires discussing what has happened in America from the time the first explorers pushed up the Missouri River toward the western ocean in a keelboat and canoes to the present, when I could travel the same route in the relative comfort of a Volkswagen camper.

Donald Jackson, the preeminent living Lewis and Clark scholar, has called the captains the "writingest explorers of their time. They wrote constantly and abundantly, afloat or ashore, legibly and illegibly, and always with an urgent sense of purpose." Write they did, enough to fill eight volumes with details ranging from what they ate and what they did each day on the trail to lengthy descriptions of the landscape, flora, fauna, and tribal customs they witnessed.

The journals, which another historian, Paul Cutright, has described as "among the glories of American history. . . . classics in the vast literature of discovery and exploration," are a mixture of straightforward reports, personal reflections, and judgments (particularly of Indian customs and society) skewed by the captains' own cultural and political viewpoints. In the same spirit, my accounts include not only descriptions of the modern Lewis and Clark trail but also some of my own opinions, based on my own beliefs and written with my own sense of urgency.

The scenery and the way of life described by Lewis and Clark began changing literally in the wake of their boats, as "civilization" rushed in behind the explorers and America reaped the mixed blessings of its Manifest Destiny. One hundred years after the Voyage of Discovery, Olin Wheeler retraced the Lewis and Clark trail and wrote a book about it. While Wheeler was early enough to include interviews with several Indians who had been alive to meet the explorers, his book, *The Lewis and Clark Trail 1804– 1904,* is a record of change. The America I traveled in the 1980s is even more different from Wheeler's than his was from Lewis and Clark's. If, as I suspect, the pace of change continues to accelerate, then the trail I have described in these pages may be vastly different even by the time of the original expedition's bicentennial in the year 2004. The scenery will have changed, and another way of life—the life of small-town, agricultural America as we know it—may have vanished.

One final prefatory note. Those "writingest explorers" Lewis and Clark wrote with their own quirky spelling, capitalization, and grammar, all of which are preserved, unrectified, in the quotations I have used from their journals. The brackets and parentheses are not mine. They are part of the editing marks made by Reuben Gold Thwaites in his *Original Journals of the Lewis and Clark Expedition,* the first publication of the actual journal entries. Anyone who has read those original journals—so powerfully precise yet colorful in their descriptions—will quickly see that, matched against Lewis and Clark's literary abilities, the only claim I can make is that my spelling and grammar are at least more standardized.

—D.D.

Contents

Contents

1

Rainbow
of Steel

The object of your mission is to explore the Missouri river, & such principal stream of it, as, by it's course & communication with the waters of the Pacific Ocean, may offer the most direct & practicable water communication across this continent, for the purposes of commerce. From Thomas Jefferson's instructions to Captain Meriwether Lewis June 20, 1803

Approaching St. Louis on the interstate, the traffic begins to thicken. At the same time, the speed in the fast lane quickens in direct proportion to the rising number of vehicles. They weave from lane to lane, maneuvering for position. A late-model Chevy darts into the opening in front of me, its muffler dragging along the pavement, sending out sparks like the electrical connection for some sort of high-speed bumper-car arcade.

My mind snaps out of an interstate-induced reverie and returns to join the rest of my body in the front seat of my camper. Back in conscious action now, ready to take command, it wants to know where we are.

My eyes and the auto-pilot portion of my brain have had all they could do just watching the road and giving basic instructions for steering. "Near St. Louis," is the best they can answer.

What happens next is what always happens in this kind of situation: I reach across to the passenger seat, sift through the layers of newspapers, plastic coffee cups, notebooks, and general debris to find the right map, unfold it across the steering wheel, and begin searching. A trace of cold sweat beads up on the back of my neck as I feel more and more unsure of my location in the tangle of map lines. My head bobs up and down, road-to-map, road-to-map; occasionally from side to side, traffic-to-signs-to-traffic-to-signs. I boost the radio volume a couple of notches. And, of course, I speed up.

ROAD RULE 1: Never stop to ask directions, unless you are completely defeated; never stop to look at a map, unless you have to stop for something else.

FIRST COROLLARY: The more uncertain you are about where you're headed, the faster you go to get there.

The chatter over my CB picks up, overriding the radio. More traffic, more truckers within talking distance of each other. And more nontruckers—"four-wheelers"—for them to complain about.

It isn't easy for the uninitiated to understand what's being said. Even after the squelch knob has been adjusted, the CB still gives off a static hiss, as if the spring corn sprouting along the roadside had already fully matured and a hard wind were blowing through brittle stalks. Several conversations are going on at the same time, on the same channel—a kind of *Donahue* show on the airwaves, without Phil Donahue to moderate.

Truckers obviously have their own Road Rules. One of them must be that to speak over the CB, you have to use a Southern drawl from roughly the West Virginia/Kentucky area. Like radio disc jockeys, they all sound alike, no matter where you are. Another rule surely says that if your rig isn't jostling you enough and if you don't have a big wad of tobacco in your mouth, you still have to speak as if you're simultaneously chewin', shakin', and talkin'.

At any rate, nothing's being said that will help me pinpoint my location:

"Cain't you git that four-wheeler off your front door?"

"They think they own the hammer lane."

"Yeah, ah heard that all right. Ev'ry once in a while, ah want to run over one."

"Wayylll, ah jes hate doin' all that paperwork."

"Ah heard all that, ah did."

The four lanes widen to six, then eight. Cars and trucks surge in from access ramps on the right, tributaries swelling the stream I'm on. There are more exits now, at closer intervals, and a lot of traffic swirls off and out of sight. Yet the pressure on this main stem still builds. We keep going faster, always faster. Rushing, but toward what? More chatter on the CB channel, now one big party line for our growing community.

". . . an' I fell in and out of love so many times, it's jes' a turrible sitcheation."

"Yeahh, I know what you're talkin' about."

A third voice: "That love. Is it spelled l-u-s-t?"

It doesn't take much listening to discover the typical trucker's chief concerns. They are, in descending order:

1. Sex
2. Four-wheelers in his way
3. His equipment

4. Problems with his wife
5. How long he's been up and driving; how far he still has left to go:
   a. Where he'll eat next
   b. Where he'll stop to take a nap
   c. What he can take to make a nap unnecessary
6. Locations of good-looking women drivers
7. Locations of the nearest police ("Bears" or "County Mounties") with radar
8. How fast his rig will go
9. Traffic information
10. Sex with his wife

I've broken through the residential perimeter of St. Louis and am clearly heading toward the heart of the city. My radio manages to come through in brief spurts, during breaks in the CB chatter. The Cardinals have won a baseball game. On the CB, they're cussing at the traffic near Busch Stadium.

"We're crawlin' up here, Crash. Back her down, back her down."

"Seems like that's all ah've been doin'."

"Yeah, but look at all the fun and money you're makin'."

A new voice joins in with some CB philosophy: "If a fella didn't have to spend any money on food, clothing, and a place to sleep, he'd have a lot more to spend on drinkin'."

Traffic information begins to predominate. It's clear where we're all headed at such speed: a traffic jam. The river of metal and rubber carrying me begins to slow, then congeal, bumper to bumper, into a solid mass. Then it just stops.

Now I can read my map.

I'm searching for the spot where Meriwether Lewis and William Clark began their historic trip west in 1804. I will retrace their trail from the mouth of the Missouri River to its source, across the Rocky Mountains and down the Columbia River to the Pacific coast. The route I plan to take—and the spirit in which it is followed—will be the same as theirs. Nearly everything else will be vastly different.

Theirs was a military, exploratory, scientific, and diplomatic mission, the pet project of President Thomas Jefferson, sanctioned and financed by the still young federal government. At various times, the size of their crew ranged from forty-five to thirty-three, including soldiers, interpreters, boatmen, an Indian woman and her infant son, even a Newfoundland dog. One member would die during the two and a half years they were gone.

I will travel alone for three and a half months, by Volkswagen camper instead of by canoe, keelboat, foot, and horse, averaging 150 miles a day to their fifteen or less. I will rely on cash and credit cards instead of hunting skills for food and on Rand McNally rather than Indian guides for direction. My only casualty will be a flat tire in Montana.

A deep gulf of time separates our two expeditions. When Lewis and Clark first began preparing for their trip, the western border of the United States was the Mississippi River; St. Louis already existed, but it was in foreign territory. From the Mississippi to the Pacific, the land was owned or controlled by either the Spanish, the French, the British, or native American Indians.

The frontier of their time wasn't too far beyond the Alleghenies. The "West" included Kentucky, Tennessee, Indiana, and Ohio, and the "westerners" living there were more concerned about moving their goods down the Ohio and Mississippi and out the foreign port of New Orleans than they were about political allegiances to the coastal states and the fledgling government so far removed from them. When the European powers weren't plotting against each other to increase their holdings on the North American continent, or encouraging Indians to resist the tide of Americans flowing west toward the Mississippi, they were financing American intrigues aimed at separating the "western" United States from the former colonies.

America's destiny was far from manifest. At the start of the nineteenth century, North America seemed more likely to be carved up like a large-scale Europe. Rather than stretching from sea to shining sea, the United States could just as easily have ended up consisting only of the original thirteen colonies, with a few more states along the seaboard—a kind of North American Brazil, sharing part of the continent with countries of Spanish, English, French, and Russian extraction.

Then, in 1803, Napoleon Bonaparte sold President Jefferson the Louisiana Territory. For $15 million, the United States got 565 million acres, covering the vast area between the Mississippi and the Rockies, except Texas. In one stroke, the size of the republic doubled. The question of whether the United States would be merely one of many nations in a Europeanized New World or a powerful and wealthy country straddling the continent was, in effect, answered forever.

Both Napoleon and Jefferson understood the far-reaching significance of their bargain. Napoleon at one time had held grand designs of empire in North America. But in 1803 he was on the verge of yet another war with England. Selling the expanse of Louisiana to America achieved two purposes simultaneously: he got some more money for his armies, and he at least prevented the well-positioned British from grabbing the territory for themselves at the outbreak of hostilities. The Louisiana Purchase, he wrote at the time, "strengthens forever the power of the United States; and I have just given to England a maritime rival that will sooner or later humble her pride."

For Jefferson, the Louisiana Purchase was more, much more, than just a solution to his "western" problem by making the Mississippi River and port of New Orleans an all-American trade route. It fulfilled a dream. Long before becoming president, he had been intensely interested in the West.

At this point in history, the West existed more in rumor and legend than in fact. Prehistoric beasts were said to still live and roam there; Jefferson the scientist was interested. A race of red-headed Indians, long-lost descendants of a Welsh race, was rumored to inhabit part of it; Jefferson the ethnologist was intrigued. Great wealth might lie in its soil and rocks; Jefferson the president wanted the wealth to be American. Problems between Indians and whites along the Ohio were intensifying with each new wave of settlers; Jefferson the statesman saw the new territory west of the Mississippi as a place to relocate the Indians peaceably and fairly, making room for the settlers on the eastern side.

Overriding all those interests, however, was the possibility of a Northwest Passage. Actually, at the turn of that century, an easy water route across the continent to the Pacific was not a possibility, it was a certainty of existing geographic knowledge. The only question was *where* the Northwest Passage was located. The most lucrative business of the time was the triangular China trade. Sea-otter pelts were purchased from tribes in the Pacific Northwest for meager trade goods and shipped to China, where they were exchanged for items of great value at home. The sea voyage around

Cape Horn was risky, long, and expensive, yet profits were still enormous. A river route across North America might reduce the time, costs, and danger—and now would be almost entirely within U.S. boundaries. Profits, American profits, would soar even higher.

Jefferson sent Lewis and Clark to find the Passage. They would go up the Missouri, the most likely river, and take it through the range of western mountains that had been described by Indians but never seen by whites at this latitude. If the Missouri didn't cut through the mountains, surely, the thinking went, a short day's portage existed to a west-running river that would lead to the western sea and its riches.

The expedition had been planned even before the Louisiana Purchase. (The men were camped for the winter of 1803–1804 in Illinois, across from the mouth of the Missouri—the western limit of U.S. territory until Lewis took part in the official transfer of St. Louis from French to American hands two months before the expedition set off.) Now that they would be traveling through newly acquired American territory, they could inform the Indians they met of the natives' new "White Father" and trading partner, as well as collect scientific, ethnological, and geographic material in the same trip. Jefferson's diverse appetite of interests could be satisfied in one expedition.

As the first Americans to travel this new part of America, Lewis and Clark led, in effect, a journey into the future. The vast expanse they would explore was unknown, unformed, and virtually untouched by white civilization. It was a potential, a slab of clay to be worked and formed by American hands. My journey along the same route will take place nearly two centuries later. I want to see what we, as a people, have made of all that potential. My concern is not the Northwest Passage, but the passage of time.

Despite the years that separate their expedition from mine, there are similarities. Like Lewis and Clark, I will count, to a great extent, on the friendliness of the natives for the success of my travels. Like the Corps of Discovery, I will encounter a terrain, people, and a way of life that differ from what I am accustomed to in New England.

Lewis and Clark and their company left the eastern bank of the Mississippi to enter a land in which nearly everything they encountered—the customs of the natives, the challenging and majestic landscape, and the exotic wildlife, such as buffalo, antelope,

prairie dog, and fearsome grizzly—was new, strange, and wonderful. My trip will be no less full of discovery. And, like the men
in the first expedition, I will take a lot of notes and report my
findings.

My map tells me that Lewis and Clark have not been forgotten.
To reach the monument commemorating their winter encampment
near the mouth of the Wood River in Illinois, I can take the Lewis
Bridge and the Clark Bridge over, respectively, the Missouri and
then the Mississippi, and then Lewis and Clark Boulevard in East
Alton, Illinois. This brings me past the Lewis and Clark Restaurant
and the Lewis and Clark Motor Lodge. A little farther south is
Lewis and Clark State Park. Within the St. Louis–Alton area are
schools, a community college, a bank, apartment buildings and
condominium complexes, some filling stations, a lung association,
an insurance agency, a real-estate office, a cinema center, and a
barber shop carrying the explorers' names. If namesakes convey
immortality, then Lewis and Clark have enough for a millennium
or two.

Still, the changes are evident. The Wood River site is bordered
by a gauntlet of oil refineries—a sight, and smell, the expedition
wouldn't recognize. The Wood River doesn't even enter the Mississippi in the same location anymore. The Wood, the Mississippi,
and the Missouri have all shifted since Lewis and Clark's time; the
precise campsite is now thought to be in the state of Missouri.

Before there was an Army Corps of Engineers—before the big
rivers of America were dammed, dredged, and tamed to follow
rigid channels—rivers were living things. The Missouri and Mississippi, particularly the Missouri, were among the liveliest. The
Missouri liked to wander as much as the frontiersmen who traveled
it. Down from the Rockies, across the High Plains, and through
the rich soil of the Heartland it coursed for more than two thousand
miles. As they struggled against its rough brown current, the Corps
of Discovery would watch in amazement as entire riverbanks collapsed into the stream to feed the Missouri's appetite for dirt and
trees. After the river valley was settled, the Missouri retained its
ancient habit, weaving from one side of its broad floodplain to
another, changing state boundaries and swallowing farms, houses,
and sometimes towns.

"Big Muddy" was its nickname. It was both: big, and muddy.

And when it finally reached St. Louis, the Missouri pushed against the Mississippi's current like some wild buckaroo coming off a long cattle drive, pushing aside an Eastern salesman at the rail of the bar, bragging about his exploits, and shaking off the dust of all those miles. Here the Missouri gave up its name only because the Mississippi had been discovered first; otherwise the Mississippi would probably be considered a tributary of the Missouri. Even now, aerial photographs show that the waters of the two rivers don't mix immediately. Instead, they run side by side for nearly seventy miles, the Missouri making its presence known and keeping its memory alive through a darker band of suspended silt on the western half of the Mississippi.

But its days of freedom have passed. The Missouri now is as much lake as river, and if the Lewis and Clark expedition left today by water, they would probably gas up at one of the refineries and push off without any concern about trees snagging their boat or riverbanks crumbling onto them. In many sections, they wouldn't need a cordeling rope for the men to walk along the shore and tug the heavy craft against the current. Maybe they could use the rope to pull a water skier behind them.

A dirt road leads off the highway to the historic site at the mouth of the Wood River in Illinois. On a late afternoon in early May, the trees are dense and so are the mosquitoes. The historical marker sits in a small clearing overlooking the spot where the sleepy Wood slowly deposits into the Mississippi. Eleven concrete slabs—one for each state touched by the expedition—rise in a circle around a stone boulder. On each slab is the name of a state and a short highlight of the explorers' time there; on the boulder is a plaque describing the entire journey. All this sits on a pile of riprap to elevate it over the occasional high-water floods that even the Corps of Engineers can't prevent.

There are cars along the road, but no people at the site itself. History isn't the attraction here. It's fish they're after, but they're thankful for the road and the access it gives them to the river. Three guys have claimed the point of land where Wood and Mississippi waters merge. Twelve poles are wedged between rocks, leaning their lines into the water. No one is talking; they're hardly moving, in fact. The buzz of an angry mosquito caught in my ear is about the only thing close to the meaningless chatter and rush of traffic I left such a short time ago. In the ranking of life's annoyances, I'll take one mosquito in the ear over a big-city traffic jam any day. So, apparently, would these guys. You can't just squash a traffic jam.

"Any luck?" I ask.

They look at me, then my camera. They look at each other. They shrug. One moves slowly off his rock to the river, reaches down into the water and pulls up a string of fish: five perch and a six-pound catfish. I take a few pictures. He puts the fish back in the water. Then he walks back to his rock and sits down to join his friends silently watching the still lines in the sluggish backwater.

A timeless communion is going on here, men on a riverbank waiting patiently for the streams of life within them to slow to the river's peaceful rhythm, until the two currents are in unison and the deep and ancient waters mingle with those in their veins.

Southward now, on Illinois Highway 3, past more refineries. The sun is getting lower in the west and pulling me back to St. Louis. National City, the sign says, population 100. Smokeless Joe's Bar-B-Q, a topless-dancer joint, two rows of houses, stockyards and a slaughterhouse. The National City police have pulled a speeder off the road. Just south of town I can see the Gateway Arch and the St. Louis skyline in the distance. I stop to look.

Between me and the sight is a jumble of squalid sheds and shacks of cast-off wood and tin. Some banty roosters are climbing onto the roofs and limbering up their necks and vocal cords to announce the impending sunset. I walk down a lane, the only straight line in this haphazard collection of structures, to where two men, watering some hogs, eye me suspiciously.

"Want to get a picture of the Arch," I say unconvincingly, and so am forced to walk a little farther to take a photograph I don't really want. There's a stench in the air that comes from pigs in close confinement, an overpowering smell of life mixing with the scent of death from the slaughterhouse on the other side of the highway.

"How's the hog business these days?" I ask. Maybe this will start a conversation.

"Bad, real bad," the man with the hose says, keeping his eyes on a pig chute. His companion has disappeared.

"Raisin' these for the trip across the street? How many you got here?"

He turns his brown eyes to me. One too many questions from a stranger stopping a minute too long. I walk on, and his companion reappears, so I struggle again for an interchange.

"These hogs headed for the slaughterhouse over there?"

"Where you get off axin' a question like that?" Suspicion has turned to anger.

"Just taking a picture."

"Well, you've taken it," he says and turns to join his partner.

Back by my vehicle, a police cruiser from East St. Louis has stopped. The way things have been going, I figure he's already written out a ticket for misplaced curiosity, so I turn myself in at his open window.

"Who lives over there?" I open with, gesturing back to the shacks.

"Just pigs and such. Unofficial stockyards, I suppose. Nobody really owns it, kind of a no-man's-land between our jurisdiction and National City. We both keep an eye on it."

"What's East St. Louis like?"

He shakes his black head. "Town with no jobs, town with no jobs."

"People cross to St. Louis to work then?"

"No jobs, no jobs." He keeps his head shaking. "They's on public aid."

Up the road, National City's finest have stopped another speeder. Going too fast or not going at all around this place brings in the police. The folks here have nowhere to go and nothing to do, and they'd rather not talk about it. Keep moving, stranger. Consider yourself lucky to have a way out, so take it.

Across the Mississippi, in a grassy park where the original village of St. Louis once stood, the Gateway Arch rises and falls in a graceful curve. It dominates the area, a 630-foot stainless-steel magnet for the eyes and imagination. The Washington Monument could be placed under the Arch with seventy-five feet of spare headroom. The combination would be a compass pointing west.

Originally conceived to mirror the curving domes created by Jefferson, the architect-president, it gradually evolved in designer

Eero Saarinen's mind as a spectacular "Gateway to the West." It is ultimately modern, yet timeless, its sweeping simplicity made possible by excruciatingly complex feats of engineering and construction.

Unlike any other monument, the Arch does not memorialize one man's life or commemorate one single historical event. It symbolizes a dream—Jefferson's first, perhaps, but then the nation's—of expansion, movement, continental conquest, and freedom. And like that dream, it contains its own contradictions: grounded in the soil, it reaches toward the ethereal heavens, bends, and returns to earth, unreal and practical at the same time. It is a silver rainbow, promising whatever it is we are seeking.

Underground is the Museum of Westward Expansion. A full-figure statue of Jefferson stands there—the only statue of Jefferson not on a pedestal—near a quotation of his from the time he made the Louisiana Purchase: "The consequences of the cession of Louisiana will extend to the most distant posterity."

From the statue, the museum extends openly in expanding semicircles, each ring marking another decade of American progress between 1803, the year of the Purchase, and 1890, the year the U.S. Census declared the frontier officially closed—ripples in the pool of history. On the curving back wall are huge photographs of scenery along the Lewis and Clark trail, illuminating selections from their journals. Jefferson's eyes are turned westward, gazing across time and space toward a picture of Pacific waves breaking near the mouth of the Columbia River, where Lewis and Clark wintered in 1805–1806 before returning to him with their findings.

Seen through the museum's design, the march of American settlement across the continent seems steady, measured, inevitable, almost well planned. This is retrospective illusion. The history recorded here unfolded more closely to a national version of Road Rule 1: movement almost for its own sake, usually without stopping to seek direction or check a map, and always in a rush toward an uncertain destination.

Tourists mill through the area, looking at the stuffed buffalo, grizzly, and beaver, touching the Indian tepee and relics, reading the excerpts from pioneer diaries and the snippets of history on the panels. The most popular attraction is the tram ride up the innards of the monument to a viewing area inside the crest of the Arch.

The most-asked question at the information booth is "Where's the bathroom?" Many tourists will later take a ride on the *Huck Finn* riverboat down at the levee and then eat at the only floating McDonald's in America. Scores of them stand on the grass lawn, arching their backs in vain attempts to fit the Arch into a snapshot. It's too big for a close-up.

For me, however, the best place to view the Arch, the place to begin my modern journey, is from East St. Louis, looking west across the Mississippi at sunset. Americans have always been beckoned by a sunset. Our heroes ride into them. Lovers stare at them. Our most expensive houses are built to watch them. The band of crimson draws our gaze, makes a restless people pause, if only for a moment, and for that moment dream of a better tomorrow rather than review the day that is ending.

Americans have always been dreamers, not contemplators; romantics, not cynics; doers, not thinkers. The purples and reds mean the day is bleeding its lifeblood out on the horizon. Today is fading into yesterday, a casualty becoming part of the past, and we are a nation not of the past, but of the future.

A setting sun calls us not to look back, but forward. Today begins in the east with sunrise, but tomorrow is over the horizon in the west. A sunset makes us look west, and westward has always been the direction of promise for America.

"Out West" is the phrase, implying unfathomed adventure. Out West is where we went as a nation to escape whatever it was we wanted to leave behind us, to discover something new, to strike it rich, to grab and settle our own plot of land—to be free. We have been a people on the move, and from the time the first colonists set foot on the rocks of the Atlantic coast our movement has been in one direction: west. Thomas Jefferson, our greatest westward dreamer, expanded the dream with the Louisiana Purchase. Out West is where he sent Lewis and Clark, and out West is where many would follow them, pursuing the American Dream as Americans settling their own land rather than as Europeans settling European colonies. This is where we would chase the sunset and the rainbow's end, creating our own myths and our own national identity—"out West," not "back East."

From East St. Louis, the Arch frames the skyscrapers of St. Louis, a gleaming city on the hill bathed in twilight colors. East

St. Louis itself—with its vacant industrial buildings, high crime, high unemployment, ghettolike homes, and palpable feeling of desperation—tells me that some of the promises have been broken, some of the hopes have been crushed, some things have been left behind and forgotten. The rainbow is pretty, but made of stainless steel. The pot of gold is not in East St. Louis. It is across the Mississippi River, through the rainbow Arch, and somewhere out West.

2

Two Ways
to Travel

*The commerce which may be carried on with the people inhabiting
the line you will pursue, renders a knolege of these people important. you will therefore endeavor to make yourself acquainted, as
far as a diligent pursuit of your journey shall admit. . . .*

From Thomas Jefferson's instructions
to Captain Meriwether Lewis
June 20, 1803

First impressions are the lasting impressions. The mind experiences something new, and it immediately starts making judgments while it processes raw information. Later, you may get more details to flesh out your initial observations, but they are still confined within the mold of opinion that was cast during the initial encounter. Only occasionally does the extra information break the mold and form a new one.

Travelers are most susceptible to this phenomenon. Drive into a new town, look around a bit, talk to a few people, drive out, and an impression is embedded in your memory.

Sheer chance determines a lot of it—which road you take into the town, at what time of day, the current weather, the people you happen to run into, what you don't see as much as what you do. Your mood is equally important. A depressed or tired traveler forms depressing impressions; the sunny opinion of the next town may be more the result of attitude or weather than factual observation.

Send two people into the same town for a couple of hours, and they'll emerge with separate portraits that agree only on the name of the location. Probably neither will do justice to the complexity and deep texture of humanity within the city limits. Travelers' pictures are mere Polaroids in the art gallery of life. The button is pushed, the snapshot pops out and is put in the glove compartment, and you move on to the next scene.

All this is a way to explain, perhaps apologize for, my bad impression of St. Charles, Missouri. Clark and his men left Wood River on May 14, 1804, and took two days to reach St. Charles, where they waited four more days for Lewis to join them from St. Louis, where he was finishing some business. Clark describes the 450 people in town as "pore, polite & harmonious." The men had a good enough time that a few had to be disciplined for being absent without leave.

I arrive in St. Charles (population 37,379) early in the morning. This is my first day on the trail. I was up before 7 A.M. at the Lewis and Clark Motor Lodge, so full of anticipation that I skipped breakfast at the Lewis and Clark Restaurant next door. Ready for adventure, instead I have been subjected to another St. Louis rush hour and an hour and a half of listening to truckers carping about the traffic jams and alerting each other to women wearing short skirts in passing four-wheelers. Not my favorite way to start the day.

The old section of St. Charles has been restored as a historic district. Brick streets lined with quaint brick buildings, including Missouri's first state capitol, have been renovated into antique stores, curio shops, boutiques, an array of restaurants and other establishments. A lot of work and civic pride went into it all.

But my problem now is breakfast. Hungry travelers become grouchy travelers, and no amount of quaintness will fill my belly and change my mood as would biscuits and gravy and a few cups of black coffee. The weather's warm and clear, so I park and walk the cobbled streets. There are plenty of restaurants—one has a sign that says *St. Louis* magazine awarded it "Best Salad of the Year"—but none is open for breakfast. Lunch and dinner are their specialties.

I walk the entire length of Main Street. About halfway up it, the quaint section ends and more modern retail and commercial establishments take over. Here, city planners decided to block traffic and make an outdoor walking mall of what was clearly the real hub of St. Charles during most of this century, until the restoration craze swept down South Main. Trees and benches stand where cars once drove. All that's missing is people. On up Main I go, four more blocks. The hike has made me all the more hungry.

At the end of the street is a small cafe. I go in with questions about eggs, sausage, orange juice, biscuits, gravy, and coffee. They answer with sandwiches and pop. It's 9:30 A.M. Back out I turn, a good ten blocks and thirty minutes of walking between me and my vehicle.

St. Charles claims to be the birthplace of the corncob pipe. Dr. William Carr lived on Main Street, turning out the pipes at five cents apiece in the latter half of the nineteenth century; the St. Charles Cob Pipe Co. moved the enterprise into big industry and raised the price to ten cents before the turn of the century. Clark himself had this to say about the soothing effects of smoking pipes in 1811: "There is no Indian trouble in St. Charles, the reason is tobacco. A few carrots of grown tobacco presented to the Indians, which they divide, giving each Indian their share, keeps peace."

These thoughts in mind, I walk into a news store, hoping maybe a pipeful will kill my hunger and bring me peace. This store is the kind of place in which history still lives, not through restoration but simply through lack of activity. You enter and feel like you've walked back into the 1950s—display bins crammed with stationery supplies, a lot of combs, air fresheners in the shape of miniature evergreens. The newspapers are about the only things that are current.

I always like to browse in these stores and usually end up buying something like a notebook that fits into my shirt pocket or a pen with three colors of ink. This day, I go with a corncob pipe (up about three bucks since Dr. Carr's time), some tobacco, and a packet of gum.

"How's business?" I ask the owner.

"Ever since they stopped traffic, lousy," he says. "Look at all the vacant storefronts on this part of Main Street. People can't drive by, so they don't see us and don't stop to walk. Everything's down on South Main or out in the shopping malls."

"They won't let you park on the brick street on the south end." I know this from experience.

"No, but you can at least drive past and decide where you're going to walk to. Don't ask me why it makes a difference, but it has. They're doing just fine, and it's only a block or two away."

By the time I reach my camper, activity is picking up in historic St. Charles. I'd probably enjoy it for lunch and an afternoon stroll, I figure, but I'm not going to hang around just to prove the hunch. I light up my new corncob pipe. The tobacco is so old and dry it burns like a brush fire three inches from my mouth, singeing my taste buds and making a small funeral pyre for my hunger. The gum doesn't help; it's more brittle than the tobacco.

But I have learned things in St. Charles: about the wisdom of eating breakfast early, when it's at hand; about the fallibility of city planning; about Americans' unshakable desire to make shopping decisions from behind the wheel before leaving the mobility of their cars; and something more.

ROAD RULE 2: Never buy highly perishable items from a store that's doing poorly or in an area built around the sale of history.

Four days of fighting the Missouri's current from St. Charles brought Lewis and Clark to a small village on the La Charette River, the last white settlement on the river and the last they would see for two and a half years. Not far away, up the gentle Femme Osage valley, Daniel Boone was building his last house in 1804, when the Corps of Discovery was heading westward. If the explorers met Boone, they didn't record it in their journals.

Boone, seventy years old by that time, had been lured to the area by the Spanish, who gave him land and authority in exchange for bringing settlers to Missouri. In the few years he had been there, the territory had passed from Spanish to French and finally to American hands. Boone finished the house in 1810 and died there in 1820. The notion of American restlessness, of moving west whenever you could see a neighbor's chimney smoke, may have been embodied in the life of Daniel Boone, but that notion certainly didn't die with him here in eastern Missouri. It is almost as if Lewis and Clark picked up the idea from him and took it with them all the way across the continent to the ocean, where it could finally go no further. In the early 1800s, this area was the westernmost fringe of American settlement; today, it is not many miles north of the nation's population center, a theoretical spot on the map where the country would balance if it were flat and every person in the fifty states weighed the same.

Modern metropolitan St. Louis, having already engulfed St. Charles, sends tentacles of strip development toward the Femme Osage, but releases its grip just before Defiance, Missouri, perhaps in deference to Boone's memory. A car parked on the roadside of Missouri Highway 94 is selling night crawlers. The sight of it, as the city vanishes in my rearview mirror, swings my mood back to one of upbeat adventure.

I am in the country at last and following a winding blacktop to Boone's home. The house, modeled after Boone's birthplace in Pennsylvania and ancestral Boone residences in England, represents the western high-water mark of English-American colonial settlement. Not only the house—with its black walnut beams and wide-board floors, thick limestone walls and hand-carved fireplace mantels—but also the surroundings of hardwood forests and gentle hills might just as easily be in Ohio, Kentucky, Pennsylvania, Virginia, or New England. Things will change farther to the west, but the terrain here is comfortable, on a human scale.

In the parking lot are school buses and tourists' cars. At the ticket office is a display of drawings for the new visitors' center and "Pioneer Village" being proposed for Daniel's crop fields. Outside the house is a huge elm tree, called the Judgment Tree, where Boone once presided as a "syndic" for the Spanish government, settling land disputes and criminal complaints. Dutch elm disease has killed the tree, Daniel's verdict on what's planned for his quiet homestead.

Inside, a tour guide takes us through the rooms: here's where Daniel slept; here's where he kept his custom-made cherry coffin under the bed where he died; here are his cupboards and desks with nifty secret compartments; this is a frontier rifle and powder horn; on the wall to your left is the Boone family tree, showing how his ten children and seventy grandchildren, including a governor of Missouri, kept his influence alive; here's the butter churn owned by his wife, Rebecca; these gun ports in the limestone walls were for fending off Indians.

My group includes grade-school children on a field trip and a Louisiana Cajun and his family, visiting relatives in the area. The kids are most impressed by the secret compartments in the chest of drawers. The Cajun is big and gregarious. He punctuates the guide's talks by nudging and poking me with his stubby finger, winking and grinning and appending anecdotes of his own life to the story of Daniel Boone.

As we walk through the house, he takes me on his own tour of history: Daniel's house reminds him of some homes in Louisiana, built before the Civil War. "We're talkin' slave tahms," he says and winks. Boone's land grant from the Spanish reminds him that his ancestors were given 120 acres by the King of Spain, but no one knows where the land is now, although the family is still searching, in hopes that it's sitting on some oil deposits. Louisiana, he reports with pride, was once "very powerful, very powerful," before it was carved up to make the rest of the central United States. And then came the Civil War, he notes with sadness; Louisiana lost only because its troops were essentially National Guard militia fighting the well-paid mercenary forces of the North. His grandmother was born in 1845 and lived to age 101, long enough to tell him of Louisiana's glorious past firsthand.

In the cellar kitchen, the tour guide tells us the story of Boone's remains. He was buried near Marthasville, Missouri, next to his

wife's grave. But Kentucky officials decided Mr. and Mrs. Boone
were Kentuckians, not Missourians, and should repose closer to
"home." The skeletons were reburied in a historic site near Frank-
fort. Boone family members who opposed the move insisted the
wrong bones were taken, and a forensic pathologist was called in
to study the skull of the Kentucky skeleton. His finding that the
skull was that of a black man seemed to bolster Missouri's claim.

This prompts the Cajun to bring me up to date on race relations
in his home state.

"Big troubles in New Orluns," he confides with a nudge.
"Verrrry dangerous. The niggers hate the foreigners. Every week,
nine or ten are killed."

"Foreigners?"

"Vietmanese. The niggers, they hate them."

"Vietnamese?" I correct him. "Why's that?"

"The Vietmanese work hard."

Out in the parking lot, he corners me one last time for a final
poke, wink, and comment. He has enjoyed the tour with me, he
says, and hopes I'll visit him some time in Louisiana. People are
a lot friendlier there, he says, than "these rednecks" of Missouri.
Then he loads up his family and drives off.

My mood swings back to darkness. Here was a man, outgoing
and friendly, open to total strangers, almost guileless and innocent—likable, yet equally open with the prejudices that crowd his
innocence. His slurs have not been the first I've heard in this still
young day. "Nigger" is a common word in the CB vocabulary.
You hear it used all the time over Channel 19, usually in a racist
joke or in a snarling tone. At the motel earlier this morning, I had
asked the clerk what people in National City do. "As little as
possible," she said, and laughed. "Most of 'em's coloreds."

The reception I got in the hog yards yesterday gave me the clear,
personal message that those on the butt end of these jokes don't
see anything funny about it. And my drive through the devastation
of East St. Louis has shown me the larger economic and social
reasons why. (Later, when I leave Omaha and enter the northern
Plains, such comments about blacks will cease. There won't be
any blacks to speak of; the racism will turn instead toward the
Indians.)

Lewis and Clark had a black man with them on their historic
journey: York, Clark's slave. He was treated as an equal among

the men of the expedition, sharing the hard work as well as the occasional pleasures of the trip. The journals refer to him as Clark's "servant."

York was a marvel to the Indians they encountered, some of whom would travel to the expedition's camps simply to see and touch him. One chief, convinced that the explorers were playing tricks, tried to rub off the grease he thought York was wearing to achieve distinction. Indian children latched onto him as their favorite.

"Those Indians wer much astonished at my Servent, they never Saw a black man before," Clark notes at one stop. "All flocked around him & examind him from top to toe."

Among certain tribes, sexual liaisons between expedition members and Indian women were considered good hospitality, as well as an important means of transferring the explorers' powers— "medicine," in the Indians' terms—to the natives. Because of his color, York was "big medicine" and therefore attracted the most offers. In one instance among the Arikara tribe, a husband proffered York his wife and the use of his lodge for the transaction, then guarded the door while it was going on. When someone came searching for York, "the master of the house would not let him in before the affair was finished."

York has been shortchanged by history, considering his unique status. He played as important a part as any of the men in the epic saga and remarkable success of the expedition. Clark granted him his freedom after their return. Yet no statues are erected along the trail to him, as they are for Lewis, Clark, the Indian woman Sacagawea, even Lewis's Newfoundland dog. I will find no streets, bridges, filling stations, or high schools named for him.

A civil war fought over the slavery issue, amendments to the U.S. Constitution guaranteeing rights to all races, a civil-rights revolution, and a historic Civil Rights Act have intervened since York's trip. Today, no motel could refuse to give him lodging, no cafe could deny him service without breaking federal law. Yet on this day in May in Missouri, I get the suspicion that were York to reappear and travel with me, he might get a chillier reception from the natives along the route than he did as a slave 180 years ago.

Missouri Highway 94 is the kind of road I like. A well-maintained two-lane, it follows the river west toward Jefferson City, giving an occasional roller-coaster ride up and down the ridges on the north side, an occasional incursion along the flat, verdant floodplain.

There are two ways to travel. One is based on getting somewhere in particular; the focus is on the destination. What's in between is merely an annoying hindrance, an obstacle to be overcome. Quickest is best. Air travel is the pinnacle of this mode. Just climb aboard, have a few drinks to quell your fears, watch a movie, and get out in a new city. If the pilot's alert and there are no clouds, you might hear, "Ladies and gentlemen, that's the Missouri River under the left wing," but even that interrupts the soundtrack on the earphones.

The land-based method for destination travel is the interstate. Interstates are the triumph of elimination, the apotheosis of uniformity. The shortest distance between two points is a straight, flat, uninterrupted line. That is the goal of an interstate: to be straight, flat, uninterrupted. It is what they don't have rather than what they do have that makes interstates what they are. No stoplights, no stop signs. No steep hills, no sharp turns. No intersections, cattle crossings, school crossings, reduced-speed zones, slow-children-playing zones, deaf-child zones, blind driveways, slow-curve signs, no-passing signs, local speed traps, bicyclists, strollers, or legal hitchhikers. No oncoming traffic. Everyone is going in the same direction, in the same hurry. The speed limit never changes, and if you are foolish enough to go that slow the only thing you have to worry about is some eighteen-wheeler swooping up behind you and flattening you like a skunk for your stupidity.

Without interstates, there would be no cruise control. But without them, there would also be a hell of a lot more traffic on roads like Missouri Highway 94. Render unto Caesar, etc., and give the devil his due.

This highway is my kind of highway for my trip, and my kind of traveling—a journey, an exploration in which stopping is a virtue, not a vice. Like Lewis and Clark, I have an ultimate destination, but the point is in the going, not just the getting there.

I stop in Defiance at Bob and Shirley's Tavern, which is also Defiance's sole gas station. Bob is sitting on the front stoop. He sells me a few supplies and gives me directions to Boone's grave. While I'm there a woman comes in to buy some pop; he puts her tab on an index card for credit because she's short of cash today.

I stop again in Augusta, at the park in the town center, and call friends in Kansas City to say I may not make it there tonight. Mothers are pushing their kids on the swings; some telephone workers are eating their bag lunches on a picnic table. The post office is closed for the noon hour.

Past Dutzow, a mere turn in the road, I stop at Daniel Boone's gravestone and pause among the cedar and ash trees to smoke a pipe (with fresh tobacco), eat a brownie, and ponder whose skull is in which cemetery. There's a historic marker—there aren't any on interstates—and I stop to read it.

Farther on, Highway 94 hugs the river. I get out to watch the current pass for a few minutes, drawing from it the same peacefulness as the fishermen at Wood River. Just west of Treloar, ten hawks are circling over a small stream and field of hay. When I stop to watch, they soar higher and higher, lifting my spirits with them until they are out of sight.

This winding road is adding a lot of miles to the trip, and the stops are making the day even longer, but I'm less, not more, weary from it. The two-lane keeps me alert. Just over each rise may be someone's grandmother out in her 1952 Plymouth going thirty miles an hour. There are tractors on the road, spitting mud from their cleats. Each farmyard has its dog, each turn its next surprise. Each town has its own character—and probably its own radar-equipped cop.

On an interstate, the surroundings are a passing blur, viewed between billboards and trucks. Hills have been blasted, gullies filled to make the roadbed as flat as possible. On the two-lane, the terrain defines the road and demands attention. Hills are climbed and gears are shifted. The roadbed swells like a sea, sometimes gentle, sometimes choppy. Curves make you brake. Straightaways invite more speed. An approaching truck may be a farmer checking whether his neighbor's corn is doing better than his own, so you watch carefully in case he eases across the center line.

This type of travel isn't for everyone, but it suits me just fine.

ROAD RULE 3: Never drive on the interstate unless there is no alternative.

FIRST COROLLARY: Stop at all historic markers. Also stop at interesting sites, unusual places or tranquil settings. Stop at all stop signs and stoplights. Stop often. (But don't violate Road Rule 1.)

SECOND COROLLARY: Never drive at night. It's too dangerous, and you miss too much in the darkness. If you must break this corollary, then you must also break this Road Rule and its First Corollary; it's safer on the interstate at night, and you can't see anything worth stopping for anyway.

The First Corollary to Road Rule 3 is only minutes old when I almost violate it. My first-day impulses are at equilibrium: one part wants to experience new things by stopping, the other wants to keep moving to cover more new ground. Gunning along a straight-away on the Missouri's floodplain, I see ahead on the left a pair of giant tractors planting corn in the damp gumbo soil. On the right, near an equipment shed, a team of two Belgian horses pulls a man and his mower cutting weeds and grass on a small sliver of land between Highway 94 and a creek. "Isn't that interesting and unusual," I think, and I'm almost past him before remembering I should stop.

A man using horses instead of a tractor can't be in any hurry, I figure. He pulls the team up to where I'm standing, tilts his Funk's cap back on his white hair, spits a glob of tobacco, and smiles a gold-filled smile.

His name is Vernon Gloe. Farming's been his life on eight hundred acres of bottomland that's been in his family since the early 1800s; horses and horse trading are his hobby and his love.

"Some people think they're pretty," he says. Before you can get the idea he's just sentimental, he spits and adds, " 'Course you do the work to put 'em in harness, some of the beauty's gone."

The fellas on the tractors across the road are his son and son-in-law. They carry on the real farming now, while Vernon tends his ten horses. His son is the only one of five who's farming, even though he could have gone into banking with his college education.

"Me, I think I would have taken the steady, good-payin' job," Vernon says. This I doubt. "By the time you pay for your seed, fertilizer, and equipment, you don't get it back from the price of your crop." This I don't doubt.

I grew up in a farming community, among farming relatives. Never met a farmer who didn't complain about the weather—too

hot, too dry, too wet, too cloudy, too sunny, too windy, too many
bugs, too many bills, too little time, too little income. Never met
a farmer who didn't talk about selling his land and giving it all
up. At the same time, never met a farmer who was rich, yet never
met one who ever gave it up unless a doctor or banker made him.

A big truck rumbles past.

"There goes another load of gold," Vernon says. He waits for
me to bite.

"What?"

"Fertilizer." He spits and laughs.

He tells me part of his family's land was an island, before the
Missouri was channelized and leveed.

" 'Course that was before my time," he adds.

"Where'd the river go before the levees were put in?" I ask, ever
the straight man in this act.

"Wherever it wanted."

Still sitting on his spring seat, reining the horses when they fidget,
he talks about how the only person he never dared trade horses
with was his father, about how TV weathermen get him angry
because their definition of good weather is no rain, about training
a new buggy horse not to spook when cars pass her on the road,
and about how his son is participating in some new seed experi-
ments in planting which Vernon thinks is just so much foolishness
since it takes up too much time. The mention of taking too much
time is his way of saying that ours is up.

"Wanna take my picture?" He nods at my camera. "Get a team
of six hooked up and everyone wants to take my picture," he says,
almost apologizing for having only two today. "I've had my picture
taken by *National Geographic*, from Japan, Memphis, Florida,
and as far west as Jefferson City."

Apparently so. He gives me advice on where to stand for the
best sun angle, and as he approaches the spot he picked for me,
yanks back on the reins to show his horses at best advantage.

When I drive off, his son has stopped his tractor in the field and
is intent on changing experimental seeds. He has time to look up
and wave.

On the southern bluffs across the river sits Hermann, a tidy town
started in 1837 by members of the German Settlement Society of
Philadelphia to be "characteristically German in every particular."

The founders disliked Philadelphia, finding it too English, and so they incorporated and headed west to begin a new colony they were confident would one day surpass the City of Brotherly Love.

Things didn't quite work out entirely as they planned. Market Street, which Hermann's town fathers designed to be ten feet wider than Philadelphia's Market Street, is an active and pretty street lined by brick and stone buildings. The neatness of the town and the names of its other thoroughfares—Goethe, Schiller, Mozart, Gutenberg—keep the flavor characteristically German. At the town museum, you can look through a pane of glass and watch the workings of the town clock, keeping punctual time since 1890. And yet, like so many other western dreams, the challenge to Philadelphia fell somewhat short. Hermann has a population of 2,695— 1,685,515 fewer than modern Philadelphia.

There were problems. In 1843, a river steamer blew up at the wharf, killing about seventy German immigrants. In 1854, the railroad was completed west through town to Jefferson City. On its opening day, a trestle collapsed over the Gasconade River and twenty-eight people died.

But the big blow was Prohibition. Early settlers had found the upland soil poor, but suitable for grapes. To promote their expansive dream, town fathers sold residents vacant lots for fifty dollars each, interest-free for five years, as long as the owner grew grapes on them. By the 1870s, the local Stone Hill Wine Company was the second largest in America, third largest in the world. Beer, whiskey, gin, brandy, and other liquors were also big business for the area. Then the Eighteenth Amendment dried up Hermann's dreams in 1920. The distilleries closed. The owners of the Stone Hill Company ordered the vineyards destroyed and the land sold. Some scraped along by growing mushrooms in the dank cellars.

Winemaking is coming back now, and Hermann is a pleasant stop, probably because it isn't the Philadelphia of the Missouri. At the Hermannhof winery and sausage factory, I buy some locally made wine, cheese, summer sausage, sweet mustard, and stick pepperoni. All but the pepperoni will make a gift for my Kansas City friends. The pepperoni—the good kind, the kind that still burns in your stomach an hour after one slice hits your belly— will not be finished until just south of Pierre, South Dakota, more than two weeks later. Hermannhof: The Pepperoni That Stays With You.

Missouri Highway 100 takes me out of Hermann, skirting the ill-starred wharf and railroad trestle. Like its sister road on the north side of the Missouri, it runs the ridges when it can, plunges briefly into the floodplain to check the river's progress, inspects the sandstone and limestone bluffs from the low side, and then ascends again to the ridges. The stack of a nuclear power plant rises over the trees on the north bank like a wine carafe bubbling white foam mist from a witch's brew.

The great hardwood forest of the Border States still holds sway here, a leafy thumb thrust into the prairies to the north and plains to the west. Trees are the predominant life form. Except on the floodplain, what open farmland there is has been won by clearing trees, and the woods stand ever poised to reclaim what was taken from them.

The highway turns due south, away from the river, but a lesser paved road, not shown on my map, promises to keep in touch with it. An official Lewis and Clark Trail sign directs me down the smaller road. In the 1960s, a federal commission devoted to the expedition adopted a logo to be erected along roads following the route. It consists of the silhouettes of two men, one in a coonskin cap leaning on a long musket, the other in a tricorne hat pointing forward with an extended arm. If I'm going to get lost, it might as well be in their company, so I abandon my map.

A Gothic tower pokes through the trees on a ridge. The road angles toward it and the town of Frankenstein—a string of houses, a reduced-speed zone, and an oversized Catholic church rather than a mad scientist's castle. Like the road that runs through it, this town does not exist on any map. The burghers are all indoors. If Frankenstein has a story to tell, there's no one out and about I can ask for it. Lewis, or maybe it's Clark, points me onward and finally delivers me back to a highway and my map.

This spring day is ending in a glow. The smell of fresh-cut hay wafts through the window. The liquid trill of a redwing blackbird, singing from a fence line to ask the sun to stay just a little bit longer, mixes into the rush of air at fifty miles an hour. Dark green shadows are lengthening across the pastures, giving higher definition to the contours. The young leaves on the trees are an infant, delicate green caught in the horizontal rays. Cattle stand as still as the wind and the glass surface of the ponds. The road dips to cross a small stream and the air cools and the startlingly sweet scent of newly spread manure jolts me like a splash of cold water in the face.

Pickup trucks outnumber other vehicles in rural America, and when there's a man and woman in one, young or old, they're always sitting close together on the bench seat. Sometimes there's a dog riding shotgun. A pickup's in front of me now. Many farmers are still in their fields, although suppertime's nearing—it's called supper here for the evening meal; dinner is the noon meal, and just as hefty. A farmer is rubbing his eyes and back while he turns his John Deere for another go-round with the harrow. In another field, three pickups have gathered and wait for a friend on a tractor to review the day and talk of tomorrow. The western rim is turning pumpkin, a band of eggshell white, then clear blue above. I'm driving through a beer commercial.

To my left, the orange sun behind him and the small cloud of dust he's raising, a man stands on a moving platform being pulled by a team of four horses. I stop, as much to savor the vision as to start a conversation. The clink of the harness and snorts of the horses approach, the man still backlit by the sunset.

"This somethin' you haven't seen?" he asks when he reaches the fence line. I decide not to tell him about Vernon Gloe.

He's short and wiry, a severe beard with no mustache, home-made clothes with suspenders, a straw hat. Across the highway, seemingly another era away from him, his neighbor is harrowing with a mighty tractor: air-conditioned, stereo-equipped cab, a gang of harrows behind it that take a quarter section of land to turn around in; a modern house with a satellite dish nearby.

"Ever wish you had one of those?" I motion toward the tractor, house, dish, the late twentieth century.

"I suppose maybe you've heard of us, the Amish," he says simply, wiping sweat from his forehead with a handkerchief.

He has ninety-one acres and about twenty milk cows, a small spread by contemporary standards but plenty to handle if you've rejected the conveniences of the internal-combustion engine as something that separates a man from his labor and his land. There are about ten Amish families in the vicinity, he tells me.

He's been standing on his harrow all day; the horses need a break. "The boy," he says, "is out plowing the other fields."

His chief interest in me, as an emissary from another life, is

whether I've seen a new movie about the Amish. He's heard a lot
of unsettling rumors about it. I give him a brief rundown: Amish
boy is sole witness to murder in Philadelphia; killers search for
boy; non-Amish Philly detective lives with boy's family to protect
witness; killers find farm; big shootout in grain silo. I skip the part
about the cross-cultural love interest. He shakes his head sorrow-
fully through the whole story and then wonders aloud how those
of his faith could ever make such a movie.

"Oh, they weren't really Amish people who made it or took part
in it," I assure him. "It was all Hollywood."

"No real Amish in it?" he double-checks.

"Nope, just actors pretending to be Amish."

He drags this notion around the fields of his mind a few times—
slowly, by horse—until confidence in his fellow believers is again
as firmly planted as his certainty that the rest of us live in a bizarre
world. He wipes his forehead again and looks down the straight
stretch of highway, where a big truck has crested a rise about a
mile away, then at my vehicle in the road.

"He's movin' right along." His signal that I should, too.

He returns to his horses, filled with enough news to keep tonight's
suppertime lively. I return to the road, knowing enough about his
faith not to ask for a picture. Besides, I've already had one pho-
tography lesson from a horseman today.

Farther north, I run into Daniel Boone's legacy once more, crossing
the river at Boonville (population 6,959), up Highway 87 to Boonesboro (population not listed), where a group of good old boys sits
on the steps of the Boonesboro Country Store and Howard County
Auto Sales. Younger fellas are working on their Trans Ams and
Dodge Chargers. The feel is more Southern than Midwestern. (As
part of the balancing act of the Missouri Compromise of 1820,
Missouri entered the Union as a slaveholding state; slavery was to
be excluded from any other state formed from the Louisiana Territory north of 36°, 30' latitude, Missouri's southern border.)

"Taiger easy," the Boonesboro clerk says after I stop to get
directions to Boone's Lick. Everyone's taking her easy—folks on
the steps, dog on the stoop, cattle in the field, even the full moon
rising lazily in the twilight—and I might as well follow suit. The
souped-up cars gathered around the garage are the only things
capable of high rpms, but I get the impression that they spend

more time parked here at the store, revving their engines, than ripping through the night like an angry scream.

Boone's Lick is a natural saltwater spring named after Nathan and Daniel M. Boone, two of Boone's sons. In the early 1800s it provided the salt essential for preserving food, and thus for settlement. The Boone's Lick Trail from St. Charles to Howard County became the main overland route west for waves of immigrants.

The salt lick is now a quiet, remote state historic site tucked in a wooded hillside, a nice place to rest as the sun disappears to the sound of more redwings. In the fading light I see a few cardinals, the last spots of brilliant color as the earth and sky turn muted gray.

Some rabbits are munching in the clearing. The sight of them eating, the thought of bushels of salt preserving barrels of pork for hungry pioneers, reminds me that so far today I haven't had a real meal. My cooler full of snacks purchased at stops along the way, even Hermannhof's finest, is not what I need. I need a restaurant, and Glasgow, Missouri, is the closest town.

ROAD RULE 4: Never eat at a nationally franchised restaurant; there's no sense of adventure, no diversity, no risk involved in patronizing them. They're uniformly bland.

FIRST COROLLARY: You can stop at nationally franchised restaurants to use their restrooms; there's no sense of adventure, no diversity, no risk involved in using them. They're uniformly clean.

I've got nothing personal against fast-food franchises. I've eaten at enough of them to know that Wendy's has the best burgers, McDonald's the best french fries, Burger King the best shakes. (I've even been known to go to all three in the same noon hour to compile the perfect fast-food lunch.) And I've gotten into loud arguments defending the honor of Pizza Hut pan pizza.

But that's at home, not on the road. Franchises are not for the traveler bent on discovery. Forsaking franchises, like forsaking interstates, means that you're willing to chance the ups and downs, the starts and the stops of gastronomy as well as motoring. It means sometimes finishing a supper so good that you order the piece of pie you hadn't realized you wanted and you're sure you don't need—

and spending the night in town just so you can have breakfast in the same place. It means sometimes sitting down with visions of America's best chicken-fried steak and rising as if a local highway contractor had poured a load of wet concrete down your throat. It means suffering as well as savoring.

Glasgow (population 1,336) overlooks a north–south stretch of the Missouri from eastern hills. It's too small for a franchise. Not that Glasgow is without distinction. It boasts the first large all-steel bridge in the world, built in 1878 for the Chicago and Alton Railroad after the discovery of a new steel alloy. The story goes that William Smith, a local engineer, met an English engineer at the Centennial Exposition in 1876 and a race developed between the two for the first all-steel bridge. Several years later, the English-man wrote Smith, asking about progress on the "proposed" Glasgow bridge. "Trains are crossing it," Smith wrote back. It's a good, American story.

At the Riverboat Restaurant and Lounge, the specials tonight are catfish and chicken-fried steak. Four or five people are sitting at the bar. An older couple has one table in a raised section in the rear. A group of eight younger folks, seven guys and one girl, have pulled two tables together in the center. She listens to the men's conversation about farming ("I ain't made anything in five years . . .") and keeps getting up to feed quarters into the jukebox. "A Stranger in My House" and "My Baby's an American Maid" come on. She mouths the words while she sits and pretends to listen to the men; so does the younger of two waitresses. A couple of other tables are filled. I take one of the few empty tables and begin eavesdropping.

The farmers:

". . . tell him about that bill he got."

"He get a big bill?"

"It ain't the bill he got that's interestin'. It's the check he wrote to pay for it."

One of the women at the bar, to the older waitress: ". . . and he said the only thing Glasgow is good for is old folks, and I said it's no good for them because's there's nothin' for them to do, and if they try, their neighbors will talk about it for four weeks." The waitress nods. "What we need is some *action*; action's what we need."

At another table, a woman orders a Coors Light. "Jule, you

want a glass of ice for that?" the older waitress asks across the crowd.

Hoping to get into the swirl of conversation, I try to engage my young waitress in the decision about supper.

Me: "Should I have chicken-fried steak or catfish?"

Waitress: "Ah don't care."

Me: "Where's the catfish from?" (A different tack; the Missouri's just two blocks away. Maybe the ones who caught it are in the crowd.)

Waitress: "Ah don't know." She turns toward the bar before I can stop her. "Hey, Debbie, where's the catfish from?!" Most heads turn toward my table.

Debbie: "What?"

Waitress: "This guy wants to know where catfish come from." All heads now turned toward me, then back to Debbie.

Debbie (To a guy eating a cheeseburger at the far end of the bar): "He wants to know where the catfish is from." All eyes on him.

Guy (To Debbie, mouth full): "Hanbl." Swallows and turns toward me, at opposite end of entire room. All eyes turn with him. "Catfish is from Hannibal, Missouri. Over on the Miss'ippi."

Me (Quietly): "I'll have the catfish."

The conversations resume. I busy myself in a salad with garden-fresh tomatoes, sip a beer, wait for my hard-earned catfish. The catfish arrives—fried whole in breadcrumbs, moist and tasty, reclining on a bed of American fries. Its eyes are the only ones looking at me as I disassemble it hungrily. I'm glad I decided to order it instead of the chicken-fried steak.

Outside, it's dark now. The peepers are croaking, having taken over from the birds in the sounds of the land. I'm about two hours from Kansas City and a free bed at my friends'. I can try to find a place to park and camp around here in the darkness, then fight the morning rush hour going into Kansas City tomorrow; or I can drive on in tonight, miss the traffic, sleep late. Surrendering to destination travel, I call my friends again and ask them to leave a light on and a door unlocked. "We proceeded on" is the phrase that recurs most often in Lewis and Clark's journals. It has become my motto for the day.

Just past Marshall, Missouri, I turn away from the river road to head south toward the interstate. Lewis (or is it Clark?) points an accusing finger down the road I am not taking. I don't feel tired until the moment I pull onto I-70. Then I slump over the wheel, pull in among the trucks, and turn on the CB in defeat.

The white lights of the city are on the western horizon. Hookers are soliciting on Channel 19:

"Breaker, breaker, one-nine. Any takers out there?"

"Come back?"

"Any lovvvve takers out there?"

"Where're you at, darlin'?"

It's past midnight when I arrive in Kansas City, now exhausted. My mistake has been refusing to choose between types of travel. I have taken the path of discovery, stopping and starting, following curves instead of straight lines. But on this first day, I have also been caught in the grip of destination travel. I forgot that my original purpose was not reaching Kansas City; it was exploring.

Lewis and Clark took six weeks to cover the distance I just did in a day, about 430 miles. The direct route from St. Louis to Kansas City, the interstate, is 257 miles and takes a little over five hours to travel; I've been on the road for more than eighteen.

3

Supplies for an Expedition

. . . repaired the Perogue cleaned out the Boat suned our Powder [and] wollen articles examined every thing. . . . our hunters killed Several Deer and Saw Buffalow, Men [employed] Dressing Skins & makeing themselves comfortable. . . . a butifull place for a fort, good landing-place. . . .   From William Clark's journal
Mouth of the Kansas River
June 28, 1804

Despite the majestic symbolism of the Arch, St. Louis is not the real gateway to the West. Kansas City is.

St. Louis is an Eastern-Southern city—as if Pittsburgh or Cincinnati had been barged down the Ohio and up the Mississippi to a new location, picking up a taste for Dixieland jazz during the last leg of the move. The early history of St. Louis, like its name, is European. Founded in 1764 by French Jesuit missionaries, it already had more than a thousand French- and Spanish-speaking residents when Lewis and Clark passed through. Even today, the feel of the city is the feeling of age. Its growth, like the older cities of the East, has been more renewal in the midst of decay than new growth.

In late June 1804, when the Corps of Discovery reached the confluence of the Kansas and Missouri Rivers, where Kansas City now stands, the nearest collection of people was a small village of Kansas Indians, some sixty miles away. Its residents were out hunting buffalo when Lewis and Clark were camped in the area.

Kansas City's name comes from the Plains Indian tribe, and its history is pure American. It was founded as a departure point for the fleets of prairie schooners setting out on the Oregon, California, and Santa Fe trails, and it became a cow town and important railhead by the late 1800s. It is the home of America's first shopping center and of all-American institutions like J. C. Penney and Hallmark Cards. Vibrant, clean, and prosperous, Kansas City has a homespun sophistication unknown in the East.

St. Louis is catfish frying; Kansas City is a steak sizzling. West of St. Louis is the rest of Missouri; to the west of Kansas City is the West.

One night during their encampment near the mouth of the Kansas River, two men in the Corps of Discovery broke into a keg of Monongahela whiskey the expedition had brought along. The two got drunk, got caught, and got court-martialed the same day. This was not an insignificant offense. The regular ration of a half gill of whiskey—about two ounces—was the only pleasure the men could look forward to during days marked by backbreaking labor fighting the river's current, the intense Midwest heat, and the plagues of mosquitoes. Everyone knew the kegs of whiskey wouldn't last the entire journey; they would empty all the more quickly if men on the night watch simply helped themselves. One of the offenders was sentenced to fifty lashes on the bare back. The other, the one who had been in charge that night, got a hundred lashes. It's easier to get a drink in Kansas City these days.

The historic Westport section of town, once the site of saloons and outfitting companies serving the wagon trains, is where most of the drinking goes on. The two-story brick buildings have been restored to their old glory and now house chic boutiques, import shops, clothing stores, and, most of all, fancy bars—a kind of Georgetown of mid-America serving, if not the westwardly mobile pioneers, then at least the upwardly mobile of Kansas City.

This is one of the yuppie nerve centers of the city, where consumption is conspicuous but always tasteful. At the Prospect, tables are set out under the sycamores in an enclosed courtyard where patrons sit and drink while they wait for dinner inside. The conversation turns on the price of foreign cars and the quality of the pesto. A lot of people are drinking Perrier. One group has just arrived from a restaurant/bar on the Plaza, the other nerve center, where they attended a special caviar tasting, chased with champagne or vodka and a new pear water; kids had been arriving in limousines, dressed for their senior prom; people with tans too dark for May in Missouri had pulled up in Porsches.

Around the corner is Fuzzy's, a bar based on a sports motif. Baseball plays on two television screens on the walls; professional wrestling and Cyndi Lauper are on another screen. A number of the young patrons are in tennis outfits, looking trim and well scrubbed, as if they had finished three sets this afternoon and then rushed home to their condominiums to shower and change into fresh tennis clothes for an evening out.

There's a western-motif bar, the Lone Star, a Mexican restaurant, a rooftop bar, a place in an old flea market with 1950s music on the jukebox. It's a warm Saturday night and the streets are filled with people milling about with determination, moving briskly on legs that jog at least four times a week.

In the center of all this, in the oldest building in Kansas City, is Kelly's Westport Inn. The corner building was erected in 1837 and was once owned by Albert Gallatin Boone, Daniel's grandson. In May 1846, as he was preparing his book *The Oregon Trail*, Francis Parkman stopped here and traded mules with Boone.

Westport in Parkman's time was crowded with settlers headed west and with Indians: "Sacs and Foxes, with shaved heads and painted faces, Shawanoes and Delawares, fluttering in calico frocks and turbans, Wyandots dressed like white men, and a few wretched Kanzas wrapped in old blankets." In a casual aside, he added: "Whiskey, by the way, circulates more freely in Westport than is altogether safe in a place where every man carries a loaded pistol in his pocket." The fashions have changed in 140 years—with the exception of an occasional spiked punk haircut—and the guns are gone, but the streets still teem with a parade of humanity. And the whiskey still flows freely.

Kelly's is at once both out of place in modern Westport and yet truer to the heritage of the area than the watering holes where the bartenders wear period-piece shirts with arm garters and bow ties and where the beers are all imported and cost a dollar fifty. History here is not a gimmick or motif. It's a sootlike accretion on the walls: sepia photographs of Conestoga wagons partially cover old mahogany veneer; these are partially covered by a THIS IS TIGER COUNTRY poster for the University of Missouri, which in turn is partially covered by an electrified waterfall advertisement for Old Style beer. Four rotating fans hang from the high ceilings. Coatracks on the center posts have handy shelves to rest your plastic beer glasses on, but low enough so your coattails don't get soaked. The wooden bar is at least forty feet long, and trash barrels for empties are placed judiciously around the floor.

Behind the bar is Pat Kelly, the young proprietor now that his father has retired. Pat has all the attributes of an Irish saloonkeeper on the frontier: a friendly smile, a hearty laugh, a biting sense of humor, a barrel-sized stomach that helps him hold the drinks he shares with his customers, and ham-hock arms that would come in handy if things got too rowdy. He takes me back to his "office"— a table, lamp, and telephone in the storeroom lined with kegs and cases of beer and a refrigerator holding his private stock—where we can talk without shouting over the din in the front room.

Over a series of beers, he tells me about the revival of Westport. There are eighteen bars within a hundred yards of Kelly's now. His place survives through its relaxed, neighborhood-bar atmosphere and lower prices for draft beer. They used to close on St. Patrick's Day because the clientele tended to get out of hand. In the cellar, where slaves were once chained when the building was a slave-trading post, he keeps "cups, chairs, and bad customers." His biggest problems now are keeping underage patrons away and new legal liability rulings that hold the bar responsible for customers who drink and drive.

When I talk about heading back to my friends' house, he insists on using a taxi service his bar and others provide free to customers who have had too much, even though I don't have my camper with me.

"Should I act drunk?" I ask as the taxi pulls up to the front door.

"You're doing a good job already," he says, and pushes me in.

I stop by the next day to tell him that, knowingly or not, he is carrying on the oldest tradition in Kansas City. A night in his bar is followed with the feeling of punishment the next morning.

Like Parkman, like the waves of westering immigrants who passed through Independence and Westport in the mid-1800s, I spend most of my time in the Kansas City area completing my purchase of supplies for my journey.

Lewis began buying supplies more than a year before the expedition set off from Wood River. In January 1803, Congress had appropriated $2,500 for the expedition. Adding the military pay for the men, an extra pay award and land warrants granted upon their return, and other expenses incurred over more than three years, scholars now peg the final cost of the historic enterprise at $38,722.25. It may have been one of the earliest examples of government cost overruns, but it was still a bargain. For as large a group as this, round-trip airplane tickets from St. Louis to Portland, plus a few nights' lodgings and meals, might cost as much today.

At the Army arsenal in Harpers Ferry, Lewis acquired rifles, muskets, tomahawks (with hollow stems to double as pipes), a few blunderbusses, some espontoons, flints, powder horns, bullet molds, nearly a quarter of a ton of sheet lead for bullets, grinding mills for corn, knives, shoes, shirts, coats, woolen overalls, knapsacks, and other necessities for a platoon of military men.

Moving on to the Philadelphia area, where he also took crash courses in celestial observations, botany, zoology, and medicine, Lewis continued outfitting the expedition. Here his purchases included compasses, a magnet, sextants, a chronometer for gauging longitudes, scales and weights, medicines, soap, fifty-two lead canisters (420 pounds) that could carry gunpowder and be melted into bullets when empty, fishing tackle, forty yards of oiled linen for tents and shelters, material for mosquito netting, and 193 pounds of dried "portable soup" for times when game would be scarce.

As gifts for Indians they would meet, he bought 73 bunches of assorted beads, 500 brooches, scarlet cloth, ruffled calico shirts, handkerchiefs, 130 twisted rolls of tobacco, and 30 gallons of "rectified spirits, such as is used in the Indian trade." The War Department provided a box of medals of various sizes (two were imprinted with Jefferson's likeness), a supply of flags, and special certificates of government appreciation to hand out to the chiefs.

A special map was commissioned, combining all the existing cartographic knowledge of the West. Most of it was vague, blank, or inaccurate. The only points of certainty were the mouth of the Missouri, the Mandan villages in what is now North Dakota, and the mouth of the Columbia River, which Robert Gray had discovered by sea in 1792.

In Pittsburgh, Lewis supervised construction of the fifty-five-foot keelboat that would take his expedition as far as the winter encampment among the Mandans. The boat cost $700. During the delays in building it, Lewis bought a portable forge, some more iron and steel sheets, and a few other supplies.

Just before they left Wood River, in May 1804, Clark wrote a "memorandum of articles in readiness for the voyage," listing the supply of food and the weight of each item:

14 bags of parched meal	1,200 lbs.
9 bags of common meal	800 lbs.
11 bags of hulled corn	1,000 lbs.
30 half barrels of flour	3,400 lbs.
7 bags, 4 barrels of biscuits	560 lbs.
7 barrels of salt	750 lbs.
50 kegs of pork	3,705 lbs.
2 boxes of candles, soap	170 lbs.
1 bag of candlewicks	8 lbs.
1 bag of coffee	50 lbs.

1 bag of beans, 1 of peas	100 lbs.
2 bags of sugar	112 lbs.
1 keg of hog's lard	100 lbs.
4 barrels of hulled corn	600 lbs.
1 barrel of meal	150 lbs.
grease	600 lbs.

Without noting their weight, Clark also listed 50 bushels of meal, 24 bushels of "Natchies" hulled corn, 21 bales of Indian goods, and "tools of every description, etc., etc."

All of this ponderous cargo, along with the considerable supplies Lewis had purchased, would be stored in the hold of the keelboat and two large dugout canoes called pirogues. One canoe had six oars, the other seven. The keelboat had a large square sail for use when the wind was favorable, and twenty-two oars for rowing. More usually, the men had to resort to setting poles or long ropes, called cordelles, to push and pull the heavy craft against the strong Missouri current. The poles, oars, and ropes often broke; the mast snapped and had to be repaired before reaching the Kansas River. A good day on the river brought them about fifteen miles from where they had camped the night before. Storms, high winds, problems with equipment and difficulties with the crumbling river-bank kept many days' progress under ten miles.

Their principal pleasures were drinking the whiskey and smoking the tobacco; their principal entertainment was dancing around the campfire to the fiddle-playing of Pierre Cruzatte, the one-eyed French boatman.

The commanders established a rotating routine for meals: "lyed corn and grece will be issued to the party, the next day Poark and flour, and the day following indian meal and pork." This was supplemented with venison and other game brought in by the hunters ("no poark is to be issued when we have fresh meat on hand"), and by wild berries growing on the riverbanks. River water was their main liquid nourishment, which one member described as "half a Comon Wine Glass of ooze or mud to every pint." Helps explain why men risked the penalty for raiding the whiskey kegs.

My preparations aren't quite as elaborate. They don't need to be. Mine is an expedition of one, not forty-five; even so, I don't need one-forty-fifth of the explorers' gear. In 1804, white settlements ended less than fifty miles west of St. Charles. From that point on—in essence, for more than 99 percent of the route—Lewis and Clark and their men had to survive on what they had brought along, what they could shoot, or what they could get in trade with the Indians. Even if they followed different Road Rules, there wasn't going to be any chance for them to pull up and order forty-five Big Macs, bags of fries, and shakes to go. My food worries will be more along the lines of "Shall I eat now?" rather than "Will there be food?"

My 1977 Volkswagen camper, borrowed from my sister, has a pop-up top that reveals a double-bed-sized platform and mattress; it features a ten-gallon water tank and sink, small cupboards already filled with cooking utensils and a camp stove, a built-in ice chest, and other storage nooks.

From New Hampshire, I have brought:

> A suitcase full of clothes
> A pair of boots
> Two pairs of sneakers
> Shaving kit
> Rain poncho
> Sleeping bag
> Binoculars
> Maps, materials from eleven state tourist offices
> Rand McNally road atlas
> The eight-volume Lewis and Clark journals
> Camera bag and equipment
> Twenty rolls of film
> Knapsack
> Compass
> Two pairs of cheap sunglasses
> A balky tape recorder, supply of cassettes
> Blank notebooks and pens
> A pipe
> My favorite pipe tobacco
> Box of cigars
> Fifteen pints of New Hampshire maple syrup (gifts)

Before I reached St. Louis, I stopped to visit my parents in Iowa, where I had the camper tuned up and new tires put on, bought a cooler, coffee, plastic cups, and paper towels, and borrowed some pillows from my folks.

My father loaned me a hatchet. A DeKalb farm cap from my grandfather became my favorite hat. My mother secretly squirreled away a box of cereal, a jar of peanut butter, cartons of granola bars and mints, and some rolls of toilet paper in the camper's cubbyholes.

I use the camper's icebox to keep my film, tobacco, maple syrup, and tape cassettes cool and dark; into the cooler go ice, pop, beer, and snack food like fruit and stick pepperoni.

Having just read John Steinbeck's *Travels With Charley*, I buy a large diaper pail and clothesline. During his trip, Steinbeck would put dirty clothes in a bucket with water and soap in the back of his truck and let it slosh and wash his garments as he traveled; the rinse cycle was in streams along the way. As it turns out, I never use the pail and line. Laundromats are more ubiquitous than in Steinbeck's time, and I'd probably be arrested by some environmental agency if caught polluting a creek with laundry detergent. The pail travels the whole route with me, however, on the theory that you always really need something the day after you get rid of it.

I also never use the camp stove. Most of my meals will turn out to be in restaurants or people's homes; on the trail I rely on cold food from the cooler. The times I'm out camping will be with people who have better equipment. One time, deep in the Elkhorn Mountains of Montana on a four-day encampment, when forest-fire dangers prevent us from having any campfires and we have brought in cold gourmet-quality food on horses, I will think of the explorers' monotonous fare of lyed corn and grease, turn to one of my companions, and say, "Oh no, not shrimp again."

Lewis had a primitive but effective form of credit card with him for the expedition: a personal letter from Jefferson that said, "And to give more entire satisfaction & confidence to those who may be disposed to aid you, I Thomas Jefferson, President of the United States of America, have written this letter of general credit for you with my own hand, and signed it with my name." I have American Express and MasterCard and a supply of traveler's checks—and a lot more opportunities to use them.

The credit cards, for instance, help me complete my supplies in Kansas City, where you're never far from a modern shopping mall

choked with shops anxious to run their imprint over your plastic.
I need a new tape recorder and buy one. Some extra filters for my
camera lens. A duplicate key for the camper and a magnetized
Hide-A-Key for emergencies my mother has warned me about. I
have a roll of film developed to make sure that my camera works
correctly. Treat myself and my friends to a dinner at Jess and Jim's,
a steakhouse featuring the first thirty-ounce sirloin I ever ate.

Lewis and Clark had Cruzatte and his fiddle. I have a tape deck
installed in the camper for the times in the sparsely populated Plains
or amid the high peaks of the Rockies when the antenna loses radio
contact with country-and-western stations.

I also decide to buy a secondhand guitar to entertain myself on
lonely nights.

You don't find secondhand guitars, or secondhand anythings,
in shopping malls. Everything in a shopping mall—from the merchandise to the clerks to the Muzak to the food to the huge plants
that seem to thrive in an enclosed, artificial atmosphere—is new,
improved, and disposable. The mall is to modern American shopping what the existence of free land on the frontier was to our
earlier citizens: where to go to replace rather than fix what you've
used up at home. Leave the old behind. Buy something new and
move on.

Secondhand guitars, like secondhand guns and secondhand jew-
elry, are the currency of pawnshops. I spend a morning in south
Kansas City, trying out guitars, listening to brokers extol their
value, haggling over prices through barred windows with men
wearing jeweler's eyepieces.

Word of mouth finally brings me to a corner store on a busy
street. A variety of signs fill the windows: "Accordions retuned,
bought, sold, traded." "Guitar necks adjusted, restrung, retuned."
"Professionally qualified repairs. 40 years' experience." "Dance band
bookings."

When I enter the front door, the burglar alarm goes off. I stand
for several minutes in the loud screech, until the owner enters from
the street, turns off the wailing, and we settle down to business.

Larry Weiskopf's life has been music. He has a music story for
every topic. Learning I'm from New Hampshire, he tells me he
played with the New Hampshire National Guard band in the South
Pacific during World War II. He had been assigned originally to
another unit as bugler, but they left him in an army hospital while

he was sick, and he was transferred to the band; his whole original unit was killed in a later battle.

He chose accordion tuning as a trade during the "great accordion boom" of the 1950s. Now hardly anyone plays them. Even fewer can tune them. "I'm one of eight men in the U.S. who can tune an accordion. I'm proud of that," he says.

He takes me to a small back room jammed with accordions awaiting his surgery and shows me why it's such a hard job: small metal reeds have to be individually adjusted (scratch the reed to make the tone flatter; file part of it off for a sharper tone) until their individual note makes an oscilloscope wave stand still. Each accordion has hundreds of reeds. He bends over and begins pumping and playing one that's out of tune. It sounds like the burglar alarm.

"Who wants to listen to that?" he shouts over the bleating. Then he plays a tuned accordion and smiles contentedly.

Weiskopf has a handful of guitars on the wall that he's taken in trade or have been abandoned by their owners. I take one down, we tune it to his oscilloscope, and I strum while he lectures me on the nuances of tuning pianos and clarinets, accordions and organs, on the pleasures of playing music, and on how he only works as much as he wants to now that he is on Social Security.

I like the guitar. He wants two hundred dollars for it. I'm looking to spend fifty. He likes me, I like him. We settle on a perfect bargain: half of what he wanted, twice as much as I intended to pay.

He escorts me out to my camper. "Drive careful in that thing," he says, patting the thin wall of metal on its front, the only shield between the driver and the outside world. "I used to have one of these. I told people that if I hit anything, at least I'd be the first one at the scene of the accident.

"Your wife with you?" he asks.

"Don't have one. That's why I'm taking a guitar."

"Go to piano bars," he advises. "Can you play popular tunes?"

"A few."

"Go to piano bars and play. Women will flock to you."

I climb into the driver's seat.

"Wait a minute!" Weiskopf shouts. He scurries into the shop and back out. He leans through the passenger window and hands me his business card.

"I wish I was going with you," he says and pulls back while I start the engine.

More advice as he waves goodbye:

"Go to piano bars, you want high-class women. Go to honky-tonks, you want—" and I nod that I understand.

I wish he was going with me.

Before I leave Kansas City, I spend a day on the river. Without the Missouri and the Kansas Rivers, there would be no city. The rivers came first. Their confluence created the reason for a city, although modern Kansas City centers on the shopping malls, banks, corporations, and the best barbecue in the nation. The rivers' chief role now is as fluid boundaries between Kansas City, Missouri, and Kansas City, Kansas. That, and as sewers for both.

The Missouri was once the principal highway of the West, an economic lifeline coiling through the Heartland. Before the railroad, before the highways, the interstates, and the airplanes, everything moved on the river. Upstream, against the current, went supplies, trade goods, settlers, dreams heading west. Some reached their destination; some sank in the muddy waters. Downstream came a different cargo: plunder from the frontier to build fortunes in St. Louis and points east, Indians persuaded to visit their new "White Father" in Washington, and broken settlers whose dreams had withered in the dry, unforgiving reality of the Plains.

Jefferson the scientist-president developed the archæological technique of slicing a site to reveal the layers of civilization in the soil. Here in Kansas City, a city made possible by Jefferson the dreamer-president, you can stand on the floodplain across from the mouth of the Kansas River and see the layered progression of transportation without disturbing the ground. The river is at your feet. On its far bank, following the cut in the hills made by the river, are railroad tracks. They came to serve the city created by the river. Above the tracks, cloverleafs from three interstates have sprouted on the bluffs. They are the busiest now, carrying trucks and commuters to the city built by the river and enlarged by the railroad. Behind you, on the projection of flat land where the Missouri bends to the north, planes are landing and taking off at Kansas City's downtown airport.

The glory days of the river are past, but there is still some activity on the water. In the shadow of one of the interstate bridges, Pete

Rozell is in the pilot house of the towboat *Sibley*, shuttling barges about a half mile between a sand dredge and a dock. He takes me on board for a few round trips.

Rozell, a stocky man in his early fifties, has been on boats on the Mississippi, the Arkansas, the Illinois, the Ohio, the Red River, and the Missouri since his teens. A Missouri River captain took him on as a deck hand and taught him to be a pilot. When he started, there were still some wooden-hull boats in service.

"The Missouri was wild and unpredictable," he says. "They always said it was a mile wide and a foot deep. They called it Ol' Muddy. Too thick to drink, too thin to plow. They said the Missouri holds the first mortgage on every farm, and sometimes it forecloses. It was seldom you could run from Sioux City to Omaha without getting hung up on a sandbar someplace."

Each river he's worked has a different personality. He knows the Missouri's best.

"This one here's got more current than most of 'em. And it's crookeder. Most of those guys who come up here from another river say, 'You come up here, you got to work.' You got to sit up here and steer your boat. You can't just set your rudders about straight and let her go. Up here you got to watch it, 'cause the currents do run different. They'll set you on a bank before you know what's happenin'."

"That ever happen to you?" I ask.

"Oh, sure. Not uncommon for anyone that's run a boat very long. He sez he hasn't run a boat aground, he ain't done much with one."

Ten to twelve hours a day, Rozell and the *Sibley* make the rounds between the sand dredge and the unloading dock, each circuit taking about half an hour. Somewhere far upstream—Rozell says some bus tokens from Omaha, more than two hundred miles upriver, have been found in the dredgings—the Missouri has claimed soil from the land and carried it south and east. Here, men reclaim the sand from the riverbed, pile it high, transfer it to trucks and move it back to the land. Most of it is used in road construction; from one old highway to another, a new cycle of life for the ancient river.

The river has its own population. "River people," I call them. They inhabit a small fringe of shoreline anywhere I stop along the Missouri. I meet them any time of day, in any weather. They sit and fish, fish and think, think and sit.

They were at the mouth of the Wood River. At St. Charles, under a highway bridge at mid-morning, there was the requisite late-model car with two long-haired "river people" sitting in it, radio playing, river passing by, light scent of marijuana sneaking out the windows. Nearby, in a pickup, was another man, taking the day off because his leg hurt, monitoring the current from his front seat.

"I used to spend a lot of time on the water," he said. "I still like to watch it."

My last stop in Kansas City is where Lewis and Clark camped, on the upstream Kansas side of the two rivers' joining. To get there from downtown Kansas City, I must drive past strip shows and porno shops, past the Italian market and old buildings housing new Vietnamese foodstores, past coal piles and railroad cars, warehouses and the city's waste-water treatment plant. Then up and over a bridge, and down along row after row of giant concrete grain silos and more railroad tracks. I get out to approach the river. An oil refinery is just upstream on the Missouri. The interstates and airport across the river create a buzz of activity.

It's hard to imagine this plot of sandy ground and its surroundings in the explorers' time. They shot deer every day they were here; saw buffalo. They built a breastwork of logs and bushes six feet high from one river to the other, just for precaution against Indians.

For three days in May 1804, Kansas City consisted of a campsite for just over forty men. Then the men moved on, and it was once again what it had been for so many centuries: two good-sized rivers meeting in the wilderness.

"The waters of the Kansas is verry disigreeably tasted to me," Clark noted. I'm not going to double-check that, one hundred and eighty years of civilizing later. The Kansas flows into the Missouri, creating eddies and whirlpools that make a sucking sound. Tires and bottles and other litter are sprinkled on the sandy point; but there are redwing blackbirds, and gnawed trunks on the small willows mean beaver still live here. A brisk wind blows from the south, curling the top of the Missouri's current against itself. A good day for a keelboat.

Parting the underbrush to emerge on the shore of the Kansas,

I run into, of course, a "river person." Don's his name, been sitting here all day, tending his lines for catfish and buffalo fish. No luck so far, but he's patient.

We sit in the sun together for a while. The traffic picks up on the expressway bridges not far away. The Kansas sucks and swirls to our left. The lines are motionless.

Don's using three types of bait: liver on one line, a premade concoction on another, and "Don's special" on a third. "Don's special" is Jell-O, cornmeal, flour, garlic, anise, and water; mix it together, cook to taste, put it on a hook. Probably better than what Lewis and Clark's men had in this same spot, but the catfish aren't interested in it today.

I tell him I'm following Lewis and Clark and should be proceeding on.

"Make sure you stop at Lewis and Clark Lake," he says. "I fish there sometimes."

"How do I get there?"

"Just take Highway 45," Don says. "It's the same one ol' Lewis and Clark took." He's seen the signs. Lewis (or is it Clark?) points the way.

4

Life in Liberty and the Pursuit of Happiness

We hold these truths to be self-evident, that all men are created equal, that they are endowed by their Creator with certain unalienable Rights, that among these are Life, Liberty and the pursuit of Happiness.   Declaration of Independence
Thomas Jefferson, author
July 4, 1776

On the corner of the small town square of Liberty, Missouri (population 16,251), sits the former Clay County Savings Bank, now a historic site and museum commemorating the first daylight bank robbery in the United States in peacetime. The James gang is suspected of committing this crime, though perhaps "credited with it" is a more precise term. Nearly $60,000 was stolen on February 13, 1866; an innocent bystander outside was shot and killed during the getaway.

During the next sixteen years, until he was assassinated by one of his own gang members farther up the river in St. Joseph, Missouri, Jesse James robbed, plundered, and murdered his way into lasting fame. A wanted man with a price on his head for most of that time, he was never captured, never jailed. Jesse was a folk hero even before he was killed, but his death pushed his standing even higher. Songs, lurid newspaper accounts, books, and movies (his son "Young Jesse" starred in the first, in 1920) transfigured the outlaw into a mythic western idol.

A few blocks away is the former Clay County Jail, now a religious shrine and modern visitor center for the Church of Jesus Christ of Latter-Day Saints. Here Joseph Smith, the founder and prophet of the Mormons, was imprisoned while awaiting trial and probable execution in the winter of 1838–1839. Through one of Smith's many revelations, the Mormons believed that Independence, Missouri, just across the river from Liberty, was the original location of the Garden of Eden, and so they had gathered in the area during the early 1830s to establish Zion, the New Jerusalem, and to await the millennium. Mormon retaliation against vicious persecution from other settlers led to the arrest of Joseph Smith and the expulsion of his followers from Missouri.

The Liberty jail was just one of Smith's many stops on his journey to martyrdom. He escaped Missouri after bribing a sheriff. In Illinois, his revelation that polygamy was to be an "everlasting covenant" stirred dissension among the faith. His activities in his Holy City of Nauvoo—including an offer to Congress to raise 100,000 troops to settle and defend new territory in the West, proposals to establish a Mormon kingdom in part of Texas, and his candidacy for president of the United States in 1844—aroused further strife, both within the church and among non-Mormons in the surrounding area. After he ordered the destruction of a local newspaper that had challenged his political rule of the town, Smith surrendered to authorities to prevent an attack on Nauvoo by the Illinois state militia. While being held in the Carthage jail, he and his brother were murdered by a mob.

There are some haunting similarities and illuminating dichotomies in the tales of the two men. Both were targets of extraordinary executive orders issued by Missouri governors, in each case calling for their "extermination." Violence, fanaticism, and bloodshed swirled around both lives like a Midwest tornado bringing sudden death and misery to innocents in its path. Both claimed publicly that they would willingly submit to trials if they could be assured of fair ones (Jesse wrote countless letters to Missouri newspapers professing his innocence and disingenuously offering to turn himself in, if the governor would guarantee his safety from lynch mobs); yet the actions of each showed a tendency to define justice according to his own personal circumstance. Neither ever received what could be considered an impartial trial—James because he was never captured, Smith because of the hot emotions his fervor ignited. Both met their ends not through the rule of law, but by the bullet; none of their murderers, although brought to trial, was ever punished.

From the vantage point of the two museums to their memories, American history, particularly popular history, comes into intriguing focus. If Jesse James had ever been jailed in Liberty, he probably wouldn't be so well remembered. If Joseph Smith hadn't been jailed there, the same would probably apply. The outlaw's shrine is a bank; the prophet's is a prison. Though charismatic in life, the everlasting fame of both men was not assured until each died a violent death, the final requirement for legends and martyrs.

We are left today with their myths and museums, monuments not so much to the tumultuous times of the past as to our national desire to sanitize our history.

At the Liberty jail, a Mormon elder with redemption gleaming in his eyes takes me to the huge display room surrounding the reconstructed prison. He presses a button and music swells while a soothing, recorded voice recounts the prophet's tribulations. Lights dim and spotlights focus on the waxed figure of Smith, stooped over a table writing down more divine revelations and church doctrine. Walt Disney could not have done a better job of combining high tech and dramatic flair.

And yet there is no sense of Smith as flesh and blood, a man who could proclaim the kingdom of heaven while planning an earthly kingdom with himself as monarch; who could write, as he did in this jail, that the Constitution is divinely inspired, and then order the destruction of a free press in his own city five years later; who could preach tolerance and then set up his own version of a church state. Standing there, as the elder presses pamphlets into my palm, I am given the choice of seeing Smith as either prophet of God or wax figure.

The bank museum isn't nearly as elaborate, although here an admission fee is charged. The bandits entered the bank, jumped over the counter, took about $60,000 and forced the teller to close himself into the vault while they escaped. The teller's handwritten account of the holdup is there: "He told me if I did not go in instantly, he would shoot me down. I went in." In a separate room are postcards, books, and hundreds of curios for sale, part of the industry Jesse's legend has fed for more than a hundred years.

His gang is suspected of robbing eleven banks, seven trains, three stagecoaches, a county fair, and one payroll manager, and of killing at least seventeen people. Although there is no evidence that he ever used the booty to help anyone but himself, and despite the fact that the only dastardly thing most of his seventeen victims ever did was to be in the wrong place at the wrong time, Jesse is remembered as an American Robin Hood, a misunderstood, anti-authority, outlaw hero.

Before and during the Civil War, Frank and Jesse James were on both the giving and receiving ends of grisly guerrilla actions. They lived in the bloodiest region of America in the midst of the most convulsively violent decades of the nation's history. Understanding those times puts the James boys in context, but the popular image ignores both context and fact. Jesse is Tyrone Power, Frank is Henry Fonda, no real blood is shed, and the only ones to suffer are the banks and railroads, which no American has ever liked unless he owned one.

"It was all northern people's money at the time," the museum attendant says. "Southerners were all broke."

The river of time takes the hard rock of a real life, moves it along through history, scraping off the rough edges as it goes, and deposits it on a distant bank as a smooth stone of myth for all to admire. Free to choose what we believe, Americans choose myth over reality every time. Americans are dreamers, and a myth, after all, is merely a dream, of the past rather than the future. Our national dreams have always edited out any nightmarish realities and rewritten popular history whenever our actions fall short of our ideals.

They feed each other, dreams and myths. Our view of the past affects our decisions for the present, which creates the future; our fervent hopes for the future reshape our sense of history until history conforms to our desires.

Perhaps that is the lesson of Liberty, just across the river from Independence.

Highway 45 takes me north from the Kansas City area, with Lewis and Clark signs pointing the way, just as my catfishing friend on the Kansas River promised. A strong wind from the northwest pushes against the flat surfaces of the camper. I have to grip the steering wheel in a constant, partial turn against the gusts from the prairies. Each time the wind pauses to catch its breath, I lurch toward the yellow center line. Then a big blow tries to force me onto the soft shoulder and into a pasture.

The camper is like the bulky keelboat Lewis and Clark sailed against the Missouri's current. It needs a name, something to give it personality, something grand to give it heroic proportions.

The *Prairie Schooner* or the *Conestoga* would commemorate the settlers and their wagons, but wouldn't relate to the Lewis and Clark voyage. The *Thomas Jefferson* would memorialize the genius spirit that made this all possible, but if I mentioned it in passing to people I meet, they might think I've slipped a bolt from prolonged periods of solitary travel and have started talking to dead presidents.

I wonder: what would the Corps of Discovery prefer? And that's the answer. The *Discovery*. My companion, my vessel into the unknown, filling in for a keelboat and forty other men all at the same time.

Now that it's named, it's easier to talk to the camper.

"How do you like your new name?"

The engine in the back purrs along. I reach forward with one hand to give a friendly pat to the dashboard when a blast of wind rocks us both.

Weston, Missouri (population 1,440), once dreamed of becoming an upriver St. Louis. Its restored antebellum mansions testify to the prosperity that riverboats once unloaded in the town, until the river shifted west. Then the railroads sent up its dreams in a cloud of faster-moving steam. Weston now calls itself "Mid-America's Most Historic City"—overlooking the reality that its size hardly qualifies it for "city" and that much of mid-America's history, like the railroad and the Missouri, passed Weston by. Still, tourists come to the stores and homes on the National Register of Historic Places, and the New Deal Tobacco Warehouse is the "only tobacco market west of the Mississippi River." (Oddly, Weston's most intriguing claim to fame goes unpublicized: a doctor in town has Albert Einstein's brain preserved in a jar.)

On the outskirts of town is the McCormick Distilling Company, "America's Oldest Distillery." A cluster of small, white buildings and several large warehouses hide in a wooded hollow, near a limestone spring that the distillery says was first discovered by Lewis and Clark. A guide takes some other tourists and me through the still, the old cavern where the whiskey once was aged and the warehouse where thousands of oak barrels now hold the clear alcohol for four to ten years until the charred wood turns it amber and it's ready to sip.

Benjamin J. Holladay, who started the distillery in 1856, was a larger-than-life figure in the West who blossomed like a sunflower on the prairie. He launched a freight-hauling company between Weston and Salt Lake City, then bought part interest in the Pony Express in nearby St. Joseph, opened his distillery, and began the Overland Stage—a stagecoach empire that eventually employed 15,000 men, 20,000 wagons, and 150,000 animals. He sold the stage line to Wells Fargo a year before the transcontinental railroad was completed and sent the stagecoach business into permanent decline. He used the profits to run a steamship company in the Pacific and build the first railroad in the Northwest. In the boom-and-bust economics of the frontier, Holladay mostly boomed.

I buy a few necessary supplies at the McCormick store, which has a special exemption from Missouri blue laws to sell liquor on Sundays, and return to my friends in Kansas City. We decide, purely for scientific research reasons, to test McCormick bourbon against the much better known brands.

From the time of the Corps of Discovery through the settling of the West, whiskey was an important element of the frontier. Explorers and trappers carried it with them; Indians traded for it; most settlements' first establishment was a tavern. So it's necessary for me to have the right bottle along as I travel. A row of clean shot glasses is lined up on the kitchen table, and the taste-off begins:

1. *Wild Turkey vs. Jack Daniel's.* Daniel's too fiery and harsh; Wild Turkey smoother, winner
2. *Jack Daniel's vs. McCormick Signature X.* McCormick wins by slight margin on third testing; a little less aftertaste
3. *Signature X vs. McCormick's B. J. Holladay Private Keep.* Private Keep wins internal distillery title; musky taste that's better, much smoother
4. *Private Keep vs. Wild Turkey.* A tie is declared. Wild Turkey a little lighter; Private Keep as smooth. Judges' reliability by now in question

On my way north the next day, I stop again at McCormick's. I figure the whiskey of the Pony Express and the Overland Stage, the whiskey Lewis and Clark made possible—could it be the whiskey of Jesse James?—should be the official whiskey of my trip west, if only for reasons of historical accuracy. I announce to the tour guide the results of the whiskey taste-off, and ask him why both McCormick and Jack Daniel's claim to be the oldest distilleries.

"Well . . ." he says, and thus begins a long tale about changes of ownership at the distillery Holladay founded, about Daniel's having the oldest "registered" distillery, founded in 1866, about both distilleries being placed in the National Register of Historic Places, and finally concluding that McCormick is the "oldest distillery in the United States operating on its original site." There's some fine print in the "oldest" claim, as there is in most claims.

Fine print or not, I stow a couple of bottles in a compartment of the *Discovery*.

Lewis and Clark Village, Missouri, is two streets along the edge of Lewis and Clark Lake at Lewis and Clark State Park. It has the look of vacation houses turned into year-round residences and retirement homes. A chalkboard on the side of the concrete-block community building, courtesy of the Sportsmen's Club, says a city meeting is coming up soon, followed by a meeting of the fire department.

Nearby is a wooden sign with the names of all the families in this town of 131. If the men of the expedition had suddenly lost interest in reaching the Pacific, had stopped, taken wives, raised one child each, and named everything in sight for their two captains, the community would be the same size.

The morning is gray and raw, and no one is on the two streets of Lewis and Clark Village. I drive through at the posted speed of 35 mph and end up doing what the Corps of Discovery did here: proceed on up the river.

On July 4, 1804, the expedition passed through this area. They began the day with a celebratory discharge of the boat's bow gun. Lewis treated one man for snakebite; a great number of geese and goslings were viewed; one creek they passed was named Fourth of July Creek; and they camped at the mouth of another creek, which they named Independence Creek, also in honor of the holiday. The day closed with another firing of the gun and an extra ration of whiskey for the men.

Independence Creek, just north of Atchison, Kansas (population 11,407), still carries the name Lewis and Clark gave it. A large hawk perches in a cottonwood, taking a late-morning nap, when I find the creek along a dirt road. Down at the mouth of the creek, Rick Lopez has taken his young son Joel fishing. This is the first time Joel has been fishing, the kind of fishing where you use a sinker and a bob and rest some extra lines and poles on Y-shaped sticks so you have a chance to talk while you wait for the fish to bite. They're using "stink bait" and worms.

Rick has been laid off from his job at the Atchison grain elevator, and it isn't the season yet for raccoon hunting, something he does for pleasure and to supplement his income. Raccoon pelts have become more valuable than beaver, he tells me, sometimes bringing up to fifty dollars apiece. One night, he and his coon dogs bagged thirteen. "That was a six-hundred-dollar night," he says.

We talk about hunting, trapping, and fishing in this area abounding with deer, fox, squirrel, rabbits, birds, coons, and even a few eagles and coyotes. He asks whether Lewis and Clark came through

before Kit Carson, the famous mountain man and Indian fighter
he seems most interested in. Christopher Columbus Carson grew
up in Missouri, but in 1826, at the age of fifteen, ran away from
his apprentice job with a saddlesmith to join a wagon train bound
for the Santa Fe trail; his employer posted a one-cent reward for
his return.

"Could someone still get by living off the wildlife like Lewis and
Clark, or Kit Carson?" I ask.

"No, not really," Lopez decides after some thought. "Oh, I suppose if a fella had a place in the country, had him a wood stove,
lived the way they used to, he might make something of a go of
it. But he couldn't live in a city like Atchison."

Joel Lopez keeps watching his lines. A rain comes up, and father
and son head for the road. Nothing has been caught. Joel has his
head down in disappointment, and his dad pats it as he shuffles off.

"That's part of what fishing's all about, buddy," Rick Lopez
tells his boy.

I remain at Independence Creek for a few more minutes to think
about the Fourth of July. The Declaration of Independence, the
revolutionary document which Jefferson wrote, holds as a self-
evident truth that among our unalienable rights are "life, liberty
and the pursuit of happiness."

That's the promise of America: to be free, free to live and free
to pursue happiness. Kit Carson pursued it to the wild mountains;
the folks at Lewis and Clark Village pursued it to a sleepy retirement lakeside. Little Joel Lopez has learned today that our freedom
is only in the pursuit. Happiness itself, like a fish in Independence
Creek, isn't part of the promise and isn't always caught.

By now it's afternoon, and before the day ends there are three
stops I want to make in St. Joseph, Missouri, across and up the
river from Atchison. In St. Joseph is the house where Jesse James's
life ended, and the stables where the Pony Express started, but
that's not why I'm pushing the *Discovery* hard against the wind,
like a rider whipping his tired mount. I've got an appointment to
tour the Stetson hat factory.

If you exclude hardware like Colt revolvers and Hawken or
Springfield rifles, Stetson hats were the first and foremost brand-
name merchandise of the West, predating the designer fads of today
by a good hundred years.

John B. Stetson, a frail son of a hatmaker in New Jersey, came to St. Joseph in the late 1850s, seeking to improve his weak lungs and his fortunes. His health turned around first. Outdoor work in a brickyard made him robust, but the Missouri River eventually flooded the business and sent Stetson on a trip to Pike's Peak. While on the trail, he impressed his companions with a demonstration of making felt from rabbit and beaver fur, which he then turned into a hat of his own design: high-crowned and broad-brimmed. A bullwhacker driving a team of oxen encountered the group, liked the way Stetson's hat provided protection from sun and rain, and bought it on the trail for a five-dollar gold piece. Within ten years, Stetson had built a factory in Philadelphia and orders were pouring in from the West for his creation, "The Boss of the Plains."

Stetsons are now made again in the Missouri town where the designer got his first start in business. The modern building sits on a bluff, safe from flooding. Robert Rosenthal, vice president of the Stetson Hat Company Group, takes me through the factory. Imported beaver and rabbit pelts are cleaned and shaved in New Jersey, turned into an oval pieshell of felt in Connecticut, and then sent to St. Joseph to be blocked into form, sanded, and polished into final products.

Some are made into gentlemen's fedoras, but 70 percent of the Stetson hats are Westerns. The amount of beaver fur in a Stetson, which indicates the amount of sheen, and therefore the price, is marked on the inside band: from 3X, the lowest, to 25X, the highest and most expensive. The two most popular styles are the 5X Rancher ("the one the Marlboro Man wears," Rosenthal tells me) and the Open Road, a narrower-brimmed Stetson you would expect an oil executive to wear to stockholder meetings. The two biggest markets are Texas, for Texans, and New York, for foreign tourists.

"Our biggest peak was 1980 and '81, what we call the *Urban Cowboy* boom," Rosenthal says. "*Everybody* had to have a Western hat. Cheap hats started flooding the market; even drugstores were selling them. Then suddenly it was like someone took a scissors to the market. But now things have stabilized. People are getting back to quality hats, and on the positive side, they got used to wearing Western hats for casual wear."

During the bust cycle following the *"Urban Cowboy* boom,"

Stetson diversified its product line to include Lady Stetson tennis visors and berets, Stetson franchises for perfume and designer clothes, an Indiana Jones hat, and a special James Dean collection.

But on the lobby walls two posters demonstrate that while Stetson's merchandise may now be moving into the yuppie market, its appeal springs from a rougher Western mythology. One poster, called MONUMENTAL MEMORIES, is a lithograph showing the disembodied head of John Wayne, wearing a Stetson, floating over mesas and buttes in a sunset of pastels. The other depicts the bottom half of a cowboy's torso with his boots and spurs dangling two feet above the ground; across the bottom is the warning: NEVER STEAL A STETSON.

At the factory store in the rear, I pick out two Stetsons for my trip west: a straw hat for the heat of the Plains, and a fine, tan 5X felt one for more formal occasions. Inside the 5X is the famous drawing "The Last Drop from His Stetson," of a kneeling cowboy watering his thirsty horse by letting it drink from the Stetson— evoking both the quality and practicality of the hat, and the sentimental side of America's signature hero, the cowboy.

My legs bow a little as I swagger out to the *Discovery* wearing the 5X, and I would stoop in front of it with the hat upturned to demonstrate my tenderness toward my modern mount, except a Volkswagen's engine is in the rear, is air-cooled, and doesn't use water.

If the mixture of myth and promotion for profit is not unique to America's West, it surely achieved its highest form there. It has been part of our fascination with the West from the very beginnings. One part of Lewis and Clark's mission was to check out the wild rumors and claims attached to the terra incognita of the West; an even bigger part was to investigate the commercial possibilities of trade. In later years, tales of mountains of gold may have been fantasy, but enough was found in the Black Hills, in Montana, Idaho, California, and Nevada, to make real fortunes and spawn real gold rushes. Immigrants were lured to settle the Plains by promotional claims of the railroads that anything could be grown on the treeless expanses of cheap land.

Peasants could become land barons, drifters could abandon apprenticeships and become famous Indian fighters, outlaws could become heroes, entrepreneurs could become millionaires—everything was wide open and anything was possible, just go West young man.

There were enough true tales of fortunes made, of acts of heroism, of epic feats, to feed a continent's hunger for validation of its dreams. And if the truth weren't enough or didn't quite square with our fantasies, *well* . . . a little blurring of the facts or outright fabrication was all right, too. The hard and lonely life of the cowboy became the essence of romance. Even today, a joke in the West goes like this: What's the difference between a fairy tale and a cowboy's story? A fairy tale begins with "Once upon a time . . ." A cowboy's story begins with "No shit, this really happened . . ."

America was a nation in its adolescence when it embarked for the West, and as the grand promotions of the frontier became self-promotions of the country, the images and values of the West became the nation's values and self-image. If anything was possible, then nothing was impossible; so if something *could* be done, it *must* be done. Expanding from sea to shining sea became more than national expansion, it was our Manifest Destiny. Anything that buttressed this divine claim vaulted automatically into the pantheon of this folk religion; anything in the way was crushed for hindering His plan. Sins were committed in its name, but indulgences were easy to come by.

The national character that emerged, so different from other nations', was exuberant, optimistic, perhaps a little innocent and naïve, unabashedly commercial, and often stubbornly blind to its darker side.

Within the life of Buffalo Bill Cody, this synthesis of fact, myth, and self-promotion took human shape. As a teenager, he rode with the Pony Express out of St. Joseph, answering their ad that said: "WANTED: Young skinny wiry fellows, not over eighteen. Must be expert riders willing to risk death daily. Orphans preferred. Wages $25 per week." He went on to earn his reputation by serving as an Indian scout for the U.S. Army, and his nickname by killing buffalo to feed the crews building the transcontinental railroad. His Wild West show toured the country and Europe, an extravagant self-promotion that etched the fables of the frontier into the world's consciousness.

Real-life heroics merged into carnival; showmanship transferred back into reality on the Plains. A friend of and former scout for George Armstrong Custer, Cody left his show to return to service after the battle of the Little Big Horn and took part in a raid on an Indian village, proudly claiming the "first scalp for Custer." A few years later, he had Chief Sitting Bull traveling with his troupe as an attraction; the two became buddies.

Frank James, Jesse's brother, and Robert Ford, who killed Jesse in St. Joseph, followed Cody's promotional model. After being pardoned by the governor of Missouri for shooting Jesse in the back of the head, Ford went on tour, playing to packed theaters as he reenacted the murder scene. Frank James surrendered to the same governor, was brought to trial, and was acquitted on several charges. He later joined fellow gang member Cole Younger—released from jail after the Northfield, Minnesota, bank robbery—to form a short-lived James/Younger Wild West Show.

Frank and Jesse's mother would welcome visitors to the family farm in nearby Kearney, complain about how misunderstood her boys had been, and then allow herself to be photographed standing next to Jesse's grave in the front yard—for a small charge of twenty-five cents. A pebble from the grave could be had for another quarter. When the mother died, Frank moved back to the family home. The last photograph taken of him shows an old man standing in front of a wooden gate; a sign behind him shows that the admission price had been raised to fifty cents. After he died in 1915, and following his wishes that his body be kept from grave robbers, his ashes were kept in a bank vault—apparently safe there now that both James brothers were gone—until Frank's wife died in 1944 and their remains were buried together in Kansas City.

After touring the Pony Express museum, I hurry to the home where Jesse was shot. Admission is a dollar. It's nearly 5 P.M. when I arrive.

"You'll have to rush through," the caretaker tells me. "An automatic burglar alarm turns on at five past, and if we're not all out of here by then, we'll set it off."

A prerecorded tape tells the story of the fateful day of April 3, 1882, when Jesse, living under the name of Thomas Howard with his wife and children, was killed. Charles and Robert Ford, members of his gang, were with him in the parlor. Jesse stood on a chair to straighten a picture and turned his back on the Fords, who had secret plans to collect the $10,000 reward the governor had posted for Jesse's capture. Robert Ford pulled his gun and fired. The bullet passed through the outlaw's head and into the wall. The tape includes the sound of a shot being fired.

The hole in the wall is much enlarged now, and has a protective cover. The caretaker says tourists used to carve out pieces as souvenirs. Somehow, that's the oddest notion of all in this tale that includes a bank robber's ashes in a bank vault, grave pebbles hawked by a distraught mother, and a burglar alarm on a bandit's home: How do you get a piece of a hole? How can something be carved out of nothing? And, I wonder, how much did it cost?

The Missouri River, hesitant to actually enter the West, runs north–south for nearly three hundred land miles between Kansas City and Sioux City, Iowa, forming the borders of Missouri, Kansas, Nebraska, and Iowa. Lewis and Clark's journals are full of descriptions of the lush land and gentle landscape.

This is farm country, not yet ranch country. Along the roadside, seed companies have small signs advertising the fact that the field of corn or soybeans you're admiring was planted with their product: Funk's, Garst, Pioneer, DeKalb. A bumper sticker on a pickup truck in front of me—with the woman snuggled close to the male driver—says: DON'T CRITICIZE FARMERS WITH YOUR MOUTH FULL.

The sight of a grain elevator and a water tower announces that you're approaching another small town; an AM radio tower beaming out crop reports and livestock prices means the town is bigger, maybe even the county seat. On the outskirts of towns, the road is lined with farm-implement dealers instead of fast-food franchises: Case, Allis Chalmers, and John Deere are the big trinity rather than McDonald's, Burger King, and Wendy's.

It's another gray day, windy and blustery again, with occasional bursts of big raindrops. On Kansas Highway 7, south of Troy, two changes in the landscape suddenly impress me, as if they had been sitting in the back section of the *Discovery* waiting quietly for the right time to move forward, tap me on the shoulder and point out the window: the road is straighter, and there are fewer trees.

The land billows like a green flag in a gentle breeze. The sky has become an important part of the landscape, with its own texture and contours. Trees can still be seen, there just aren't as many as there were across the heart of Missouri: clusters of elms and oaks near farmhouses, locusts along the fencerows, cottonwoods outlining the banks of streams and rivers. The highway is more interested in getting to the next town than in following the bends of the river. It dips with the terrain, but turns reluctantly and only occasionally.

Beauty here is found in subtlety: a meadowlark's yellow tummy, the curve of an erosion ditch along the contour of a small hill, the slow, swinging gait of a line of cattle heading out to pasture, the lilting names of the rivers: Nodaway, Tarkio, Big and Little Nemaha, East and West Nishnabotna. The rivers cut through the sod as if they would sink all the way to the center of the earth if only the banks would hold up. Another mental tap on the shoulder: no rocks. When and where did they disappear?

A few miles north of White Cloud, Kansas (population 210), with a guy on the radio explaining the impact of foreign-currency exchange rates on the farm economy, Highway 7 just up and ends, and a muddy dirt road takes over.

ROAD RULE 5: Never retrace your route, unless you are completely defeated, or at a dead end. Keep moving forward. And don't forget, you can't stop to ask directions or check your map.

The *Discovery* splashes ahead with courage. It shimmies through soft spots in the road and slides around a few corners. A wet grime has covered the rear window to prevent looking back.

"This road has to lead somewhere," I tell it, trying to sound confident. The river appears on the right for reassurance. After a half hour of mud, the road turns to gravel, and then meets a paved highway. The "somewhere" we've been headed is Nebraska.

Straight highways lead me to Brownville, Nebraska (population 174), "Nebraska's Oldest Town"—another river town with big dreams that were never fulfilled. When Congress passed the Kansas-Nebraska Act of 1854 and opened the areas for settlement, Richard Brown had already found a stone ledge along the west bank of the Missouri that would make a fine steamboat landing. Here he founded the town that bears his name.

The town newspaper, the *Nebraska Advertiser*, began promoting Brownville to prospective settlers in the East: "Brownville is one of the most flourishing towns in Nebraska, of the most rapid growth and flattering prospects as it enjoys a situation perhaps surpassed by none and enjoyed by few in America." By 1870, the paper claimed that 3,500 people lived in Brownville. Schools were built, a college was started (and soon closed), a lyceum featuring prominent speakers was formed, and Brownville started calling itself the "Athens of the West."

Town fathers decided Brownville's ticket to the future was a railroad and convinced voters to approve a $275,000 bond issue to lay enough track west to lure a major line from the East. The contractor put down a few miles of ties and iron, but no train ever moved west over them and no eastern link ever arrived. The townspeople were left with a staggering debt, the county seat was moved to Auburn, and most of the people and businesses, including the *Advertiser*, moved out.

The town now consists of some old houses, a short stretch of brick buildings, and a nice little restaurant, the Brownville House, where I stop for a cup of coffee and a piece of homemade bread.

I pay and exit along with a young guy wearing a jacket that says Livingston, Montana, on its back.

"You from Livingston?" I ask as we walk out.

"Yeah. But I'm here, and tryin' to get out of this miserable place."

"What brings you here?"

"Nuclear plant."

"They building it, or is it done?"

"I do maintenance."

"When you heading home?"

"I tried to leave this morning, but they wouldn't let me go."

Brownville may not be the Athens of the West, but any place with homemade bread as good as the Brownville House's doesn't deserve this kind of surliness, even if leaving Brownville is a time-honored tradition. He roars off in a hot Chevy; the *Discovery* and I head across the river for one last slice of Missouri.

The sign near Rock Port, Missouri (population 1,511), promises the "World's Largest Selection of Fireworks." The warehouse-store is about 150 feet long, there are shopping carts to push down the aisles of rockets, firecrackers, and even hand grenades ("They just give off smoke," the clerk tells me. "If they went *boom* we'd sell a lot more."), and they accept credit cards for the purchases. It's the biggest array of fireworks I've seen, yet I suspect that somewhere in the world there's a larger selection than in Rock Port.

The clerk's advice on rockets is to go for color instead of noise. "Any that have a red, white, and blue combination?" I'm feeling patriotic. The Fourth of July is less than two months away.

"No, but that's a good idea," the clerk says. Must not be any in the whole world, if you believe their sign. I consider questioning their claim, but figure the clerk will start with, "*Well* . . ." and I'll be stuck here longer than I want to be.

Twenty dollars' worth of rockets gets stored next to my supply of McCormick bourbon—firewater and fireworks—in the compartment under the upper mattress. I make a mental note to remember not to smoke my pipe or cigar in bed.

Whenever I cross the state line into Iowa, the state of my birth and upbringing, I am gripped with desire for a tenderloin sandwich, one of Iowa's many gifts to a hungry nation. The tenderloin in a tenderloin sandwich differs from a tenderloin offered at steakhouses in two important respects: first, it is thin and lightly breaded, not thick and juicy; second, and this often comes as a shock to unsuspecting cafe patrons, it is pork, not beef. Some places in other states call them breaded pork loin sandwiches, or pork fritter sandwiches, but in Iowa, the nation's number-one hog-producing state, tenderloin sandwich says it all.

The standard against which I have held all tenderloin sandwiches is set by the Crouse Cafe in Indianola, Iowa, my hometown. The pork itself is thin and moist—you get the impression someone in the back of the kitchen has worked it over pretty heavily with a big mallet—and it isn't overly breaded (overbreading is a common mistake). The breaded tenderloin is at least twice the diameter of the large bun that covers the center of the circle of pork. This is critical for a proper tenderloin. It transforms a lunch into a two-course meal: eating the edges of the loin; then, when you reach the bun, eating a sandwich. Four courses if you eat the french fries first and have a piece of pie for dessert. If everything but the pie comes in a plastic mesh basket lined with waxed paper, you're in store for a treat for both the eyes *and* palate. Have the soft drink of your choice.

I'm wondering why the Crouse Cafe doesn't promote itself as "Home of the Nation's Best Tenderloin Sandwich," when U.S. 275

enters Iowa. A possible setback for my taste buds: the first town is named Hamburg.

As I get gas for the *Discovery*, I ask the pump jockey where I can get a good tenderloin. (For some reason, when I travel, too often I end up asking gas-station attendants for meal recommendations and waitresses for directions, rather than vice versa. The results are so erratic, this practice should not be considered a Road Rule.)

Following his suggestion, I pull up at the Frontier Steakhouse Lounge and Bowling Alley in the tree-lined downtown of Hamburg (population 1,597). The brief panic that he may have sent me to a steakhouse because he was thinking of the *other* tenderloin passes when I see the menu.

The clientele is a mixture of farmers, Hamburg merchants, and grandparents with their grandchildren. The fragments of conversation that float over to my table are about democracy and the free-enterprise system, farm problems and weather, and how nervous one person becomes when he gets off the wrong exit of the interstate and ends up in a black section of Kansas City. It's noon; no one is bowling in the other part of the building.

The tenderloin I'm served is Crouse Cafe–sized and of proper tenderness, served with fresh onion, tomatoes, lettuce, and pickles; the fries are thin and good; and the apple pie with ginger in its crust makes me consider driving back to the gas station and personally thanking the attendant.

The *Discovery* and I now both have full tanks and can sluggishly proceed on.

Nebraska City, Nebraska (population 7,127), about fifteen miles north and across the river from Hamburg, bills itself as "Tree City USA," something you wouldn't expect in a state that doesn't have a state forest. J. Sterling Morton moved here in 1855 to run the local newspaper. The house he built that year was the only frame house between the Missouri River and the Rocky Mountains.

Later, as head of the state board of agriculture, he promoted the idea of setting aside a day each year to plant trees. In 1885, the Nebraska Legislature designated April 22, Morton's birthday, as Arbor Day. In 1891, Morton planted a grove of white pines to prove to the governor that pines would, in fact, grow in Nebraska. The grove that stands today at Arbor Lodge Historical Park—part of a sixty-five-acre arboretum and therefore the closest thing Nebraska has to a state forest—was replanted in 1937. Drought killed Morton's grove. His son, Joy, had completed the mansion, donated it to the state, and gone on to found the famous salt company.

Nebraska City's other chief promotion is John Brown's Cave. The Kansas-Nebraska Act of 1854 lit the fuse for the Civil War by determining that each territory would decide its own question of slavery through an election. Slave-holding Missourians assumed that Nebraska would be a free territory and neighboring Kansas a slave territory; New England abolitionists, angered that the Act violated the provisions of the Missouri Compromise, began financing "free-soil" settlers moving into Kansas.

The border erupted in violence. "Border Ruffians" from Missouri would cross the river to stuff ballot boxes and burn homesteads; "Jayhawkers" from Kansas would retaliate by raiding western Missouri farms. Kansas became known as "Bleeding Kansas." A cauldron of bloodshed swirled for ten years, through the end of the Civil War, inflicting a vicious and barbarous punishment on civilians unsurpassed in American history until the weapons of righteous fervor were united and trained on the Plains Indians a decade later.

John Brown, the uncompromising warrior of abolition, used southwestern Iowa and southeastern Nebraska as his staging ground in the fight for a free Kansas. After a small army of Missouri Border Ruffians sacked Lawrence, Kansas, in May 1856, Brown and his four sons went to Pottawatomie Creek, near Lawrence, pulled five proslavery men from their cabins in the middle of the night, and hacked them to death with sabers. Three years later, he led a band of men to raid the federal arsenal at Harpers Ferry, hoping to spark an insurrection of slaves. Robert E. Lee, an officer in the U.S. Army at the time, captured Brown, who was tried for treason and hanged.

The Brown fever of the 1850s has cooled by now. About the closest thing to fervor along this former region of zealotry is a particularly vivid fundamentalist broadcast on school prayer over a small-town radio station, or a call-in discussion about the prospects for the Kansas City Royals' winning the pennant.

John Brown's Cave site is a small cabin on Nebraska Highway 2. Nearby is the John Brown's Cave Cabin Museum, John Brown's Camper and Trailer Site, John Brown's Family Restaurant, and

John Brown's Cave Gift Shop, which has a huge billboard promising that the gift shop is "one of the largest in the state." Dwarfed
by all this—a "*Well . . .*" whispered against the shouts of the billboards—is a small historic marker erected by the state and county
historical societies. It states that the cabin was a stop on the Underground Railroad and was used by John Kagi, one of Brown's
men killed in the Harpers Ferry raid, that Brown passed through
Nebraska City five times, "but it is only by inference and legend
that he visited the cabin area."

As I try to pull back onto Highway 2 from the marker's turnoff,
a big semi is leaving the gift shop parking lot. One of us is going
to have to yield. Remembering Larry Weiskopf's story about being
the first one at the scene of an accident in a Volkswagen, I decide
not to challenge the truck for a spot on the highway.

ROAD RULE 6: Never call the bluff of an eighteen-wheeler, a
Greyhound bus, a highway grader, a Buick or Cadillac with
heavy chrome bumpers, a teenager driving any motorized
vehicle, or a tractor pulling a wagon loaded with manure.

FIRST COROLLARY: The road of history is littered with facts
that ignored Road Rule 6; whenever myth and reality collide,
myth rolls on.

Back on the Iowa side, Interstate 29 hogs the floodplain. U.S.
Highway 275 gives it about ten miles' berth and keeps to the higher
ground farther east, out of sight of the river and the heavy truck
traffic. North of Sidney, Iowa, the cultivated fields have been
terraced to prevent erosion. The hills look like the deeply lined
face of a man who has been poorly shaved the morning after a
hard night: stubble in the clefts, smooth on the flat spots, and a
few gouges.

"Welcome to Tabor, A Friendly Town," the sign says, followed
a few feet later by SPEED ZONE AHEAD. Tabor (population 1,088)
is so friendly that virtually every store in the one-block downtown
uses a first name: Jerry's Tavern, Jim's Food Mart, Stan's Radio
& TV, Smitty's Lounge, Mel's Insulation Service, Nancy's Gifts
and Notions, Bev's Beauty Salon. William's Hardware and Reed's
Drug could be either first or last names. Mr. C's, a small coffee
place, seems a little stuffy and formal in this group, but a guy
entering it as I drive by gives me a friendly wave.

At the end of the commercial zone is a combination DX gas station and convenience store—the kind of place that has spread across the nation and taken root like kudzu, where you pump your own gas, buy a can of pop, a premade ham sandwich, and a bag of potato chips, and hit the road. A hand-painted sign on the road says this is "Tabor's #1 Mini-Mart," an indisputable fact proved by the forty-five-second drive through Tabor's downtown. The clerk tells me John Brown's headquarters was next to the town park, and there are tunnels connecting the surrounding houses from the days of the Underground Railroad.

Mrs. Wanda Ewalt, a smallish woman with gray-blond hair, a housedress, and functional black shoes and white socks (she reminds me of my mother), gives me a tour through the Todd House, where Brown stored his weapons for the Kansas free-soil fight. On a day when I've become numbed by claims ranging from "America's oldest" this and the "world's largest" that to, the last straw, "Tabor's #1 Mini-Mart," Mrs. Ewalt is a breath of fresh, honest air.

The small, white two-story house, now a museum, was built in 1853 by the Rev. John Todd, who founded the town and established Tabor College as a Christian college. In the parlor is a square grand piano, which, a notecard on it says, was the "first piano in Tabor and the first to be shipped up the Missouri."

"At least that's what they told us," Mrs. Ewalt says.

"What about the tunnels I heard about?"

"*Well* . . ." she says and takes me to the front door. Here we go again, I say to myself. She points across the square park to two houses with a street between them. "They said there was a tunnel between them. Now, as a girl, I played in that brick house, and there was a root cellar down there . . . I think it was just a root cellar. Other people say it was a tunnel and caved in. And people say there was a tunnel from here across that park over there. Well, *I* don't think that ever, ever happened."

Brown drilled his men and encamped in the park during one winter. He hid a brass cannon and two hundred Sharps rifles—called "Beecher's Bibles" after the Rev. Henry Ward Beecher said there was "more moral power in one of those instruments so far as the slave-holders were concerned than in a hundred Bibles"—in the Todd House cellar.

Mrs. Ewalt tells me a few stories about Reverend Todd. He dressed a runaway slave in his wife's clothes to escape capture one night; when slave owners stopped at the town's hotel (when Tabor had a hotel), Todd and the townspeople would convince the slaves to seek freedom and hide them in secret rooms in his home. But she is careful not to overstate the case.

"There were some exciting times here," she says, "but nobody actually fired a shot. It never came to a fight in Tabor. It did down in Percival [farther south]. There was some shooting down there."

Brown's exploits finally were too much for the abolitionists of Tabor.

"He was allowed to speak at church as a rule," Mrs. Ewalt says. "But they wouldn't let him that last time—after the murders— and he left in a huff."

Wanda Ewalt politely declines my request to take her picture outside the Todd House with the gentle statement: "I'm not dressed for any picture-taking."

I remark on the bad weather.

"Well, it depends on your point of view," she says, honest to the end. "It's been cold and miserable, that's for sure, but we don't mind the moisture." She climbs into a pickup truck and heads home.

When I pass Tabor's #1 Mini-Mart on my way out of town, bound for Omaha, I consider and then drop the idea of having a sign painted on the side of the *Discovery*: "The Best Volkswagen Camper That Ever Followed the Lewis and Clark Trail."

Well . . .

5

Through the Looking Glass

We value too much the lives of citizens to offer them to probable destruction. . . . we wish you to err on the side of your safety. . . .
From Thomas Jefferson's instructions
to Captain Meriwether Lewis
June 20, 1803

The Situation of our last Camp Councile Bluff or Handsom Prarie appears to be a verry proper place for a Tradeing establishment & fortification. . . . The air is pure and helthy so far as we can judge.
From William Clark's journal
August 3, 1804

The Voyage of Discovery reached the mouth of the Platte River on July 21, 1804, more than three weeks after the expedition had left the Kansas River. Lewis and Clark were anxious to meet the Plains Indians of the area and to initiate what would become a three-part diplomacy among the tribes: inform them of their new "White Father" in Washington and impress them with his power; encourage peace among the constantly warring tribes; and lay the foundation for the American traders who would be following.

All three hopes were dashed by the expedition's failure to find any local tribes at home. Most villages were vacant while their inhabitants were out either hunting buffalo or raiding neighbors. After remaining for five days at a spot they named Camp White Catfish, about ten miles north of the Platte, the expedition moved slowly upriver to another campsite, Camp Council Bluff, roughly twenty-five miles north and across the river from present-day Council Bluffs, Iowa. Here they waited again, until a small delegation of Oto Indians arrived to parley on August 2.

Just south of present-day Omaha, Clark described the terrain as "well situated for Defence." Later, he recommended the area of the Council Bluff campsite as a "proper place for a Tradeing establishment & fortification" because it was near Oto, Pawnee, and Omaha villages, had soil suitable for making bricks, and a "great deel of timber." On the journey between the two camps, he remarked on an unusual scene of devastation: a band of flattened trees, "apparently the ravages of a Dreddfull harican. . . . many trees were broken off near the ground the trunks of which were sound and four feet in Diameter."

The men were pestered by increasing numbers of mosquitoes and by boils from their constant exposure to the river water, but Clark found it "worthey of observation to mention that our Party has been much healthier on the Voyage than parties of the same number is in any other Situation." Their diet of venison had broadened to include elk, beaver, and, as the name of Camp White Catfish indicates, what they could pull from the river. One of the

men killed an animal curious to the explorers—a badger—which
they stuffed for preservation.

Food and fortifications, nature's plenty amidst the possibility of
awesome destruction—Omaha still has the elements Lewis and
Clark witnessed in 1804. The city is home of the Omaha stockyards
and the command headquarters for the nation's nuclear arsenal.

Anyone who thinks the railroad is dead in America should visit
Omaha, Nebraska (population 311,681). The Union Pacific lines—
Omaha is the railroad's headquarters—refuse to be relegated to
the mere outskirts and industrial sections of town, as they are in
most cities. They parade through downtown Omaha, secure in the
knowledge that without them and the stockyards they serve, there
probably wouldn't be any city in the first place. The tracks seem
to tell the residents: You don't like us, move to Brownville.

Down at the stockyards themselves, I join seventh- and eighth-
graders from Wayne County, Nebraska, who are getting the grand
tour of the hundred-year-old institution and learning what will
eventually happen to the heifers, steers, and hogs the schoolchil-
dren are raising for the 4-H Club. "By" Phillips, the voice of the
stockyards on forty radio stations that broadcast daily livestock
prices, is the tour guide.

The stockyards are a "livestock hotel," Phillips says. The pens
are jammed with "slaughter livestock," already fattened and being
sold to one of the eleven packing firms in Omaha. Under a system
called "private treaty selling," buyers for the slaughterhouses tour
the pens, one firm at a time, and submit bids on the cattle. "That's
what we call competition," Phillips tells the youngsters. Up to
twelve thousand cattle and fifteen thousand hogs are traded this
way each week.

Today there will also be a general auction of about two thousand
"feeder cattle." These will be shipped out to feeder lots for fattening
and then brought back again for another stay at the livestock hotel
on their journey to America's dinner tables.

The auction arena is a 40-by-20-foot oval of sawdust, rimmed
by a wooden amphitheater. An electronic tote board behind the
auctioneer's podium flashes the program number and weight of the
next 900-odd pounds of hamburger on the hoof, a metal gate opens,
the steer is prodded into the arena, and the auctioneer launches

into his rapid-fire bidding spiel that, to the uninitiated, might just
as well be a Federal Express commercial in Arabic for all the sense
it makes.

The buyers on the bleachers, some of them consulting on telephones, seem equally divided between those who wear cowboy
hats and cowboy boots and those who wear farm-implement caps
and work boots. But everyone is wearing a hat. Finding someone
in this place with an uncovered head is about as easy as finding a
vegetarian-plate special in the stockyard cafeteria. Bids are made
by an indifferent flick of the wrist, and I'm afraid to swat a fly
away from my face for fear of ending up as the owner of a half-
ton steer at sixty-one cents a pound. It would never fit in the
Discovery.

The auctioning of one steer takes thirty-two seconds. The newly
sold steer is goaded through a gate at the other end of the arena,
chased by horseback through the maze of pens and chutes to an
awaiting cattle truck, and before I have a chance finally to shoo
that fly, another animal is tramping the sawdust, and the auctioneer
is cranking his voice up for another attempt at the North American
oral speed record.

Outside, where the May morning is gray and raw again, the
"private treaty selling" is going on. The pens are arranged to provide a variety of perspectives on the cattle: from the fence rails,
from the chutes, and from catwalks strung about fifteen feet above
the red-brown backs of the cattle. Each steer—most of them are
white-faced Herefords—has a plastic tag on its left ear, with an
identification number in large numerals. The cattle mill about,
shoulder to shoulder, staring at each other's identification tags with
an open-eyed, almost stunned, expression on their faces, like rural
delegates at their first convention in a big city. I'm tempted to ask
them how they like their "hotel" accommodations and whether
they've seen what's on the menu for the concluding banquet.

About thirty years after the Lewis and Clark expedition, the German Prince Maximilian of Wied and the Swiss artist Karl Bodmer
traveled up the Missouri River as far as central Montana. They
met with Clark in St. Louis, and the explorer loaned them a set
of his maps. They even wintered among the same tribes—the
Mandans and Hidatsas—who had welcomed the Corps of Discovery. The detailed journals and diaries of Maximilian, added to the

Lewis and Clark journals, provide historians and ethnologists with the most extensive existing description of the life of Plains tribes before the onslaught of white acculturation. Bodmer's watercolors and sketches are probably even more valuable; they are to early nineteenth-century Indian culture what Walker Evans's and Dorothea Lange's photographs are to the Depression: vivid images that portray more than words could ever describe. The journals and pictures, owned by the Internorth Art Foundation, are on permanent display at the Joslyn Art Museum's Center for Western Studies in Omaha.

Dr. Joseph Porter, curator of western American history and ethnology for the center, takes me through the collection. We peruse Bodmer's watercolors: stunning landscapes of the eerie White Cliffs region of the Upper Missouri, scenes of Indian village life, including a picture of the interior of a Mandan earth lodge, and portraits of chiefs adorned with eagle feathers and porcupine quills and with their chests painted to demonstrate their battle victories. One watercolor, of the Hidatsa chief Addih-Hiddisch, shows the tall Indian wearing a peace medal handed out by Lewis and Clark; another depicts Charbonneau, the French interpreter who, with his Indian wife Sacagawea, accompanied the explorers to the Pacific Ocean and back, introducing Maximilian to tribal leaders.

The area of the Missouri River so carefully drawn in the Bodmer collection still lies ahead of me. Looking at the pictures takes me forward in geography to what is awaiting and backward in time to what has vanished since the voyage of Lewis and Clark. A few weeks after Maximilian and Bodmer left the Mandans and Hidatsas, Sioux raiding parties wiped out two Hidatsa villages; three years later, the smallpox epidemic of 1837 left the Mandans on the verge of extinction. A Corps of Engineers dam built after World War II put most of what was left of the tribal lands under water.

One of Porter's specialties is U.S. military history in the West. He has just finished a biography of Captain John G. Bourke, who served on the staff of General George Crook, the Army leader the Plains Indians both feared for his skill in the field and revered for his honesty, so rare in their dealings with whites. Like Bourke, the man he wrote about, Porter has spent enough time among Indians to acquire a respect for them individually and a sympathy—clear-eyed, not weepingly sentimental—for the way Manifest Destiny pulverized their culture. During one of his stays with the

Mandans and Hidatsas in North Dakota, he brought along slides of Bodmer's prints.

"Imagine what it's like for them to look at these pictures," he says. "An Indian goes to school, sees pictures of Washington and Jefferson, and wonders: 'What happened to my old people? Don't we have any famous people? Aren't there any pictures of my ancestors?' For us, this collection is valuable for historical research; for them, it's a vital link to their own past."

"Kind of like family movies," I suggest.

"Yeah, it was." Then he puts it more academically. "It was a visual documentation that Indians are often deprived of."

Porter has also written about the West as a "romantic horizon," and about how artists like Bodmer, George Catlin, Alfred Jacob Miller, Frederic Remington, and Charles Russell simultaneously provided the East with realistic portraits of life on the Plains and with the stirring images that helped form a national mythology. His own family history reflects the frequent clash of myth and reality.

"My grandfather had TB," he says. "The cure at the time, like the cure for so many things, was to move west. So he packed up the family and went to the South Platte in Colorado."

"Did it work?"

"No. My grandfather died out there."

The Great Plains Black Museum is much smaller than the Joslyn Art Museum, and in a different section of Omaha. When I walk in, I bump into another school tour. (It's getting near the end of a school year, and teachers have realized that by mid-May the most they can hope for from students is that the kids are at least willing to file on and off a yellow bus.) Students from the ethnic-studies class at Millard South High School are roaming through the small rooms of the makeshift museum.

"You in a hurry?" a voice calls to me as I sign the guest book. I turn to face a short, smiling black woman. The students and other adults are all white.

"No," I answer.

"Good," she says quickly. "I like to meet people who aren't in a hurry." She reaches out her hand. "I'm Bertha Calloway: owner, founder, director, proprietor, and janitor. I'll be your friendly tour guide."

She gathers the students around her commanding yet exuberant presence and begins a ten-minute speech about the West, and the role minority groups played in its development. She mentions black slaves helping the Mormons in Salt Lake City, the Chinese and Irish building the railroads. Her tone and choice of examples seem to build a sense of pride and camaraderie for those history may have overlooked.

"All through our history you will see that there were many minority groups that played an important part," she tells the students. "Trace your own roots. You will be surprised that there were a lot of poor people that came to this country 'cause they were looking for a better life."

She returns to the subject of blacks in the West: black cowboys—there were a significant number after the Civil War—who rode the long cattle trails; the "Buffalo Soldiers" (named by the Indians because of their dark, tightly curled hair) who were stationed in the Plains and Southwest during the end of the Indian Wars and into the World War I era; and Billy Pickett, the rodeo cowboy who invented the bulldogging event and once did it as a command performance for the Queen of England.

"When it all comes together," she says, "there's no doubt in my mind that people are beginning to realize more and more that the West wasn't all white."

Knowing my particular interest, she elaborates, and occasionally exaggerates, for the students about York, the black man with Lewis and Clark. He was valuable to the expedition, she says, and the Indians were very fond of him. "They could call him a slave or whatever they wanted to call him," she says. "In our museum we call him the Trailblazer, the Pathfinder."

Mrs. Calloway senses the extent of the students' academic fervor in May, and she has her own broader purposes of ethnic understanding when she suggests that the class spend the last half hour of their field trip not in the museum but touring the stores of the neighborhood. The Millard South ethnic-studies class heads out the door; she and I talk a little more. We're standing outside when the kids return, and she grabs two students to pose with her for a picture.

"Don't make me look too much like Lena Horne; I can't leave my museum to go to Hollywood," she says, and then turns to the girls: "Anyone bother you?"

"No," they say.

"Don't I have a nice neighborhood? Come back sometime and spend some money."

Before I depart, she takes me aside.

"Sometimes, we have to write our own history, Mr. Duncan," she confides—proudly, not apologetically.

"You're doing it pretty well," I tell her.

"I hope we are."

And Bertha Calloway goes back into her museum.

A thumbnail history of Offutt Air Force Base, just south of Omaha, is the story of the chain-reaction acceleration of events and technology during the last century. As the eastern terminus of the Union Pacific Railroad, Omaha was a logical site for a military post when the Plains were the remaining largely unsettled frontier of the nation. A fort was completed in 1896 and named Fort Crook to honor the renowned Indian fighter and Civil War hero. America's first air unit, the 61st Balloon Company, was assigned to the fort during World War I. In the 1920s, it was renamed Offutt Field in the memory of First Lieutenant Jarvis Offutt of Omaha, who died in 1918 while with the Royal Flying Corps in France. A bomber plant at the base built the *Enola Gay* and *Bock's Car*, the B-29s that ended World War II by dropping atomic bombs on Japan. Since 1948, it has served as headquarters of the Strategic Air Command.

If thermonuclear war between the superpowers ever breaks out, the recommendation to the president of whether to launch America's land- and submarine-based missiles and its nuclear-equipped bombers, and the implementation of the president's orders, will come from an underground command center here. In the sequence of cataclysmic attack and retaliation that would occur in an all-out war, as the history of mankind on earth turned to cinder, Omaha, obviously a prime Soviet target, would be one of the first places incinerated.

Some citizens of Glenwood, Iowa, just across the Missouri River from the base, are taking one of the special evening tours of the headquarters periodically arranged by SAC Joe Porter and I have been permitted to join them. They are a collection of farmers, some in bib overalls and caps, and their wives, and a few businessmen from the community of 5,280. We wait for our guide in a lobby lined with scale models of B-52 and B-1 bombers, KC-135 tankers, the new Cruise missile, and an SR-71 reconnnaissance plane. The chaplain's is the office closest to the exit.

Before taking us to an upstairs conference room for an hour and a half of briefings, our guide asks us to walk single file through the corridors, close to one wall, in case the guards are sent running through the halls with their M-16s as part of a test alert.

A young captain gives us the first half of the briefing, an overview of SAC. He's friendly and has a relaxed, almost unmilitary bearing—like your next-door neighbor's oldest son—and begins by chatting with us about how much he and his wife like the Omaha area, how warm it seems compared to his last stint in North Dakota, how thankful he is to see trees again when he jogs.

The captain explains SAC's resources of missiles and bombers and the Navy's missile-equipped submarines. Scattered across the Midwest and Plains—as far inland from both coasts and therefore as far from enemy attack as possible—are clusters of underground launch-control centers, each manned round the clock by two-man crews, and each in charge of ten Minuteman missiles in underground silos within miles of their vicinity. Two keys must be turned simultaneously to launch the missiles, he says, and they are twelve feet apart in the underground capsule to ensure that one person, for whatever reason, doesn't unleash a warhead into the atmosphere; for extra security, a launch also requires key-turns from a separate command capsule.

His tone is personable and reassuring—the lecture is punctuated heavily with phrases like "as you probably know . . ." and "people I talk to . . ." to make us feel comfortable with it all. On the screen behind him flash silent photographs and short movie reels of bombers in formation and missiles trailing white plumes into azure skies, as mesmerizingly beautiful, despite the horror they imply, as the Bodmer prints Porter had shown me this morning.

The conference-room lights come back on, and the second part of the briefing, on the Soviet threat, begins with a new lecturer. This one is a major who talks in clipped, forceful sentences, one arm crooked behind his stiff back and a wooden pointer in his other as he rocks back and forth on the balls of his feet.

"I've been watching the Russians for fourteen years," he tells us at the start, and the point of his talk—reinforced by his bearing, so different from the captain's—is that the Russians aren't like us at all; they are hard to understand and not to be trusted. While the impression left by the captain has been that our missiles are in the hands of people just like the rest of us, more or less an extension of the Glenwood Rotary Club rather than a separate military establishment, the major's implication is that watching the Russians and making decisions about their actions is something better left to professionals like himself.

According to his view, the Soviets backed down during the Cuban missile crisis because the United States had them outgunned, something they vowed would happen "never again." Since that time, he says, they have armed themselves unceasingly. Now, by his balance sheet, we are outnumbered in manpower, oil supplies for naval vessels, missiles, fighter planes, radar installations, surface-to-air missiles, antiballistic missile installations, hardened silos, tanks, artillery, ships, hardened bunkers and hangars, military research and development funds, and devices for chemical, biological, and radiological warfare. The United States, he says, prevails in some of its technology and the accuracy of its missiles.

"The balance of power has shifted, and I want to make sure you know I'm quoting *them* now," he says. "Once and for all, and irrevocably." But SAC's continuing preparedness, he says, is making sure that every day when "Ivan and Gregor sit down in their basement to figure out the balance, Ivan turns to Gregor and says: 'Not tonight, Gregor, not tonight.' "

Keeping in single file and hugging the wall, we descend a series of stairs and hallway ramps, past several guarded checkpoints, through some openings that can be closed with two-foot-thick doors, to the underground command center. As we're poised at the final checkpoint, waiting for clearance to enter, the guide informs us that this huge bunker would not actually withstand direct nuclear bombardment; but it could function as a self-contained fallout shelter for thirty days. Unless "Ivan and Gregor" are either much more poorly equipped or worse shots than the major has portrayed them, it's hard to imagine a nuclear exchange that wouldn't have the SAC nerve center near the top of the list of targets.

This news clearly baffles a number of us, as does the slide on one of the five big screens that form the long wall we face from the command balcony, where the generals would sit and filter the magnified information on the screens as they make decisions on the fate of the globe. The slide gives an official SAC welcome to the residents of *Denison*, Iowa. It's a minor mistake, to be sure, but as I sit in the balcony with the residents of *Glenwood*, Iowa, I think back to the first lesson I learned at a small newspaper, where my job was to write obituaries. My editor insisted that I double-check the spelling of the name of the deceased, rather than relying on the notice provided by the funeral parlor.

"Obituaries are one thing everyone reads and everyone understands," he would tell me when I objected to the extra work. "A misspelled name gets them thinking that if the paper can't even get the name of a dead man right, they can't believe anything else in the paper. It ruins our credibility." And my guess is that the talk in downtown Glenwood tomorrow is not going to be about the impressive technology and displays we've been shown as much as how anyone could possibly mistake Glenwood for Denison.

For us civilians, some of the logic of the bunker world seems turned upside down. We've been assured that, on the American side of the nuclear battlements, every possible precaution has been taken to prevent careless mistakes; and then one is made. On the other side, we've been told, the people with the missiles are untrustworthy and war-happy, just waiting for the right moment to strike; and now, apparently, they're so far ahead of us in weaponry that they're not going to. In the major's lexicon, bomber planes were "birds" and nuclear-tipped missiles were "rascals"; the latest, biggest, and most accurate offensive missile in our arsenal was the "Peacekeeper." While nuclear war is described by some as "survivable," the command post for our side isn't built to last beyond the first volley.

Peace is reigning on this evening in the bunker. From our perch behind the glass in the balcony, we look down on a long bank of communication stations, dimly lit in the darkness of the room. Clocks above the screens give the time for Omaha, Zulu (Greenwich, England), Moscow, and Guam. Things are quiet and unhurried beneath us; Joe thinks he sees one man balancing his checkbook. Our tour guide tells us to make ourselves comfortable for the presentation.

"But if a red phone next to you rings, don't answer," he jokes. "It's probably for someone else, anyway."

A man on the floor, speaking through a microphone, reiterates the captain's details about SAC's mission, the multiple safeguards against an unauthorized nuclear launch, the weapons in the arsenal, and the redundancy and survivability of the "command-control." There are more slides of planes and missiles on the screen, and the lecturer has one of the men call an Air Force base in Alaska to demonstrate the instantaneous communications available to the top brass. The report from Alaska is that the weather's cold.

An airborne command post, called "Looking Glass," is constantly flying an undisclosed, random pattern across the central United States, the lecturer says. If Washington and Omaha were turned to rubble in a surprise attack, the Looking Glass commander could still communicate a launch order to the missile silos from his modified Boeing 707 and settle the score. The lecturer asks a radio man to demonstrate their communication to the plane.

"Looking Glass, this is SAC, over?" we hear on the speakers. There's a long pause.

"Looking Glass, this is SAC, over?" Another span of silence.

"Looking Glass, this is SAC, over?" Still nothing. The lecturer goes on to another topic. Several minutes later, Looking Glass reports in and gives us a short summary of their equipment. The tour guide with us in the balcony says the plane must have been doing some "silent running" when we first tried to reach it, and that the lapse of time is nothing to worry about. Something more for coffee conversation at a Glenwood cafe tomorrow morning.

Back outside, Porter and I notice the clouds of the last few days have cleared. *The air is pure and healthy, as far as we can judge.* The stars twinkle in the timeless black void of the night sky. On a clear evening in 1804, when an air gun was sufficient to impress potential adversaries and repeating rifles were yet to be invented, Lewis and Clark would have looked up and seen the same thing. For them, camped on the edge of the known world, the stars at night and the next day's sunrise were the only unshakable certainties. In a different time, on the edge of a different unknown, I look to the stars—seemingly the only unchanged sights in our two journeys—seeking the same certainty. But it's not there. Not tonight, not tonight.

6

Against the Current

Children. The great chief of the Seventeen great nations of America, impelled by his parental regard for his newly adopted children on the troubled waters, has sent us out to clear the road, remove every obstruction, and to make it a road of peace between himself and his red children residing there; to enquire into the Nature of their wants, and on our return to inform Him of them, in order that he may make the necessary arrangements for their relief. . . .

Children. We hope that the great Spirit will open your ears to our councils, and dispose your minds to their observance. Follow these councils and you will have nothing to fear, because the great Spirit will smile upon your nation, and in future ages will make you out-number the trees of the forest.

From Captain Meriwether Lewis's
speech to the Oto Indians
August 3, 1804

The Missouri River floodplain is wider between Nebraska and Iowa—from six to fifteen miles of bottomland between the higher ground on either side—and the hills and bluffs that define its limits are gentler. The river itself, running north–south here, is the boundary for more than states. It is the border between those places where rainfall is taken for granted and those where the word "moisture" pops up in conversations with a tone of concern. West of the Missouri, the concept of lushness begins evaporating until it is dried from thought at the Continental Divide; the eastern side of the river usually gets all the rain it needs.

On the Iowa side, the bluffs are scalloped, rounded, and dimpled. Driving toward them from the river is like traveling across the bottom of an empty pieshell toward the raised edges of the crust. The hills are a range of pygmy mountains, with a false treeline on the slopes below the bald tops. A silo on a farm nestled along the hills rises to half the height of the "peaks" behind it, exposing the true scale of things. Thousands of years ago, fierce winds blowing across the south face of the glaciers of the Plains carried tons of silt, depositing it on the east side of the river. The result was this line of bluffs, called Loess Hills by geologists, and the rich soil of the cornbelt on the downwind side: Iowa, which produces one tenth of the nation's food by itself, even though it is the smallest of the eleven states touched by the Lewis and Clark trail.

State Highway 183 passes a sign saying: SKI CRESCENT HILLS. It's not often that you look across a half mile of cornfield toward a ski resort.

Crescent, Iowa (population 284), has a satellite dish dealer selling the television receivers (they look like oversized birdbaths turned on one side to dump the dirty water) that are now as common to rural America as mudflaps on pickups. They point toward the heavens, plugging every farmhouse into an international Chautauqua. Each time I pass one, I imagine a family hurrying home from a church social and arguing whether the kids can see the latest rock videos on MTV, or whether Dad can watch something on a twenty-four-hour sports network, and later, when the kids are in bed, Dad trying to get Mom to join him on the living-room davenport for some soft porn from Sweden.

Honey Creek, Iowa, is a small post office, a bar under renovation, and two or three houses—a lovely name for a town, but not enough residents to have its population listed on the map. Checking the map on the move to learn this, I drive through Loveland, Iowa (also no population listing), without even seeing the town.

More than half of Iowa's 99 counties have lost population since the 1980 census. Harrison County, which I enter just after blinking and missing Loveland, is one of them.

"A lot of good people are going down the drain," says Gary Guge, the county's agricultural agent for the Cooperative Extension Service, when I meet him in Missouri Valley (population 3,107).

He's talking about farmers, but in this part of America, when the farmer suffers, everyone suffers. Enough good farmers go down the drain, and a rural society based upon them gets sucked under in the same swirl.

A bank in Woodbine closed its doors this winter: too many loans to too many farmers who could no longer keep up. In Dunlap, there once were five implement dealers, three car dealerships, and two lumberyards; now there are none. Stories are told of farmers who once supplied food to a soup kitchen for the poor now being its patrons. Main streets of the small towns have vacant storefronts that look like missing teeth in what once was a wide smile. At regular intervals along the country roads are empty houses, and FOR SALE signs stand next to the mailboxes of many of the occupied ones.

The depression sweeping over the prairies began in the early 1980s. Farmers survive on credit—they have to borrow money for equipment, for livestock, and for the crop they put in the ground. They use their land for collateral. During the seventies, farm exports were booming, government policies encouraged fencerow-to-fencerow plantings, and inflation propelled many farmers to expand their holdings. Then the bottom fell out.

"It was like running a train into a brick wall," Guge says.

The bricks in the wall included: a distortion of the gap between a farmer's costs and the price he gets for his product (for instance,

the price of corn dropped a lot more than the price of fertilizers or
tractors), a plummet in farm exports, which built up domestic
surpluses and dropped farm prices even further, a series of bad-
weather years that decreased yields, and land prices—the collateral
for the loans that carry the pumped-up interest rates of the inflation
years—that fell by a half.

As the rest of the nation recovered from a deep recession, the
farm belt slipped further into a long depression. Our constantly
improving ability to grow more food with fewer people, combined
with policies to keep food cheap for consumers, is like an economic
neutron bomb on agricultural America: the verdant land and the
buildings are untouched; only the people are hit and disappearing.

"The bad farm managers were weeded out a long time ago.
Some real good farmers aren't farming this year, and some real
good people will have the plug pulled on them this fall, once their
crop is in," Guge says. Across the nation, almost half of the 2.2
million farms are expected to go under by the year 2000, when it
is predicted that fifty thousand big operations will grow three fourths
of all the food and fiber we need.

I think of Lewis and Clark as they traveled up the river along
this stretch, finding some Indian villages abandoned because of
smallpox epidemics, raids by hostile tribes, or hunts to follow the
buffalo migrations.

"What would I find here if I came back in twenty years, on the
two-hundredth anniversary of their journey?" I ask.

Guge has spent twenty-one years with the farmers and farm
communities of Harrison County. He says this has been a good
crop year, maybe things will stabilize a little. Then he talks about
a banker friend who has confided, like a desperate confessor, that
his bank has loaned money to some good farmers this year only in
order to get one more crop from them before foreclosing. He talks
about the ascendancy of giant corporate farms, the possible survival of small part-time farmers who have income-producing jobs
away from the land, and the disappearance of the mid-size farm
that has been the foundation for a way of life since the settlers first
turned the prairie sod. As he talks, his eyes turned away toward
the wall, he works his way around an answer he is fighting against
having to give. Then his gaze returns to me from the writing on
the wall.

"I don't particularly look forward to just dealing with the president of General Motors," he says.

State Highway 300 takes me north along the river side of the Loess Hills, through a small town called California, through Modale, and into Mondamin (population 420). The single-block downtown has a small-engine garage, an American Legion post, a Montgomery Ward catalogue sales center, Vic's Place and Grill, Country Store Antiques ("open by chance or appointment"), a post office, a Laundromat, a flower store, and a clothing and hardware store that also serves as a bus station. Amidst these faded stucco and brick buildings from the 1920s is the Mondamin Savings Bank, the only newly renovated structure in town.

Jim Unruh, the young president of the bank, has a small glassed-in office that sticks into the lobby—a desk, phone, two chairs, and a computer terminal. Ninety percent of his business is agricultural loans, he tells me. Virtually all of the farm operators couldn't pay off their loans last year, so they were rolled over into this year.

"Half of 'em would be done this year, if the crops are no good—and that would take me out as well," he says. "It looks like a good crop this year, but that will just allow them to make payments on debt they didn't used to have. It took just two years to get into trouble; it takes a lot longer to get out."

The same forces impelling the farms toward larger acreages worked by fewer people are bearing on the banking business, Unruh says. ("Get big or get out" is a phrase you hear a lot in Harrison County.) There are equal traces of bitterness and resignation when he talks about small banks like the one in Woodbine being closed by the government while a giant bank in Chicago gets bailed out: "It's all a matter of where you are and how big you are."

He thinks corporate farms, with one farmer working three thousand acres as an employee, are inevitable. And that means the end of small towns like his.

"Like the farmsteads—they're just about all gone now—small towns are next," he says. "I'm out of business then, too. Maybe it will take another forty years. The handful of small-timers who survive will do well; they'll reap some benefits when the big-timers have enough control to raise farm prices. But that's what's going to happen."

The talk is of "structural change" in agriculture: breakthroughs in science that increase yields that create surpluses and depressed prices instead of feeding the world; greater mechanization to till the land; tax laws that draw corporations into farm-owning precisely because they need the losses against nonfarm profits; international markets and national policies for which small farmers and small farm towns and small banks are unimportant commodities as long as there're still cattle going to the slaughterhouse and grain being grown for sale.

It's called a "shakeout" of the farm economy, a "realignment." The terms are coldly impersonal. The forces at work, slowly depopulating a region and closing a chapter of rural life, seem as unanswerable and inevitable as the winds and glaciers that created the loess, as far removed as a satellite beaming TV signals to a little house on the prairie.

Two other men I meet in this region are on opposite ends of the "shakeout." Both are in their late thirties, both were raised on farms, both have wives and children, both have the sunburn on their lower arms and on their faces from the shadow line of their caps to their chins that are as emblematic of farming as the dirt in their fingernails. Both agree to talk to me only on the condition that their names and locations not be disclosed. A sense of shame at his circumstances is the reason for one man's insistence on anonymity; a slight tinge of guilt is the other's unspoken motive.

The first farmer lives on land homesteaded by his grandparents. A copy of the land patent, signed by President Rutherford B. Hayes in 1878, is framed on the wall of the kitchen, next to a certificate honoring the farm for being in the same family for a hundred years.

The initial moments of our talk are awkward. He brings out a small plastic box and opens it on the kitchen table. One by one, he pulls out ribbons and medals he won in his youth in 4-H and the Future Farmers of America: one for gardening, two for leadership, several for cattle judging, a ribbon and medal awarded at the state fair. He lingers over the explanation of each one, lays them on the table, and stares at them. In the silence, I realize this is something he has done as much for himself as it was to show me his professional credentials. He is seeking answers from the ribbons, because he is losing his family's farm and can't figure out what he did wrong, where he failed, why this is happening to him.

He's played by the rules he was taught, but the game has changed and may soon leave him with nothing but these mementoes.

The farmer looks up at me, seeing an Easterner at his table, and an Easterner means a city person in his mind. This turns him angry.

"You ever clean a cow that hadn't cleaned when her afterbirth or placenta hasn't come out right? You ever do that?" he demands.

"No."

"You ever have somethin' go wrong with a sow that can't have her pigs, and it's snowin' and the vet isn't going to get over here? What're you going to do then?"

"I don't know."

"Well I'll tell ya what you'd better know," he says, his voice rising and quavering. "You better know how to get them pigs out. Now if you're going to have a veterinary do this work, this is fine, but he's gonna demand veterinary wages. He isn't going to go borrow that money to pull that cow or pull them pigs. He ain't gonna do that.

"You tell me about independent agriculture, I'm going to tell you somethin'. I wouldn't—" and he loses his train of thought in an explosion of frustration. "I'm so goddamned mad at you people in the city. If some man is starvin' and says he's got to have some food, I'll say, 'Okay, here's a damn shovel. You go and you work your ass off here and I might give you somethin' to eat.' This is involuntary slavery. They're tellin' me if I want to save my ancestors' farms then . . ." and he trails off again, ". . . then I'm going to do whatever it takes."

I tell him I was born and raised in a small town in Iowa. This information—or perhaps the thought that he's just blown up in his kitchen, with his 4-H ribbons listening—calms him down, and he explains his situation. The bank he did business with has been taken over by the Federal Deposit Insurance Corporation to protect the bank's depositors. The bank had too many uncollectible farm loans on its books and was headed for insolvency. The farmer's was not one of the bad loans; he had always made his payments on time. But when the FDIC took over, their concern was the good depositors, not the good borrowers, and there has been an interminable maze of paperwork in trying to get a loan to operate this season. He needs the loan to put crops in his field to raise feed for his cattle and hogs; the FDIC wants more collateral, but the value of his collateral, his land, is going down, not up. Things looked like they'd work out, but the FDIC personnel running the bank are stretched thin—so many bank failures to supervise. The person he was dealing with just left on a two-week vacation, leaving his crisis in the IN basket.

"I've had it with this mad runaround," he says. "I don't know how many miles I've put on going into town, going to the bank, going to an attorney, trying to find some sanity in this mess." His lawyer has fifteen other clients in the same fix: no loan, no crop; no crop, no feed; no feed, no livestock; no livestock, no income to pay back the loan and mortgage. The farmer has sold off most of his livestock to pay his bills. The FDIC garnishees his checks, requiring that they be made out jointly to him and the bank. "They're literally telling you, you can farm without receiving an income," he says.

He's done everything the way he was taught, he says. He never overexpanded his land holdings, never bought fancy equipment when times were good. He had running water and a new bathroom put in the house when he took it over from his parents, bought a TV for the kids, but not much more.

"I think the land-grant colleges that emphasized increased production forgot that you've got to sell your production," he says. "It would be like Ford or Chrysler constantly running their plants at maximum production whether there was a market or not. It's a sad situation. We hear of people starving all over the world, even here in the United States with the street people. They ain't got enough to eat every day. But again, I can't produce without dollars—for fuel, repairs, veterinary supplies, equipment."

"Do you think your kids will farm?"

"Hope not," he answers. "I don't want 'em tied into involuntary servitude."

"What will you do?"

"I have no idea. I don't want to leave, and I can't stay. I suppose, had I stayed with fifteen cows and went and got a job someplace instead of borrowing money to farm—" He pauses to rephrase. "I guess *that* was what I was supposed to have done instead of thinkin' I got somethin' with these dumb awards from 4-H and FFA."

The other farmer who doesn't want his name used talks with me in his office. Raised on a farm and educated in agronomy, he doesn't have a farm of his own; he manages and farms other people's land. A majority of his clients are absentee owners or, increasingly, banks that need someone to run the farms they've just foreclosed.

He tells me how commodity prices have dropped while farming costs haven't. "Farmers are in a Catch-22," he says. "They're losing money but they have to produce to make their payments and minimize their losses."

"Adjust" is a word he uses often. The price of fertilizer and equipment and seed and fuel—the farmer's costs—won't adjust down. Prices paid for commodities and meat—the farmer's income—won't adjust up because of surpluses and increased international competition. Only two things are left to adjust. Land values, a "hard asset but only worth what someone will pay for it," he says, have adjusted. They've adjusted down, taking the loans and some of the banks with them. And the number of farmers is adjusting. "We'll end up producing the same bushels, but selling for less," he says. "But the ones who can't sell for less will be adjusted out."

He sees it as an inevitable process. "I don't think the rest of society will bail out 4 percent of us," he says. "We don't have the right to ask for it, anyway. There's no God-given right to be the head of a $1.5 million business, and that's what farming is now, a business. Family farms aren't subsistence farms anymore. They raise one crop. They're a business and business is risk. What's the difference between them and a guy who buys a McDonald's franchise and then the street is abandoned? Are we supposed to rescue him?"

And so every day he goes out to the land that now belongs to the banks or to investors far away and does what he was taught in 4-H and FFA: he farms. He tills the soil, driving a tractor past the empty houses of people who have been "adjusted out." He asks again to make sure I won't reveal his name or the county where he works. What he does is a "sensitive subject right now," he says. Some people might not understand that he's just doing his job. The rules of the game have changed, and he's adjusted to them.

I ask him about the farm he grew up on. His father is retiring from it, he says, and his oldest brother will be taking it over.

"If I had the opportunity, I'd probably prefer to be home with my father, if I could make a living at it," he admits.

"Why?"

"Don't know for sure. I ask myself the same question. It has a certain draw to me."

The first meeting between Plains Indians and official representatives of the United States took place about fifteen miles north of present-day Omaha, on August 3, 1804, when Lewis and Clark received a small delegation of the Oto and Missouri tribes. The men of the expedition paraded for the Indians, and then Lewis, standing under the keelboat's sailcloth erected as an awning against the August sun, stood to deliver a long speech. A flag with seventeen stars, one for each of the states in the union, fluttered nearby.

The captain explained that the land now belonged to a new "White Father" whose "cities are as numerous as the stars of the heavens, and whose people like the grass of your plains, cover with their Cultivated fields and wigwams, the wide Extended country, reaching from the western borders of the Mississippi, to the great lakes of the East, where the land ends and the Sun rises from the face of the great waters."

In his speech—which would be repeated to every tribe the Corps of Discovery would meet for the next two years—Lewis addressed the guests as "children," in accordance with the prevailing attitude toward the people who had been inhabiting the continent centuries before European whites had even realized that the earth wasn't flat.

Lewis employed a combination of promises and threats to make his points. The new American father expected his red children to make peace among themselves and to trade exclusively with the St. Louis merchants who would be following the expedition, Lewis said. If they did not, he warned, they would receive no trade goods and "bring all the Calamaties of want upon you"; the ferocious might of the "Seventeen great nations of America" would be turned against them and "consume you as the fire consumes the grass of the plains."

But, he said, if they heeded their new father, "the only friend to whom you can now look for protection . . . he will take care that you shall have no just cause to regret this change; he will serve you, & not deceive you." Delegations were invited to visit Washington to meet the president and see for themselves the wealth, power, and happiness that could be theirs.

As would happen throughout the journey, the Indians were not particularly impressed or concerned by the display of American power shown by the small band of explorers, nor would lengthy oratory bring an end to the cycle of intertribal raiding and fighting that was as much a part of Plains life as the buffalo hunt. But they were interested in trade. The whites could provide things the Indians wanted—ornamental beads, finer-grade tobacco, whiskey, and, most important, machined goods like rifles that they needed for hunting and warfare. The meeting ended with the presentation of gifts and medals from the explorers and a demonstration of Lewis's airgun: the carrot and the stick.

A little farther up the river, near the current Omaha Indian reservation, a meeting with the Oto and Missouri chiefs who had missed the first council vividly demonstrated the gulf between the two cultures, white and red, that would mark U.S.–Indian relations on the Plains for the next nearly two hundred years.

That barbarity and civilization are in the eye of the beholder was made clear when the parley with the chiefs was delayed while the captains dealt with the court-martial of Moses Reed, who had deserted two weeks earlier and had just been brought back to camp. Reed was found guilty and sentenced to run a gauntlet between the men of the party four times, while they all lashed his bare back with switches. The chiefs, appalled by this measure of punishment and humiliation for a man, petitioned for Reed's pardon, prompting a short speech from the captains "explan'g the Customs of our Countrey" before the punishment proceeded.

On the other side of this cultural divide, Lewis and Clark's naïve plans for peace among the Indian nations were put into clearer focus when the chiefs explained the nature of their disputes with neighboring tribes. Two Missouri warriors had been killed trying to steal horses from the Omahas; their deaths demanded vengeance. Similarly, the Otos and Missouris believed the Pawnees would soon be retaliating for the theft of corn from a Pawnee village. The captains' lofty rhetoric would have as much effect on quelling these blood feuds as would a minister's exhorting the Hatfields and the McCoys to turn the other cheek.

More misunderstanding resulted when the captains unintentionally slighted a high-ranking Missouri chief with lower-grade gifts, when the chiefs' proposal that a supply of whiskey might keep them from attacking the Pawnees and Omahas was rejected, and when the Indians felt that most of the keelboat's supplies were being saved for their upriver enemies, the Sioux. On the positive side, the Otos and Missouris finally agreed to let the captains arrange a peace between them and the Omahas; but the Omahas were out hunting buffalo, and the explorers never made contact.

The years that followed the Corps of Discovery's journey did nothing to alleviate the cultural differences between these two worlds. The divine plan of Manifest Destiny had but a single hue in its rainbow—white. As the demand for furs and pelts obtained from Indians declined in the mid-1800s and settlers and miners pushed on to the High Plains, the increasingly outnumbered Indians became a hindrance to "progress." Having never been considered a culture to be understood and accommodated, the first Americans lost even the status of economic trading partners. If coexistence was ever possible, it was never attempted. Instead, the policy of the United States—which even in Jefferson's Declaration of Independence refers to native Americans as "the merciless Indian Savages"—was one of relentless conquest and subjugation. They were rounded up, relegated to reservations, and, still considered "red children," made into welfare wards of the government, expected to be neither seen nor heard.

The Oto and Missouri Indian tribes, the ones who had been told that if they followed the councils of their new white father would "outnumber the trees of the forest," are no longer here. The remnants of the two tribes live in Oklahoma, where there are even fewer trees than in Nebraska. Their combined population is 2,249.

As I pull into the Omaha Indian reservation at Macy, Nebraska, I don't have to worry whether anyone will be around. The buffalo are gone now; no one will be out hunting them. An unemployment rate of 70 percent keeps most people home.

The center of Macy is a few miles off U.S. Highway 75. The buildings—a small store, a gas station and garage, trailers, and government-built houses—are in various stages of disrepair. A large, brick school is newer, as are the tribal headquarters and health center on a hill overlooking town. Packs of sullen dogs crisscross the streets in front of the *Discovery*.

On the left side of a dirt street, trailers used for the reservation's Head Start program are enclosed by high steel fences with barbed wire on top. On the right are residential trailers. One of them is the home of Dennis Hastings, an Omaha Indian working on several projects dealing with tribal history.

Hastings is a large man with a soft voice and a shy smile, a veteran of both the Vietnam war and the symbolic Indian occupation of Alcatraz when he was a college student in California. He has about him the aura of a radical who has mellowed, someone who probably once had youthful, angry plans to overthrow an unfair world and now is determined instead to work quietly, even gently, with his people to pick up the shattered pieces of their culture and slowly rebuild a sense of pride and dignity against the ghettolike despair that pervades reservation life.

"The white man's way hasn't worked for the Omaha people," he says. "Their spirit's broke."

For Hastings, the way for recovery points in two directions: to the past, where the Omahas can rediscover self-worth through their former traditions; and to the future, where his people may someday combine the best of the Indian world with the best of the white world, rather than the worst of both.

"Who, really, are we? How do we control our own destiny? These are the questions we're asking ourselves," Hastings says. "We need to work on the future: what do we want? We haven't done that since the late 1800s. The Bureau [of Indian Affairs] has run our destiny since then.

"We're like gerbils here, you know. The government opens the cage, throws the government money in, shuts the cage, and we go gerbiling around doing whatever we were told to do."

He takes me to the school, where we meet Dr. Lawrence Cummings, the superintendent. Cummings, who came here from a suburban district in Colorado, says the Macy school district ranks highest in the state in unemployment and the percentage of disadvantaged homes. Most of the students, he says, don't know the Omaha language and don't learn English. "They're functionally illiterate in both languages," he says.

Cummings has started a native heritage program to instill pride in the youngsters, but his main emphasis has been on the "basics" of education, especially among the younger students. Using methods he describes as "very crude, very Skinnerian," a point system was started throughout the school; students win varying amounts of points for showing up for class on time, behaving in class, doing their work. In the school's hallway is a long, glassed-in case displaying items ranging from candy to toys to a television set. Below each item is its worth in points. Students can trade in their points for the items whenever they want.

Not only has this system improved attendance, punctuality, and performance, the superintendent says, it has had an unintended side effect. "Originally, the kids spent their points each day for candy bars," he says. "Now, they're saving them for larger items. They've learned the concept of 'delayed gratification.' "

Saving money and "delayed gratification" are not traditional concepts for the Plains Indians. For centuries before the whites arrived, the natives' culture was based on taking what was needed to survive—and nothing more—from the environment around them: the buffalo and other game, the wild berries on the riverbanks, fish, and some cultivated plants. In their harmonious cosmology, humans were merely another part, not the masters, of the earth. The idea of money was as foreign to their thinking as the notion that a human being could claim ownership of the land.

When the white world overwhelmed the Indians shortly before the start of the twentieth century, the adjustment was, not surprisingly, unsuccessful. Money paid for land taken from treaty lands was spent within days; land allocated to individual Indians (who didn't believe it could be owned in the first place) was often sold to white farmers, and the money spent again. BIA policies, at least those that were enacted to protect rather than exploit the Indians, began the cycle of dependence that endures today.

Given the reality that the ancient Indian life cannot be totally restored—the fences on the Plains are not going to be removed and the buffalo allowed to roam again, the vast hunting grounds that are now privately owned farms or coveted coal and oil deposits are not going to be given back to the tribes—the point system at the Macy school is a way for one culture to learn a basic tenet of another.

Dennis Hastings has a teenage daughter, Rainbow, a good student and outstanding athlete who has amassed three thousand points. This is more than enough to buy herself a television set, but she confides to me that some of her points will go toward a present for her father. Respect for elders and generosity being honored Indian traditions, this must be what Hastings means by combining the best of both worlds.

I return to Macy every morning for several days. Sometimes with Hastings as an intermediary, sometimes without him, I talk to a lot of people. One Omaha man, a former member of the tribal council, takes me into his kitchen and for nearly two straight hours recites a bleak history of his people: lands diminished, traditions lost, dignity denied. His assessment of the present is equally bitter: lack of education, rampant alcoholism, broken families, fractious bickering on the tribal council. Throughout the litany, there is no mention of possible solutions to the complaints he is listing.

"Our whole life has been terrible," he says. "Don't look at the rosy side."

I ask him what Lewis and Clark would notice most if they returned.

"Pollution," he answers. "The worst thing would be the pollution. And if he met the people, then, of course, he wouldn't recognize them, because of the change in their stature, their physical characteristics.

"I have diabetes, like many Indians," he says. "We used to live on buffalo. We lived on vegetables, mushrooms, milkweed, wild berries. We looked forward to all these things and the different things we ate in season. The sweetest thing we ate was honey, wild honey—just a little of that. We were geared to that food over centuries and centuries. Now everything is sugar."

He lets that thought sink in, as if giving me time to ponder the human consequences of a twenty-degree change in the world's temperature, and then adds: "I'm on Weight Watchers."

Another man talks about government-sponsored economic development projects as examples of failures of the BIA and tribal council to provide long-term employment. One project was starting a shop to customize exotic sports cars. The contractor, he says, used the development money to build the factory and then disappeared before the reality of the utter absence of a market for the product became clear.

Standing in his garden, his grandchildren playing at his feet, an elderly Omaha explains the ceremonies of the Native American Church—a religion begun in 1918 that mixes elements of Indian ceremonies, Christianity, and the vision-inducing peyote from Mexico.

"A lot of younger people are getting interested in it," he says.

"Why's that?"

"Searching," he says. "Searching for a better way of life, more meaning."

Sensing that I may not agree that hallucination is a practical response to the cultural disintegration I've encountered, he turns the tables on me. Indians aren't the only ones searching.

"Are you a hobbyist?" he asks.

I tell him I don't know what a hobbyist is. They're whites who like to dress up in painstakingly authentic Indian costumes and dance authentic Indian ceremonial dances, he says. He saw them once in New England, where I come from.

"Boy, those suckers could dance," he says. "And sing! I know good dancin' when I see it and good singin' when I hear it, and they could sure do it." He chuckles at the prospect of whites reincarnating ceremonies of a way of life their race has all but destroyed. "Amazing," he says.

When I tell Dennis Hastings about the conversations I've had on the reservation, and when I say that each time I pull into Macy I wonder how any society can cope with 70 percent unemployment, he becomes concerned I'm missing the "positive" signs he thinks are now beginning to appear among his people. He invites Porter and me to a gathering that evening of the Hethu'shka Society.

The Hethu'shkas were one of several societies among the Omahas; this one was restricted to warriors and was meant to encourage a heroic spirit in the people. A group of primarily older men revived it a year ago.

Three long tables are stretched across the kitchen and dining room of a house on the floodplain when we arrive and join a group of about thirty men, women, and children at the home of Charlie and Genevieve Holt. Platters of roast beef, corn, mashed potatoes, and gravy, handfuls of plastic utensils, and Styrofoam cups of coffee are passed down to everyone.

Hollis Stabler, a World War II veteran and president of the society, asks Elmer Blackbird to give the prayer before we eat. Blackbird—a tall man with an eagle nose, pursed lips, dark, limpid eyes, and the angular lines painters like Bodmer etched into the visual stereotype of an Indian's face—stands and begins the prayer. He speaks in Omaha in a lengthy, rhythmic oration interrupted by occasional grunts of approval from some of the older people at the table. His soft voice has a gravel timbre underlying it that I have already learned to recognize as typically Indian. The only recurring English words are "Jesus Christ."

After we eat, one by one nearly everyone stands and gives a short speech, thanking our hosts, praising Blackbird's prayer, and expressing the importance of the Hethu'shkas in keeping alive Omaha traditions and customs. Their tone is respectful and dignified.

The society is planning a dance ceremony on the weekend. A young man explains that he and several others intend to reenact a "buffalo run" and will arrive in time to help start the dance ceremony. Elmer Blackbird rises to inquire whether the rumor is true that they will be carrying a bundle of tobacco with them. He has heard this, and it troubles him. Tobacco is a sacred item, he says, used in prayer and important ceremonies; it would be inappropriate for "buffalo runners" to carry it. The society's ceremonial pipe has been lost to time, he explains, "but we still have tobacco, probably the only sacred thing we have left on the reservation." The young man agrees that his group, now knowing the tradition, won't carry a tobacco bundle.

Hollis Stabler says that an American flag presented to his family after his brother was killed in the battle of Angio will be flown. (A higher than usual percentage of male Omahas have seen military service, primarily in accordance with the honored role warriors traditionally played in their society, but partly as a way out of the suffocating economic conditions of the reservation. The same is true on all reservations.)

In the middle of the discussion, someone mentions that there has been a death on the reservation. Blackbird rises again. According to custom, he says, a dance celebration would not be respectful of the mourning family, even though they are not members of the society. The Hethu'shkas conclude their business by deciding to postpone the ceremony, and an elderly woman stands to praise the society for setting such a good example for the tribe.

Porter nudges me and then stands. He thanks the group for allowing him to attend the dinner, explains his job at the Joslyn Art Museum, and expresses his desire to learn more about the

Omahas and his hope that they can cooperate to bring Omaha artifacts now in Eastern museums back to the region for an exhibition.

When he sits, I rise. (Am I the modern Lewis and Porter Clark?) Following the other speakers' examples, I thank the Holts for their hospitality. I tell the group that I'm following the route of Lewis and Clark and, like the explorers, am far from my home and depending upon the kindness of strangers. I say their dinner has reminded me of family reunions when I grew up, and how my cousins and I used to listen to my grandfather's stories which taught us all a deep respect for him and, through his example, for ourselves. Looking over toward Hastings, who is sitting impassively as I talk, I tell the Hethu'shkas that what I have seen this evening is a "positive" sign for their tribe and something they can all be proud of.

As everyone is leaving, I talk briefly with Elmer Blackbird near his pickup. "I'm concerned about our people losing our customs and traditions," he says. "The Hethu'shka Society wants to retain what traditions we have left and revive some of them. So I think we're going in the right direction." I ask him more about the role of tobacco. "It was considered the greatest gift anyone could receive," he says.

Before he pulls away, I go to the *Discovery* and dig out one of the pouches of the tobacco I have brought from New Hampshire and hurry back to give it to him. Dennis Hastings is smiling contentedly when I get back.

On my final day in Macy, I want to visit Blackbird Hill and ask Hastings to go there with Porter and me. Blackbird was the Omaha's most notorious chief. Before the smallpox epidemic of 1800 decimated the tribe, weakening forever its power over Missouri River traffic and taking Blackbird's life, the chief was feared by other tribes and white traders alike. Nothing moved up or down the Missouri without his sufferance. A good part of his power was gained by his possession and use of arsenic, obtained from the whites, against his tribal enemies. After his death, he was buried, sitting astride his favorite steed, on a hill with a commanding view over the river.

Lewis and Clark visited the grave. They found a six-foot-high burial mound and a tall pole holding the scalps the chief had taken. As a token of their visit, they attached a red, white, and blue flag to the scalp pole. George Catlin, the artist and aspiring Indian ethnologist, painted the hill in 1832—and then dug up the chief's skull and brought it back to Washington.

With Hastings's massive frame filling the passenger seat of the *Discovery* and Porter on the bench in back, we drive down muddy roads along the rolling hills. Hastings confers on me an honorary Nebraska-reservation driver's license for not getting stuck. We stop first at a collection of five earth lodges and fourteen tepees recon- structed in a gentle swale of pasture for the filming of a public television show about the Omaha tribe. The show will be part of a series on Nebraska's history; it will depict the Omahas of the past, not the present. Hastings helped tribal members build the village, using some scant archaeological findings to relearn a craft and, he hopes, a bit of self-pride that had been lost. The work on the television project has been "like looking in a mirror and seeing an image of yourself" for the Omahas, Hastings says—probably like the Mandan and Hidatsa Indians of North Dakota looking at the Bodmer paintings that Porter showed them.

Near Blackbird Hill, we park the *Discovery*. A makeshift road has been bulldozed to the site from the county road we're on, but Hastings worked with other tribal members to get the council to stop any further work on it. "There's no reason anyone needs to drive in," he says as we walk, pointing to bits of human bone exposed by the bulldozer scar. "After all, this is a graveyard—not just for Blackbird but for a lot of our ancestors."

There is no longer any burial mound, no pole with scalps, no flag to mark the final resting place of Blackbird and his horse. The river itself, which used to curl tightly against this rounded bluff, shifted several miles east years ago. Oak trees that recurring prairie fires once prevented from growing now climb the slopes and crowd the clearing on the crest. A brisk west wind bends the treetops and makes the green pasture grass writhe. White cumulus clouds, the rearguard of the weather system that brought the previous days of rain, move east toward Iowa in the deep blue sky. If there are spirits here today, they are the spirits of change, moving, like the wind and the course of the Missouri itself, away from the Omahas.

The three of us, leaning into the wind, walk around the site a few minutes and pay our respects to the chief buried somewhere beneath us. "He was a good man; he became a visionary for his people," Hastings says. "Power corrupted him."

Later this day, back on the Iowa side of the river, as I drive north through Sloan and Salix, two more dying rural hamlets, my thoughts return to Macy, Nebraska, and to Harrison County, Iowa. In one, the people are struggling to inch out of the rubble left years ago when the machine of Manifest Destiny bulldozed its way across them. In the other, the cycle of "progress" seems poised to repeat itself on yet another population tied to the land. The society of small farmers and small towns of the 1980s is the world of the Indians, a hundred years later.

I think about the Indians and farmers, about promises made, explicitly and implicitly, and promises broken, about peace medallions and 4-H ribbons. I think about one farmer losing his ancestors' land, and another going out to farm it for the banks and investors, and this reminds me of what General Crook said when he was asked if his campaigns against the Indians were hard work. "Yes, they are hard work," he answered. "But the hardest thing is to go out and fight against those who you know are in the right."

Then I remember Dennis Hastings, always working for the positive, telling me: "Sometimes you get discouraged, but you just get back into the trenches." In his soft voice was a trace of resignation to the relentless, indifferent flow of history, but also determination and some hope.

The word "Omaha," he told me, means "against the current."

7

Happy Feet

*the Scioues Camps are handsom   of a Conic form Covered with
Buffalow Roabs Painted different colours and all compact & hand-
somly arranged . . . each Lodg has a place for Cooking detached,
the lodges contain from 10 to 15 persons. a Fat Dog was presented
as a mark of their Great respect for the party of which they partook
hartily and thought it good and well flavored.*

From William Clark's journal
Calumet Bluff encampment
August 29, 1804

Onawa, Iowa (population 3,283), says its 150-foot-wide Main Street is the widest in the United States. Onawa is an Indian word from Longfellow's *Song of Hiawatha* meaning "awake." So when I get up in the morning in nearby Lewis and Clark State Park, hungrier than usual, it seems to make sense to drive the *Discovery* into Onawa, down the wide Main Street, in search of breakfast.

The choices are the Happy Chef, a restaurant next to a motel outside town, near an interstate exit; the downtown Onawa Cafe; or Helen's Cafe, just north of the business section. Hungry as I am, these kinds of decisions can not be made lightly. I'm willing to cruise the length of Onawa before making a choice.

A friend once told me to avoid truck stops, because a trucker isn't looking for good food as much as a big parking lot for his rig, proximity to a gas station, and the hope of seeing other truckers. Besides, he reasoned, they aren't from the town. Look for police cars, that's his theory: cops are from the same locale, and they find the place with the best food at the best price and just keep returning. Of course, he's a policeman himself and says "a good cop is never wet, cold, or hungry."

William Least Heat Moon, in *Blue Highways*, gauged restaurants by the number of calendars on their walls; the more the better. Steinbeck avoided the whole topic and bought groceries for himself and his dog Charley and cooked them in the back of his truck. I don't cook much, even though the *Discovery* is equipped for it, and I've always felt a little embarrassed walking into a crowded eating place and counting things on the wall before deciding whether to sit down or walk out.

I've had to develop my own theories.

The first involves a restaurant or cafe's name. "Cafe" is better than "restaurant," for starters—and much better than "family restaurant." I'm told by more sophisticated friends that in France the terms "cafe" and "restaurant" delineate specifically different eating establishments. In small towns in America, however, the differentiation is more a matter of the whim of the owner when the place gets named. Still, there seem to be some minor differences, and my personal whim is to lean toward the cafe.

My experience is that a cafe is more likely, in addition to booths and tables, to have a counter with stools, allowing a person eating alone to sit with other people; to have a communal local paper for patrons to read and discuss; to have small boxes of cereal stacked on a shelf across from the counter, which are something to read if someone else has the paper (but should never be ordered—they're more for decoration); to have a placemat that either has a map and short history of the area or brief news blurbs from a local radio station; to have a toothpick dispenser at the cash register; to have fresh pies in a stainless-steel-and-glass compartment in full view; and to have easily overheard conversations about what's going on in town. And the food? Often as not, it's better than a restaurant's, and it's always cheaper.

I don't have any problem with families eating in the same place I am, but I've learned that "family restaurant" generally means you can't get a beer with your meal. Even if I'm not in the mood for a beer, the euphemism bothers me. I wouldn't go to a "singles restaurant" either, for that matter (or stay at any "adult motel").

More important than "cafe" or "restaurant" is what goes in front of them to form the name. There are four categories, in order of preference:

1. *First-name cafes*. John Doe opens a cafe in Anytown and names it "John's Cafe" (or just "John's"). Given the name, you can usually assume that John is still around and in charge. His name's up there in front of the public, so he's more likely to make sure they're satisfied. Joint-name or initial cafes are in this category: John and his wife, Louann, call their business "Lu-John's Cafe" or "L and J Cafe."

2. *Last-name cafes*. "Doe's Cafe"—or, more likely, "Doe's Restaurant." A little more formal. The other problem is the possibility that John and Louann may have retired years ago, leaving John Jr., who never liked the restaurant trade to begin with, but is holding onto the business he inherited until he can sell it and move out of town.

3. *Place-name cafes*. "Anytown Cafe" or "Anytown Restaurant." It can be as good as the first category, and a certain

sense of pride and place is carried in its name; or, again, it may have gone through a series of owners and be hanging on more by tradition than menu.

4. *Generic-name cafes.* "Sunrise Cafe," "Oxyoke Restaurant," "The Chuckwagon," etc. Take your chances. At least it isn't a franchise.

I lump a fifth group of small-town restaurants in with national franchises, and simply refuse to eat in them. These I call the Ks, places that use a *k* in their name when they should use a *c*—Korner Kafe, the Koffee Kup, the Kozy Korner. I don't see the sense of it (the same goes for any "kampground" or "kwik mart"), and it grates on me like the '60s radicals' spelling of "Amerika." I avoid them on principle.

Nearly all of the cafes and restaurants I encounter have one of two recurring signs on the front door, sometimes both: "No shirt, no shoes, no service" and "We reserve the right to refuse service to anyone." I always think I'd like to be there when a particularly famished ACLU lawyer arrived wearing only Bermuda shorts.

Ruling out places with those two signs on the front door would leave only fast-food franchises; they aren't a measure of the quality of the place, anyway. But there are other things to consider in choosing a place to eat, and I mentally go through the list in my search for breakfast in Onawa.

BAD SIGNS:

1. An empty parking lot
2. A parking lot full of out-of-state cars
3. A billboard promoting the salad bar
4. An aged HELP WANTED sign in the window
5. A video game instead of a jukebox
6. A "microwave oven in use" notice
7. A menu that tries to be cute or artistic, instead of straight-forward and legible
8. Nametags on the waitresses
9. No toothpicks near the cash register
10. Watery ketchup in the bottle

GOOD SIGNS:

1. Pickups in the parking lot
2. Police cars in the parking lot (my friend's right)

3. Softball trophies behind the counter
4. A view into the kitchen through the order window
5. A separate handwritten and photocopied note on the menu with the day's special
6. A list of the pies available, written with chalk on a slate
7. A lot of calendars (William Least Heat Moon's right)
8. Older, rather than younger, waitresses
9. The first dollar bill the cafe earned, in a frame on the wall behind the cash register
10. A big clock with rotating advertisements for local insurance agencies, banks, hair stylists, and auto body shops

Helen's Cafe in Onawa serves me two eggs, two juicy sausage patties, two pieces of toast, and two cups of coffee for $2.68. The communal paper, from Sioux City, has a big story about the governors of Iowa, Nebraska, South Dakota, and Wyoming meeting with the president of the Omaha district of the Farmer's Credit Association; all four governors are predicting more farm liquidations unless something is done about low prices and high interest rates. At a large table in the corner, the group is constantly mixing as farmers pull up in their pickups, have a cup of coffee and a homemade breakfast roll, and talk over the weather and government programs with the others still at the table.

I'll never know if the Onawa Cafe or the Happy Chef has a better breakfast. All I know is my system worked for me in Onawa this morning (it isn't foolproof), and Helen's gave me what I wanted in the setting I was looking for. With the double satisfaction that comes from good food and good theories, I head north toward Sioux City.

ROAD RULE 7: Devise your own system or theory on choosing where to eat. It's less important what the theory is (as long as it rules out national franchises) than it is that you have one and that you follow it.

FIRST COROLLARY: You don't have to follow your theory in towns that have only one place to eat.

One of the many remarkable facets of the Lewis and Clark expedition is the fact that only one member died during the trek. For nearly two and a half years, this group ventured eight thousand miles through wild, unknown, often unfriendly territory—more than thirty people exposed each day to the harsh elements, undertaking exhausting and potentially debilitating tasks in rushing rivers and stark mountains, encountering dangerous beasts and warlike tribes—with only their strength and wits standing between them and extinction.

One young member, Private George Shannon, became separated from a hunting party and was lost for sixteen days in the South Dakota–Nebraska region. A poor shot to begin with, Shannon ran out of bullets after four days and survived on grapes and a rabbit for two weeks before rejoining the group. He got lost again, in Montana.

On numerous occasions, storms and high winds nearly swamped the boats on the raging Missouri, which would have surely caused drownings. The winter in North Dakota included severe cases of frostbite among men sent out to hunt buffalo.

During the second year of travel, the explorers had with them a young Indian woman, Sacagawea, and her four-month-old son— an act that might get them all arrested today by child welfare authorities. Across Montana, close escapes from grizzly bears became an almost common experience. A buffalo bull rumbled into camp one night while the men were sleeping; Lewis's Newfoundland dog alerted the explorers and scared off the bull, but in the resulting melee several men came within inches of being trampled to death. In the arduous portage of the Great Falls, the group battled rattlesnakes, more grizzlies, and the withering heat of the High Plains summer. Clark, York, Sacagawea and her baby, and her husband, Charbonneau, had a close escape from death when a sudden thunderstorm sent a flash flood down a gully.

The entire contingent was on the verge of starvation when they emerged from a two-week crossing of the snowy Bitterroot Mountains in Idaho; and then the sudden shift to a rich diet of salmon from the Nez Perce Indians nearly killed them all again with sickness. Some of their horses had died in tumbles down mountainsides, and some were eaten when the food ran out, but the men survived. Along the Columbia River, they shot down cascading rapids the local Indians would never dare attempt.

On the return trip, a small group led by Lewis fought with a band of Blackfoot Indians in northern Montana. Two of the Blackfeet were killed; Lewis and his three men escaped. Not long afterward, Lewis was shot through the left thigh and right buttock when a hunting companion mistook the buckskin-clad captain for an elk; luckily, no bones or arteries were severed.

When the expedition arrived back in St. Louis on September 23, 1806, they received a well-deserved triumphant greeting: having heard no word from the expedition since it left the Mandan villages in the spring of 1805, the world had long since given them all up for dead.

Both Lewis and Clark were skilled in frontier medicine. Across the continent, they treated themselves, their men, and often Indians (in exchange for supplies when their trade goods ran out) with boiled barks and berries and herbs for common complaints. Lewis had also taken a crash medical course from Dr. Benjamin Rush, the nation's most renowned physician of the time, during his preparations in Philadelphia. Following the doctor's advice, Lewis brought with him a large supply of purgatives, emetics, and diuretics to give his men, including fifty dozen pills known as "Rush's thunderbolts." Nearly any medical problem was treated with these purgatives, prompting more than one Lewis and Clark scholar to joke about a double meaning to the phrase, "walked on shore today," that shows up so often in the journals.

These were the times when doctors believed that few treatments were more effective than a healthy loss of blood by the patient. Lewis had some lancets with him and from time to time would bleed a sick explorer. Dr. E. G. "Frenchy" Chuinard, a Lewis and Clark buff and author of *Only One Man Died: The Medical Aspects of the Lewis and Clark Expedition*, has told me that, given the propensity of doctors of that era to resort to extensive bleeding for the slightest ailments, the survival of members of the Corps of Discovery was probably enhanced by the absence of a physician.

But no one could have saved Sergeant Charles Floyd when he died on August 20, 1804, near present-day Sioux City, Iowa—the first American soldier to die west of the Mississippi River and the expedition's sole casualty. Clark described Floyd's illness as a "bilious Chorlick," which is now believed to have been a ruptured appendix. Since the first appendectomy in the United States was not performed until 1887, Floyd could have been in Dr. Rush's office instead of nearly a thousand miles from the nearest settlement, and he still would have perished in 1804. If the expedition passed through today, however, the chances are that Floyd would survive (and Dr. Chuinard would have to change the title of his book). The two hospitals in Sioux City routinely perform about two hundred appendectomies every year.

Floyd's travails did not end with his death. The expedition buried him on a bluff with military honors. They named it Floyd's Bluff, as it is still known; it is just south of Floyd's River, and just north of Sergeant Bluff, Iowa. Stopping there on September 4, 1806, on their return trip, the men "found the grave had been opened by the nativs and left half covered." They refilled the grave, replaced the cedar marker and moved downriver. In 1857, a flood undermined the bluff and the grave spilled part of its contents into the river. The skeleton (with the exception of Floyd's forearms and part of his midsection, which were never recovered) was reburied with military and religious ceremony, and then forgotten.

A revived interest in Floyd caused local historians to dig him up once more (they knew they had the right skeleton because of the parts that were missing), place the bones in urns, and bury them again on August 20, 1895. Prior to the reburial, the skull was photographed, and a local lawyer, C. R. Marks, inscribed identifying marks, including Marks's signature, on Floyd's troubled brow. Five years later, on August 20, 1900, the remains were unearthed yet again and deposited under a cornerstone for a final monument. The hundred-foot obelisk was completed for a dedication ceremony (this would be the sixth time solemn words had been spoken over his complete or partial remains) on Memorial Day of 1901.

The day is sunny and warm when I pull up to the Floyd Monument, the first Registered National Historic Landmark in the United States. From its perch on the bluff, the obelisk looks down on railroad tracks and Interstate 29 and the Missouri River. The waters roll south, as they did when they carried Floyd's forearms, bobbing and waving in the current, past Chief Blackbird's headless but horse-borne skeleton, past the site where Daniel Boone's bones rest, separated now from those of his wife.

"I am going away. I want you to write me a letter," Floyd told Clark, and then died before he could dictate it. We'll never know what words he would have left to posterity. I tell the obelisk and the graffiti-laden skull beneath it that I'm willing to take the message and write it down, since the ghost has no hands.

ROAD RULE 8: If you're at all famous, don't let them bury you on the banks of the Missouri River.

I have decided that I'm going to like Yankton, South Dakota (population 12,011), before I even get there. Radio station KKYA, which starts coming in loud and clear about thirty miles out of town, is the best country-and-western station I've heard. In one uninterrupted stretch, it plays Don Williams, Conway Twitty, Barbara Mandrell, Merle Haggard, Emmylou Harris, the Bellamy Brothers, Elvis Presley, and Willie Nelson—no commercials and not even a disc jockey to announce the songs: these people don't need any introduction for us aficionados, anyway. There's a short break to announce who's in the local hospital, and then another twenty-five minutes of nonstop heartbreak, honky-tonk, and cheatin' songs. This is, as we used to say where I grew up, Hog Heaven.

In the early days of the Dakota Territory, before the area was split into north and south states and the state capitals were established in centrally located Bismarck and Pierre, Yankton was the territorial capital. The buildings in the downtown are of Victorian vintage, still proud and well kept. One has a small historic marker on the side (I stop for a reading: it's a Road Rule) saying that here Jack McCall was brought to trial for shooting Wild Bill Hickok in the back in a saloon in the Black Hills. A vigilante court in Deadwood had released McCall, but he bragged so much about the murder that he was rearrested, tried in Yankton (four witnesses said Wild Bill had forgotten to sit at the poker table with his back to the wall), found guilty, and hanged just outside of town. You've gotta like this town.

On Third Street, a giant black shoe reaches out from a shop door: Boston Shoe Repair. In big, block letters on the plate-glass window: GOOD BOOTS CHEAP. My right hiking boot ripped a seam on Blackbird Hill, so I stop. Besides, the name reminds me of New England and home.

Dennis and Ann Menke inspect the injured boot and pronounce it salvageable. Ann takes it back to a stitching machine in the corner; Dennis and I start talking as I eye the supply of cowboy boots enviously.

Menke's step-grandfather, a Greek immigrant, started the business here on Third Street seventy years ago. He had admired Boston, his port of entry, on his way west, so he gave his shop the city's name. Menke, an outgoing man of thirty-seven, says he apprenticed under his grandfather and father, starting at age nine.

"I was born into it, so I didn't have a choice," he says. "She," he gestures to Ann, a girl from the East, "married into—"

"—so I didn't have a choice," Ann chimes in from the stitching. They both laugh. Choice or not, it's clear they like their work.

I say I've read stories about the Old West, when men used to bring women out from the East for brides.

"What do you mean *used* to," they say, and laugh again.

I pick up a particularly handsome pair of brown cowboy boots. Dennis informs me they're on sale today. We talk about the Missouri River that I'm following. Menke and a friend once took an eighteen-foot canoe from Pierre to Kansas City. It took them sixty-five days, aided by a sailing attachment. "That's when I got into sailing—when I learned you didn't have to paddle," he says. They have a twenty-one-foot sloop on Lewis and Clark Lake, the impoundment behind Gavins Point Dam near Yankton, and their dream is to sail it to the Gulf. He points out the quality of the boots I'm holding. "They'll last you thirty years if you take care of them," he says.

Some customers come in to drop off or pick up repaired boots. The Menkes talk at length with them all. Dennis has prepared two one-page sheets on how to take care of shoes and how to select and break in a new pair of boots. He gives me the second one as I try on the cowboy boots. It says to try them on before noon, because feet are the most sensitive and their truest size in the morning; that a snug fit across the ball of the foot is important; and that the best way to break in cowboy boots is to apply silicone each day for three days and to walk around in them at home for a few hours each day wearing damp socks: "The silicone softens the leather and the damp sock makes them memorize your foot shape." Both Dennis and Ann think the boots look good on me.

We talk some more about Yankton, the Missouri, and the shoe business. "I hope we can preserve some of this," Dennis says, sweeping his arms to include the shop, and possibly more. "That's the thing about America, we're so set on always *changing* things. Well, I'm not. That's why we've kept this building pretty much the way it always was. Seventy years is a long time around here."

Another customer enters, is attended to by the Menkes, and leaves. "We try to think long-term with people, give them a little extra care," Dennis says. "You can't just scoot people in and out the door and take advantage of 'em. In a small town like this, you'd be through in a year."

Ann has finished stitching my hiking boot and has applied a good coat of oil to it and its mate. They look almost new. Both Ann and Dennis, wearing their cobbler's aprons, give the mended boot a final inspection before handing it across the counter. I ask again about the cowboy boots. Dennis says the sale price is just above his cost. A sale is made.

I'm going to wear the new boots out of the store, but Dennis won't allow me to until I take them off and let him apply a layer of silicone, buff them, treat them, caress them for about ten minutes. When I put them back on and prepare to leave, I tell the Menkes I've never learned so much about boots and feet.

"Keeping feet happy is my business," Dennis says. He and Ann smile and wish me luck on my travels. "Remember to take good care of them," he says as I walk out.

Gavins Point Dam, the farthest downstream of the six major dams on the main stem of the Missouri, is near the site where Lewis and Clark held council with the friendly Yankton Sioux at the end of August 1804. When two representatives of the expedition approached the Yankton camp a few miles up the James River to issue an invitation to parley, the Indians offered to carry the white men into the village on buffalo robes, as a sign of honor. The offer was declined on the grounds that such distinction should be showered only on the captains, but a special feast of roast dog was accepted. The next day, a large delegation of Yanktons moved to the Missouri to camp opposite the expedition. Gifts and speeches were exchanged for two days, and several Yankton chiefs expressed an interest in visiting Washington. The captains' journals describe pleasant meetings during the day and enjoyable nights around the campfire, as the Yanktons performed ceremonial dances to loud drumbeats and warriors gave orations about their feats of bravery and horse stealing.

A gold wafer sun is beginning to sink into the Lewis and Clark Lake when I descend the tailrace road at the dam to reach the Chief White Crane Unit campground. Howard Smith pokes his head out the window of the registration booth at the campground entrance.

"You got space?" I ask.

"Sure do."

"Hot showers?"

"You bet."

"How much?"

"Eight bucks."

"Sign me up."

Howard and his wife, Ermal, give me a short personal history while I sign in and pay my fee. Originally from Webster City, Iowa, they began roaming America in their camper when Howard retired. During these wanderings, they made two decisions: they would buy a retirement home in the Rio Grande Valley of Texas ("In Webster City, you can't sit out in your shirtsleeves on Christmas Day," Howard explains), and they would bid for the job of running the campground registration at one of the federal campgrounds ("It's seven days a week, but we like meeting the people," Ermal confides). They picked this particular Corps of Engineers campground because one of their children lived in Nebraska; but, and Ermal rolls her eyes as she tells me this, the kids were then transferred to Dallas.

The Smiths migrate north every spring, and live in their camper during the summer here at the Chief White Crane Unit, where they're a combination of First Family of the campground and kindly aunt and uncle to everyone who shows up. A pickup stops by the booth. The driver has caught a big northern just below the dam. Howard chats with the man about bait and lures and Ermal comes out of the booth to inspect the fish and make a guess at its weight (about six pounds). I've finished my registration form when they return.

"New Hampshire; you're a long way from home," Ermal says and takes my money. Having received the modern equivalent of a buffalo-robe greeting, it doesn't feel that far.

This is a vastly different kind of encampment among the cottonwoods from the time when Chief White Crane and his Yankton people set up their tepees to meet Lewis and Clark. The modern nomads, mostly retired couples or families with small children, have large trailers or self-propelled campers (the *Discovery* is the smallest vehicle in the campground) with kitchens, beds, toilets, and televisions. Colored Japanese lanterns strung from trailer to tree are popular; a good number have bug zappers wired to their power supply that give off a soft purple glow and short bursts of *brzzzzts* as mosquitoes, gnats, and larger insects are electrocuted. The Indian names on the aluminum and steel "tepees"—Apache, Winnebago, Cherokee—are the only link to the past. The dogs that will be eaten tonight are hot dogs; the four-legged kind are required to be kept on leashes.

Campgrounds have an informal code of friendliness. You check out your neighbors' license plates, make small talk about your homes, the weather, the bugs, and your camper, and retreat to your own site. People walking by on the looping drive always get a wave and a hello from folks sitting on their folding chairs next to their rig. Two men from the big trailer next to me are in the public restroom the same time as I am. They're from Nebraska, here with their wives.

"Come here often?" I ask.

"This is our third time this year," says one.

"Doin' some fishing?"

"No. We just come here to take 'er easy. You from Texas?"

"No, it's not my VW. I'm from New Hampshire."

"You're a long way from home."

We walk back to our campsites in the dark. Through the windows of the Apaches and Winnebagos I can see people playing cards at the kitchen table, a woman knitting and a man pouring himself a drink, a couple silhouetted in the bluish aura of a TV set. Most people seem to be doing what they do at home; only the setting has changed.

There are still a number of empty campsites on the loops, but three or four cars with trailers keep cruising slowly around the roads—late twentieth-century settlers in gas-powered Conestogas, convinced that the campsite around the next corner will be a little better than the one at hand. Americans on the move, just for the sake of it.

"You alone?" one of my walking partners asks.

"Yeah," I say.

A long pause.

"So you can go just about wherever you want."

This doesn't sink in until I ask them, knowing they're not here to fish, if they're going to explore around the area tomorrow.

"We'll probably take in the town. Do some shopping," he says as they shuffle off. "Good night."

In the back of the *Discovery*, I sit beneath the white light of a fluorescent flashlight, catching up on my notes, sipping Missouri bourbon, and reading the explorers' journals. (Sergeant John Ordway, describing the meeting with the Yanktons near this very site: "they Camped along side of us & behaved honestly.") Our little village is quiet in the darkness, and mine is the last light out when I turn it off and go to sleep.

Tomorrow, I'll go wherever I want.

8

Ponca Creek

. . . make yourself acquainted . . . with the names of the nations
    & their numbers;
the extent & limits of their possessions;
their relations with other tribes of nations;
their language, traditions, monuments;
their ordinary occupations in agriculture, fishing, hunting, war,
    arts, & the implements for these;
their food, clothing, & domestic accomodations;
the diseases prevalent among them, & the remedies they use;
moral & physical circumstances which distinguish them from the
    tribes we know;
peculiarities in their laws, customs & dispositions;
and articles of commerce they may need or furnish, & to what ex-
    tent.

From Thomas Jefferson's instructions
to Captain Meriwether Lewis
June 20, 1803

Highway 12, a gray ribbon un-
furled on the rumpled green carpet of northern Nebraska, stretches
west toward the horizon. A speck appears in the far distance and
grows into a pickup truck, approaching at 55 mph. Twenty yards
in front of the *Discovery*, the right hand of the pickup's driver lifts
from the steering wheel. *Whoosh.* The truck is gone but the image
of a friendly wave shimmers on the pavement ahead of me like
the mirage of an oasis on the desert. Fifteen minutes later, another
pickup and another wave. A meadowlark perched on a fencepost
lifts his head, warming his golden belly in the morning sun, and
gargles a liquid song of greeting. Crofton, Nebraska—"the friend-
liest little town by a dam site"—rises in the windshield, then sinks
in my rearview mirror. I'm ready when the next vehicle appears
and return the wave.

Genuine friendliness and hospitality are a function of the wid-
ening disparity between the big geography and sparse population
out here. Feeling alone against the vast elements, you grab any
opportunity for communion, however fleeting. The same applies
to the notion of neighborliness, a deep and honored tradition.
Neighbors in these parts aren't the folks you lean out your apartment window to shout at across the alleyway to keep their kids
quiet or to stop putting out their garbage in bags instead of cans.
Neighbors here are the ones you count on for help when your truck's
broke and you have some fence wire that has to be moved today,
or the ones who bring over a hot covered-dish dinner when there's
sickness in the family. Keep a pot of coffee on, in case someone
drops by, and have some pie ready in the icebox.

As the land and the elements get more immense, the towns get
smaller, not larger. Omaha will turn out to be the last city of more
than 100,000 people along the Missouri River—in fact, the last
city even approaching that size along the Lewis and Clark route
until I reach Portland, Oregon, roughly three thousand trail miles
later. Small towns, widely scattered, are the rule. Most have fewer
than a thousand residents.

The progression of town sizes begins with a one-bar town. Every
town has a bar, even if it doesn't have a post office or any other

stores. A one-bar town may be big enough for a post office/store or post office/filling station/store, but the bar came first. A two-bar town will include a post office, a cafe, a couple of stores, a filling station/garage, a filling station/store, and a grid of four streets. Three-bar towns have more of the same, plus a restaurant to compete with the cafe, a three-block-long Main Street, and a motel on the edge of town. Beyond that, and you're probably in a county seat with more than two thousand people and maybe even a traffic light. Anything from a two-bar town up will have at least one place to rent videotapes of movies—I've seen them in gas stations, drugstores, even the bars—which in the last few years have become as ubiquitous as satellite dishes.

Visitors in the small towns of the Plains are greeted with a friendly curiosity, instead of the suspicion and reticence of an Eastern hamlet, or the callous indifference of a big city, or even the Chamber of Commerce boosterism of a medium-sized Midwestern city ("Let me show you the Eyetalian fountain down at the city park—cost $25,000 and we're *real* proud of her"). Just the same, it's wise to watch what you put on postcards to mail out from the local post office; it might already have become the chief topic of conversation at the cafe when you walk in for supper.

Lynch, Nebraska (population 357), is a two-bar town sitting along a double bend in Ponca Creek. I'm feeling road weary and looking for a place to stay for more than one night. Given all the strangers' waves on Highway 12, Lynch seems like a good bet.

ROAD RULE 9: If you want to meet people and learn about a town, the two best places to go are bars and churches. Bars are the only institutions in our society created for the specific purpose of conviviality; churches have a broader purpose, but doctrine requires the congregation to take in strangers.

FIRST COROLLARY: Bars are open more days and longer hours than churches.

"As a young buck, I was rough and tough and hard to bluff. I still am . . . well, not young anymore." A man in his sixties wearing striped overalls and a white T-shirt is standing next to a crowded booth in the D & L Corral bar in Lynch telling them about the time he swam across the Missouri River to get to a dance in South

Dakota. Like every other male in the bar, he's got a cap on his head, only his is turned sideways. (Somewhere along the trail— I'm not sure where it happened—I passed the point where men take off their hats indoors.) The group orders a pitcher of "red ones"—draft beer and tomato juice, a popular drink in both Lynch bars—and the old man continues his story about picking a spot a mile upstream from his destination, stripping off his clothes, plunging into the Missouri, and swimming diagonally with the current, clothes held aloft with one arm, to the Dakota side.

"Bet I could still swim that sumbitch today," he says. "Anyone want to try me?"

Lacking any takers, he returns to the bar rail, where I'm sitting. We start talking. His name is Cabool Chambers, and there's a story with his name.

"Boone, where'd you find this little feller?" an old geezer asked when Boone Chambers stepped off the train in Lynch with a seven-year-old he had adopted in Missouri.

"Found him in a hollowed-out log in Cabool, Missouri."

"Cabool. Cabool. That'd be a good name for him." And so he's been called ever since.

I buy us a round of red ones. We talk some more. He buys a round of red ones. He learns along the way that I have no story to go with my name (even though we both share first names with cities), and no place to stay in Lynch, so he offers the front yard of his trailer home to park the *Discovery* for as long as I want to stay in town.

On the other side of me, slowly sipping his draft beer, is another man, in his late seventies and wearing the same uniform as Cabool, only his cap isn't on sideways. His name is Pete Mulhair, and *his* story deals with his last, not first, name. When his grandfather and father applied for homestead patents in 1892, "someone in Washington, D.C." misspelled the name Mulhare as Mulhair. "They didn't want to go to no more damn trouble with it," he says, and so it's been Mulhair ever since.

Pete Mulhair is a short, gritty man—like Cabool, probably still willing and able to swim the Missouri, despite his age—who tilts and thrusts his head toward you when he speaks. I allow as how Lynch seems to be a nice town.

"Sure is," he says. "Wish there was something here that could keep people working. One year, I kept track of the young kids that got married here in town. There was twelve weddings and not a one of 'em stayed here. They all had to go away to get a job 'cause there's nothin' to do around here.

"The farmers was all starvin' to death—a little farmer ain't got a chance, and a big farmer ain't got a chance unless he's got his dad to get him started. I don't know how many big farmers sold out in the last two years. Sold my own; just got disgusted and said the hell with it and moved to town."

He pushes his face a few more inches forward and tells me about a recent drive he took in the surrounding country: "I went out east for two miles and counted nine houses that were vacant. Then I went two miles south and counted seven more."

He remembers when Lynch had nearly six hundred people, and I ask him what the town was like. Mulhair turns to stare at his beer, an image of the past rising with each air bubble in the glass.

"About five stores . . . two doctors . . . a hotel . . . two hotels . . . two or three garages . . . a train station . . ." He pulls back from the beer vision and looks at me. "Now we don't even have a car salesman—a new-car salesman—in the whole county."

Across the street, at the Nite Owl, a game of four-point pitch is in progress at a side table. In time, I get dealt in. I've learned enough by now to keep my DeKalb cap on while I play.

David Lee, a young man in his thirties, left the life of a road musician to return to Lynch, not for the money ("*Nobody* gets rich here," he says) but to raise his family and do carpentry work. One man playing with us says he likes small towns versus cities of, say, eight thousand, "because people around here will take care of you when you're down and out."

The players talk about hunting deer, wild turkeys, jackrabbits, pheasant, and quail. One of them, a guy in his twenties, is intensely interested in what it's like in New England: how are the houses built, what kind of trees grow there, are there any farms, and, reflecting his own experience, whether the old buildings are still around or abandoned and falling down. He raises cattle on family land. "Ain't no way anybody could start a farm unless his dad already had the land," he says. "Ain't no way, no way."

The bartender brings a draft beer over for me and says, "That'll be fifty cents." "Fifty cents!" I exclaim. "Yeah, I know, I know,"

he shushes me. "I raised the price about six months ago, and people
are still complaining."

Ponca Creek flows southeast out of South Dakota and then roughly
parallels the Missouri and the Niobrara, a long and lovely river
that is completing its journey through Nebraska's haunting Sand
Hills, as it slices across Boyd County, Nebraska. The effect of the
three streams slowly wedging together, each with its own rolling
hills and bluffs and rich bottomlands within just a few miles of
each other, is one of tender, almost exquisite beauty in late May.
The pastures and hayfields are a deep green; cornstalks, a lighter
green, have pushed up in straight rows out of the dark soil; plum
bushes grow in confusion along the fencerows; cottonwoods tower
over the cattails on the riverbanks, each mimicking the other, one
with brown trunk and green top, the other green stem and brown
head; cedars and burr oaks climb slopes too steep to till.
     My desire to linger here seems reaffirmed the next day by the
vista overlooking the Ponca valley in the gentle light of morning,
and, as it turns out, is firmly grounded in history. Others have felt
the same emotion.
     In 1877 the government decided to remove the Ponca Indians
from this land to Indian Territory in Oklahoma, where the sudden
change from a dry, cooler climate to the humid heat combined
with malaria and just plain homesickness to kill a third of the tribe
within a year. After permission to return was repeatedly denied,
two hundred surviving Poncas decided to walk back to the land
they yearned for, leaving in January 1879 and getting as far as the
Omaha reservation by spring. There, the army intercepted them
and began marching them back to Oklahoma until legal proceed-
ings—inspired by some prominent citizens of Omaha and even the
army officer outraged at the unfairness of the orders he had been
given—stopped the second removal. The resulting case, *Standing
Bear* vs. *General George Crook*, became a landmark, establishing
for the first time that Indians are persons within the meaning of
the law; prior to the ruling in 1879, they weren't. The Poncas
received a cash payment for their lost lands. Their descendants
live in Oklahoma.
     Reluctant departures have marked the area since that time. The
sole exception was the land boom when homesteaders of diverse
ethnic origins—Irish, Swedes, German-Russians, Danes, and Bo-

hemian Czechs—staked out quarter-section farms and built communities in the 1890s. Towns sprang up about every ten miles, the distance a farmer could buckboard in to shop and return the same day. Lynch, Monowi, Bristow, and Gross each grew to populations of about 600 or 700, peaking just after World War I, and then began a steady decline. Their populations at last count are, respectively, 357, 16, 127, and 2. Boyd County has 3,331 residents; the largest town is Spencer, population 596.

When it became impossible to support a family on 160 acres, homesteaders sold out to farms of 320 acres, which gave way to full-section farms, and so on up the scale. Coinciding with this, buckboards gave way to automobiles. The fewer farmers on the bigger farms could travel farther distances to do their shopping, so the towns in between became fewer and smaller. Now, there are no towns of more than 20,000 people within a hundred-mile radius of Lynch.

The whole story of this beautiful county, from the time of the Poncas on, is the American Dream in reverse.

Steve Holen, a young archaeologist and historian married to Cabool's stepdaughter, is visiting Lynch with his family and becomes my companion for the next four days. His job is in southern Nebraska, but his heart is along Ponca Creek, and he'd move here if only there were a living to be made. Compounding the long-term trend of decline, he says, are two more immediate factors: the severe agricultural crisis and move toward corporate farms, which are accelerating what was already happening; and the growing age of the people remaining behind—the average age in Lynch is between forty-five and fifty, compared with a national average of thirty.

"When they're [the old people] gone, the small towns are really going to be abandoned," he says. "The towns will just dry up and blow away."

The Bakery Cafe is Lynch's only year-round eating place (there's a hot-dog and ice-cream stand open in the summer, near Highway 12), so there's no need to run through the cafe theories on the way to breakfast. The inside is basically just a square, low-ceilinged room with an array of portable tables and chairs. The wide door to the kitchen is always open, which in addition to the large pass-through window allows Donna, the young proprietress, and her waitresses to be part of any conversation going on out front, or to keep track of the shows on the television back by the stoves.

Signs on the walls announce an upcoming school potluck picnic, a healing service at the Catholic Church, a meeting of the Lynch Boosters, a performance of Irish Dancers, Kolack Days (a Czech celebration) in Verdigre, an open bridal shower for a prospective bride, and the fact that "smoking is permitted in this entire establishment."

For most people in the area, breakfast is something you either have at home or don't have at all, but the Bakery Cafe serves as a spot to drop in for a cup of coffee and maybe a breakfast roll. The coffee pot sits on the low counter in a corner; patrons pour their own and drop a quarter in a bowl.

A center table seating eight is the focal point of the morning crowd. Public conversations take place here, sometimes reaching out to include the satellite tables. The center table is all male—when two married couples come in, they divide by gender: men to the center table, women to a satellite where two other women are sitting—and the standard uniform includes a cap and a small attachment on the belt for a pair of pliers. Weather, bad crop prices ("too low for what we sell, too high for what we buy"), more weather, and the fact that Lynch High School will be graduating only eleven students next week are the chief topics of discussion. A notice from a farm foreclosure sale held near town a few days ago is passed around with a lot of head-shaking and little comment.

When I order coffee and a piece of cherry pie in a bowl of milk for breakfast (a taste I acquired from my grandfather), it becomes the topic of conversation—not derisively, just out of curiosity: is that what people back East eat every morning? Donna is a premier pie baker, whipping up two or three a morning, and I ask for a whole banana cream pie for my departure in four days.

"It won't last two days in your cooler," she warns.

"I don't intend it to," I tell her.

It's a sunny Saturday—intimations of summer in the warm, steady breeze. A good day for a desultory tour of the Lynch area. Up a gravel road from Ponca Creek I stop at the home of Ray and Esta Davy. A 1947 International truck in better condition than the *Discovery* rests in the driveway. Ray and Esta are sitting on chairs in the shade of tall cedars and walnut trees, Esta knitting around the plastic holders from a six-pack of pop to form potholders.

Ray, a week away from his eighty-eighth birthday, tells stories of days gone by in a soft voice that wheezes a little when he laughs, which he often does. His eyes sparkle in his stubbled face as he talks about playing hooky from school to be in the woods, of adding a second engine to a Model T and waiting for wagons to head up a river hill so he could roar up and around them, of building a boat out of scrap lumber after the harvest in North Dakota in the 1930s and rowing home on the Missouri River with two friends.

I ask them how they met and how long they've been married, prompting more wheezing *heh, heh*s from Ray and girlish giggles from Esta.

"Sixty-three years," she says demurely.

"We're not either one of us spring chickens," Ray says and winks.

"I don't feel bad, though," says Esta. "I had finished tenth grade and wanted to finish school, but he said, 'No, you're notta gonna finish school . . .' "

". . . I was never no lover of school to start with," Ray says.

". . . and so I didn't," she continues. "I would have liked to finish school."

"How old were you when you got married?" I ask.

Esta pauses from her knitting and leans forward to whisper, as if a large crowd were trying to eavesdrop.

"Seventeen."

Ray lets out some more *heh, heh*s.

"Wasn't that *awful*?" she says, laughing and returning to the potholders. "I felt like I was an old lady, though, at the time." They raised three children. One died in his thirties; the two others have moved away from Lynch.

Ray shows me his workshop, Esta goes into the house and returns with old pictures of the two-engine Model T, and they tell the story of buying the International brand-new in 1947 and driving it to Michigan for a wedding in 1951 and sleeping in the back ("It was sort of the first camper," Esta says, comparing it to the *Discovery*). When I pull out of the driveway, they're sitting on the back bumper of a truck two years older than I am. Esta is knitting.

Fay Christensen is knitting, too, when I stop at the house she and her husband, Clemen, built when they married in 1917. Cle-

men was born a half mile from this house, in 1892, when his parents
arrived from Denmark and started a homestead.

Fay moved to the area from Wisconsin with her family in 1909,
when she was sixteen. She taught in a one-room schoolhouse just
down the road. There were twenty-six students in the elementary
and junior-high grades when she was preparing them for high
school in Lynch. Fifty had been there when Clemen attended. The
school closed years ago and the building itself is gone now. The
couple have two daughters, in Omaha and New York.

Listening to the Christensens in their living room is to hear
firsthand the complete story, from the beginning to the present, of
white settlement of the area and to understand a comparatively
youthful regional history that can be encompassed by one person's
life—like being able to stop at a home near Plymouth Rock and
talk to Miles Standish.

"What wasn't plowed was blue-stem prairie," Clemen says. "That
blue stem, unless you know what it's like I don't know how to tell
it to you. It was a good grass. When it headed out, it would be
waist-high on a man. It was wonderful pasture for summer. It was
no good for winter—I don't know, it must have got woody or
something. But it made pretty good hay, a lot of hay, and it was
good hay."

There were trees on the south side of the Ponca, he remembers,
but none on the north side, between it and the Missouri. Prairie
fires had kept the trees out between the watery borders.

The settlers came. "It took four homesteader families to occupy
one square mile," he says. "It was really a lot of people here. You
might say polluted with people. They've thinned out now."

Lynch? "It wasn't much of a place until the railroad came in in
nineteen hundred and two." He remembers; he was ten years old.
"Then, of course, it made a boom. It really boomed for a while."

Monowi? "In June, before the railroad got there in August, they
had a town site sale of lots. They built about two of everything.
They had two lumberyards, they had two blacksmith shops, they
had three grocery stores at one time, and a drugstore and a bank.
Livery barn. Two hotels."

Clemen leans back in his easy chair and ponders it. Fay is
knitting in a rocking chair.

"I seen 'em lay the track into Monowi and I seen 'em tear it out of Monowi." A pause. A lifetime and a town's history passes like a ghost through the quiet house. "Seventy-six years in between."

Monowi (an Indian word for "pretty little prairie flower") lies on the north shoulder of Highway 12. There's no reduced-speed sign to slow down passing traffic, just a sign that says you're entering Monowi town limits and that the population is 20. If there once were six hundred or more people living here and two of everything, as Clemen Christensen remembers, you wouldn't know it to look at what's left of the town: just a few houses, some vacant lots overgrown with weeds and lilac bushes, an abandoned school-house, and an abandoned town hall. It's even hard to imagine that twenty people live here, and, in fact, only sixteen did at the last census.

At the intersection of a gravel road and the highway is a two-story wooden building with no sign announcing what it is. Five or six pickups are splayed haphazardly across the gravel road, as if the volunteer fire department had been summoned to what turned out to be a false alarm. It's a bar—the only commercial establishment in town and reportedly the only bar in Nebraska that still has outhouses. A hand-printed sign next to the telephone inside explains the parking pattern outside: it's for quick getaways, not arrivals.

Just left	25 cents
On his way	50 cents
Not here	$1.00
Who?	$2.00
Still not here	$5.00
Tell wife you've left but you're still here	$7.50

A game of pinochle is in progress at a side table. The players look up from the cards briefly as Steve Holen and I walk in, nod to Steve, whom they recognize, and resume play. We're looking for Dave Lee, who lives in Monowi, and for reasons that can be understood only within the logic of warm Saturday afternoons, have stopped here first instead of at his house, only a block away.

Rudy, the bartender, tells us Dave's not here. As we walk out, I wonder whether this means Dave now owes Rudy a dollar.

When we arrive at Dave Lee's house—the sole occupied dwelling on a block that once was the heart of Monowi; it belonged to his grandfather—he is at work in the side yard, digging up the sewer line for repair. The kind of work anyone likes to have interrupted by visitors. Peering into the back of the *Discovery* as he talks to us, he spies my guitar. Five minutes later, he has his own guitar out and we're sitting in his backyard, trading songs.

His wife, Debbie, comes out onto the newly built, still unpainted back porch, realizes in one look that the sewer line won't be fixed today, and offers us iced tea.

Lee grew up in the Lynch area and then left for thirteen years to attend college, join the armed forces, and travel in a band. He and Debbie are something of an anomaly along Ponca Creek: they moved back.

"It's the life style, I think," he explains. "We kinda burned out on city life. There's not so many people around here. Just a lot easier livin' is all."

Chickens, dogs, kittens, and his two young sons are all underfoot as we play in the backyard. Does he worry that his boys won't be able to stay in the area when they become adults? It doesn't matter, he says: "at least we've given them a chance to see what it's like here." Eric and John chase a hen around a corner of the chicken coop. Dave soaks in the scene, warming himself in it like afternoon sunshine.

"Not a bad place to grow up," he says.

The town of Gross sits on the high land between the Ponca and the Missouri. Before the coming of the railroad, when supplies reached the area by riverboat and were brought to Gross for distribution, it was the largest town in Boyd County, reaching nearly seven hundred people. Nancy Hargens, the bartender/chef at the Nebrask-Inn in Gross, shows me a picture of the town in 1904: the houses, barns, and buildings crowd the edges of the photograph, even though it was taken from a considerable distance.

The owner of the bar has died recently. Nancy, who has worked here for ten years, since she was nineteen, is managing things until the estate is sold. The estate includes the deceased woman's house, the bar, a vacant garage, the old schoolhouse, and several acres of empty blocks—everything in Gross, in fact, except the town hall, town park, and one other house. The woman's death dropped the population of Gross to two. It's called the smallest incorporated town in the world. The other resident is mayor and town clerk; Nancy is treasurer and cop.

"Ever have to make an arrest?" I ask her.

"Nope, but I've thrown my share of people out of the bar."

The three other farmers at the bar nod knowingly.

"How often are the elections? Wouldn't they all be one–one ties?"

She turns from the grill, where she's making cheeseburgers for Steve Holen and me, as if to ask Steve with a look whether he wants to be tossed out with me.

The cheeseburgers are good, and when I order a red one to wash it down, Nancy seems to decide that I'm okay. She becomes more talkative. Besides running the Nebrask-Inn in the evenings, she works at the bank branch office in Lynch and helps her grandfather farm near Gross. Since starting here, the only times off from work she's had are Christmas Eve, Christmas Day, and New Year's Day. She's looking forward to someone else buying Gross and taking over. The pace is wearing her out.

"How much they asking for the town?"

"I heard $30,000," she says.

"Sounds pretty high," one of the farmers interjects.

"I know," she answers.

Back in Lynch, there's a Saturday-night traffic jam on Main Street. Not something you'd expect in a town of 357. Actually, it's not a jam, because the traffic's constantly moving. It's more of an un-official parade of about eight vehicles, all driven by teenagers. A car starts at the intersection at the south end of the downtown, drives up Main Street past the Bakery Cafe and the two bars, across the principal intersection and up one more block to the telephone office and Shaw's repair shop; then it makes a wide U-turn and proceeds the two blocks back down Main to the starting point, makes another U-turn, and heads back up again.

A couple of boys driving loud Dodge Chargers, a girl in a Camaro with fur around the steering wheel, another girl in what must be her father's big Olds, a pickup with the body jacked up two feet above the axles, a Ford Escort with five kids, another pickup, and a few more cars—up two blocks they go at 15 mph, turn around, down the same two blocks, turn around, up two blocks, etc., etc.

I take a seat on a bench near the Lynn, the movie theater made from a small metal Quonset hut ("You don't want to pay for a movie during a hailstorm," I was told; it's open three nights a week), and watch the cars pass. I check my watch when the Camaro passes and when it returns: a minute and a half.

As a northbound vehicle meets a southbound one, they honk at each other, as if it's been a long time since they've seen each other and they're surprised by the encounter. They could park the whole caravan and get out to talk—still not creating much of a crowd, but saving a lot of gas and making a lot less noise—but up and down they go for hours, circling and honking like a small flock of geese in some sort of mating ritual, as night settles over Lynch.

In the Nite Owl, which the kids outside are too young to patronize, I learn that the cruising goes on every Friday and Saturday night until nearly midnight, when the youngsters go out into the seclusion of the country for a beer party. Long before that, I leave the bar, find a break in the parade, ease the *Discovery* into line for one spin up and down, and then break out to head for Cabool's.

When I shut out the lights in my camper, the faint honking from downtown helps lull me to sleep.

Sunday begins with the sounds of mourning doves, not geese—an alarm clock I can't turn off any more than I can shut out the light of dawn illuminating the canvas sides around the camper bed. It's Ascension Sunday. Time to get up and get ready for church.

Steve Holen and I go to the Bakery Cafe for coffee and to kill time before church. We are accepted at the center table, where there's more talk about weather, crops, and prices. Tales of drought in South Dakota have several men planning on being able to sell some Ponca Creek hay for extra cash this summer.

With still more than an hour before the service, Steve and I walk up Main Street, and as we pass the Nite Owl he sees Glen Stewart sitting at the bar, so we go inside to get out of the hot morning sun. Without asking, Glen buys us both a beer, which we accept on the basis of already being up for three and a half hours, then he ushers us out to his pickup for a drive along the Missouri River bluffs.

Stewart, seventy-eight, has lived here since he was six months old. His father came to the area in a covered wagon from Missouri. He still operates heavy equipment—trucks, graders, and bulldozers ("I could give you a shave with a bulldozer," he tells me)—the business he's been in since the advent of refrigerators drove him out of the ice business ("I used to put up six to eight tons of ice a year," he says) in the 1920s.

As he drives and talks, he alternates gestures with his right and left hands, swift movements as if he's brushing away a gnat from the dashboard. He tells us tales about the old days: when three passenger trains, six freight trains, and occasional locals stopped in Lynch each day; when a mill on Ponca Creek put out its own brand of flour; when Lawrence Welk would play for dances in town; when one of the five general stores would ship in a year's supply of merchandise by the train-car loads; and when he used to go swimming in January in an enclosed pool created by a warm artesian well ("The biggest artesian well ever dug in the state of Nebraska").

I mention last night's caravan on Main Street, and he talks about young men racing horses up the street for wagers and about the times when farmers would come in to shop on Wednesday and Saturday evenings. "You couldn't even find a place to tie your team up," he says. "You had to shoulder your way down Main Street, it was so crowded."

From the high ground overlooking the river to the north of us, he points out a place where the river changed course years before the Fort Randall dam was built just upstream, washing out two houses on the South Dakota side and creating a long island now filled with cottonwoods.

As we descend back into the Ponca valley, we cross Whiskey Creek on the approach to Lynch. "I'll tell you how Whiskey Creek got its name," he says with a gesture. "A guy walked out of one of the bars one winter night, drunk, and fell off the footbridge and froze to death."

On Main Street, as he parks his pickup, he looks up and down the quiet street. "Lynch is a good place to live," he says. "But all it's good for is to live so you can die."

He goes back into the Nite Owl. Steve Holen and I head for church.

—

Four blocks away is the Lynch United Methodist Church, and the two of us enter the wide doors and take seats in the back while the congregation is singing "All Hail the Power of Jesus' Name." Several things stand out as I survey the congregation. The crowd is small (twenty-eight people, filling up less than a third of the small church), nearly all female (only eight men, including Holen and myself), and aging. There are no children present and only one couple under roughly age forty-five. We rise to sing "Trust and Obey." The piano begins in a key set for a soprano, and the sound we send ascending through the rafters is principally high, wavering voices, birdlike and frail.

A laywoman reads the sermon ("Does My Church Have Spirit?") because the minister's on vacation. After the collection, the responsive reading, prayers, and some more hymns, the service ends with the announcement that next week's service will be held in a church in Bristow, about twelve miles to the west.

Perhaps I had unconsciously expected the churches to be immune to the forces of change so evident everywhere else along Ponca Creek. In my mind I had envisioned a small but crowded church, hymns of faith sung full and deep-throated, mothers holding fidgety, well-scrubbed children while a prairie preacher held aloft a Bible, warning of the brimstone for those who failed to heed the Word and promising the glory for those who would trust and obey.

Having entered with hopes of finding some sign of eternal certainty, a reassurance of continuity, I leave the church instead with thoughts of the Ponca tribe, vanished from this land and bewildered why the Great Spirit had not protected them.

Afternoon is spent in a canoe on the Missouri River. We are "river people." Any unsettling thoughts from the morning are as remote as the sweaty exertions of the explorers who battled this current instead of surrendering and drifting with it as we do. Ours is the only vessel on the water. A warm silence surrounds us. Floating at the same speed as the current, it seems as if the canoe and water are stationary and the scenery on the shoreline is unrolling slowly in some gigantic 3-D Cinescope. Cottonwoods have dropped their white fluff on the Missouri's surface; it moves steadily and quietly with the canoe. Along the bank, wild turkeys, blue herons, and deer pay no attention to us as we pass.

After two hours, we turn into a winding backwater, at times

paddling straight into the drooping sun—three suns, all blindingly bright and gold: one in the sky, one reflected in the smooth water, and one lingering in an afterimage on the backs of our eyelids when we blink. Around a bend and a beaver slaps his tail on the water to warn of our approach to a mud-and-stick lodge. As we pull up to the bank to get out, startled carp rustle the mud in the shallows next to the canoe and swim toward deeper water.

We grill some hamburgers, savoring them along with the last, juicy drops of rose-colored daylight. Wisps of steam rise like wraiths from the warmer backwater and migrate downriver, fleeing the sunset instead of chasing it, and thereby repeating the contrary history of this place.

I spend two more days along Ponca Creek, not so much out of a sense of needing to learn more about it as a desire to remain as long as possible with the friendly people and the soothing beauty of the land. Perhaps it's out of fear that by the time I pass through on my return trip, the people and towns will be gone entirely.

At the Lynch school, Dale Merritt, the superintendent, tells me: "My biggest concern here is chewin' tobacco; and then alcohol—keg parties out on the river. Drugs aren't much of a problem." Declining enrollments have forced him to change to eight-man football, and with only six girls out for basketball "if you get in foul trouble, you're hurtin'." The state is pushing for even further consolidation of regional schools, but Merritt says "losing your high school in a small town means losing your small town." More than six hundred people came to graduation ceremonies for the eleven seniors last week, and four hundred are expected at the potluck lunch in a few days.

Dean Frank, a younger farmer in the area, tells me about problems created when the bank in Verdigre was closed. He takes out a 1967 Nebraska map, lays it out on his kitchen table, and we compare it to my more recent map. A lot of towns from the area on his map are missing on mine: Middle Branch, Star, Dorsey, Walnut, Sparta, Venus, Opportunity. What are they now? "Nothing, zero, zilch," he says. "I don't know if there's anything at Opportunity."

We have a cookout in Dave Lee's backyard, and play guitars late into the night. Catfish at Cabool's. A steak dinner for five bucks at the Dew Drop Inn in Verdel. Donna's pie and coffee at the Bakery Cafe. Pete Mulhair gives me radishes and peanuts from his garden.

On my last morning in town, I give Cabool a bottle of maple syrup and thank him for his hospitality. "Stop by any time you're in this country; you know where I live," he says. "You can shit, shower, shave, or shampoo here whenever you want. You're as welcome as the flowers in May."

I have one more cup of coffee at the center table of the Bakery Cafe and pick up my banana cream pie from Donna.

As I'm climbing into the *Discovery*, Pete Mulhair sees me and insists on buying me a beer in the Nite Owl. He's just finished moving some steers for a rancher. Before I can leave Lynch, he takes me east of town to see Little Red, a mare he got in trade for a trucking job nine years ago.

On the way back in his two-ton Ford, he tells me he bought the truck used, because nothing new is worth the price. It had 80,000 miles on it when he bought it five years ago. Now it has 280,000 miles to its credit—40,000 miles a year with Pete behind the wheel.

"How'd you keep it going so long?" I ask when we get back to the *Discovery*.

"Goin' slow," Pete says, pushing his head forward toward me and squinting under his cap. Pete's seventy-eight years old and still trucking. "Goin' slow's the secret."

Maybe he speaks for more than himself, and his last words to me mean that the story of Ponca Creek is a story of survival instead of surrender: "I let anyone who wants to pass me by."

9

Dakota Spirits

Do they ever petition the Good Spirit *to interfere with his power to avert or relieve them from the evils which the* bad Spirit *meditates or is practicing against them[?]*

From "Inquiries relitive to the Indians"
Thomas Jefferson's instructions
to Captain Meriwether Lewis

When they pushed up the Missouri past the mouth of the Niobrara River in early September 1804, the Corps of Discovery entered a new land: the High Plains. They were now west of the 98th meridian, where everything is different. The climate is semiarid—an average rainfall of 10 to 15 inches, versus 20 inches or more east of this dividing line—so the sky is clearer. The land is flatter, so there is more sky. The tall prairie grass gives way to short, steppe grasses; with the exception of cottonwoods along the rivers and occasional small cedars, the trees disappear: even more sky. With few hills or trees to slow its progress, the wind is forceful and constant.

For the explorers, the strangeness included more than changing topography and climate. Almost every day, they encountered new animals and new plants—in a two-week period, six mammals, two birds, and eight plants never before described and recorded for science. A prairie-dog burrow was flooded by the men, until one of the small mammals floated up and was killed and preserved to be sent back to Jefferson. Pronghorn antelope appeared on the grasslands, and pages of the journals were devoted to their markings, their habits, and their remarkable speed. The long-tailed magpie, previously believed to inhabit only Europe, was discovered. The coyote, mule deer, plains gray wolf, jackrabbit, and sharp-tailed grouse, all new to science, became commonplace sights as the expedition headed northwest along the river.

"This senery already rich pleasing and beatiful was still farther hightened by immence herds of Buffaloe, deer Elk and Antelopes which we saw in every direction feeding on the hills and plains," Lewis notes on September 17, 1804. "I do not think I exagerate when I estimate the number of Buffaloe which could be compre[hend]ed at one view to amount to 3000."

With the exception of the elk and wolf, I will see all of these animals in the Dakotas, although not in such mind-boggling numbers. For the modern explorer, however, the big change is the landscape. The opening up of sky and horizon that has been steadily proceeding since Kansas City suddenly accelerates, a virtual explosion that blows away hills and trees to expose you to the raw and powerful forces of nature that are now so starkly revealed.

The treeless plains roll out before you, not a monotonous flatness but an undulation, like the well-toned, tanned back of a muscular Mother Nature. On and on it stretches, without end, without relief. The road disappears in the distance, not from changing direction but because it has narrowed to a thin line that the gaping jaws of the horizon have swallowed.

The only thing competing on the same scale is the sky, which meets the earth out there at the horizon in every direction. The sky has its own terrain, a reminder that, like the earth below, it is a force of its own. Brilliantly white clouds float through like an armada of airships headed with determination toward some mission of cosmic importance. Storm fronts move in, not big enough to fill the entire canopy, but adding texture and new shades of gray and pink to the spectacle. Rain can be seen at a distance that must be counties away, and lightning punishes a butte or the top of a knoll for trying to impede the front's inexorable movement. Even on clear days, when it seems the sky is a bell jar resting on the horizon, a strong and steady wind pushes against the side of the camper, telling me that this is a land and these are forces too immense to be confined.

You don't feel any smaller. You simply realize that the human scale of the East and even of the Midwest has been a deception, hiding you from the true scale of nature and the forces it commands. And now you must confront those forces, deal with them in some way or another.

The Plains Indians responded by aligning themselves with nature, incorporating their lives and beliefs with their surroundings—the terrain, the four winds, the other animals inhabiting the vastness. They made themselves part of, neither more nor less important than, the natural forces.

Off in the distance, caught in the middle of the two elemental forces of sky and earth, a small white church sits as a monument to a different human response to this immensity of scale: the white man's religion. If these forces threaten to dwarf and overwhelm you, then ally yourself with a being supreme enough to have created it all—a God who cares more for you than for the forces He has unleashed against you.

Unlike the Indians, for whom the Great Spirit was both creator and creation, the whites had a God who considered humans (at least converted humans) special, more special certainly than the earth and the animals upon it, and more special than other humans who didn't believe in Him. God was on *our* side, and *our* Father could whip their Father.

Later I see another response. Earthen dams stop the Missouri River and back it up for hundreds of miles; irrigation systems the size of a giant's toys bring water to the dry plains; grain elevators rise as if the skyscrapers of New York have gone on a Fresh Air Fund vacation; freight trains of grain cars and coal cars extend for more than two miles; a coal shovel for the open pits reaches down and lifts out a chunk of earth the size of several house lots; power plants send strings of high-voltage lines into the distance to feed the electricity addiction of cities thousands of miles away.

This is direct competition with the elements, head to head, without invoking any supernatural assistance. Channel those forces to do man's bidding. Dam the rivers to provide the water for farming that Nature won't drop on your land. Tame the river that washes away your topsoil. Level the hilltops; parcel the prairies into manageable portions for cattle; open the mountains and extract their treasures; take what trees there are and use them to create your own environment, small enough and kind enough for human comfort. Ride the high-spirited bronc as it bucks, spurring it in the flanks to greater and greater exertions until it finally tires and, panting and sweating, is subdued.

ROAD RULE 10: The theology of the road forms its own religion, combining bits and pieces of other beliefs. It relies on technology (a vehicle), yet respects the forces of nature. Its deity is the Road Spirit; its principal practice is the pilgrimage.

Five minutes into South Dakota on Highway 18 and I see a cock pheasant strutting on the roadside. He strains his head forward and his wings backward as he runs to get out of the way, like a sprinter in the final strides of a hundred-yard dash. A prairie dog sits upright on his small haunches, peering over the grass to the pavement and the greener grass on the other side. He drops down to all four legs, wiggles his tail as if he's cranking up a balky motor—or his courage—and then darts across the highway, his tail pointed straight up. Next on the roadside is a black, white, and red sign marking the location of a fatal accident. It says: x

MARKS THE SPOT. WHY DIE? Maybe the animals can read in South Dakota. Turning north at Pickstown, Highway 50 takes me for a hundred miles, past more Xs and death-defying pheasants and prairie dogs.

Near Chamberlain, I'm forced to break a Road Rule: the only way to cross the Missouri on my way to Pierre is to take Interstate 90 west for fifteen miles. A clutter of billboards blocks the expansive vista I've become accustomed to. Instead of the majestic sweep of the Plains, the view from the interstate is of gaudy advertisements for Reptile Gardens, the Rushmore Borglum Story, Casey's Cafe, Al's Oasis, the Old West Museum, Flintstone's Family Fun, and Wall Drug.

FIRST COROLLARY: Don't disobey the Road Rules. In the theology of the road, as in most religions, sins bring down retribution.

The billboards should be punishment enough for a Road Rule violation. They aren't. Under an overpass, a hen pheasant decides to make a last-minute flight across the westbound lanes. She rises slowly, like an overloaded jumbo jet, and passes the right front of the *Discovery*, turning her dark eyes toward me in the driver's seat. In a half second of slow-motion time, as we both seem to realize what is about to happen, her eyes ask "Why die?" and mine answer "I'm sorry." A dull thud sounds just under the left front headlight, the hen drops to the pavement. A semitrailer hammering down the fast lane finishes her off. I take the first exit in a blackened mood. "I'm sorry," I say again.

SECOND COROLLARY: Confession is good for the soul and the only hope for forgiveness.

Between Chamberlain and Pierre is the Big Bend of the Missouri, a peninsula of 6,500 acres that, on the map, looks like a big tonsil in the throat of the river. Lewis and Clark established its measurements: a thirty-mile loop of river to progress only two thousand linear yards. In the riverboat days, passengers would often disembark, take a pleasant walk across the land, and wait for the vessel to arrive via the longer water route.

The Road Spirit is still angry with me. As I approach the Big

Bend, the two-lane blacktop turns to gravel, then to dirt, then to a path into a fallow field at the tip of the peninsula, where it stops. Somewhere in the town of Lower Brule I missed a turnoff. Breaking another Road Rule, I flag down a farmer on a tractor and ask directions for Pierre. He points me back to Lower Brule, so I break yet another Road Rule and retrace my route. On the way to this dead end, I was on the upwind side of the gravel and dirt roads; there was no traffic. On my way back, in the downwind lane, three or four pickups meet me, and I have to drive through the columns of dust in their wake. A thin film of tawny dirt covers everything on, and in, the *Discovery*. When I get back on the right road at Lower Brule, I have combined the worst of both worlds at the Big Bend: traveling the longer distance of the water route, eating the dust of the land route.

THIRD COROLLARY: Confession helps, but is not a substitute for atonement.

The Dakotas, South and North, aren't twins, despite their names. The differences are most apparent in their capital cities. Pierre, South Dakota (population 11,973), is a Western cow town surrounded on three sides by high-bluff plains. A sweep of dust at the corner of one of the downtown streets gives you the impression that if you turn too hastily, you might encounter a cattle drive and be stuck in its midst for hours. It was named for Pierre Chouteau, who knew Lewis and Clark and followed their path a few years after the Corps of Discovery to establish fur-trading posts along the Missouri. Locally, the city's name is pronounced Peer, not Pierre (no one in town can explain why).

Bismarck, North Dakota (population 44,485), radiates prosperity from its hills overlooking the Missouri, and its traffic jams are neither imagined nor caused by beef. The German immigrants of North Dakota named the city of Bismarck in honor of the Iron Chancellor. Dust isn't allowed, and no one dares mispronounce the name.

You get the feeling that while the people of South Dakota were involved in range wars, Indian wars, and gold rushes in the Black Hills (which brought on another round of Indian wars), the good burghers-turned-sodbusters to the north were perfecting a better hybrid strain of winter wheat.

South Dakota is one brash tourist promotion after another, from the Corn Palace in Mitchell to Mount Rushmore in the Black Hills, not to mention places like Reptile Gardens, Wall Drug, and Flintstone's Family Fun. Both states have spectacular Badlands, but South Dakota's are the ones you hear about. North Dakota's big attractions include the International Peace Garden, a seventeen-story state capitol building that looks like a cross between a grain elevator and an insurance-company headquarters, and the geographical center of North America. Its latest promotion is billboards on the Montana border that say: "When Custer left North Dakota, he was still alive."

The state bird of North Dakota, like that of Kansas and Nebraska, is the meadowlark. South Dakota's is the pheasant, the only state bird on the trail that has a yearly hunting season on it. Wild Bill Hickok was gunned down and buried in South Dakota, next to Calamity Jane; Lawrence Welk was born in North Dakota.

South Dakota also has the D & E Cafe in Pierre, which would be enough for any state's reputation.

It's after 8 P.M. by the time I start looking for a place to eat in Pierre, having already checked into my first motel since Wood River, Illinois, made a much-needed stop at a Laundromat (an old man pulled out seven farm caps from a washer and sat them on the counter to dry), and scouted around both Pierre and Fort Pierre (population 1,788), which straddle the Missouri.

Now it's getting late, and I want a good supper. One thing's for sure: I'm not about to break another Road Rule and risk getting food poisoning.

On a side street a few blocks from the center of Pierre is the D & E Cafe—a subcategory of First Name Cafe, a good sign. Pickups are parked outside, another good sign. Even at eight-thirty (a late hour for supper around here), it's crowded inside—still another good sign. More good signs: older waitresses, a framed dollar bill on the wall behind the cash register, pieces of pie in a glass cabinet, and a good look into the kitchen via the pass-through window.

Things are looking up. Then I see the prices on the mimeographed menu and immediately suspect a cruel trick is about to be played on me by an unappeased Road Spirit:

Large T-bone	$3.65
Shrimp	$3.00

Small T-bone	$2.60
Small Rib Steak	$2.05
Plain Pork Chops	$2.00
Breaded Pork Chops	$2.05
Half Fried Chicken	$2.45
Quarter Fried Chicken	$1.45

There has to be a catch, I'm thinking as I order the small T-bone. It must be a no-frills meal. What's the catch, I wonder when the waitress brings a small bowl of chicken soup. I ask myself the same question when she places a tossed salad in front of me. Must be a skimpy entree. Then she takes away my finished soup and salad and brings over a plate with a steak nearly hanging over the edges, hash browns, two pieces of toast, and a small side dish of green peas.

Besides being overwhelmingly filling, the food is good. Business is brisk. The waitresses are hustling from the kitchen window to the full tables. I seem to be the only one searching the walls for the hidden Candid Camera.

"Are you ready for your ice cream?" the waitress asks. "It comes with the supper."

I decide the trick must be in the other desserts.

"How much is the pie?"

"Fifty-five cents."

"Is it homemade?"

"Every day."

The piece of cherry pie she brings me has a crust like a thin, chewy sugar cookie—nearly on a par with Donna's finest. There are two small scoops of vanilla ice cream on it. They came with the dinner.

Stomach full and wallet lightened by less than four dollars, I waddle into the street to the *Discovery*.

FOURTH COROLLARY: Great are the rewards for those who have strayed but return to the Rules, were lost but now are found.

The second best thing about Pierre is that the Missouri River separating it from Fort Pierre is also the line between the Central Time Zone and Mountain Time. "When the bars close in Pierre, there's still an hour left in Fort Pierre," the clerk at the motel tells me. "First we go to the Longbranch, then cross the bridge to the Silver Spur."

Since the days long ago when I became hooked on Western movies, I've had two fantasies about saloons. In one, I sidle up to the bar, shake off some trail dust, and say, "Whiskey, and leave the bottle." In the other, someone in the saloon lifts his cowboy hat and shouts: "Drinks on me for everyone!" and the place erupts with whoops and hollers.

As I enter the Longbranch, the band has just started playing "Honky Tonkin'," and the crowd is whooping.

"You're just in time," the bartender says. "George is buying a round for the house. What'll it be?"

Figuring that asking for whiskey, leave the bottle, would be pushing my luck, I order a draft beer. You don't want to tempt the Road Spirit by getting too greedy when you're on a roll.

George is out on the dance floor. I deduce this by the way people lift their glasses to him when he and his partner sashay near their table—that, and because it says GEORGE on the back of his leather belt. A lot of the patrons, men and women, have their names on the backs of their belts, as if we're at a convention of memory-loss sufferers and need reminders of who we just talked to once they start walking away.

Most people are wearing cowboy hats. George and his dancing partner each have one. A guy I saw prodding bulls at an auction this afternoon is dancing, and he has a black cowboy hat on his head, wider-brimmed and shinier than the dusty one he wore in the pit. He's the best dancer of the evening and is out on the floor with a different girl for each song the band plays. They do the cowboy jitterbug. He rocks back and forth on the heels of his cowboy boots (the less foot movement the better) and swings his partner out and back, around and over, a nearly constant loop around the center pivot of boots and undisturbed cowboy hat—a lariat display using women instead of rope—and then he flourishes at the end by a series of twirls, tangling and then untangling her arms around him with a final, sudden dip while he takes his hat off with a free hand, protecting it from possible harm, and emerges from under the arch of her arms, hat securely back in place. It's hard to know whether he changes partners so often because he's popular or just wearing women out.

The clientele is a real mix: old and young, Indians and whites, drinkers and dancers, groups and loners, singles and couples. Married couples are easy to spot: they're the ones who stare over each other's shoulders as they dance and then return to their tables to drink their beers in silence.

The crowd keeps building, and George buys two more rounds for those who were in place when the band started, relying on the waitresses and bartender to know who gets the free drinks. The band is playing "Hey, Bartender" when I leave for Fort Pierre, where the night is an hour younger.

The Silver Spur is bigger and rowdier than the Longbranch. The bar is longer, there's more space for the pool table, more room to dance, and even a big-screen TV in the far corner, although no one is watching it. Regulars have their names burned into wooden plaques, the "Silver Spur Hall of Fame," hanging along one long wall. Cowboy hats and names on belts are even more prevalent.

During "happy hour" drinks are two-for-one; that is, they set two drinks in front of you and charge you for one—if it's draft beer you're drinking, they serve it in large Mason jars. Happy hour is from 4 to 9 P.M. I arrive after it's over, and there's a harder edge to the crowd than at the Longbranch. In my youthful fantasies, this would be the place where the barroom brawl takes place.

A rancher who looks and sounds exactly like Slim Pickens is next to me at the bar. He buys me a beer and we talk. He has 2,400 acres, 240 of them "under plow" and the rest rangeland for 100 head of cattle; his father homesteaded the land in 1909 and he's in the process of passing it on to his son, 160 acres at a time.

"I'm a cow man," he says, his voice scratchy, like wind over sand. "I could put two thirds of my land into crops, but I'd have to buy half a million dollars' worth of goddainged equipment, and I'd have to sign up for government programs. I won't have a goddainged thing to do with the government. That's what I believe."

He learns I'm from New England, which reminds him of a joke: A proper New England woman is visiting a Western ranch and gets disgusted by the cruder ways of the people she meets. "In Boston," she huffs to a cowboy, "breeding is everything." "Well, mam, we do it out here too," the cowboy answers, "but it isn't *everything*."

The rancher slaps the top of the bar, flashing his equine teeth as he laughs, and orders us another beer while he launches into a long speech about the virtues of his John Deere tractor versus his neighbor's Case: "Put them sumbitches tow-bar-to-tow-bar and that goddainged John Deere would just walk away. I do believe it."

During the second beer, I learn about buying bulls, the best way to cut and stack hay, how many days in a row the temperature was below zero in the winter of 1936–37 (forty straight days), and a few more good things about his John Deere tractor and bad things about the government.

The leftover drinking crowd from the happy hour is being supplemented by the dancing crowd from across the river when I leave before midnight. The jitterbugging cowboy has arrived and is out on the dance floor, still the best bull in the pit.

As I cross the Missouri back to the Central Time Zone, it strikes me that I could have an extra hour of sleep if my motel was in Fort Pierre instead of Pierre. But I can't complain. I've had a good dinner and a long night on the town for less than five bucks.

When I wake up the next morning, I'm unsure of the time, but certain where I'll get breakfast.

FIFTH COROLLARY: Repeated obedience to Road Rules is repeatedly rewarded.

Reading the breakfast menu at the D & E Cafe prompts me to consider standing up, lifting my cap, and shouting: "Breakfast on me for everyone!" It would be cheaper than George's generosity, even though the cafe, as always, is packed with customers. Full breakfasts, including coffee, cost from ninety-five cents to a dollar forty-five. A cup of coffee by itself is fifteen cents.

I splurge on a top-of-the-line breakfast, reinforcing the Western belief that Easterners are big spenders. With newspaper and tip, it comes to two dollars.

North of Pierre is the Oahe Dam, a large earthen blockade and part of the string of dams that has turned the main stem of the Missouri into more or less one long lake across the Plains. This, coupled with the same extensive damming of the Columbia River system, is probably the most striking physical change along the route since Lewis and Clark took it between 1804 and 1806.

"The key to this century is power—power on the farm as well as in the factory—power in the country as well as in the city," President John F. Kennedy said when he dedicated the dam in 1962. The Army Corps of Engineers display at the Oahe powerhouse says that the six main dams generate enough electricity to serve the city of Boston, and they create lakes stretching 836 miles with combined shorelines exceeding the American shorelines of the Atlantic and Pacific oceans and the Gulf of Mexico.

Here human projects assume the titanic scale of nature itself. Plans have been made to pump Lake Oahe water one hundred miles east to irrigate 100,000 acres of South Dakota prairie; a similar project exists for Lake Sakakawea in North Dakota. Other Missouri River–basin states have entered into a legal wrangle with South Dakota over its desire to send more Lake Oahe water west to coal fields in Wyoming, where it would be used for a coal slurry extending from Wyoming to Arkansas.

On the eastern shore of the lake, the last glacier of the Ice Age scraped the land flat and smooth, as if the Corps of Engineers had turned loose all the bulldozers at its disposal. Huge irrigation sprinklers revolve around pivots at the center of each square 160-acre quarter section, turning the brown land green in 130-acre circles that from above look like St. Patrick's Day cookies spread across an endless baking sheet. Corn grows where man provides the moisture that nature wouldn't. What was once rich bottomland is now hundreds of feet below a lake surface crisscrossed by water skiers and fishermen. The mighty turbines at the dam rumble like distant thunder; the lightning they produce is sent along lines carried by metal towers that march across the Plains like giant kachina dolls, totems of the triumph and power of science.

On the western, nonglaciated side of the Missouri, the grasslands are massive humpbacks that heave and roll as if a whale migration in a prehistoric sea had been arrested in mid-motion for eternity and then covered by a coarse horsehair blanket. Here one man has worked to replace what mankind nearly exterminated. Roy Houck owns fifty-five thousand acres, where three thousand buffalo roam in the second largest herd in North America.

For the Plains Indians, the buffalo represented food, clothing, shelter, and more. The animal was an integral part of their belief system. Buffalo skulls, hides, tails, raw parts, and viscera, even buffalo chips found their way into nearly every religious ceremony and many medicines. Believing the buffalo and the earth to be indivisible, the Teton Sioux of South Dakota would never speak poorly of the buffalo for fear the earth would tell the buffalo and bring misfortune to the speaker. Existence itself—both temporal and spiritual—was inextricably linked with the bison.

When Lewis and Clark explored the Louisiana Territory, the buffalo were so numerous they sometimes had to stop their river travel while a huge herd forded the Missouri. As late as the mid-1800s, an estimated 30 to 40 million grazed across the West.

But then buffalo robes became fashionable back East, buffalo tongue grew to be considered a delicacy in Europe, the crews building the railroads across the Plains needed to be fed, passengers on the rails thought it was great fun to shoot buffalo simply for the sport of it, and, finally, the white man realized that if the buffalo herds were eliminated, the Indians could be more easily subjugated and confined to their reservations. By 1889, there were fewer than a thousand buffalo, most of them either in protected parks or in Canada.

After Roy Houck's cattle ranch was inundated by the waters of Lake Oahe, he moved to the dry, less hospitable, high ground on the western shore. In 1959, he decided to raise buffalo, not out of sentimentality but to adjust his business to the new land he owned. He culls about a third of his herd each year for slaughter. Like the Indians, he uses every part of the buffalo: hides, skulls, bladders, and meat are all sold. The appeal of buffalo meat, besides its novelty, he says, is that it is lower in cholesterol than regular beef. Also, since buffalo are not constantly inoculated, as cattle are, some people with allergies prefer buffalo meat.

"I like them," he says of his buffalo. "I appreciate an animal that's qualified to take care of himself. Buffalo can sure do that. They're individualistic. They like to do things their own way, to be left alone. I'm probably the same way. Maybe that's why we're together."

Roy Houck's eighty-year-old face, like the land he owns, has been corrugated by time and weather, etched by lines that sculpt his features into a terrain at once gentle and strong. Over coffee in his kitchen, he talks of the buffalo's size, power, and deceptive speed (a buffalo can outrun a horse over sustained distances and reach 40 mph on a short burst), of an angry cow ramming his pickup (only the pickup was damaged), and of his hassles with the federal government over whether transporting his buffalo will spread brucellosis to neighboring cattle herds.

On the wall of his living room is the head of a buffalo bull that weighed more than a ton and dressed out to 1,200 pounds of meat. The head has a wide-eyed look, as if the bull had reached top speed, tried to lunge into the house, and, surprised to find itself staring at a television set and the twentieth century, froze in its tracks.

After coffee, Roy bids farewell and heads out to check part of his herd on his balloon-tired, motorized Kawasaki three-wheeler. He disappears over a rise and down a gully—his Stetson is the last thing I see—crossing an eerie landscape seemingly from another planet, in pursuit of beasts from another era.

My last meal in Pierre is lunch at the D & E Cafe, and I am filled with questions as I look at the menu.

Fried egg sandwich	$ .70
Hamburger	$ .70
Cheeseburger	$ .75
Denver sandwich	$1.10
Double cheeseburger	$1.30
Steak sandwich (fries, salad)	$1.40

How can this place survive on these prices? Is it just the plaything of some millionaire who doesn't need to make a profit? A front for some other money-making enterprise? An experiment in nutrition by some charitable foundation? Meals made from road kills along the X-dotted highways of South Dakota?

I want to ask for answers, but something holds me back. Like the Plains Indians after a bountiful buffalo hunt, I simply give thanks for the sustenance instead of questioning its source.

I pay my bill, take one final look at the dollar on the wall, and leave.

SIXTH COROLLARY: The theology of the road, like all others, contains many mysteries. Our role is to trust and obey.

The northwestern quarter of South Dakota—an area roughly 180 miles by 110 miles, or equal in size to the combined land masses of Connecticut, Massachusetts, and New Jersey—includes only four towns of more than a thousand people. All four sit on the perimeter of the rectangle (the two largest, Sturgis and Belle Fourche, are tourist towns near the Black Hills), so a minor adjustment of this imaginary line would leave essentially the same area with a total population of fewer than 40,000 people—not even two per square mile.

Driving west along U.S. 14, I come upon a large steel shed painted on one side with a red rose and the words: "Hayes International Airport . . . Rose Spray Service." A windsock along the dirt runway shows the breeze is strong and from the south today. Bill Rose and John Mitchell are filling the tank of a 600-horsepower Thrush with insecticide to spray for grasshoppers when I wheel the *Discovery* into the yard.

Bill learned to fly from his father, Houston Rose, a former Navy pilot. John, whose father runs the flying service in Pierre, also knows how to fly, but because he's blind in one eye can't get a license. They pause from their work long enough to give me several pieces of information.

The chief secret of spraying, Bill tells me, is "don't have any wrecks." He's survived three already—one when he was flying low and the propeller hit the ground, one when his engine just quit running, and one when he tried to land on a gravel road and lost control. His business is spraying to kill weeds or grasshoppers, and searching for cattle on the huge ranches. With both spraying planes in action, he says, they can cover four thousand acres in one day.

A small cluster of houses, Hayes, is about a half mile away, and I ask John how many people live there.

"Let's see," he says. "There's me, Bill and Barb and their boy, Caleb . . ." and goes on to count the town's inhabitants by their first names. "About thirteen, I guess."

The plane is loaded with insecticide and Bill is getting ready to take off. Before he gets into the cockpit, I ask how he can call this shed on the prairie an international airport.

"A guy from Canada landed here a couple of years ago," he answers, and takes off.

Turning north on Highway 63 just past Hayes, across a treeless terrain that makes me yearn again for Ponca Creek, I see my first sagebrush of the trip, dried balls of twigs pinned by the wind against a barbed-wire fence. Heavy alkaline concentrations in the soil—a phenomenon noted by Lewis and Clark—leave a white band around the small drainage ponds, nature's equivalent of ring around the collar. More pheasants on the roadside, meadowlarks on fencepost perches, a hawk pointed into the wind in a stalled glide, some jackrabbits bounding across the fields, and a small herd of butterscotch-and-white antelope standing at attention on a rise— but no people in sight, or sign of people except the fences on both sides of the pavement. The tailwind pushes me along at 70 mph.

The road drops into a mile-wide gully cut several hundred feet deep into the Plains by the Cheyenne River, a listless brown stream where a blue heron stands in the shallow water. A porcupine lies dead on the bridge; his last vision would have been the cottonwoods and willows on the winding bottoms. Then the road climbs back to the plateau, and the trees and water and steep slopes of the river breaks are a memory quickly evaporated into the clear, huge sky.

The water tower of Eagle Butte, South Dakota (population 438), rises on the horizon like a manmade moon. Time for a stop.

At the *Eagle Butte News*, a weekly paper with a circulation of 1,850, one of the three women employees is getting a permanent from a second one in the back room when I walk in. It's Friday; this week's paper is out and there's five days until the next deadline, so editor Helen Clausen, the third woman, has time to talk.

"I sell the ads, get the news, and catch the hell," she tells me and watches as I scribble in my notebook. "How long have you been traveling since you left St. Louis?" I answer, and she scribbles in *her* notebook. My visit is going to be featured in the next edition. As things turn out, she asks me more questions than I ask her. I take a picture of her and the other two women standing in front of the *Eagle Butte News*; she takes a picture of me standing in front of the *Discovery*.

The entire exchange is reminiscent of the artist Karl Bodmer's meeting with Yellow Feather, a Mandan chief. Believing it to be "bad medicine" to have his likeness captured on a piece of canvas and kept by another person, Yellow Feather would not consent to sitting for a portrait until he had made a sketch of Bodmer to hold as insurance against any tinkering with evil spirits. Helen Clausen and I are each protected.

North of Eagle Butte on Highway 63, a string of flatheaded buttes appears in the far distance. There is more sage—both the dead, brown bundles tumbling across the road and growing plants, aquamarine against the tawny baked earth. A towering dust devil swirls like a mini-tornado across a flat stretch of empty range two miles away. The valley of the Moreau River has even fewer trees than the Cheyenne, and the tan sides of the river breaks are streaked with pink scoria. Across the false horizon of a hilltop to the west, a herd of horses moves in single file and disappears, leaving a curtain of dust behind them.

Just past the Moreau River, my radio can not find any AM, FM, or CB signal to keep me company in this vastness. This is where my preparations in Kansas City pay off. I fish out a tape of the late, great Marty Robbins and have him sing to me of cantinas in El Paso, gunfighters with the "big iron" on their hips, cattle stampedes, and cool, clear water. It fits the scenery. The rear engine of the *Discovery* hums along when I join in on one of the songs.

> The shadows sway and seem to say
> Tonight we pray for water—cool water.
> And way up there He'll hear our prayer
> And show us where there's water—cool, clear water.

On a bluff overlooking the confluence of the Grand and Missouri rivers, a plain concrete obelisk pocked by bullet holes commemorates Sacagawea, the Shoshoni Indian woman who accompanied Lewis and Clark from the Mandan villages to the Pacific coast and back. A hundred yards away is a polished granite base over the grave of Sitting Bull; the stone bust of the Sioux chief that once rested on the granite has been recently vandalized and has been removed for repairs. I learn that there will be a Memorial Day service at the grave on Monday and think to myself it would make a good stop, if only it didn't mean I'd have to retrace my trail to attend. Mobridge, South Dakota (population 4,157), has a Pizza Hut, but my craving is quelled by my adherence to Road Rules.

Where paved roads parallel the Missouri River, both South and North Dakota have designated them Highways 1804 and 1806— Highway 1804 on the east side, in honor of the Corps of Discovery's journey up the river; Highway 1806 in honor of their return trip downriver. Lewis (or Clark?) points the way as I go north on Highway 1806 and cross the state line.

At Fort Yates, North Dakota (population 771), is another grave marker for Sitting Bull. He was buried here first, but we know by now what happens to famous people buried along the Missouri River. In 1953, a group from Mobridge convinced some of Sitting Bull's descendants to request a reburial in South Dakota. When the requests were rebuffed, the Mobridge group snuck in under cover of darkness, dug up the skeleton, trucked it across the state line, and buried it securely under a heavy concrete slab. By the next day, stores in Mobridge were selling T-shirts that said: "Mobridge, S.D. Sitting Bull Sleeps Here." South Dakota has always stolen the march on North Dakota when tourists were at stake.

It's 8 P.M. as I push north from Fort Yates, but the sun is still about thirty degrees above the horizon. Dark clouds have moved in from the northwest. Rain is coming—maybe someone heard Marty Robbins and me. The western rim is pink; a gash of eggwhite cuts across the northern horizon. The sun itself is hidden behind one of the clouds but sends golden shafts of light down to illuminate disparate points of earth. It reminds me of a pastel painting entitled *The Revealed Hand of God* that used to hang on a wall in my grandparents' home. The flathead buttes are much closer, looking like a mountain range that has been lopped with a hedge trimmer for neatness' sake.

South of Bismarck, the upper reaches of Lake Oahe give out and river takes over. Across the wide bottom, giant cottonwoods block my view to the east in the twilight, the closest thing to a forest I've seen since Missouri and a pleasant surprise.

By the time I find supper and a motel in Bismarck, the storm that I saw approaching two hours ago has just about arrived. As I unload the *Discovery* in the parking lot, I sing the line from Marty Robbins once more:

> And way up there He'll hear our prayer
> And show us where there's water—cool, clear water.

A crooked arm of lightning streaks from the dark sky to the ground in the north, bright enough to light up the prairie but still too far away for its thunder to be heard. The rain hits a few minutes later.

Saturday of Memorial Day weekend is spent with the ghosts of George Armstrong Custer and the Seventh Cavalry. Custer's last station was Fort Abraham Lincoln, across the river and south of Bismarck. From there, in 1874, he led an expedition into the Black Hills—an area sacred to the Sioux and at the center of a huge territory that had been reserved by treaty "for all time" for the tribe—and discovered gold. The resulting gold rush touched off another Indian War. So in the early summer of 1876, Custer and the Seventh marched out once again to punish the hostile Sioux and Cheyenne encampments in Montana.

At Fort Lincoln, before he left on the 1876 expedition, Custer told some of his Arikara scouts that a victory would assure him of the presidency (the Democratic convention was coming up, as was the nation's centennial celebration). This campaign, he told them, would be his last, would bring him great fame and would put him in the White House. He was right on two of the three predictions. He never became president, but it was his last campaign, and being wiped out by Sitting Bull, Crazy Horse, and Gall on the bluffs of the Little Big Horn made him famous, more famous certainly than Rutherford B. Hayes, who won the election of 1876.

The original site of Fort Lincoln is a state historic park, where I spend the afternoon on the grassy hillside that once held barracks and officers' housing. A historic marker notes the place where the entire Seventh, including the five doomed companies, marched out past their wives and children to the tune of "Garryowen" and "The Girl I Left Behind Me." The day is overcast and cold. The wind is the only music.

During the evening, I take a cruise on the *Far West*, a replica of the paddlewheeler that brought back the wounded from the Little Big Horn and the news of Custer's defeat. We head a few miles upriver toward a refinery and power plant, then downstream, under a railroad trestle and interstate bridge to a point opposite the old fort, and then back to the mooring. A band plays below decks, and the one blackjack table (two-dollar limit) is lined three persons deep. It's just as well that I can't get to the gambling table, wrapped as I am in Custer's memory: I'd probably have the modern version of his luck, lose my gas money, and have to *stay* in Bismarck.

I go up to the top deck to smoke a cigar and watch the night scenery. There's only one couple out here, combating the night chill by necking on a bench. Something—my presence, my cigar, the spirits following me—prompts them to get up and leave to join the rest of the crowd down below. Alone on the stern, I listen to the churn of the paddles against the current and let it keep the beat as I try to remember the tune of "The Girl I Left Behind Me."

Products of eighteenth-century Enlightenment, Lewis and Clark, like Jefferson, were deists. According to their religious view reason, not divine revelation, proved the existence of God, who had created the universe but had then left it alone to be governed by its natural, orderly laws. God was an absentee architect-owner, not a building superintendent.

The expedition celebrated two Christmases on the trail—at Fort Mandan in North Dakota and at Fort Clatsop on the Pacific coast. The men sang songs, fired their guns and cannon, and danced. They had an extra ration of rum the first Christmas; the supply of liquor was gone long before the second winter. But there is no mention in the journals of any religious ceremonies, even a prayer, on those days.

Lewis describes Charbonneau "crying to his god for mercy" during a near-disaster on the boat, and later writes that upon reaching the river's headwaters at the Continental Divide one of the men "thanked his god that he had lived to bestride the mighty & heretofore deemed endless Missouri." It's interesting that in these, two of the rare references to God in the journals, Lewis seems careful to distinguish that the deity being petitioned is not his own, and that he uses a lowercase g both times.

For Rev. James Kraemer's congregation at the Church of the Nazarene in Mandan, North Dakota (population 15,513), God is neither remote nor an abstraction. Thanking and petitioning their God is a continual process for them. And He answers them.

The Sunday evening service has nearly filled the small church with families, most of whom were here this morning as well. There is a prayer service at seven-fifteen every morning, an evening service on Wednesdays, and regular prayer meetings in church members' homes during the week.

Early in the Sunday evening service, Reverend Kraemer calls upon his flock to stand and give testimony. One by one they rise to recount ways He has entered their lives and answered their prayers: from helping a teenager on a math test to comforting a heart-attack victim, from filling one parishioner with hope and joy to helping a family find a camping spot at a crowded state park.

The service is filled with songs of praise—"Sing of the Mercy of the Lord," "If That Isn't Love," "Let's Just Praise the Lord," "Living by Faith," "A Mighty Revival Is Sweeping This Way," "I Want to See My Savior First of All"—and few people need hymnals to remember the words.

Reverend Kraemer, a young man with a broad, constant smile, is part of a group of evangelical ministers seeking signatures on a petition to change a North Dakota law that permits small grocery stores to open on Sundays. Their concern is that unless they protest this limited law, the legislature eventually will allow other establishments to operate on Sundays, and some of their parishioners will face the choice of working and missing church or attending services and losing their jobs. Reverend Kraemer asks his congregation to sign the petition and to boycott any grocery store that opens on Sunday. "Let's keep Sunday a special day," he tells them.

After the sermon from the Gospel of Mark ("If thou canst believe, all things are possible to him that believeth"), the minister calls on those who wish to come forward to the altar rail. At first, about seven walk up and kneel to pray silently; some are sobbing and shaking quietly. Then more join them. Reverend Kraemer bows down with a young girl, a mother comes forward to kneel next to her son and gently rubs his back. Two older women clasp their arms around each other while the pianist plays softly. Back at the pulpit, Reverend Kraemer raises an arm and says: "Lord, we are thankful that your power is at work in our lives. And Lord, we *do* believe that a mighty revival is sweeping our way."

Outside the church after the service, while scores of children play in the front yard, virtually every adult member of the parish comes up individually to talk with me; several invite me home for supper with them.

I feel much the way Lewis and Clark must have during their encounters with the Arikara Indians near the modern South Dakota–North Dakota border. The Arikaras' beliefs and customs were vastly different from the explorers', just as this congregation's religion is not mine. The Arikaras rejected the expedition's offer of whiskey, wondering why anyone would offer them something that made them act foolishly; their view of hospitality and the transfer of spiritual "medicine" prompted them to proffer the pleasures of their women to the travelers; and when the captains ordered a disciplinary lashing of one of their subordinates, a shocked

Arikara chief informed them that his nation might punish an offense with death, but would never whip someone, not even an
unruly child. And yet Lewis and Clark recorded these alien customs
drily and straightforwardly, without making judgments or editorial
comments.

In one remarkable journal entry, Clark describes some stones
resembling two humans and a dog to which the Arikaras paid
reverence with votive offerings. According to tradition, these rocks
were once a man and woman who loved each other but were not
allowed to marry. The man went off to mourn and the girl he left
behind him followed with a dog. All three subsisted only on grapes
until they eventually turned to stone. "On the river near the place
those are Said to be Situated," Clark notes matter-of-factly, "we
obs[erve]d a greater quantity of fine grapes than I ever Saw at one
place."

SEVENTH COROLLARY: The theology of the road is a tolerant
religion. Other beliefs can be observed, but should not be
questioned or ridiculed. They should be treated with respect;
they may work better than your own.

Tomorrow is Memorial Day, and the curiosity of attending a
service at the grave of a man who handed the U.S. Army one of
its greatest defeats on home ground becomes a mighty temptation,
even if it does mean retracing my route to Mobridge, South Dakota.
Having spent a day with Custer's memory, I decide, Sitting Bull
deserves equal time.

There are still two hours of late-May twilight left, and it's two
hours from Mandan to Mobridge: I can make it without any night
driving. After checking my map, I plot a course that will return
me to South Dakota mainly on different highways than my northbound route.

I get into the *Discovery* and head southeast. The storm system
of the last two days is breaking up. The rain has cleaned the
highway of dust, and the rangeland has responded by showing a
tender green along the gullies. Through a beautiful, peaceful, windless evening the camper purrs along Highway 6. The Cannonball
River valley, lined by purple and pink buttes, looks like Arizona's
Monument Valley with grass.

As I approach Mobridge, for the first time on my trip the sun sets toward my right rear instead of to my left or in my windshield. Lewis and Clark, I remind Anyone who may be listening, made one major backward trip in the Bitterroot Mountains and probably survived because of it. Unscathed and unpunished, I check into a Mobridge motel and sleep like a baby.

EIGHTH COROLLARY: With proper theological rationalizations, as in any religion, exceptions can be made for any Road Rule without paying penance.

10

Two Indians

. . . your woman who accompanied you that long dangerous and
fatigueing rout to the Pacific Ocian and back diserved a greater re-
ward for her attention and services on that rout than we had in
power to give her. . . .
William Clark's letter to
Toussaint Charbonneau
August 20, 1806

These are the vilest miscreants of the savage race, and must ever
remain the pirates of the Missouri, until such measures are pur-
sued, by our government, as will make them feel a dependence on
its will for their supply of merchandise.

William Clark's description
of the Teton Sioux
Winter 1804–1805

The bullet-hole-ridden concrete obelisk near Sitting Bull's grave that memorializes the Indian woman who accompanied Lewis and Clark has a plaque that says her name was Sakaka-Wea, that she "guided" the expedition to the Pacific Ocean, and that she died and was buried at Fort Manuel in South Dakota on December 20, 1812.

Well . . .

The Corps of Discovery was as fascinating a collection of humanity on an epic mission as history can provide. First, there were the two young captains. Lewis: Jefferson's protégé, only twenty-nine years old when the expedition left Wood River, the better educated of the two, introverted and sometimes moody, more prone to philosophize and rhapsodize in his journal entries, a natural botanist and zoologist. Clark: four years older than his co-captain, more experienced in military matters, the better riverman and frontiersman, extroverted and even-tempered and at ease with both the enlisted men and Indians, a cartographer of first rank despite his lack of formal training. Contradicting military orthodoxy, they shared command of the expedition without any evidence of dissension or stress. That so few emergencies arose—and that those that did were so skillfully handled—during the trek across four thousand miles of uncharted wilderness and back is a testament to the captains' intelligence and leadership. They made the expedition's achievement seem almost easy. In fact, it was extraordinary.

There were the men who braved constant hardships and perils, yet lost only one of their number: the black slave, York, who intrigued the Indian tribes and who became such an accepted equal during the journey that he was allowed to vote with the other men in deciding where to build their fort on the Pacific Coast; Shannon, the young private who was twice separated from the main party for extended periods; Drouillard, whose hunting skills impressed even the Indians and were credited by Clark as crucial to the expedition's survival; the Field brothers, Reuben and Joseph, who were selected for virtually every mission of importance or danger; the one-eyed French boatmen Cruzatte who entertained the troupe with his fiddle playing and nearly ended Lewis's life by mistaking him for an elk during a hunt; even the Newfoundland dog that survived the withering heat of the Plains summers and had a moment of glory by chasing out a buffalo bull that had rampaged into camp one night.

But none of them has captured the imagination of writers and the public as has the Indian woman Sacagawea. And, in the never-ending battle between reality and myth, fact and fiction, none has sparked as much controversy.

Students of Road Rules will not be surprised to learn that myth and fiction have prevailed. Sacagawea probably has better name recognition among the public than Meriwether Lewis or William Clark; certainly the novels about her have sold better than books about the expedition as a whole. She is said to have more statues in her honor than any other woman in American history.

Her role in the expedition, the date and place of her death, even her name are hotly disputed.

Most people know her as Sacajawea (SACK'-a-ja-wee-a); in the Dakotas, she is called Sakakawea (Sa-CA'-ca-wee-a). Leading Lewis and Clark scholars, the Lewis and Clark Trail Heritage Foundation, the Bureau of American Ethnology, and the U.S. Geographical Names Board refer to her as Sacagawea (Sa-CA'-ga-wee-a, rhymes roughly with Chicago-wea).

The issue about her name is whether it came from her native Shoshoni tribe and means "boat launcher" (or "boat pusher"), in which case Sacajawea would be correct; or whether it derived from the Hidatsa language and means "bird woman," which translates to Sakakawea, or, more uniformly, Sacagawea. Lewis, in a journal entry on May 20, 1805, writes that they have named a creek in Montana "Sah ca gah wea or bird woman's River," and that settles the matter for most historians, although a question has been raised as to whether the explorers simply misunderstood some sign language: the difference between the Shoshoni sign for "boat launcher" and the Hidatsa sign for "bird woman" is merely a nuance of hand and arm movement.

Notes by a trader at Fort Manuel and by Clark as Indian Agent for the Missouri Territory clearly state that she died at the fort and was buried in 1812, at about the age of twenty-five. But, Fort Manuel being along the Missouri River and Sacagawea being an important historical figure, it was only a matter of time before

Road Rule 8 would catch up with her. A novel by Grace R. Hebard
in the 1930s and a recent novel by Anna Lee Waldo began and
perpetuated the myth that Sacagawea (they both call her Sacajawea) was not the woman who was buried near the Missouri. They
contend the heroine went on to further exploits and died an old
woman on the Wind River Reservation of Wyoming in 1884, more
than seventy years after Clark pronounced her dead.

Sacagawea's true role in the expedition is substantial enough,
and some of the incidents she was involved in dramatic enough,
to make good reading and to earn her a place in history. Embel-
lishments aren't necessary.

At the age of twelve or thirteen, she was captured by a Hidatsa
raiding party at the Three Forks of the Missouri. By the time Lewis
and Clark arrived at the Hidatsa and Mandan villages in North
Dakota, Sacagawea and another Shoshoni captive had been sold
to the French trader Toussaint Charbonneau, who, according to
custom, had made her one of his wives. On February 11, 1805,
Lewis attended to the birth of her and Charbonneau's son, Jean
Baptiste.

The explorers had learned enough from the Hidatsas to know
they would need horses from the Shoshonis to cross the mountains.
They therefore hired Charbonneau as an interpreter, with the understanding that his wife would come along to help with the Shoshoni negotiations. The infant, dubbed "Pomp" by Clark, became
the youngest member of the Corps of Discovery. Sacagawea was
seventeen.

To call her a "guide" of the expedition is a gross overstatement;
the bulk of the territory covered by the group was as foreign to
her as it was to the men from the East. As the explorers neared
the land of her people, however, she did confirm familiar landmarks, and on the return trip she directed Clark to what is now
Bozeman Pass in the Rocky Mountains. But most of the time she
was not blazing the trail.

In a coincidence that would strain credulity in a fictional account, the first band of Shoshonis the expedition bumped into in
the Bitterroot Mountains was led by Cameahwait, Sacagawea's
brother, and included a woman who had been captured in the same
Hidatsa raid as Sacagawea but had escaped to rejoin their people.
In the negotiations for the acquisition of the all-important horses,
Sacagawea served as interpreter.

More intangibly, throughout the journey her very presence and that of her child, as Clark notes in a journal entry, "reconsiles all the Indians, as to our friendly intentions. A woman with a party of men is a token of peace."

The simple fact that the teenage mother, nursing a baby all the way, was able to keep up with the expedition and survive its ordeals is remarkable in itself.

Lewis and Clark scholars say these facts, which firmly establish Sacagawea's unique spot in history, should satisfy any hunger for heroine worship. Hebard's and Waldo's novels, however, prove otherwise—particularly since it is their wildly exaggerated fictional accounts that have hit the best-seller lists.

What Hebard started in her book, filled with tenuous evidence of a Sacagawea who lived into her nineties, Waldo stretches even further. She even includes a spicy affair between Sacagawea and Clark, complete with an angry and brutal fit of jealousy by Charbonneau.

Historians and Lewis and Clark buffs have churned out paper after paper in scholarly journals to refute what they believe to be, as Irving W. Anderson, who has specialized in the Charbonneaus, has called it, "a serious negative intrusion upon the integrity of U.S. history." To their dismay, their efforts have made as much impact on the popular conception of Sacagawea as the bullet holes on the Sakaka-Wea obelisk near Mobridge: the monument stands, the plaque calls her the expedition's guide, and the public considers anything that says otherwise vandalism.

Lewis and Clark's first tense confrontation with Indians occurred in the middle of South Dakota, when a large band of Teton Sioux tried to prevent the explorers from proceeding farther upriver. The firmness and coolness of the two captains—and the display of the small cannon on the bow of the keelboat—are credited with extricating them from the situation without a fight.

While the journals generally exhibit respect for the tribes the expedition met, the harsh comments in them about the Sioux stand out in sharp contrast. "These are the vilest miscreants of the savage race," Clark writes about them, "and must ever remain the pirates of the Missouri, until such measures are pursued, by our government, as will make them feel a dependence on its will for their supply of merchandise."

Sixty years later, in a telegram to President Grant, General William Tecumseh Sherman displayed a similar opinion of the tribe, and then proposed a more extreme policy: "We must act with vindictive earnestness against the Sioux, even to their extermination, men, women and children. Nothing less will reach the root of the case."

Of all the tribes of the High Plains, the Sioux fought the encroachment of the white man the longest and hardest in the 1800s. They handed the U.S. Army one of its worst military defeats at the Little Big Horn in 1876, when Custer and more than two hundred men were annihilated; and they suffered one of its grisliest massacres in 1890, when five hundred members of the Seventh ringed a village of about two hundred Sioux, two thirds of them women and children, and killed virtually all of them at Wounded Knee. The long series of Indian wars was buried there in a mass grave.

Dakota (or Lakota, as the western portion of the seven tribes pronounce it) is the name the Sioux ascribed to themselves. It means "allies" or "alliance of friends." The word "Sioux" is a French extrapolation of the name the Dakotas were called by their enemies, the Ojibwa Indians. It means "cutthroat" or "little snake."

Within this single, bitter irony—that the whites gave the Sioux this derogatory name and made it stick, and then gave the Dakota name to the land they took from the Indians—the complete history of America's treatment of its first inhabitants is told. As a people they were cheated, humiliated, killed, and cruelly subjugated; at the same time, as a symbol, they have been grandly enshrined.

In no other instance is the disparity between reality and our popular myths at greater variance. To our school mascots, our vehicles, even our states we have transferred Indian names—as if, in a twist of Indian belief, we could thereby transfer the "medicine" of their strength and stoic nobility to a football team or a four-wheel-drive stationwagon. (Sherman himself, the ruthless Indian fighter, was named for the Shawnee leader Tecumseh, who tried to create a confederacy of tribes to fight the whites. "Unless each tribe unanimously combines to give check to the avarice and oppression of the whites," the chief said in 1812, "we will become conquered and disunited and we will be driven from our native lands and scattered like autumn leaves before the wind." Tecumseh's plan for a united Indian front had failed and he had been dead seven years before his white namesake was born.)

Myth. Myth is the Jekyll-and-Hyde image that has oscillated through fiction and movies: the Indian as barbarous savage impeding the march of civilization, then the Indian as gentle, romantic, and noble savage—either way a caricature.

Reality. Reality was somewhere in between. The Indian cosmology and sociology were in many ways more "civilized" and noble than the whites', but native customs also included practices like taking body parts from the mutilated corpse of a slain enemy or enslaving and selling women captured in a raid.

Modern reality is the reservations: pockets of cynicism and despair in a region otherwise notable for its friendliness and spunky optimism, rural versions of East St. Louis inhabited by the survivors of a race of people who weren't merely left behind by the sunset-chasing quest of the American Dream and then denied access to it. No, the Indians weren't left behind; they were in the way.

Their culture, based on harmonizing with the often harsh and relentless elements of nature, encountered a new force, equally harsh and relentless but intent on conquest, not harmony: the machine of white civilization, fueled by concepts foreign to America's natives—private ownership of property, material wealth, and exploitation of nature's treasures. This mighty machine simply rolled westward across the prairies and crushed anything and anyone in its path.

In Jefferson's Enlightenment view, the Indians were little different from the whites, just at a lower stage of civilization in a great chain of development because of their wilderness environment. Given time, he believed, the Indians could be persuaded to exchange their hunting grounds for small farms, and the white and red bloods would eventually commingle in complete assimilation.

The Louisiana Purchase fit into Jefferson's plans. Tribes east of the Mississippi could be relocated into the new territory to begin the slow process of "catching up" with the whites; meanwhile, the lands to the east could be settled without the conflicts that normally arose between the two cultures. The pressures of national expansion and his plan for gradual acculturation of the Indians could both be accommodated, if there was enough land and enough time. His policy also had a pragmatic side, reflecting his duties as president. "The Indians can be kept in order only by commerce or war," Jefferson said. "The former is the cheapest."

Whether Jefferson's policy might have worked, we'll never know. The vast new area of the Louisiana Territory became too much of a magnet for a nation of people with an insatiable appetite for cheap land. Settlers swarmed westward across the Mississippi long before the Indians became friendly farmers with red skins. By the time Andrew Jackson became president, Indian policy was reduced to pushing them out of the way of white settlement.

As far as the Indians were concerned, of course, there was little difference. To them, Indian removal, whether motivated by a benign concern for their "development" or by sheer greed for their lands, was the same thing: an uprooting to places the whites didn't want for the moment.

For Jefferson, Indians were "our brethren, our neighbors; they may be valuable friends, & troublesome enemies. Both duty & interest then enjoin, that we should extend them the blessings of civilized life, & prepare their minds for becoming useful members of the American family."

For Jackson, a quarter of a century later, they had "neither the intelligence, the industry, the moral habits, nor the desire for improvement which are essential to any favorable change in their condition . . . they must necessarily yield to the force of circumstances and erelong disappear."

Government policy has seesawed back and forth between these two basic views through the present. One administration violates treaties by ceding Indian lands to homesteaders; another tries to preserve "surplus" lands for the tribes. One gives tribes the right of self-government on the reservations; another proposes to terminate reservations altogether.

The result is a mixture of the worst of both. At a Sioux reservation in northern South Dakota, a tribal officer complains about the debilitating level of alcoholism among his people; later he tells me he owns the local liquor store. Tales of vicious political infighting are related to me at every reservation along the trail, worries that the dark side of self-determination—that council members dole out government jobs (often about the only work on a reservation) as patronage to their family and friends—is undermining its purpose. A member of the Cheyenne River Sioux council tells me: "Once people realize their civil rights, things will improve."

Then he refuses to comment about his support of a decision that "forever barred" three council candidates from holding appointed or elective offices because they had just won primary races against the incumbents.

White merchants of agency towns, the towns where tribal headquarters and federal agents are located, reflect the same schizoid attitude. They complain of bad debts, troubles with employees, and high insurance rates because of vandalism; yet they often get into bidding wars with other towns for the location of the headquarters. "This town would have dried up just like the other towns in the county if it hadn't been for the Agency," one businessman confides.

The halls of tribal offices and the discussions at council meetings I attend are dominated with the acronyms of federal programs: BIA, HHS, TERO, HUD, EPA, WIC, EDA. In a depressing fulfillment of Clark's call for a "dependence" on the government, grants have replaced the buffalo as the principal means of subsistence.

And yet at every reservation I visit are seeds of hope in the barren landscape of reservation life. Younger tribal members, often college-educated, are returning to their reservations and committing themselves to helping their people—returning by choice, not necessity. Dennis Hastings, working "in the trenches" to rebuild self-pride with the Omahas. A woman educator in North Dakota, who tells me: "What does 'Indian education' mean? It's not beadwork and tanning hides all day. It's learning by doing and it's still applicable. When you become educated, you don't necessarily have to lose your traditions. If you truly want self-determination and self-sufficiency, you have to set your standards and take responsibility." Gerard Baker, a young Hidatsa who has risen to a supervisory position in the National Park Service, who hopes his career can be an example and a proof to whites and members of his tribe alike that an Indian is not a caricature. A Nez Perce in Idaho whose work on interpreting history is part of keeping the best traditions of his tribe alive. And a Cayuse woman along the Columbia River in Oregon, trying to forge white–Indian cooperation in the tangled web of fishery management, and hoping her efforts will advance women's rights on her reservation at the same time.

For them, the choice is not between a romantic myth or a despairing reality, idealized nobility or disintegrated culture. It's the harder work in between. "We have to understand where we came from," one tells me. "But we're never going back [to the way things were] and we can't stay where we are. We've got to progress—without bitterness, without self-pity."

America's love-hate relationship with Indians, the penchant to ennoble a race of people while subjugating them relentlessly, fused in the life and death of Sitting Bull.

The Hunkpapa medicine man was among the Indian leaders who rejected the Fort Laramie Treaty of 1868 and refused to move his people to the reservations it created. With Crazy Horse, Two Moons, and Gall he formed the confederation of Sioux and Cheyenne—the greatest massing of the "hostile" Indians in our history—that overwhelmed Custer at the Little Big Horn. A shocked nation cried out for revenge. As fragmented bands of the confederation were pursued, beaten, and forced to return to the reservations, Sitting Bull moved his band across the border into Canada. (Crazy Horse surrendered in May 1877 and was killed while under arrest that September.)

Rumors swept the country: Sitting Bull had attended West Point; he was fluent in French; he wasn't really an Indian, he was a halfbreed with blue eyes; he wrote erudite poems to the Nez Perce Chief Joseph; Sitting Bull had studied Napoleon's military strategies. These were the only ways to explain—or accept—his stunning victory. None of the rumors was true.

Finally, in 1881, with the remains of his band on the verge of starvation, Sitting Bull and 186 of his followers turned themselves in at Fort Buford, North Dakota. The steamboat that carried him to imprisonment near the Nebraska border was named, ironically, the *General Sherman*. The captain of the boat that later brought him back upriver to the Standing Rock Reservation and Fort Yates was the same one who had piloted the *Far West* when it carried the wounded from the Little Big Horn to Bismarck.

The obdurate chief who had once scolded reservation Indians, telling them that "you are fools to make yourselves slaves to a piece of bacon fat, some hardtack, and a little sugar and coffee," was given a hoe and a plot of land to farm. He is said to have attended the ceremony when the cornerstone was laid for the territorial capital in Bismarck in 1883. A picture of the day's festivities shows some Sioux men wearing feathered headdresses marching behind a parade placard that says: MARCH OF CIVILIZATION. Sitting Bull is believed to be the one carrying the American flag.

Buffalo Bill Cody—Pony Express rider, Indian scout, buffalo hunter, hero of Ned Buntline's dime novels, star of his own world-famous traveling show, embodiment of the West as a marketable entertainment commodity—had joined the punitive expedition following the Little Big Horn to avenge the slaughter of his friend, the general the Indians called Long Hair. In a scene he reenacted later in his Wild West Show and immortalized in a huge-selling lithograph, Cody had taken the "first scalp for Custer." A few years later, Buffalo Bill was bringing Sitting Bull along on his tours as a prime attraction. The chief, once the scourge of America, was packing in adoring crowds and getting a dollar per autograph—more than Frank James ever received.

In the late 1880s, a great spiritual revival called the Ghost Dance swept through the demoralized tribes of the Plains. Its followers believed that the world would soon end, the vanished buffalo and dead Indians would return, and the whites would be eradicated. Some believed that wearing a ghost-dance shirt made them invulnerable to bullets. Not surprisingly, this movement alarmed the whites, particularly when they learned that Sitting Bull had joined the believers.

On December 15, 1890, forty-three Indian police surrounded his house to bring him in again. Sitting Bull was killed resisting arrest, or was assassinated, depending on which version of the day's events you care to believe. His house was shipped to Chicago in 1893, where people paid admission to view it at the World's Fair.

There are many theories about what happened to his bones. Some say that they were not the ones buried in a box at Fort Yates, that his followers, fearful of future depredations of his remains, buried them secretly. If that story is true, the fears were well placed.

A photographer in the early 1900s dug up the skeleton under the Fort Yates marker for a picture, took a bone as a souvenir, and later gave it to the North Dakota Historical Society. It turned out to be the femur of a young woman. The monument and grave at Fort Yates were moved several times. In the 1960s, as the Corps of Engineers was building a dike in the former cemetery, it came across a casket holding a box of bones that fit the description of

Sitting Bull's. North Dakotans claim the Mobridge group dug up the wrong grave and buried the wrong skeleton under twenty tons of concrete in South Dakota. So they maintain their own monument at Fort Yates.

Mobridge thinks otherwise. Prior to the surprise exhumation, when legal channels were being pursued to move the chief's grave, the *Mobridge Tribune* editorialized on March 26, 1953: "It's true, Sitting Bull's fame makes a monument of this sort a great tourist attraction, but that is purely incidental to this project." The editorial says the rising waters of Lake Oahe are endangering the Fort Yates grave, and money is already being raised for a more fitting monument and bust at the new site in South Dakota.

The *Tribune* had pictures of the early-morning raid of April 8, 1953, showing five men with hand shovels and a tow truck lifting the cement slab from the Fort Yates grave. Under a banner headline saying

Local Drama Draws Wide Publicity
All World Knows Now That Chief
Sitting Bull Is Buried Near Mobridge

a story begins: "Perhaps not since war broke out in Korea has an incident received so many bold headlines and inches of space in newspapers and been so thoroughly aired on the radio. Much magazine publicity is yet to come." By September, the memorial was ready to be dedicated. Politicians spoke, a ninety-six-year-old Cheyenne survivor of the Battle of the Little Big Horn was among the one thousand Indians from nine states who gathered on the bluffs, three granddaughters of Sitting Bull attended, the Mobridge High School Band played.

The *Tribune* this Memorial Day weekend is filled with stories about tomorrow's upcoming service at the monument that will "honor the great Sioux leader Sitting Bull and that will remember those Indian and White soldiers who died while in the service of the United States," the first such service of its kind. It reports on the response to a Chamber of Commerce fund drive to repair the bust (someone had pushed it off the pedestal, breaking off the feather). The lead editorial in this paper that had trumpeted the grave-robbing some twenty years earlier is devoted to praising the outpouring of generosity to restore the bust—and to criticizing anyone who could commit such senseless vandalism.

Just what the promoters from Mobridge had in mind for a Memorial Day service at Sitting Bull's grave is not clear. A handful of representatives from the town's American Legion, VFW, and Chamber of Commerce are present, plus a few white reporters, but the overwhelming majority of the seventy-five people gathered around the monument on this cloudy and windy day are from the Standing Rock and Cheyenne River Sioux reservations, and they have very definite plans for the ceremony. They have come to set the record straight.

Reginald Bird Horse, a tall man with a long, single braid of coarse hair, takes the microphone attached to two loudspeakers mounted on a truck, and welcomes the crowd in Lakota, then translates his words into English. He compares Sitting Bull to the white man's Washington and Lincoln. "It's a good feeling when members of the VFW, the Legion, do an honor to one of our leaders," he says. "We appreciate that. I know that this is something that should have been done quite some time ago. I feel that this a good beginning. We need a good relationship and this is a good start."

Three men begin a Lakota song, a high and mournful chant, while Isaak Dog Eagle, a descendant of Sitting Bull, fills a ceremonial pipe with sacred tobacco. Bird Horse explains that the chant is to the four directions, to the Great Spirit above and to Mother Earth, and that the pipe is important to start any ceremony.

A leader from the Cheyenne River reservation talks about the long military tradition of the Indians (all five of his father's sons were in the armed services; one died in Korea), about the need for unity against current federal Indian policies, and about his tribe's respect for the great leader of their neighboring tribe, the Hunkpapas. Another man explains that Sitting Bull was originally buried without any military ceremony. The chief gained an "international and national reputation as a Sioux hero and a patriot for resisting subjugation of his ancestral lands," he says, and Sitting Bull died "defending this cause, just as many of our fallen warriors of all wars have—in defense of our country's freedom."

An honor guard of Fort Yates veterans, half of them in ceremonial headdresses, fires salutes into the midday air. "Taps" is played.

A local parish priest, who says his father was a homesteader, compares the problems of local farmers with those of the Indians. "Many farmers are losing their land, and now have an idea of what it must have felt in the heart of the Indian to lose this beautiful country to other people," he says, then recites an ancient Indian prayer from the Oglala reservation at Pine Ridge.

Joe Flying By, an old Indian in faded jeans and jean jacket, removes his brown Stetson, uncovering a gray, braided head, and delivers a combination of oration and chant in Lakota. Bird Horse translates. History has different versions, he says. It took ninety-five years to realize that here was a great leader, he says, "but now we have come together to honor this man. . . . I hope this is just a beginning." But he warns: "We can never live the white man's way, because we are Indian people."

Isaak Dog Eagle, the Sitting Bull descendant, urges people to write to Congress for just compensation for the lands that were taken from the Sioux. "It seems the United States government has forgotten its promises to the Indian people," he says. "Please, if you want the land so bad, please honor the land, for the land is our mother. The land is where we eat from, the land is where we grow from, and that is where we go home to." He says Sitting Bull was misunderstood, was buried twice without proper ceremony, and gives thanks for today's service. "It's about time they brought flags over here in his honor," Dog Eagle says, "because the Hunk-papas, under the leadership of Sitting Bull, we're the only ones that can claim we defeated the United States of America's great armies and have captured that flag."

Four men, standing around a large bass drum, sing the "Chief's Song," which Bird Horse translates as they chant to a slow beat:

"You people, my people, there is a long life ahead of you. Try to honor all things. Be brave. Myself, I no longer exist. I have lived my life and am no more. So please remember what I have said: be brave, continue being a Lakota person throughout. Chief Sitting Bull has stated this and has gone to the Spirit world."

11

Winter
Interlude

*last night was excessively Cold the Murkery this morning Stood at
40° below 0. . . . [a boy] Came to the fort with his feet frosed and
had layed out last night without fire with only a Buffalow Robe to
Cover him. . . . we had his feet put in cold water and they are
Comeing too. . . . Customs & the habits of those people has anured
[them] to bare more Cold than I thought it possible for man to en-
dure.*

From William Clark's journal
Fort Mandan
January 10, 1805

By the time Lewis and Clark were north of what is now Bismarck, they had to begin preparing for winter. It was only late October, but the weather was turning cold, and already there were occasional snows. Their plan was to winter among the Mandan and Hidatsa Indians near the mouth of the Knife River, near present-day Stanton, North Dakota. Here they would build their winter quarters, Fort Mandan, and await better traveling weather. Ice began appearing in the Missouri River on November 13, 1804, and the river was frozen solid by the end of the month; they would not be able to depart until early April 1805.

During the six winter months the explorers spent with these tribes they pursued a number of objectives: preparing reports for President Jefferson on their expedition so far, studying the customs of the village-dwelling Mandans and Hidatsas, seeking as much information as possible on the route they would be taking in the spring, trying to forge a peace between the Arikara tribes to the south and their winter neighbors, and promoting the notion among the tribes that they should trade with the representatives of their new "White Father" in Washington rather than with the English traders from Canada.

Of course, other necessities of survival also took much of their time: finding food (including several buffalo hunts), repairing and making equipment for the next year's travel; being neighborly with the Indians (venereal disease outdistanced frostbite as one of the chief medical problems by midwinter); and just plain struggling to keep warm. The swing between weather extremes in the High Plains is unknown to other regions of America—temperatures top 100 degrees in the summer and crack 40 degrees below zero in winter. References to the cold weather seep through the journals like the frost through the Dakota sod.

Nearly two hundred years later, one thing that time has not changed is the weather. Winters are still brutal in North Dakota.

I probably could have established this simply by checking the national weather maps in the newspaper while sitting by a warm woodstove at home in New England. But a desire, perverse perhaps, to *experience* a High Plains winter as Lewis and Clark did brings me to Bismarck in early February. Gerard Baker, a young Hidatsa Indian, has arranged for us to spend a few nights in an earth lodge, a reconstruction of the kind of dwelling his people used when the Corps of Discovery was among them.

I arrive in Bismarck by airplane, and the checkout attendant at the car-rental stand gives me the first lesson in the difference between intellectual conception and experience when she hands me a thick coil of wire with the car keys. "Plug it into the car engine and an outlet at night so your car will start in the mornings," she says.

A bank thermometer in downtown Bismarck pegs the unofficial temperature at 19 below at 9 P.M. With the frigid weather is a clear night sky. Thirteen miles from Bismarck, I can still see the city's lights across the rolling plains in the rearview mirror; ahead, to the north, an aurora borealis shimmers on the horizon. The few cars I meet on the road have cardboard sheets across their grilles with a single, small hole punched in the center—this is to allow a little of the winter air into the car's radiator, but not too much. It's best for people to breathe the same way, in short gasps instead of a full inhalation that could seize your engine with pneumonia.

Like people everywhere who live where winters last half the year, North Dakotans try to turn adversity into virtue. Unable to change the weather, or escape from it, they brag about it. "This isn't so bad," the motel clerk tells me when he sees I'm from out of state. "You should have been here last week. It was forty below."

Stanton, North Dakota (population 623), is a town that time has tried to pass by. When river traffic carried people and heavy cargo, the town's location near the confluence of the Knife and Missouri rivers gave Stanton an importance that ended abruptly when the first railroad bridge was built across the Missouri downstream at Bismarck in the last decade of the 1800s. Stanton is still the county seat of Mercer County, but Hazen, about twelve miles west, has a billboard proclaiming itself the largest city in the county, thanks to the boom in the coal business. Even farther west, billboards on the outskirts of Beulah advertise that town as "Lignite Capital of the World." Alternate Route 200, the main highway in these parts, is pulled northwest toward Hazen, missing Stanton entirely. Stanton's a two-bar town with far fewer people living here now than there were in the immediate area when Lewis and Clark encamped for the winter among the nearly four thousand Mandans and Hidatsas.

Just south of town, a highway sign announces a "scenic turnoff." From the parking space you look down at a bend in the Missouri, an actual river here in the traces below the Garrison Dam upstream and still a number of miles above the outer reaches of the massive Lake Oahe. To the south and east is the smokestack of a coal-burning electric plant. To the north stand two more plants, one on the site of a Mandan village visited by the explorers, surrounded by hills of lignite coal. Just west of these, the tops of giant cranes can be seen as they drag out coal from the bottom of an open pit and place it on a long conveyor belt for delivery to the plants. Electricity is one of North Dakota's chief exports (the state uses only about 40 percent of what it generates). If this is a "scenic turnoff," it must be using slang from the 1960s: it turns me "off," not "on."

Near the parking space is a huge stone, smooth and oval like a pebble you might pick up on the riverbank and fondle in your hand before tossing it into the water, except that this one is about six feet high and twelve feet long. There is no official sign to explain the stone, just the random graffiti from some passerby who probably found the scenic wonders of the coal plants uninteresting and happened to have a few cans of spray paint along to ease the boredom. This stone used to rest on the western bluffs above the river before the highway department moved it down and across the road to anchor the scenic turnoff.

To the Mandan Indians, it was a sacred shrine, intertwined with their legends about the river and the beginnings and ends of things. In this legend, one of several giant turtles that had come from the river to protect and advise the Mandans was convinced not to return to the Missouri. The turtle became the rock, in which state it would remain until just before the end of the world. When the Indian Armageddon arrives, the Mandans are to gather at Turtle Rock and sing on its top. The rock will turn back into a turtle and once again protect the people and advise the survivors. One of the signals that the End is near was to be a split in the rock. The giant stone survived its transfer from the bluffs to the parking lot, but sometime in 1984 two fissures inexplicably appeared that opened its top like a loaf of warm bread. The graffiti survived intact.

—

When Lewis and Clark reached this area in 1804, the Mandans were already in decline. Continuous wars with other tribes, particularly the Sioux, and a devastating smallpox epidemic in 1782 had seriously reduced their numbers, and, accordingly, weakened the tribe's influence in the Upper Plains. Before the beginning of the nineteenth century, they had moved up the Missouri to live in close and generally friendly proximity to the Hidatsas near the mouth of the Knife River. Like the Hidatsas, the Mandans were village dwellers, not nomads; they lived in semipermanent earth lodges instead of tepees and were noted primarily for their skill in farming rather than following the buffalo herds, although the buffalo was as integral a part of their lives as it was for every other tribe in the West.

With the Hidatsas, the Mandans were the middlemen of the complex trade network of the Upper Missouri. James Ronda, a scholar of Lewis and Clark's relations with the Indians, has called the villages the "great Missouri River country store." They provided not only the produce, principally corn, for other tribes, but also the location for goods to be exchanged: Cheyenne horses and leather products, Assiniboin and Crow furs, goods from the Arapaho and Cree, English-made guns and manufactured items, even buffalo meat from their enemies the Sioux were part of their trade.

In 1837, one of the things they got as part of their trade with the whites was another round of smallpox. Because they lived in villages rather than in scattered camps across the Plains, the disease was particularly deadly to the Mandans. It is also said that the hostile Sioux took advantage of the situation, camping a war party in the area to discourage Mandans and Hidatsas from venturing away while the pox took its toll. In one season, the Mandans were reduced from 1,500 to 150; the Hidatsas went from about 2,000 to 500. Following this catastrophe, the Mandans moved upriver again with the Hidatsas, where they were later joined by the Arikaras.

The Mandans and Hidatsas were unique among the Plains Indians in their steadfast loyalty to the United States government. They never fought the whites. Yet their reward was the same: constant treaty violations and neglect from the government they had befriended and had grown to depend upon. By the mid-1800s they often could not hunt buffalo because the military wouldn't protect them from the increasingly belligerent Sioux. "When we listen to the whites," one chief said in 1870, "we have to sit in our villages, listen to [the Sioux] insults, and have our young men killed and our horses stolen, within sight of our lodges." The women didn't even dare pick wild berries outside the villages.

By the 1880s they had moved upstream again, forming communities along the rich bottomland of the Missouri in northwestern North Dakota. Although their reservation was constantly reduced in size by the government, they began once again to prosper and grow on their ranches and farms. Theirs was a self-sufficient society, not a cash economy. The Depression of the 1930s had little impact on their people, and in the 1940s and early 1950s, only 6 percent of the tribes' members were on public welfare.

But in 1952 the Garrison Dam was completed, and the bottomland, villages, homes, farms, schools, churches, burial grounds— the social and economic base for 85 percent of the people of the Fort Berthold Reservation—gradually disappeared under the new Lake Sakakawea. The three tribes, scattered now on the far less productive high rangeland in five distinct segments of the reservation that sprawls around the serpentine lake, are still struggling to recover. Unemployment and alcoholism, the twin scourges of modern reservations, rose with each foot of lake water.

Nothing much is left of the Mandans as a distinct tribe. The Missouri River, before it was tamed, claimed one village visited by Lewis and Clark; the coal plant sits atop another; and the dam took care of their later villages. Intermarriage with their neighbors the Hidatsas and Arikaras after the smallpox decimated their numbers has resulted in what scholars say are no more full-blooded Mandans, although some people on the reservation claim otherwise.

Just north of Stanton, however, is the Knife River Indian Villages National Historic Site, which encompasses the three Hidatsa villages that were inhabited when the explorers wintered in the area. Huge, circular depressions about forty feet in diameter mark where the earth lodges once stood in the Golden Era of these people. Next to the visitor center is a half-size replica of an earth lodge, built by Gerard Baker in 1979. It will be our weekend home.

At the age of thirty-one, Gerard is an interesting blend of white and red cultures. He has steadily worked his way up the ladder of the National Park Service from an interpreter of native culture to

one of the few Indian district rangers with management and supervisory responsibilities. He has a college degree in criminology,
which, combined with his size, his even temperament, and his
proficiency with weapons, has made him part of the Special Events
Team, the Park Service's law-enforcement equivalent of SWAT.
Gerard is constantly studying and practicing some of the old Indian
ways, partly as an intellectual inquiry into his own roots but mainly
as a conscious decision to lead his life by gleaning what he thinks
is best from the two, often contradictory, societies. His sources are
books, long talks with older people on the Fort Berthold Reservation, and simply trying things out on his own—like building an
earth lodge.

Extended conversations with him can range from quotations
from the journals of traders at the fur posts in the 1830s to stories
of Indian spirits, from hell-raising tales of his days as a basketball
star in high school and college to deep thoughts on the future of
his tribe. A day in his life might include paperwork at his office,
a horse ride to check the park's buffalo herd, scraping and tanning
some deer or elk hides, then a nighttime refresher course in car-
diopulmonary resuscitation to maintain his emergency-medical-
technician license or a meeting with fellow deputy sheriffs in
McKenzie County.

He is now district ranger at the Theodore Roosevelt Memorial
Park North Unit in the Badlands area more than a hundred miles
west of Stanton, but many people in Stanton still remember him
from his days starting out with the Park Service at Knife River.
In addition to his park duties, Gerard had coached some junior-
league basketball teams in town, and his friendliness and sense of
humor had made him well known to and well liked by the locals.
Besides, Gerard Baker tends to stand out in a crowd, even in towns
larger than Stanton. He's six foot five inches tall and weighs about
230 pounds, has long, braided locks of black Indian hair, and is
as apt to be wearing leggings he made from some hides he tanned
as he is his forest-green park uniform. The historic site nearby,
the remnants of the largest of the three former villages, is called
"Big Hidatsa." The term could as easily be applied to Gerard.

When we hook up in Stanton, he has on elkskin leggings, a
deerskin shirt decorated with porcupine quills and a few beads, a
red cloth sash for a belt, and a red *voyageur* cap.

"Do those Indian clothes really keep you warm?" I ask him.

"You bet," he says, then picks up his parka and smiles. "But not as good as ol' Eddie Bauer."

Part of the Indian way, according to Gerard, is teasing, especially as a way of disciplining children. In their culture, uncles and aunts help direct their nieces and nephews toward proper behavior by chiding, kidding, and just plain making fun of the kids. In 1846, when Francis Parkman traveled the West to write *The Oregon Trail,* he remarked with disgust on the way the Plains Indians parents never rebuked or spanked their children. Teasing by relatives was the Indian substitute Parkman apparently never noticed. In a good-natured way it is also the basis of Gerard's sense of humor.

My knowledge of the camping/outdoor life is rather rudimentary, reduced to three basic rules:

1. Turn down all offers to go snipe hunting
2. Check the direction and force of the wind before relieving yourself outside
3. Watch for a twinkle in the eye of anyone offering suspicious-sounding advice

All three serve me well in the weekend with Gerard. He tells me we might have a "sweat" during one afternoon. We will have to cover willow saplings, bent to make a tiny hut; build a fire to heat some rocks; put the rocks in a hole in the hut's center; cover the saplings with tarps and blankets; disrobe and sit inside while we drip water on the heated rocks and wait to start sweating.

"Hidatsa sauna," Gerard explains. "And then when it's so hot we can't stand it anymore, we jump out and dive into a snowbank."

I look skeptical. The forecast calls for high temperatures in the single numbers.

"You'll go first," he adds. "Indian custom."

A full-size earth lodge was large enough for an extended Indian family of five to twenty-five persons, their personal belongings, and even a few prize horses. The half-size replica Gerard built at Knife River looks like a sod igloo. We have to crawl through the extended entryway to get inside. Four six-foot cottonwood posts, at the corners of a five-foot square, hold up the center. About five feet from them is a ring of smaller posts, between three and four feet tall. Laid across the beams which the posts hold up are cottonwood saplings, then willow branches, prairie grass, and finally a foot of earth. Most of the smoke from the fire we build in the lodge's center escapes through a two-foot-diameter hole at the top. Most, but not all. Enough smoke lingers inside to sting our eyes when we stand near the center.

"Keeps the mosquitoes out," Gerard says, admiring his work while a midwinter snowstorm blows outside.

We spend the gray afternoon getting settled in the lodge. Erik Holland, an archaeologist from Fort Clark and a friend of Gerard's, is with us. We cover the opening of the entryway with a tarp to keep the snowdrifts out and drape a second tarp across the inner opening for good measure. A stack of cottonwood, sap willow, and ash logs rests in one corner of the dirt floor. Keeping the fire roaring for several hours has warmed the interior enough so that we can sit with our winter parkas off, even though the mercury outside is already below zero and still falling.

Gerard takes out a small twined rope of sweetgrass, which he ignites in the fire and then blows out, smudging the lodge in each of the four directions, and finally places the remainder over the southern entrance.

"For the spirits," he says. His ancestors are buried nearby.

It's getting dark now, and the driving snow has abated, replaced by a driving wind under a cloudless slate sky. Gerard puts a large pan on one edge of the fire and begins boiling potatoes, onions, some red peppers, and buffalo tripe. Rather than the mere stomach lining of the buffalo, this is not just tripe, it's the buffalo "book," thin leaves of membrane that assist the beast's digestion and look like a medium-sized encyclopedia unfolding in the boiling water.

Gerard considers it a delicacy. "Hidatsa lobster," he calls it, in honor of my New England home. He scoops out a bowl of the concoction and hands it to me across the yellow cone of firelight.

"You go first," he says, and watches intently as I take a few tentative bites. I catch a twinkle in his eyes before he turns to Erik and says, "I guess it's not too hot for us to eat," and fishes out two more servings. I wouldn't rate buffalo book with boiled lobster, but the hunger that accompanies a North Dakota winter day only adds to the adage that beggars can't be choosers. We eat the greasy, rubbery meal with our hands; it makes more sense than chasing it around our plates and the earth floor with forks and knives.

Gerard has brought five buffalo robes with him to the earth lodge. He tells me to place one on the ground, fur up, and use the other four, fur down, over me for the night. Before I can ask him how he plans to keep warm while he sleeps, he starts unrolling his down-filled sleeping bag near the fire, opposite the entryway. Erik Holland has one as well.

When I inquire about the relative warmth of buffalo hides and sleeping bags, Gerard shrugs and says the hides served the buffalo and the Indians pretty well in the winters of the past. "I do know my sleeping bag's guaranteed to twenty below," he adds.

He then starts concocting Indian traditions for my benefit. For instance, he says whoever has the most buffalo robes in an earth lodge is responsible for keeping the fire going throughout the night.

After we lie down to sleep in our respective places, there is a long silence; then I hear his voice, muffled through his sleeping bag.

"Can you tell the difference between sap willow and cottonwood by their feel in the dark?"

"No," I answer. "Why?"

"Just curious. They'll both burn okay, but sap willow pops in a fire. A spark landing in the wrong place can play hell with an old buffalo robe. Good night."

Fully clothed in my long underwear, insulated socks, jeans, shirt, sweater, and stocking cap, my rolled-up parka as a pillow and the oppressive weight of four buffalo robes on top of me, I go to sleep, listening to the rush of the wind across the smoke hole. The wind's wail is interrupted by the occasional pop of a sap-willow log.

About two and a half hours into the night, something wakes me up. Coldness. Not a chill. Not some little shiver that comes when you shift your feet under the blankets at night and the move from the envelope of body warmth makes you grunt and toss in your sleep. Coldness—as if frost is trying to work its way into you from the top of your head and the bottoms of your feet. Painful coldness.

The fire has burned down to embers. It gives off as much heat as it does light, a mere memory of both. I lie awake and wait, hoping either Gerard or Erik will wake up and feed the fire. Nothing happens. The frost line creeps another tenth of an inch into my body. Gerard was right: the person with the most buffalo robes is the one who tends the fire, *if* everyone else is in goose down and nylon. Buffalo robes don't carry the same guarantee. I shed the robes and feel my way to the woodpile, drag some logs to the fire, and get back under the buffalo hides. The flame builds up—with a few pops from some sap willow—and creates just enough heat to let me go back to sleep. The same routine repeats itself twice more during the night.

Cold feet, even colder than during the night, wake me early in the morning. I have the choice of closing my eyes, lying still, and failing to get back to sleep because my feet won't let me, or staying awake while I move them back and forth under the hides to warm them up. Eyes shut or open, moving my feet or not moving, it's still not sleeping. At least the second option might ward off frostbite. Gerard and Erik are still asleep. I can tell this by the slow, rhythmic puffs of breath that rise from one end of their sleeping bags, smoke signals to me that their feet are warm.

As I lie on my back, sort of jogging in place underneath the buffalo robes, I watch the morning arrive through the earth lodge's smoke hole. A box elder tree hovers over the opening. The changing contrast of colors between the tree branches and the sky marks the passage of time to daybreak: black sky with even blacker branches gives way to dark blue, then silver etches against a slate background, then tawny lines across gray, and finally brown tree branches in the robin's-egg blue of day. From nightmarelike Rorschach test, to Impressionist painting, to some sort of nature color photograph through a peephole, the scene unfolds, like the awakening of conscious thought in a human being—the changes imperceptible as they occur and made known only by the uneasy sense of loss of what preceded. Through it all, the box elder twitches and shudders in the blasts of wind.

There's enough light inside to look around the lodge. The top inch of water in our plastic bucket is ice, even though it was only four feet from the fire. I can see now the reason for my frozen feet: a small drift of snow angles in from the entryway, coils behind the woodpile, and stops in a heap next to the bottom of my buffalo hides. Someone must have been sloppy in readjusting the tarp when he returned from answering a call of nature in the night. It's something that can be easily understood and forgiven if you've ever tried to unwrap yourself from a warm cocoon, put on boots, crawl

out of an earth lodge into twenty-below darkness, do your business
in 30 mph winds, and retrace the whole thing in the space of 2.3
seconds or less.

My ballpoint pen is too frozen to work. The cold has sapped
the life out of my tape recorder's batteries. So I busy myself building
the fire into an inferno and pondering the winter spent by the
explorers. Their journals offer at least the company of cold misery.
"Sent out 7 men to hunt for the Buffalow   they found the weather
too cold & returned," Clark writes in mid-December. Temperatures
of 20 below zero, "74 degrees below the freesing pointe," minus
21, minus 40 are noted. One entry is particularly intriguing and
relevant to the night I've just experienced: "this day being Cold
Several men returned a little frost bit, one of [the] men with his
feet badly frost bit   my Servents feet also frosted & his P---s a
little." I don't feel so bad in comparison.

I will always remember Erik Holland fondly. Gerard and I are
up and talking about boiling coffee grounds in the unwashed tripe
pan, when Erik's voice interrupts us from his sleeping bag.

"I'll buy breakfast for everyone at the Riverside," he says.

Less than fifteen minutes later, we're in Stanton ordering ham
and eggs, drinking good black coffee, and the two of them are
telling me about waking up in the middle of the night and waiting
silently for someone else to put more wood on the fire.

"One of you could have done that miserable work," I complain.

"You go first," they say in unison.

At least I wasn't the one who left the tarp half open, I tell them.

"How do you know?" Gerard asks.

"I must have gone first."

The chief topics of conversation among the other patrons at the
Riverside are the basketball team and the weather. Both have fallen
on cold times, and there seems to be nothing anyone can do about
either, except talk about them. The Stanton High School teams
are nicknamed the Sioux, a particular irony. Imagine the reactions
of the spirits of the Hidatsa and Mandan warriors, buried less than
a mile away, when they hear the yells from the gymnasium each
Friday night: "Let's go Sioux!" No wonder the team seems jinxed.

Breakfast finished, we head down Alternate Route 200 so we can
cross the river and visit the reconstruction of Fort Mandan, Lewis
and Clark's winter quarters. Erik is driving, I'm in back. Gerard,

in the shotgun seat, is playing some ceremonial Hidatsa chants and songs on the tape deck. "Hidatsa Top Ten," he shouts back at me over the blare and returns to singing along. Each song is different, he tells me, which I have to accept on faith. They're all indecipherable to my ears—just a series of "*hey*-yay-yay-yah, *hey*-yay-yay-yahs" at various pitches—and sound the same to me. Now I know how my parents felt about the rock and roll I played to them as a teenager.

We stop briefly at Turtle Rock, where Gerard explains the Mandan legend and disdainfully inspects the graffiti. Erik points out the location of the principal Mandan village during the explorers' time, now under a power plant and coal slagheap. The car is still running, and the tape of chants is audible from where we're standing by the rock. Off in the distance, the other coal plants send their smoke signals pluming hundreds of feet into the cold blue sky, communicating the new order of the universe. Conical piles of strip-mined coal sit like menacing Sioux tepees on the bluffs overlooking Big Hidatsa.

The sun is now high in the sky, with no clouds in sight except those created by the smokestacks, yet the temperature is still two below zero. It's as if the sun had given up trying to warm North Dakota. An incessant wind blows thin lines of snow across the highway, spirits on a hurried journey to join compatriots in the drifts wherever the ground dips.

The fissure in Turtle Rock is supposed to signal the Coming of the End. Maybe it's already arrived, not in some sudden cataclysm, but in the passing of a people and their way of life. Maybe the Turtle waited in vain for nonexistent Mandans to gather on its back. Freed from its stony prison and without any people to protect, perhaps the Turtle slipped silently back into the Missouri, where it now plies the waters between two symbols of the greater Spirit that defeated it, the Oahe and Garrison dams.

A local historical group has built a replica of Fort Mandan among the cottonwoods on the east bank of the river. The actual location is a little ways upstream and under water, a victim of the earlier, wandering days of the Missouri.

"You go first," Gerard tells me as we trudge through the town toward the palisades of the fort, "in case someone's still there. They might get the wrong idea if they see an Hidatsa in buckskins."

This gives him the idea for my Indian name. According to Indian tradition, a person is given a name by his elders, usually in conjunction with some event in the person's life or some personal characteristic.

"Man Who Sleeps in Buffalo Robes" or "Buffalo Robe" was his first idea last night. Then "Smells Like Tripe" became a favorite. But now he settles on "He Goes First"—*Ee zeek' ah nets,* it sounds like in Hidatsa—and it sticks.

The fort is triangular, a design Clark learned during his military campaigns in the Ohio River valley before the expedition. Two sides of the triangle form living quarters, the outside walls tall and the roofs sloping toward the center courtyard; the third wall is a twenty-foot palisade with a gate. Compared to our half-size earth lodge, it seems commodious, though cold and barren sitting uninhabited. Filled with a company of forty-five busy men, it was no doubt crowded and at least as warm as we were last night.

In something like this the explorers had spent a long, frigid North Dakota winter, becoming friendly with the large villages just upstream, waiting for spring, and preparing to venture into territory no whites had crossed before them.

"He Goes First." I like the name, despite the jokes about my own experiences it implies. It makes me feel closer to Lewis and Clark than I've felt so far in their footsteps.

New Town, North Dakota (population 1,335), the Fort Berthold Reservation agency town, was created when Lake Sakakawea inundated the river towns of Beaver Creek, Nishu, Charging Eagle, Lucky Mound, Shell Creek, Independence, and Elbowoods.

New Town is a four-bar town without a stoplight. The local movie theater, the Trail, is open only Thursdays through Sundays, but videos are available every day at the Rexall drugstore. A gas station offers a free video rental with every ten gallons of gas. Two evenings in a row, I lose money at the two-dollar blackjack table at the Steak 'n' Stein. The Sunset Motel, where I pass a few nights, is inexplicably on the east side of town. Gerard has warned me away from two of the bars in town unless I am willing to fight my way out. There was no twinkle in his eye when he gave me this advice, and so I follow it.

Throughout the reservation the housing—much of it government-built—consists of small ranch-style homes on barren sites.

They look more solitary and exposed than the rounded humps of a cluster of earth lodges must have appeared when Lewis and Clark visited the area.

Alyce Spotted Bear, the chairwoman of the Three Affiliated Tribes (Mandan, Hidatsa, and Arikara), brings me up to date on the tribes' history. Besides flooding their bottomland farms and unalterably ending the tribes' self-sufficient existence, the Garrison Dam and Lake Sakakawea dispersed the tribal members onto upland sections of the reservation separated from each other by drives of two to four hours, she says. In her view, the sociological havoc wreaked on their communal spirit by the dam since the 1950s has been as devastating as the smallpox epidemic of 1837.

Her two main hopes for economic recovery are employment at a giant coal gasification plant near Beulah and fostering tourism—including a casino—on tribal lands near the lake.

A resort hotel is already complete on a treeless plain west of New Town. It is named Four Bears Motor Lodge, after the great Mandan chief. Before going to sleep one night there, I take out one of the books about tribal history that Gerard has loaned me and happen upon the last speech Four Bears ever gave. He was on his deathbed from smallpox in 1837:

> Ever since I can remember, I have loved the whites. I have lived with them ever since I was a boy and to the best of my knowledge, I have never wronged a white man. On the contrary, I have always protected them from the insults of others, which they cannot deny. The Four Bears never saw a white man hungry, but what he gave them to eat, drink and a buffalo skin to sleep on in time of need. I was always ready to die for them, which they cannot deny. I have done everything that a red skin could do for them, and how they have repaid it! With ingratitude! I have never called a white man a dog, but today I do pronounce them to be a set of black-hearted dogs. They have deceived me. Them that I always considered as brothers have turned out to be my worst enemies.
>
> I have been in many battles, and often wounded, but the wounds of my enemies I exult in. But today I am wounded, and by whom, by those same white dogs I have always considered and treated as brothers.

I do not fear death, my friends. You know it. But to die with my face rotten, that even the wolves will shrink with horror at seeing me, and say to themselves, "That is the Four Bears, the friend of the whites."

Listen well to what I have to say, as it will be the last time you will hear me. Think of your wives, children, brothers, sisters, friends, and in fact all that you hold dear. All are dead, or dying, with their faces all rotten, caused by those dogs the whites. Think of all that my friends, and rise together and not leave one of them alive.

Before turning out the light for the night, as a white tourist at the resort lodge named for Four Bears, I get up from the bed to make sure the door is locked.

Gerard introduces me to some of the older tribal members, who describe life before the dam. Each time, as one talks of the bottomlands—men often mention good winter shelter for their cattle and horses, women the wild berries and fruits of summer—the dark eyes of the old person glisten with mist.

Gerard's mother feeds us a meal in her country home that reminds me of dinner at my grandmother's: fresh-baked rolls, heaping slabs of roast beef, plenty of vegetables, and a cake for dessert. Mrs. Baker stands near the table and watches approvingly as Gerard and I, his wife, Mary Kay, and their three children devour the food she has prepared. According to older customs, she will eat only after everyone else is done.

Paige Baker, Sr., Gerard's father, was a member of the reservation council, a tribal judge, and on a number of North Dakota boards and commissions. He and his wife, Cora, insisted that their four children get a good education. Fred Baker, their oldest child, is now an administrator for the Public Health Service at the Rosebud Reservation in South Dakota; Paige Jr. is completing a doctorate in administration at Penn State University; and Mary is dean of academic affairs at the United Tribes college in Bismarck.

Their home, where the Bakers relocated when the lake flooded Independence in 1952, a year before Gerard was born, sits in a wooded draw on the western edge of the reservation. The small living room is filled with the iconography of a close-knit family: graduation pictures of the children, photos of the grandchildren, childhood mementoes, a Catholic crucifix. One photograph shows Paige Jr., dressed in traditional Hidatsa clothing, meeting Pope Paul; the cover of an outdated North Dakota state map features Mary in a colorfully beaded buckskin dress. (A Baker relative served as the model for the Sacagawea statue that stands near the state capitol.)

Gerard loans me a tape cassette of some conversations with his father, made before Paige Baker, Sr., died of lung cancer. The tapes are filled equally with reminiscences and fatherly advice. At one point, Mr. Baker tells of his grandmother taking him to an ash tree in 1921 and crying that the spiritual things of the tribe were being lost; then, with her grandson next to her, she implored the tree to give her grandchildren some of its strength to survive.

"Now everything is lost," Mr. Baker says on the tape. "We don't believe in the white man's way and we don't believe in the Indian way. So what the hell are we? We're not anybody." He coughs several times, and it's easy to imagine him collecting his thoughts before turning to his youngest son with words to remember once he's gone: "You're going to run into trouble; you're going to look for something. You'll wish you had a god or something more powerful than you are to pray to and then hang on to, which you're not going to have if you don't practice it now and learn about it. But if you learn about it, then when the time comes that you need that help, you'll know you've got it. Hang on to things like that."

When Paige Baker, Sr., died, Gerard tells me, their small herd of horses arrayed themselves in a straight line facing the road when the hearse with his father's body passed by on its way to the cemetery. The elder Bakers were practicing Catholics, but knowledgeable and respectful of the Hidatsa ways; Gerard reversed the order.

He started learning the "old ways" and began believing. He read books about his heritage—the Lewis and Clark journals, diaries of fur-company traders, Prince Maximilian's writings, anthropologists' studies. He looked at Bodmer's drawings. He started collecting oral histories from older tribal members. He skinned animals and tanned their hides, made traditional clothing, built tepees and earth lodges and sweat lodges, became an expert marksman with a black-powder musket.

He spent long times outdoors, fasting for several days and going off alone into the eerie buttes of the Badlands to wait for spirits to approach him. The first one was a man coughing behind him as he sat on a hillside at night. While he was singing Hidatsa songs in a coulee one day, a woman's voice started singing with him. Birds spoke to him in his dreams.

His life became not a rejection of the white man's way or the Indian way, but a unique synthesis of both. One morning, after he has told me about his belief in spirits, he goes outside to the basketball hoop in the driveway to teach his nine-year-old son Bobby a hook shot.

Like the Mandans and Hidatsas with whom Lewis and Clark spent their North Dakota winter, Gerard is generous with his hospitality toward me. And like the explorers, who gleaned information about their hosts through persistent questioning, I compile Gerard's life story not from his offering it up—self-promotion or bragging is unseemly to the ways of the Hidatsa—but through constant probing on my part. His hospitality includes answering a guest's questions honestly and directly, regardless of how many or how personal they may be.

"Everything on this earth, including trees, including rocks even, everything that's here has a spirit, and therefore we should respect it," he says during one conversation. But the spirit I grow to respect the most during these two weeks is his.

On my last day in February with Gerard, we drive along a winding road on the high bluffs overlooking the Little Missouri River. When we get out of his truck, there is a pungent sulfurous smell in the air from escaped gas at the wellheads of the oil rigs ringing the park. Three buffalo bulls are grazing about a quarter mile from us, and we walk a hundred yards in their direction so I can get a picture of them.

"You can earn an eagle feather by pulling one of their tails," he jokes.

I raise my camera and look through its long lens. We are upwind from the threesome. Smelling us, they lift their massive heads and begin trotting in our direction.

"They seem to be headed our way, Gerard," I say, standing my ground to snap the pictures. "Gerard—?"

When I turn around he is already halfway to the truck at a dead run, motioning me to follow.

"You can earn your feather in the summer," he tells me back at the truck. "We'll take a sweat and then go see the buffalo."

During the airplane ride back to New England, people near me seem to wrinkle their noses. I am a different kind of synthesis of white and Indian ways. My parka still reeks of earth-lodge smoke and buffalo tripe.

But I wear the scent, like my new name, with a certain pride. When we arrive at the airport gate and it's time to walk off the plane, I go first.

12

Buffalo
Hunt

I returned last Night from a hunting party much fatigued. . . .
From William Clark's journal
Fort Mandan
February 13, 1805

ROAD RULE 11: The straighter the road you're on, the more
your mind wanders a curving path. As your vehicle hurtles
forward in space, your thoughts meander backward in time,
often stopping to linger with a memory as if it were a historic
marker on the roadside.

FIRST COROLLARY: Each place you stop exists in layers of time
as well as space. The present is merely an intersection of the
winding roads of the past.

The highways that take me from Mobridge, South Dakota, to the north unit of the Theodore Roosevelt National Park in western North Dakota must have been easy work for the crews that painted the yellow center lines. U.S. 12 west, North Dakota Highway 22 north, Highway 200 west, and U.S. 85 north rarely bend. The painters could have locked the steering wheel of their truck, set the paint machine on automatic, and taken long naps across fifty-mile stretches while their job got done.

Within a half hour from the end of the Memorial Day service at Sitting Bull's grave, the *Discovery* has taken over the task of travel, allowing my mind to return to my winter stay with Gerard Baker. Dirty white clouds cloak the May sky—the same color and texture as the snow on the North Dakota plains in February.

Memories of the cold weather, the gold plume of smoke rising through an earth lodge's center hole into the winter night, the walk through deep snow to Fort Mandan, the buffalo that chased us back to our truck: those are the mile markers of my thoughts while the camper's odometer clicks off the distance on the straight pavement.

A change in the road snaps me briefly out of the past and into the present. About fifteen miles south of Watford City, North Dakota, U.S. 85 crests a lip of plains and plummets into the Badlands of the Little Missouri, a jumble of eroded coulees and towering buttes whose vertical sides are lined with strata of sandstone, bentonite clay, shale, and veins of lignite coal. The setting spring sun paints the surrounding scene in soft tones of pink, yellow, blue, and purple. A sign welcomes me to the Theodore Roosevelt National Park's north unit. It transports me back in time once more.

Beginning thousands of years ago and continuing into modern times, lightning bolts against the buttes have set the layers of lignite on fire, sending smoke out of fissures in the hillsides and baking the neighboring seams of sand and clay into a red scoria.

General Alfred Sully, chasing the Sioux through the area in 1864, called the landscape "hell with the fires out." Nineteen years later, a young man from the East touring the Badlands for different purposes had the opposite reaction. Theodore Roosevelt had come from New York to hunt buffalo and strengthen his asthmatic lungs in the semiarid air of the High Plains. Within just a few days along the Little Missouri, he decided to start a cattle ranch in the Badlands. "Here," he said later, "the romance of my life began."

For roughly a decade Roosevelt divided his time between his ranch in North Dakota and his interests back East. His months at his Elkhorn ranch on the west bank of the Little Missouri would be spent in cattle roundups, long rides across the broken landscape, hunting expeditions, and even a notorious capture of three Dakota desperadoes (like Gerard, Roosevelt was a deputy sheriff). Back East, he would dine with the intellectual and social elite of the upper classes, write essays and books, and engage in reform politics.

The Badlands cowboys first called the scrawny, bespectacled Easterner "Four Eyes," but his grit and boundless energy soon changed that to a respectful "Mr. Roosevelt." The transfer of influence went both ways. Life on the frontier of the West profoundly shaped the views of the man who would become president. His dual existence worked its own synthesis on Roosevelt and his thinking, which found its expression in his theories of Americanism.

"Like all Americans," he told a Fourth of July rally in Dickinson, North Dakota, in 1886, "I like big things; big prairies, big forests and mountains, big wheat-fields, railroads, and herds of cattle too, big factories, steamboats, and everything else. . . . I am, myself, at heart as much a Westerner as an Easterner."

On his way to the White House, Roosevelt would write a glowing biography of Senator Thomas Hart Benton of Missouri, the champion of Manifest Destiny, and a multivolumed *The Winning of the West,* which glorifies the "restless and reckless hunters, the hard, dogged, frontier farmers" who pushed the nation's boundaries to the Pacific coast.

Becoming president eleven years after the Census Bureau declared the official close of the frontier in 1890, Roosevelt exercised his Americanism abroad by making the United States a muscular world power, and at home by fostering the creation of national parks and wildlife refuges. In both—his love of wild places and

his restless, some would say reckless, expansionism—the influence
of his days in the West reverberated for generations.

The long drive from Sitting Bull's grave to the park has cramped
my shoulders; the even longer travels in time have turned my mind
to mush. I'm ready for a "sweat" when I pull into Gerard Baker's
driveway. Within minutes of my arrival Gerard, his son Bobby,
and I are traveling to his mother's house, where Gerard already
has the willow saplings bent to form a sweat lodge next to the
horse corral.

We start a fire with old ash fenceposts and cover the lodge frame
with tarps and blankets. Gerard has invited two of his younger
cousins to join us. Their admiration for him is clear in the deference
they pay him and the way they listen to his stories. He teases them
constantly.

The northwest corner of the sky is black with storm clouds.
While we heat stones in the open fire, the family's string of horses
gallops into the draw, and one of the cousins asks Gerard why
they're running.

"Storm coming," he says. "Change in pressure." Three dogs
round the hill, nipping at the horses' heels. "That and the dogs,"
Gerard adds.

Mosquitoes start biting us as we disrobe to enter the sweat lodge.
"Storm coming," Gerard says as he slaps one. "Change in pressure,"
we all answer.

The sweat lodge is too small for all five of us. Gerard and I go
first. We shovel some of the red-hot stones from the fire into a
small hole at the lodge's center and crawl in, closing the tarps
behind us, and sit cross-legged and stooped in the tiny enclosure.

It is dark inside, except for the glow of the rocks, which draws
my stare deeper and deeper, much as the intense heat draws my
perspiration each time Gerard drips some water on the rocks. We
are cleansing "bad spirits" from our body, Gerard says, and then
he relates another tale from tribal mythology about the end of the
world. The Lone Man, a dominant figure in their lore, told his
people the end would be near when four things happened: when
the Missouri River (called the Grandfather) ran backward, when
the prairie grass turned upside down, when the trees turned to
show their roots, and when the field mice grew antlers.

Dams have pushed the river back over the tribes' homeland,

farmers have turned the sod, and coal shovels have opened giant pits where trees once stood, Gerard says; all that's left is some sort of mutation of field mice, perhaps by atomic poisoning or genetic experimentation.

The glow of the rocks deepens. Gerard drips on more water, and we sit and sweat in silence until the heat finally forces us out into the night. Bobby and the cousins crawl in to take our place. Gerard and I stand naked in the dark coolness.

"Storm coming," he says again. The wind picks up and big drops of May rain wash our bodies.

My night's reading from the journal includes Clark's entry at Fort Mandan on January 5, 1805:

A Buffalow Dance (or Medeson) for 3 nights passed in the 1st Village, a curious Custom   the old men arrange themselves in a circle & after Smoke[ing] a pipe which is handed them by a young man, Dress[ed] up for the purpose,   the young men who have their wives back of the Circle go [each] to one of the old men with a whining tone and request the old man to take his wife (who presents [herself] necked except a robe) and---(or Sleep with her)   the Girl then takes the Old Man (who verry often can scarcely walk) and leades him to a con- venient place for the business, after which they return to the lodge; if the old man (or a white man) returns to the lodge without gratifying the Man & his wife, he offers her again and again; it is often the Case that after the 2d time without Kissing the Husband throws a new robe over the old man &c. and begs him not to dispise him & his wife   (We Sent a man to this Medisan Dance last night, they gave him 4 Girls)   all this to cause the buffalow to Come near So that they may Kill them.

The buffalo dance was not an exercise in promiscuity for the Mandans of Lewis and Clark's time. It was a religious ceremony whose purpose was to transfer the "medicine" of respected elders or visitors from other cultures to the buffalo hunters. The custom was abandoned by the tribe long ago.

"Did you dream of your girlfriend?" Gerard asks me in the

morning. "If you did, it'll help us find the buffalo." He knows I read the journals last night.

Two of the 150 buffalo under Gerard's supervision have escaped the parks' reinforced-fence boundaries. Regulations springing from concern about loose buffalo destroying ranch fences and trampling crops require him to find them. If they're still close enough to the park, he tries to herd them back; if they're too far away, he has to shoot them.

An attendant at park headquarters calls with the news that a rancher spotted the two buffalo southwest of the park early this morning. Gerard puts two hunting knives, a 30.06 rifle, a box of ammunition, and a bow saw in the pickup; Mary Kay hands us a sack lunch as we head out the door. The morning is clear and hot. Last night's rain has scrubbed the buttes of the Badlands, and the wet sage gives off a sharp, sweet smell.

"They're just like us Indians, the buffalo," Gerard says as we drive off. "They've lost everything they used to have. They've dwindled down. They've been put down in confined areas just like we are. They're protected, they're taken care of by Uncle Sam. Back home it was the same way—they gave us commodities and canned food to eat. Sometimes the buffalo are a pain in the ass. I imagine sometimes we're a pain in the ass, too. But they're still proud, boy, those old buffalo."

We cruise back roads about five miles from the park for an hour, looking in vain for two dark humps in the tan coulees. The gravel roads are straight. My eyes scan the distances; my mind recedes to the past.

That the buffalo could have gone from more than thirty million to a few hundred and the brink of extinction in the space of a half century is a staggering notion. Never mind the degree of senseless slaughter it implies, it seems a logistical impossibility. But it happened, and not by chance of nature but by design of man.

First came the market forces. Buffalo Bill Cody made a good living providing buffalo meat to the railroad crews and leading Army generals and European aristocrats on extravagant hunts. In one season alone, he boasted of having singlehandedly killed 4,280. Lucrative as the buffalo-meat and buffalo-robe business was, however, the big money was made in the 1870s, after new technology in tanning created increased demand for the buffalo hides. Buffalo leather was used in everything from machinery belting to home furniture. Now the slaughter was unceasing. Fortunes could be made.

During the depression after the panic of 1873, buffalo hunting was one of the few profitable businesses; hunters and skinners swarmed over the Plains. Hunters perfected a new technique: the "stand." Rather than chasing a herd on horseback, a hunter would use the terrain and wind to his advantage, sneak up on a herd, and begin a slow, deliberate shooting of the lead animals. If he was a good enough shot, he would drop the beasts one by one while the others grazed without stampeding. One hunter set a record by killing 120 buffalo during one "stand" of forty minutes. The barrel of his rifle finally overheated from the rapid firing.

The herds thinned. In 1873, only a year after reporting that there was "apparently no limit to the numbers of buffalo," Colonel Richard Irving Dodge found rotting carcasses in their place. "The air was foul with a sickening stench, and the vast plain, which only a short twelvemonth before teemed with animal life, was a dead, solitary, putrid desert," he wrote.

Such reports spurred the House and Senate in 1874 to pass a bill prohibiting the killing of a buffalo cow by anyone except an Indian and making it illegal to kill more animals than could be used for food. But President Ulysses S. Grant, more concerned with hostile Indians than dwindling buffalo herds, stopped the bill with a pocket veto. Government policy would finish what the marketplace started.

When the Texas legislature was poised to pass its own bill protecting the vanishing herds in the state, General Phil Sheridan, Grant's chief agent in handling the Indians, hastened to Austin to address a joint assembly. Sheridan, who coined the phrase "the only good Indian is a dead Indian," persuaded the Texans against the legislation with this argument:

These men [buffalo hunters] have done in the last two years, and will do in the next year, more to settle the vexed Indian question than the entire regular army has done in the last thirty years. They are destroying the Indians' commissary; and it is a well-known fact that an army losing its base of supplies is placed at great disadvantage. Send them powder and lead, if you will; but for the sake of a lasting peace, let them kill, skin and sell until the buffaloes are exterminated. Then your prairies can be covered with speckled cattle and the festive cowboy, who follows the hunter as the second forerunner of an advanced civilization.

Sheridan suggested that instead of being stopped, the hunters should be given bronze medallions "with a dead buffalo on one side and a discouraged Indian on the other." Years later, with both Indian and buffalo reduced in number and safely confined, a different version of Sheridan's medallion would be circulated by the government in the form of nickel coin. The buffalo on the nickel was alive and standing; the Indian on the other side looked rather noble.

By the time Roosevelt first came to North Dakota in 1883, the hide companies were bankrupt from the virtual disappearance of their source of supply. For several cold and rainy days Roosevelt and a guide scoured the Badlands. They saw only a few buffalo. Teddy fired on one, but his shot hit the animal too far back from its head. As the wounded and angry bull charged, Roosevelt's pony panicked and knocked his rifle against his head; luckily, the buffalo veered off and disappeared. Roosevelt escaped with a bloody face. (Accidents like this were not unusual: in the scramble of a mounted hunt, Custer had once misfired his gun, killing his wife's favorite horse underneath him.)

Characteristically undaunted, Roosevelt continued his hunt. Caught without shelter during a night's rainstorm, lying in blankets in a puddle, the Easterner surprised his guide by turning to say: "By Godfrey, but this is fun!" Later in the month, he finally bagged a bull.

After a survey of the West in 1894 found only eighty-five free-ranging buffalo (about a thousand more were in parks, zoos, and private herds), Congress passed a law protecting the survivors. In 1905, the American Bison Society was formed to encourage the preservation and propagation of buffalo. Theodore Roosevelt, by then president of the United States, was named honorary president of the society.

An excited rancher flags us down from his pickup. He's seen the two bulls and directs Gerard to their location. When we get there, we can barely see them from the gravel road, two black dots a half mile distant and moving steadily northwest along a creek bed. Gerard checks his map and comes up with two pieces of bad news: they're already more than twelve miles from the park perimeter, getting farther with each step; and the closest road in their direction is another fifteen miles away. To follow them, we'll have to take the Dodge pickup into the rough breaks; since they're so far from the park, he'll have no alternative but to shoot them when and if we catch them.

Gerard talks to the park headquarters through his two-way radio, telling them our location and dispatching another crew to start west and head off the buffalo in case our pursuit fails. We open a gate and start across the rangeland. It's noon.

A mile of bouncing between sagebrush and cow pies brings us to a problem. A tributary of the creek the buffalo and we are following enters from the left. We're hemmed in on two sides by seven-foot drops to the stream beds. No problem for the buffalo, who can descend and climb like oversized mountain goats. Big problem for the pickup, even if it had four-wheel drive, which it doesn't. The buffalo are now more than a mile in front of us, walking a steady gait in a straight line, as indifferent to the danger we represent to them as they were to the ditch that has stopped our progress.

We turn ninety degrees to the left of the bulls' path—our only option other than giving up and going back—in hopes of finding a place to cross the tributary. Instead, we find a tributary to the tributary, another deep gully that forces us left again and heads us at an oblique angle to the projected course of the two buffalo. The bulls have long since disappeared behind a broken string of buttes.

Last night's rain has settled the dust of the sandy soil in the valley. But in some of the low places of the faint trace we're following, the earth is deceptively muddy. Several times we nearly get stuck, a prospect both of us dread this deep into the Bad-lands.

"One of us is going to have to walk in front of the truck to watch for wet spots," Gerard says. It's a park truck; he's the only park employee. A faint twinkle starts to form in his brown eyes, but I beat him to the punch.

"I'll go first," I say and climb out, "but I think in the old days it was the other way around. The Indians did the scouting."

"Did I ever tell you that you can earn an eagle feather by pulling the tail of a rattler?" he shouts from the truck window as I start a half trot ten yards in front.

For about an hour our strange procession loops and winds toward higher ground and a creek crossing, a late twentieth-century miniature wagon train led by someone who's never been in this country before. After several dead ends, false trails, half circles around solitary buttes, climbs and dips, crossings and recrossings of shallow gullies, we emerge on the opposite side of the line of buttes where we last saw our quarry. Just before two o'clock we find a break in the chain, I get back into the truck, and we drive through to the main stream bed. The two bulls are 150 yards in front of us.

The truth is, I *had* dreamed of my girlfriend last night.

The buffalo seem unconcerned about our presence behind them. They just keep walking at their steady gait—about 5 mph—swishing their long tails as they lumber along. Their sides are mangy and spotty from shedding their winter coats. The smaller, younger bull, about the size of a big ox, occasionally swings his massive head to the side to look at the pickup trailing them. The older bull, half again as large as his young companion, is in the lead and never once looks back.

As if this were their destination all along, and they had been wondering when we'd show up to join them, the bulls round a small hummock and stop next to an untended oil well. The two buffalo begin grazing on tufts of short grass. The pump at the well rocks back and forth, dredging the liquefied remains of the buffalo's prehistoric ancestors hundreds of feet below us.

Gerard uses this pause to check his map. The well is too recent to show up on the map grids marked in ownership sections of green (Forest Service), blue (state land), purple (Park Service), and white (private land). Still, it's easy to estimate our approximate location, despite the wandering path that brought us here. Most of the oil production in this region is on leases from the government; we're on a square green island in a sea of surrounding white sections on the map. The Theodore Roosevelt park is at least twenty miles of broken country to the east, and the buffalo clearly aren't heading back. Once they move from this well site, they'll be walking deeper into private lands and deeper into trouble. A red-scoria access road curls into the pump station. If Gerard is going to have to kill the bulls and have any chance to remove their carcasses, this is where it will have to happen.

He calls the patrol car he dispatched earlier on his radio, then park headquarters for another pickup to haul the second carcass. He radios the sheriff's dispatcher for McKenzie County to see if any deputies are nearby with rifles, in case the second bull takes off at the first shot; the dispatcher tells him it would be more than an hour before a deputy could show up.

The bulls have finished grazing and follow the scoria road for a few hundred feet and then start up the side of a barren hill. We flank them in the truck and stop. Gerard loads the rifle with 150-grain shells, opens the truck door, and draws a bead on the big bull, using the open window as a brace. He mutters something in Hidatsa before he pulls the trigger.

The first shot hits the older bull in the side of the head. He lifts his head and shakes it, as if startled from sleep by a troubling dream. Then he turns his rump toward us, and remains stationary on his feet. The younger bull has jumped, but settled, from the report of the rifle. Gerard says something again in Hidatsa, takes aim, and fires. The young one, which the bullet hits right behind the ear, breaking his neck and killing him instantly, crumples to the ground.

The old bull has turned again now, offering a clear second shot. He is coughing gallons of brilliant red blood onto the sandy soil. More Hidatsa from Gerard, another loud crack from the rifle, and the bull drops like the other one, chin on the ground, body turned with his legs out stiff.

Gerard takes out his hunting knife, and the two of us walk the two hundred feet to the motionless bodies on the hillside.

"What were you saying before you shot?" I ask him.

"Hidatsa prayer," Gerard says. "The buffalo's got a powerful spirit. I don't want him to suffer. I was asking for a clean, quick kill that will release the spirit without too much pain."

He bends down next to the larger bull, sticks his knife into its neck, and severs the jugular vein to bleed the carcass. A deep gurgle comes from the body as the soil turns dark underneath it. Gerard repeats this with the second one, and we return to the truck.

He radios the sheriff's dispatcher to say he won't need another deputy, tells his crews that the buffalo are down, and then calls his supervisor at the park's south unit to find out who will get the carcasses. A list is kept of nonprofit organizations that want the meat and are willing to pay the butchering costs. The Fort Union National Historic Site, a former trading post near the confluence of the Yellowstone and Missouri rivers, takes the heads and robes. The top of the list today includes the Jamestown Chamber of Commerce, a local Catholic church, the Fort Berthold Reservation, and the state industrial school. The supervisor says he'll contact them in that order to see who can pick up the carcasses; Gerard says he's already arranged to bring them to Watford City, where they can be ready by tomorrow.

We drive out the access road to find a county road and meet Gerard's patrol car and the other pickup. On the way, Gerard stops at a farmhouse, where he asks the rancher to bring a tractor with a front-end bucket to lift the carcasses onto the pickups, and he calls the Piggly Wiggly supermarket in Watford City to tell the butcher he'll be bringing in two buffalo by this evening.

Our new wagon train—two pickups, a sedan, and a big tractor with an enclosed cab—returns to the buffalo. Gerard and Jimmy Olson, the head of maintenance for the park, begin work on the smaller bull. They slice circles around the bull's ankles and begin skinning the hide by pulling on the coat and cutting the fatty tissue holding the robe to the meat. It is hot, messy work done to the sounds of ripping flesh, knives being periodically sharpened on whetstones, occasional faint gurgles from the bull's windpipe, and buzzing flies. Their hands became caked with dark, dry blood. Gerard finds a third knife and gives it to me to help out. He instructs me about tugging and peeling back the hide while I slice. The skinning is harder labor than it looked.

We turn the dead bull on its back and open the chest cavity, removing the heart and putting it in a plastic garbage bag. Olson carefully slits the thin membrane near the belly, and the casing around the bull's four stomachs balloons through the opening, as if someone inside the bull had pulled the cord on an inflatable raft. Gerard, at the lower end of the abdomen, is making a cut toward Olson's, trying to be sure he doesn't rupture the full bladder. When the two cuts meet, the bags of stomachs and lungs and coils of intestines spill onto the ground.

Kristi Korb, a young park attendant from Ohio on her first day of work for the summer season, is turning a pale green as she watches us. "We always had the women do this work in the old days," Gerard tells her. "We men would go sit on the hilltop and watch for enemies."

The liver and kidneys are now exposed. Gerard slices off a piece of brownish-purple liver and offers it to the bystanders. They all decline—Kristi's answer being a wave of deeper green across her face—so he turns to me.

"You go first," he says. "It'll give you some of the buffalo's strength." He watches intently as I chew the slice of liver: warm, a little crunchy, and surprisingly sweet and strong tasting. Then he eats a piece. We do the same with small slices of kidney. Gerard removes the kidneys and liver, and cuts off the bull's testicles and long penis. All but the penis are placed in the garbage bag with the heart.

Olson attaches chains to the hind legs of the carcass and has the rancher drive his tractor closer. The chains are wrapped around the tractor's bucket, and the carcass is lifted so the head is dangling just above the ground. Twisting and strenuous cutting remove the horned head. It falls in a heap with the hide, a broad, soggy, furry blanket. The bucket lifts and turns and places the skinned carcass in the bed of Olson's truck. I heft the heavy head and hide in next to it. Kristi and another attendant take the truck and first carcass to Watford City, and we start in on the older bull. It's four-thirty.

Our knives are duller, our arms are more tired, the day is hotter, and this bull is bigger than the first. Blood smears our hands, forearms, shirts, and parts of our foreheads where we have tried to wipe sweat away. We follow the same procedure—skinning the hide, opening the chest and abdomen, saving the heart, liver, kidneys, and sex organs in the garbage bag. Probably because we're trying to hurry, one cut goes too deep and the bladder breaks, spewing its contents on Olson and Gerard.

Shortly after six o'clock, we have the second carcass, the hide and head, and the heavy bag of organs in the back of Gerard's pickup truck.

Olson heads back to the park in the sedan; the rancher rumbles off in his tractor. Gerard and I take one more look at the stomachs and intestines on the hillside—"Dinner for the coyotes tonight," he says—and begin the hour's drive to the Piggly Wiggly. The pump at the well nods farewell.

—

The two carcasses hanging from spikes in the supermarket freezer weigh 948 pounds and 671 pounds, not counting the heads, hides, and viscera. The butcher tells us the Jamestown Chamber of Commerce and the reservation have already called, asking when they can pick up their meat. A ranger from Fort Union carts off the heads and hides. We still have the bag of organs and one of the penises in the truck bed, my "reward" for my scouting duties. Gerard has plans for them: cooking the former for tomorrow's breakfast; nailing and drying the latter on a board, until it is ready to be used as a cane.

In the Piggly Wiggly parking lot, where a small crowd gathered to watch the buffalo being unloaded, several men are still gawking at something in the back of Gerard's truck.

"What's that?" one of them asks Gerard, pointing to a three-foot-long pole of cartilage.

"What do you think it is?" he answers.

"Is it the tail?" The man doesn't want to mention what he thinks it really is.

"No," Gerard says. "What does it look like?"

"It's not *that,* is it?"

"You bet," Gerard says.

The man's eyes are twenty times the size of a buffalo nickel as we pull away. Gerard's blood-caked face looks a little like the profile on the coin's flip side.

I awake the next morning in Gerard's house to the aroma of testes, kidneys, and small buffalo steaks frying in the pan. The smell is distinctive and overpowering, the same smell from the hillside where we skinned the hides.

"I'm trying to decide what that smells like," I tell Gerard, searching for descriptive images and comparisons.

He turns to me from the frying pan and fixes me with a look like Roosevelt's guide must have during their rainy hunt a hundred years ago—a look wondering if Easterners know anything about anything.

"Buffalo," he says. "It smells like buffalo."

13

Big Sky

we were now about to penetrate a country at least two thousand miles in width, on which the foot of civilized man had never trodden; the good or evil it had in store for us was for experiment yet to determine. . . .   From Meriwether Lewis's journal
Departure from Fort Mandan
April 7, 1805

The sky *is* bigger in Montana. But of course, everything else in Montana is bigger as well. The semiarid climate, the general lack of air pollution, the gradually increasing altitude of the High Plains as they approach the Rockies to the west, and the sweeping horizons conspire to make daytime skies that are deep and azure, and nighttime skies in which the stars shine like high-beam headlights of an approaching truck convoy.

It took Lewis and Clark four months to travel westward across the expanse that is now Montana. In that time, they did not encounter a single other human being, red or white. Nearly two centuries later, Montana is still remarkable for its size and its sparse population.

How big is Montana? Some statistics help comprehend its size and remoteness. Consider: Montana is the nation's fourth largest state; yet it ranks forty-fourth in population. Consider: Its northeast border marks the change from the Central Time Zone to Mountain Time; its northwest border is the changeover to Pacific Time. The state engulfs an entire time zone.

How big is Montana? Consider: Montana newspapers carry nine different weather forecasts to cover its varied weather zones. Consider: The state government maintains 13,000 miles of paved roads; no one knows how many miles of dirt and gravel the counties take care of. Before 1974, the legal speed limit in Montana was defined as "careful and prudent," which local residents say meant about 80 to 85 mph. Federal laws required a change. Now, if you're stopped for driving over 55 mph during the day and weren't driving recklessly, you'll get a five-dollar fine but no mark on your driving record. "You just can't get around Montana at fifty-five," a local tells me.

How big is Montana? Consider: The main stem of the Missouri River, not even counting its headwater tributaries, travels 733 miles *within* the state's borders. That is the distance from Baltimore, Maryland, to Savannah, Georgia; or the distance from Savannah to the Texas-Louisiana border; or the Louisiana border to Chicago; or Chicago back to Baltimore.

Rainbow of steel:
the Gateway Arch,
St. Louis

Vernon Gloe and his team of Belgian horses, Hermann, Missouri

LEFT. Livestock hotel:
cattle at the
Omaha stockyards

BELOW. Bertha Calloway,
Great Plains
Black Museum, Omaha

Sit and fish, fish and think, think and sit: a "river person" at the mouth of the Kansas River, Kansas City

LEFT. Making feet happy: Dennis and Ann Menke, Yankton, South Dakota

OVERLEAF. Ponca Creek: downtown Lynch, Nebraska

BELOW. Howard and Ermal Smith, Chief White Crane Campground, Yankton, South Dakota

ABOVE. The ribbon road unfurls: Highway 12, northern Nebraska

BELOW. Buffalo herd, Houck Ranch, Pierre, South Dakota

Memorial Day service, Sitting Bull's grave, Mobridge, South Dakota

Cabool Chambers,
Lynch, Nebraska

Ray and Esta Davy,
Lynch, Nebraska

ABOVE. "He goes first": Dayton Duncan, Earth Lodge, Stanton, North Dakota

OPPOSITE. Corn bins, Pierre, South Dakota

BELOW. Gerard Baker skins buffalo, Theodore Roosevelt National Park, Badlands, North Dakota

TOP. Scenes of visionary enchantment:
White Cliffs of the Missouri River, Montana

ABOVE. Fry Pan Jack, king of the hoboes,
Helena, Montana

OPPOSITE. Rocky Mountains, east of
Lewis and Clark Pass, Montana

Modern mountain men:
Jack Schilla and Phil
Walsh, Three Forks of
the Missouri, Montana

ABOVE. Where the
Passage myth was wounded:
the *Discovery* at Lemhi Pass,
Montana-Idaho border

RIGHT. Canadian Club
search team: Joel Bernstein,
Lee Hames, and Don Keysser,
Beaverhead Rock, Montana

LEFT. Cowboy Joel
Bernstein, Bitterroot
Valley, Montana

BELOW. Good Sams:
Del and Daisy Davitt,
B. J. and Alta DeGarmo,
Samboree, Lewiston,
Idaho

RIGHT. Down the Lolo Trail: Lochsa River, Bitterroot Mountains, Idaho

BELOW. Desert and crops: irrigation and sagebrush, eastern Washington

Kathryn Brigham
and her dip net,
Bridge of the Gods,
Columbia River

The Dalles, Columbia River

The "grandest and most pleasing prospect": Pacific Coast, Cannon Beach, Oregon

How sparsely populated is Montana? Consider: There are fifty-six counties. Only eight have more than 20,000 residents; fourteen have fewer than 3,000. An area larger than the state of New Jersey is devoted solely to wheatfields. The average ranch/farm size is 2,588 acres. Cattle outnumber people by twelve to one.

Perhaps the best way to consider Montana's size and population is this: All six New England states join with New York state and three quarters of Pennsylvania to form the boundaries of a single state. Everyone except those living in Hartford, Connecticut, is told to get out by sunset. The next morning, the people of Hartford are told to disperse and inhabit the new state. That's Montana.

From Fort Mandan, the captains dispatched a contingent of men back to St. Louis with the keelboat, loaded with animal and plant specimens and letters for Jefferson. The reduced Corps of Discovery—including Charbonneau, Sacagawea, and the infant—now numbered thirty-three. Once they passed the mouth of the Yellowstone, Lewis and Clark and their party entered a territory where no Americans had been before. They were the first U.S. citizens to traverse Montana, the first to see the Rocky Mountains, the first to cross the Continental Divide, the first to reach the Pacific Ocean by land. Unlike them, 180 years later, I have the advantage of good road maps to lead me, books about the territory (beginning with their journals) to prepare me for what to expect, and tables of statistics to quantify what I have yet to experience.

But I have to verify for myself the vastness of Montana. It takes me only one very long and taxing day.

ROAD RULE 12: You can learn a lot from books, maps, and statistics, but the road is a better—and sterner—teacher.

The rains have returned when I leave Gerard Baker's house, filled with a breakfast of buffalo. Forty miles west of the Theodore Roosevelt park, the *Discovery* and I cross the Yellowstone, broad and muddy like the Missouri, which it joins a few miles north. A flock of pelicans is flying north in a broken chevron just above the Yellowstone's current. Dark and nasty clouds are sweeping in with a gusty northwest wind, rupturing sheets of rain across the plains.

At the Montana border, North Dakota Highway 58 becomes a dirt road and crosses the Missouri on a single-lane bridge shared with a railroad track. Dust is dehydrated instant mud, and there seems to be nothing in between those two extremes in the High Plains. As the *Discovery* wallows through eleven more miles of mud before reaching U.S. 2, I register a silent vote in favor of dust.

My radio welcome to Montana is a news report saying that a section of an interstate in the south-central part of the state is closed because high winds have overturned a tractor-trailer; roads in the northwest and southwest corners are closed by snowdrifts. This is the thirtieth day of May.

Here in the northeast corner, the rain is collecting in the rutted depressions of Highway 2. The camper planes and jerks in the puddles. I have to hug either the center line or the shoulder to straddle these long lakes; the bursts of wind keep trying to force me either into the oncoming lane or back into the water. For the first time since the heavy traffic of St. Louis and Kansas City, small beads of sweat gather on the back of my neck as I lurch westward. But I don't think it's just tension. It feels like a cold coming on.

In Poplar, Montana (population 995), after I decide against a stop at the Chief Kwik Way convenience store for some cold medicine, the cultural center for the Fort Peck Indian Reservation catches my attention, so I pull in for a short tour. In the course of a conversation with Gerald Red Elk, a sixty-five-year-old tribal member, he mentions that he has a plant root that can fend off my cold, if I'm willing to use it. Having eaten raw buffalo liver off a bloody hunting knife for strength less than twenty-four hours earlier, I figure chewing on a root to fight a cold makes sense.

Red Elk takes me to his small house a few blocks from the cultural center, where he tells me about other tribal "medicines": how a plant called blue root can cure a malarial fever or ease the pain of a toothache, how the ginseng root is good for heart ailments, how a smudge from burning Russian cabbage can clear the sinuses, and how he believes participating in a sun dance put his cancer in remission.

At Fort Mandan, when Sacagawea was having her first child and her "labour was tedious and the pain violent," Lewis was told that a small portion of the rattle of a rattlesnake, ground up and administered with water, helped induce delivery. They tried it. Ten minutes later, little Jean Baptiste Charbonneau was born. "Whether this medicine was truly the cause or not I shall not undertake to determine," Lewis writes, ". . . but I must confess that I want faith as to it's efficacy."

"We all want the same thing: health, strength, and the courage to go on," Red Elk tells me. Besides using Indian medicines, he is also a practicing Mormon. "It's all the same God, but there are different ways of praying to Him. The important thing is faith, believing."

He hands me the dried root, acquired from Sioux Indians in South Dakota in barter for the blue root. It is brown and gnarled, about the size of my little finger. "Grate it up to make a tea, or chew small pieces of it as you travel," he says. "It's strong and bitter, but it'll kill that virus in your system. Don't be surprised if it makes you sweat."

West of Poplar, struggling against the water and wind to keep the *Discovery* in the correct lane of Highway 2, I gnaw off the end of the root, chew it well, and swallow. The initial taste is turpentinishly harsh, like eating pine bark. Then a strong minty flavor works its way from the roof of my mouth and up through my tingling nostrils. After a few more bites, more sweat beads form on the back of my neck. It's either from my tight grip on the steering wheel, the cold progressing, or the cure working its way through my body. Maybe all three. Who knows? I take another bite and try to believe.

Near present-day Nashua, Montana (population 495), Lewis and Clark crossed a river they describe as "being about the colour of a cup of tea with the admixture of a tablespoonfull of milk." Accordingly, they named it Milk River, which it is still called. When I pause on the roadside to see that its color, like its name, has not changed, two cars stop to inquire whether my vehicle's broken down and I want some assistance. I wave them on, not knowing that later this evening I'll need that kind of friendly helpfulness.

From Fort Peck to Fort Benton, approximately two hundred air miles, there is no road that closely follows the Missouri. For much of this distance, the river is bordered on both sides by the Missouri River Breaks, a wild, rough, inhospitable, and chiefly uninhabited terrain that makes a river road both impossible and unnecessary to build. Only one paved highway crosses the river in this distance—U.S. 191, which runs north–south and bisects this stretch of the Missouri at the western edges of the lake formed by Fort

Peck Dam. West of the highway crossing is the White Cliffs region of the Missouri, protected by Congress as a "wild and scenic river," and the only portion of the river untouched and unchanged since the days of the explorers. My intention is to take a canoe trip from Fort Benton through the White Cliffs with a group of Lewis and Clark enthusiasts.

But first I have to get to Fort Benton by road. U.S. 2 arcs northward away from the river, across the rolling wheatfields near the Canadian border. State Highway 200 parallels the Missouri about fifty miles south of the river and will get me to the mountains earlier. At Fort Peck, I turn south on Highway 24 to take the lower route. Like Lewis and Clark, by this time on my journey I'm anxious for mountain views.

The highway crosses along the top of the huge crescent of Fort Peck Dam, the largest earthen dam in the world when it was built in the 1930s, which the Corps of Engineers claims saved the cities of Omaha and Council Bluffs from the disastrous flood of 1952. The lake it formed has a 1,600-mile shoreline.

Highway 24 is a patchy stretch of asphalt through choppy buttes and valleys, the same kind of terrain Gerard and I traversed to follow the buffalo. There are few trees, not even much sage. In the fifty-nine miles between Fort Peck and Highway 200, I see seven cars, two ranch houses, and an unending string of barbed wire near both shoulders. Twenty-five miles north of Highway 200, the *Discovery* loses radio contact with the world again. I switch to the tape cassette. Merle Haggard sings, "Turn me loose, set me free, somewhere in the middle of Montana . . . Big city, turn me loose and set me free."

Lewis (Clark?) points me west at the highway intersection. It's still another thirty-six miles to Jordan, Montana (population 485), the first town in ninety-five miles since I left the Missouri at Fort Peck.

The gray canopy of the storm system is breaking up into lines of white clouds that look like the trail of steam puffs from a giant locomotive. The lowering sun behind them makes each ball of cloud opaque, with pink veins and traces of purple—an ornamental egg or a buffalo's testicle.

As it winds and curls ten miles for every linear mile, Big Dry Creek cuts through a valley seemingly too broad for such a little amount of water in it. A dozen pronghorn antelope lift their heads from the streambed as I pass. Two mule deer in the highway right-of-way raise their big ears and large tails to attention as the *Discovery* approaches and then leap the barbed-wire fence in an effortless bound.

Several pickups are parked outside QD's in Jordan when I pull in for dinner. Quinn and Darlene have attached personal messages to the menu: "Your patronage is our existence. Thank you. We appreciate your business." The chicken-fried steak I order covers its large plate and is accompanied by a mound of hash browns on a plate the same size. Even the portions are bigger in Montana. The restrooms are marked "Doe's" and "Buck's." I make a pit stop at the "Buck's" and climb back into my vehicle.

A quick check of my map says fifty more miles will bring me to Mosby, on the banks of the Musselshell River. I should get there by 9 P.M., before nightfall, and I tell myself that I'll treat myself to a well-deserved motel room there as a reward for fighting the winds, the rain, and my incipient cold. I take a few more bites of Red Elk's root. It raises a little more sweat and scours the last traces of dinner from my mouth.

What I forgot to check on my map was Mosby's population. Mosby turns out to be a small house, a boarded-up gas station, and a pay phone. There is still enough twilight to read the historic marker on the roadside by the Musselshell and to recheck my map. Like most of the other towns in the table at the corner of my map, Mosby exists as a pair of coordinates—D-9 in this case—and a dot on a piece of paper. Towns with populations as low as 164, 120, 91, even 61 are listed, but no population for Mosby, or a majority of the other towns for that matter. They're just too small.

Montana roadside historical markers are a folksy collection of information. One I saw earlier in the day at Wolf Point states that the town got its name when trappers poisoned several hundred wolves one winter and stacked their frozen carcasses near the boat landing, to await the spring thaw and the opportunity to skin them. "It taught the varmints a lesson," the marker says. "No one in Wolf Point has been bothered by a wolf at the door since." (Much later, near Mullan Pass west of Helena, a marker commemorating Capt. John Mullan, who built a military road through the area to Washington state, contains this advice of his on the care of pack mules: "Never maltreat them, but govern them as you would a woman with kindness, affection and caresses and you will be repaid by their docility and easy management.")

The Musselshell marker explains the history of Fort Musselshell, at the river's mouth, from the days of Indian trading to cattle drives. "The Assinniboines and Sioux regarded this post as an amusement center where bands of ambitious braves could lie in ambush and get target practice on careless whites," it says. "During the cattle days of the '80s the mouth of the Musselshell became a cattle rustler's hangout but after a Vigilance Committee stretched a few of them they seemed to lose interest."

When Montanans say their state has a colorful history, their emphasis is on colorful.

Winnett, Montana, is twenty-two miles farther west. By the time I reach it, the sun has dropped through the drainage hole of the western horizon, sucking the last swirls of color down with it. The massive storm front that has plagued me all day and smothered my view of the big sky of Montana is now behind me. A few evening stars are twinkling in the vastness above me; a near-full moon rises in the rearview mirror like a pale gas balloon.

A quick tour of Winnett (population 207) turns up no motels. Winnett is the county seat of Petroleum County, but its few gas stations are already closed for the night. My gas gauge has just touched empty.

I've had a number of cars, campers, and trucks in my life. Each one's gas gauge required its own translation: "empty" has meant anywhere from two to five gallons in the tank. Lewistown, a veritable metropolis of 7,104 people, is fifty-three more miles down the road. It will surely have motels and gas stations, so I pull back onto Highway 200 and move on.

Six miles west of Winnett, the *Discovery* sputters to a stop. With a certain German precision, "empty" on this particular Volkswagen gas gauge means exactly that.

FIRST COROLLARY: The lessons of the road are taught by practical, workshop methods, not by lectures. They're more effective that way.

Here's where I think my CB can come in handy.
"Breaker one-nine. Anybody with their ears on?" Silence.

"Breaker one-nine. Anybody listening?" Nothing.

I sit for a few more minutes behind the wheel, promising the Road Spirit/Teacher I'll get fuel each time I eat from now on, mustering up a few fragments of German epithets I still remember from school for the *Discovery*'s sake, and wondering how often people run out of gas in Petroleum County.

The only thing to do is hike back to Winnett and hope I can roust someone to open their gas station. I turn on the hazard flashers, grab my flashlight, climb out and start walking east, the *Discovery* blinking goodbye from the highway shoulder. The moon and stars are bright enough to light my way.

About a mile later I hear the high whine of truck tires. Two headlights appear in the distance and I begin waving the flashlight. The whine gets higher as the truck shifts down, and a big cab pulling two long grain trailers grinds to a halt next to me. The passenger door swings open and I climb the ladder to peer in and ask for a ride to the closest open gas station. The trucker waves me in, and we rumble west, passing the *Discovery*, which looks like a toy vehicle from the vantage point of the truck cab.

Inside the cab are two padded seats, a small bed behind them, two mounted fans, a CB, tape deck, radio, and an array of gauges that light the interior with a gold glow, like embers of a fire. The trucker is youngish, slim, with long hair, a beard, red cap, and a black T-shirt advertising Harley-Davidson motorcycles. The extra weight from the second trailer jerks and jiggles the cab on the rough pavement.

I try to start a conversation above the noise of the mighty engine, the whir of the fans, the thwapping tires, and the cackling buzz of CB static.

"Hauling grain?"

"What?"

"Hauling grain!?"

"Yeah."

A long pause.

"Where to?"

"What?"

"Where to!?"

"Moccasin."

Another pause.

"You own this rig!!!?" I'm tired of repeating myself.

"Nope, just drive it."

He slips a tape of rock and roll into the cassette player, turning up the volume and turning off the conversation. I watch the scenery, he watches the road, and we bounce for twenty miles until he pulls in at a truck stop in Grassrange (population 139).

He turns down the tape low enough for me to thank him and ask one more question before I climb out.

"How do your kidneys survive all that punishment?"

"Oh, I ride motorcycles on my time off," he says. "This here's nothing compared to that."

The truck stop is about to close for the night, the clerk counting the day's receipts and the cafe waitress cleaning the tables. Both of them are cute young women, and my mind, a little overactive from a month alone on the road, races ahead on a traveler's fantasy: one of them will drive me back to the *Discovery*, ask me if I have a place to stay for the night, invite me to the small ranch she's trying to run on her lonesome in addition to her job at the truck stop, and years later I'll be entertaining our children with the story of how running out of gas in Petroleum County brought their mother and me together.

I buy a four-gallon plastic container, fill it with gas, pay my bill, and explain my predicament. This is the moment when the fantasy is supposed to kick in.

"Any chance one of you is heading east?"

They both shake their heads, no, and go back to their work.

SECOND COROLLARY: The main course of study in the classrooms of the road is not romantic fiction.

My face must look crestfallen—as much from the prospect of a twenty-mile hike as from a fantasy shattered—because the clerk looks at me with pity and picks up the phone. Ten minutes later, Deputy Sheriff Ron Rowton arrives in a station wagon to take me back to the *Discovery*.

Rowton has a neatly trimmed mustache, a cowboy hat, and a tan sheriff's uniform. He's a deputy for Fergus County, which sprawls from the Missouri River south for seventy-five miles and is fifty-five miles from east to west borders, but he's willing to venture a few miles out of his jurisdiction to help a stranded stranger. He's more willing to talk than the trucker was.

"What kind of things do you handle besides out-of-gas Easterners?"

"Just about everything," he says. "Burglary, theft, minor stuff mostly."

Remembering the historic marker at Mosby, I ask if there's any cattle rustling these days.

"Still some," he says. "We caught a few not too long ago." They were pulling trucks up to ranges in broad daylight and carting off calves. The deputies caught them because their methods—their "M.O.," he calls it—were repetitive. "They did the same thing the same way once too often."

"Do you still string them up?"

He looks over from the steering wheel, the same look I got from Gerard early this morning. For a minute, I think I've ended our chat.

"No," he finally says, "but they're doing a few years of hard time."

A pair of deer appear in the corners of the headlights' beam. Rowton tells me they cause quite a few accidents, mostly in early evening and early morning as they're moving to and from a feeding area.

"I've only hit one in the last five years, so I consider that pretty good for this area," he says and then offers some advice for night driving: "Just look out at the edge of your light [he squints and points], and if you see anything moving just slow 'er on down and get ready to stop."

He tells me about growing up just north of Mosby in a two-room log house with an sod roof and no running water. He walked more than three miles to a one-room school and remembers when his home got electricity when he was six.

"How old are you?" I ask. These are the kind of stories my mother used to tell me about her childhood.

"Thirty-five," he says, the same age as mine.

The *Discovery* is still blinking when we reach it. Luckily for me, Rowton has heard me ask enough stupid questions by now to wonder if I'm capable of getting the gas in my tank, so he doesn't just drop me off and head home.

The container's mouth is too big to fit in the gas line. I begin mentally reviewing my physics lessons about creating vacuums and siphons with a plastic tube. Meanwhile Rowton removes the batteries from his cylindrical flashlight shell and starts pouring gasoline through it into the *Discovery* before I can remember the theories of fluidics.

"That ought to get you the fifty miles to Lewistown," he says, handing me the empty container.

I thank him and the good people of Fergus County and we part company. With luck, I'll get to Lewistown just before midnight. Driving west, I'm careful to watch the fringes of my headlight beams. I've learned enough Montana lessons for one day.

East of Lewistown (named for the explorer), Highway 200 begins an ascent toward the stars. The temperature drops as the altitude climbs, and the scent of pine wafts into the camper. To the south, moonlight shines on a line of white. Clouds again, I think, then look a second time. Not clouds, but a snow-capped ridge of mountains—the Little Snowy Mountains, part of the Lewis and Clark National Forest. This is not exactly how I had planned to celebrate my first view of the mountains.

Just after midnight, I find a motel on the outskirts of Lewistown, named, appropriately enough for this long day, the Trail's End.

Besides the lessons of the road I've learned, this day will be significant by the end of my trip for two other reasons: it's the last day of significant rainfall until I return to Kansas City more than two months later; and it's the day Gerald Red Elk's root killed the cold I never got.

According to my odometer, I have covered 445 miles since this morning—more, even, than that first long day from St. Louis to Kansas City. On that earlier day, however, I crossed the entire state of Missouri; today's miles have taken me only to a point somewhere in the middle of Montana. The stars overhead are as bright as the lights of Kansas City, a metropolitan area with more people than the state I'm in. *Big city, turn me loose and set me free.*

14

Works of Nature, Works of Man

*As we passed on it seemed as if those seens of visionary inchant-
ment would never have and [an] end; for here it is too that nature
presents to the view of the traveler vast ranges of walls of tolerable
workmanship, so perfect indeed are those walls that I should have
thought that nature had attempted here to rival the human art of
masonry had I not recollected that she had first began her work.*

From Meriwether Lewis's journal
White Cliffs of the Missouri
May 31, 1805

From Fort Benton to Great Falls is only about fifty miles, but it took the Corps of Discovery a month and a half to get through this area of Montana. Part of the time was spent resolving a nettlesome question of geography; the bulk was consumed in an exhausting portage around a gauntlet of five waterfalls.

From the end of May to the middle of July 1805, the explorers saw the most spectacular scenery and suffered through the most arduous physical labor since the expedition had left St. Louis. Clark and a small party nearly perished during a flash flood in a steep gully; several men had close scrapes with murderous grizzly bears; Lewis's cool head saved one of the men from slipping to his death off a canyon wall. At different times, Lewis, Sacagawea, and later Clark became sick with fevers and pains, Sacagawea almost to the point of dying. Lewis's folk remedies for the ailments ranged from concocting a dark tea from chokecherry branches and drinking from a sulfur spring to bloodletting and prescribing Dr. Rush's purgative "thunderbolts." In some cases the treatment was probably as life-threatening as the illness, but all three survived and improved. In an incident of particular importance to the men for the remainder of the trek, the Corps celebrated its second Fourth of July on the trail by drinking the last of the whiskey.

But for the intelligence of the two captains, the expedition would have turned to follow a tributary of the Missouri, mistaking it for the main stem, and would have found themselves in the midst of the forbidding peaks of modern-day Glacier National Park with winter hard on their heels. Whether they could have survived this detour is only conjecture. At best, the expedition would have been delayed a year; at worst, Jefferson's pet project might have vanished through the combination of the harsh elements and hostile Blackfoot Indians of northwestern Montana. Possibly, the Corps of Discovery would have been forced to return to the East without reaching the Pacific.

When they emerged from the White Cliffs section of the Missouri, the expedition came upon what seemed a fork in the river. From the north a river entered, a broad river, brown and muddy like the Missouri had been up to this point. The river flowing from the south was clearer and faster, more of a major mountain stream than a plains river. The men were unanimous in their belief that the northern fork was the Missouri and therefore the path to the Pacific that the Hidatsa Indians had told them about at Fort Mandan. Lewis and Clark deduced the opposite from the same information. If, as they had been told by the Hidatsas, the Missouri came from the "Shining Mountains" and over a large waterfall, it would be the swifter, clearer branch. (The dilemma arose because the Indians had not mentioned this fork in their descriptions.)

Lewis was sufficiently confident to name the northern fork the Marias River, in honor of his cousin Maria Wood, but the captains were concerned enough about the morale of their men, and about the possibility of wasting valuable time by leading the expedition into an explorer's cul-de-sac, to make them decide to check their theories. While the main party waited at the fork, Lewis took a small group by land along the southern branch. When he discovered the Great Falls on June 13, he had the proof he needed that this was, in fact, the Missouri and the way to a Northwest Passage. The Corps of Discovery could now, to borrow the phrase they began to use once more, "proceed on." Clark and the others soon joined him and began the difficult portage around the falls, which took nearly a month to complete.

Great Falls, Montana (population 56,725), is one of the state's newest cities—it was incorporated in 1888—and until recently it was Montana's biggest. People here tell you it's a "planned city." The streets and avenues are laid out in grids and, with the exception of Central Avenue, the city's main drag, virtually all have numbers for names. This makes it easier for a stranger to locate addresses, but I find myself yearning for some of the imaginative names Lewis and Clark gave to sites as they traveled through Montana: Rattlesnake Creek, Ash Rapids, Teapot Island, Blowing Fly Creek, Windy Island, Slaughter River, Flattery Run, Portage Creek, and the myriad of topographical features that were named for members of the expedition, important historic personages, and notable occurrences.

White Bear Island, named for its infestation of grizzlies, where the expedition camped upon completion of the portage, still carries the name Lewis and Clark gave it. And the Great Falls itself, the largest of the five cataracts, retains the same name, if not the majesty, of 1805.

Lewis was elated at his discovery of the falls, since it settled the expedition's navigational conundrum. But this emotion was soon overpowered by sheer wonder as he sat down to describe the falls for the first time.

The cascade, he writes, "formes the grandest sight I ever beheld. . . . the irregular and somewhat projecting rocks below receives the water in it's passage down and brakes it into a perfect white foam which assumes a thousand forms in a moment sometimes flying up in jets of sparkling foam to the hight of fifteen and twenty feet . . . from the reflection of the sun on the sprey or mist which arrises from these falls is a beautifull rainbow produced which adds not a little to the beauty of this majestically grand senery."

When Paris Gibson saw the string of falls in 1882, he envisioned something else: dams and hydropower. Two years later, a town site had been drawn for the "planned city." By 1890, the first of five dams was in place and a copper smelter was using its power. The Anaconda Company grew to employ 60 percent of all working Montanans, and Great Falls became the state's biggest city. But then Anaconda pulled out of Great Falls and out of Montana, leaving behind nothing but an empty smokestack and closing another chapter in the boom-and-bust history of the West. To the dismay of the people of Great Falls, who considered the refinery's giant smokestack, the world's second tallest, a tourist attraction at least, the manmade wonder was later dismantled. Malmstrom Air Force Base, home of the 24th North American Air Defense Command and a couple of hundred Minuteman missiles, is now the largest employer in town. Billings, Montana, riding the crest of the newer oil and coal boom along the Yellowstone River, has replaced Great Falls as the largest city in the state.

When I visit the Great Falls and stand at the same spot from which Lewis first saw the cascades, the marvel of the view is not from showers of spray and pretty rainbows, but the near-total absence of water over the rock cliffs. The towering walls of Ryan Dam loom just upstream, shunting the Missouri through a turbine house and a concrete sluiceway before the water is discharged back into its channel downstream.

If you're looking for scenery worth seeing in Great Falls these days, you have to settle for the art gallery and old studio of cowboy artist Charley Russell. The smokestack is gone, and the grandest sight Lewis ever beheld has been turned into kilowatts.

Having been denied the scenic pleasures that Great Falls once offered, I am determined at least to reenact a few of the explorers' experiences. At the end of a long hike near the mouth of the Marias River, Lewis mentions having a "hearty supper of our venison not having taisted a mosel before during the day; I now laid myself down on some willow boughs to a comfortable nights rest, and felt indeed as if I was fully repaid for the toil and pain of the day, so much will a good shelter, a dry bed, and comfortable supper revive the sperits of the waryed, wet and hungry traveler." And, after all, this is the area where the expedition finished its supply of liquor.

My twentieth-century reenactment consists of finding a motel room and going out for a night on the town.

ROAD RULE 13: A good explorer is able to adjust to new information and make the most out of the surroundings. One fork in the road or river may end in disappointment, but the other fork can get you back on track.

FIRST COROLLARY: Sometimes the best fork to choose is the one next to a plate and a drink.

The motel clerk tells me the only rooms left have waterbeds, which add four dollars to the price.

"Is it worth it?" I inquire.

"Haven't you ever slept on one?" she answers, her preconceived biases about the differences between New England and, say, California hardening before my eyes.

A young woman sitting in the tiny lobby pipes up: "It's more relaxing. Your whole body relaxes."

I'm getting interested. "Do you have one at home?"

The woman nods. "I absolutely love it. Nothing falls asleep until your whole body falls asleep."

I ask if she insisted on a room with a waterbed at the motel.

"No. I'm here for a convention, and they ordered the cheaper rooms. I sure wish I was in a waterbed room."

Needless to say, by this time I've signed the registry for a waterbed, and another traveler's fantasy is already leapfrogging ahead in time, out of control. (I refer to this condition as "Road Fever.")

"What convention are you here for?" In my fantasy, the correct answer is the Montana Assocation of Physical Therapists or the Big Sky Hospitality Hostesses Annual Convention.

She smiles politely. "Church of the Nazarene."

Quietly, I take my room key and ask the clerk for recommendations on a good restaurant for someone eating alone.

ROAD RULE 14: There are many strains of Road Fever, and an even greater number of folk remedies.

FIRST COROLLARY: My most common treatment is a cold shower.

My supper is taken at the kind of upscale restaurant/bar you can find in any city of the nation with more than thirty thousand people, regardless of the region. The decor is a mixture of white oak, brass, glass, and hanging plants, with artwork and piped-in music in the restrooms. The menu's format puts more emphasis on cuteness and calligraphy than on clarity; desserts and wine, being as important as the entrees, have separate menus. The posters on the walls of the lobby are for a "Run for Fun" and advertising golf shirts or T-shirts with the restaurant's logo.

The bartenders are young, healthy, well-scrubbed men, usually with a tan in any season and wearing the latest in casual wear— in this case, a bright Hawaiian-style shirt (a few tufts of chest hair showing through the V of the open collar), pleated pants, and running shoes. Their banter is witty, like the menu and like the waitresses, who are also young, physically fit, fashionably yet casually dressed, and friendly. This is Montana, but a number of male patrons at the bar are wearing raw silk sports coats with the sleeves and collars pushed up, demonstrating the pervasive and homogenizing influence of the satellite dish that brings them the latest vices from Miami.

Adjusting to my surroundings, I order the seafood linguini, spinach salad, broccoli with melted cheese, a glass of Chablis, coffee, and a dish of Häagen-Dazs ice cream for dessert. The food is all right—certainly different from and more expensive than what I've grown accustomed to—and they accept credit cards, something I haven't had the chance to use for a couple of weeks.

—

The night's tour of the bars and dance halls of Great Falls is a fuzzy memory by the time I return to my waterbed. Some incidents, questions, and observations stand out, however:

1. People with cowboy hats are better dancers than those without them
2. If both members of a couple are wearing cowboy hats, can they kiss without one of them getting poked in the eyes?
3. Watching people try to do the cowboy two-step or Western swing to a rock and roll song called "Man Down Under" is a funny sight
4. So is watching people try to rock and roll to "Tumbling Tumbleweed"
5. While men will come alone to a bar, women usually arrive at least in pairs; and if one of them is particularly pretty, the other(s) isn't (aren't)
6. Crowds at country-western bars are friendlier than those at discos
7. No modern expedition needs to worry about running out of whiskey in Great Falls; the Lewis and Clark Distillery is just downriver in Helena

At one bar, a salesman from Seattle starts talking to me about the women of the area. In his opinion, they're a little beefier than in his home base—"Big Thigh Country," he calls Montana—but the way his eyes keep scanning the crowd convinces me he suffers from his own brand of Road Fever. Learning about my trip, he tells me to stop at a natural hot spring along the route I'll take in Idaho. "Great place to pick up girls," he says. He's in his early twenties, and when he abruptly leaves me at the bar rail to dance with a pretty girl I feel like an aging gunslinger who never got the chance to tell a young whippersnapper that there's more to life than putting notches on your belt.

8. Most of the men wearing cowboy hats in Great Falls bars are salesmen and shop clerks, not cowboys
9. And the ones in raw silk sports coats are salesmen and shop clerks, not officers from *Miami Vice*
10. Part of Great Falls's problem is that it's too big to be a cow

town; but its biggest problem is that it wants to be a city
in a state that doesn't want cities

The waterbed takes me in its embrace, and puts my whole body,
filled with linguini and some Lewis and Clark whiskey, to sleep.

11. Lewis was right about the restorative effects of a "dry
bed," even if it is filled with water

On a back road from Great Falls to Fort Benton, rounding a corner
on a plateau southeast of the Missouri, I come upon a flat area of
about an acre surrounded by chain-link fence. The site has a square
slab of concrete in the center and a few small radar transmitters
at the corners. (They look like miniature satellite dishes, only there's
no house or dwelling to imply a television.) No sign tells what this
place is, but I recognize it from my briefing at SAC headquarters
in Omaha. It is an underground missile silo.

Beneath the concrete sits a nuclear-tipped ICBM, waiting in dark
silence for a signal to send it into the big sky toward some other
point of earth, coordinates probably marked with numbers and
letters which translate into what? Moscow? Stalingrad? Some equally
impersonal site among wheatfields on the Russian steppes housing
a missile pointing at New York, Washington, or this wheatfield in
Montana? Is there someone half a world away at this moment,
looking at a chain-link fence and radar dishes and wondering the
same things I am, filled with the same questions of wherefore and
why, and with nothing and no one to answer them?

Inside this deep, vertical grave with a horizontal, concrete tomb-
stone is a device that makes the mind circle and reel in logical
contradictions: made by man, unlike anything ever made before,
for the purpose of never being used; hidden from view, but achiev-
ing its purpose by the knowledge of its existence; meant to preserve
life by threatening extinction; a culmination of human history that
allows history to proceed because of its prospect of bringing history
to an end in the space of twenty minutes; a crowning achievement
of mankind whose proper place is this, a desolate, unpeopled plot
of ground.

The only thing poking through the ground today is wheat, which
is destined this summer to wither in a parching drought. When

the farmers look anxiously to the skies, their prayer is to see rain falling from the heavens or at least that they make it through to the next season. As I look up, my prayer takes a different form, learned in the bunker at Omaha: "Not today, Gregor, not today." Let it rain or not rain, but let there be another season.

Farther along, the river breaks begin and the road descends to the Missouri, where it ends abruptly at the rolling water. Across the river, a man leaves his house and walks to a flat platform made of thick planks and attached to a cable stretching over the water to my side. The putter of a small engine starts, and the platform moves slowly toward me.

This is the Carter Ferry, and the man is Mel Lammi, whose job it is to transport cars from one shore to the other whenever they show up. Lammi was in the Navy for twenty-two years, serving on destroyers, cruisers, and two aircraft carriers.

"This is a little smaller," he tells me as we travel across the Missouri. "Don't think I can land any aircraft on here."

Mel's father, Atrin "Speed" Lammi, ran this ferry for twenty-four years, until he died and Mel took over this spring. His father lost the ferry twice when it was overloaded—once with a load of cattle, once with a load of wheat. The cattle survived; the wheat didn't.

The technology making the ferry possible is, like that in a missile silo, hidden from view—in a small shed on the side of the platform instead of a concrete bunker. Lammi opens the door to give me a peek inside: a Farmall tractor hooked to a cable pulley.

"It's really pretty simple, isn't it?" he says as we land.

"Sure is," I answer and drive off.

Fort Benton fits Montana better than Great Falls. Maybe because it's smaller: 1,693 people. Maybe because its boom and bust was a hundred years ago, so it doesn't have the pretensions Great Falls still clings to. Maybe it's because Fort Benton's history is much more colorful than the choking of a waterfall or the erection and dismantling of a refinery smokestack.

Joel Overholser, the retired editor of the local paper, walks me along the town's riverfront downtown area, reeling off tales of Fort Benton's past. Originally named Fort Lewis until the honor was transferred to Senator Thomas Hart Benton, Fort Benton served as the western terminus of Missouri River traffic from 1847 until the railroad ended its days of glory in 1887.

The goods shipped in and out of town by keelboat and then steamboat reflected the changing economics of Montana in the last half of the 1800s. Beaver pelts and wolf skins from the Indian trade gave way to gold in the 1860s, as miners flooded the territory, replacing the mountain men. Supplies for the mining camps were shipped to Fort Benton, where bullwhackers and their teams of oxen took over the final portion of transportation. The figures are staggering: in one year alone, ten thousand miners disembarked at the riverfront; the steamboat *Luella* took two and a half tons of gold dust back downriver in one trip, and its captain was paid $1,200 a month for his efforts; as many as a thousand oxen could be seen on the town's streets, waiting to pull their wagons to the mines. Profits were immense. At one point, miners were willing to trade gold dust for equal weights of tobacco. Some steamboat companies cleared $65,000 a trip.

When the gold rush ended, Indian trade in buffalo robes took over. Traders would take a quart of whiskey and add to it muddy Missouri water, chewing tobacco, cayenne peppers, molasses, and ginger to make a gallon or more of "Indian whiskey." Then they'd follow the Whoop-Up Trail to the Canadian border, where they'd exchange the firewater with the Blackfeet for buffalo robes. One company shipped out 23,256 robes from Fort Benton. Canadian Mounties started showing up to bring the whiskey trade under control; Fort Benton got the contract to supply the Mounties and prospered again.

Fort Benton was the New York of the West. Anything or anyone coming in or out had to pass through. The buffalo disappeared, but sheep and cattle boomed in Montana; Fort Benton prospered. Supplies were needed for the railroad crews; Fort Benton benefited from the business.

Then the railroad itself was completed in 1887, the river traffic evaporated, and Fort Benton was left with the colorful stories Joel Overholser tells today: like the time a drunk cowboy tried to ride a horse to the second floor of the Grand Union Hotel, or when Madame Moustache ran out of her establishment waving two pistols at a steamboat captain to keep him from landing his smallpox-infested vessel, or when an Englishman visited the "bloodiest block in the West" at the riverfront and reported that men played keno with their six-shooters displayed on the table.

Overholser estimates that about fifty men were murdered on the block during a ten-year span, "and that's not counting Indians." The owner of the Occident gambling house came downstairs one morning, looked out the back door and didn't see the usual corpse in the alley, and supposedly said: "Hell, I'm getting out of here. This dump's getting too civilized. I'm going West."

Fort Benton's river traffic is different these days. Bob Singer's Missouri River Outfitters company runs canoe and large-boat expeditions down the 150-mile reach of the river that has been protected by Congress from dams, dikes, and development. For three days and two nights, I join a canoe tour he is outfitting for a group visiting Montana specifically to view historic Lewis and Clark sites.

Singer and I, and Larry Cook, who will assist Singer with the chores of the trip, cart seven canoes, a shallow-draft motorboat, boxes and coolers of food, and other supplies from Fort Benton to Coal Banks Landing, where we meet the tour bus. The tour organizer is Steve Ambrose, a history professor from New Orleans who wrote Eisenhower's biography and usually leads summer tours of the World War II battlefields of Europe, but is equally interested and informed about the Voyage of Discovery. His group of thirteen includes his wife, Moira, their daughter and son-in-law, Stephenie and John Tubbs, and people from scattered parts of the country.

Traveling with the Missouri's current instead of against it, an afternoon's paddling brings our flotilla fifteen miles to our first night's campsite. We are on the western edge of the supernatural White Cliffs area, a stretch of the river bordered by eerie and magnificent white sandstone and dark igneous rock formations that have fascinated travelers and challenged writers' descriptive powers since the day Lewis emerged from them on May 31, 1805, and sat down—at the very spot we are now camped—to try to paint the scenery with words for the first time. While Singer and Clark begin cooking dinner, Ambrose has the rest of us sit facing the river and, sitting behind us, starts reading Lewis's journal aloud:

The hills and river Clifts which we passed today exhibit a most romantic appearance. The bluffs of the river rise to the

hight of from 2 to 300 feet and in most places nearly perpen-
dicular; they are formed of remarkable white sandstone which
is sufficiently soft to give way readily to the impression of
water; two or thre thin horizontal stratas of white freestone,
on which the rains or water make no impression, lie imbeded
in these clifts of soft stone near the upper part of them; . . . The
water in the course of time in decending from those hills and
plains on either side of the river has trickled down the soft
sand clifts and woarn it into a thousand grotesque figures,
which with the help of a little immagination and an oblique
view, at a distance are made to represent eligant ranges of
lofty freestone buildings, having their parapets well stocked
with statuary; collumns of various sculpture both grooved and
plain, are also seen supporting long galleries in front of those
buildings; in other places on a much nearer approach and
with the help of less immagination we see the remains or ruins
of eligant buildings; some collumns standing and almost entire
with their pedestals and capitals; others retaining their pedestals but deprived by time or accident of their capitals, some
lying prostrate an broken othe[r]s in the form of vast pyramids
of connic structure bearing a serees of other pyramids on their
tops becoming less as they ascend and finally terminating in
a sharp point. nitches and alcoves of various forms and sizes
are seen at different hights as we pass. . . . the thin stratas
of hard freestone intermixed with the soft sandstone seems to
have aided the water in forming this curious scenery. As we
passed on it seemed as if those seens of visionary inchantment
would never have and [an] end. . . .

Lewis concludes with the observation that nature seems to have
tried its hand at masonry here, until he remembers that nature did
her work first.

Others, from Prince Maximilian to Father Pierre-Jean DeSmet
to John Neihardt, have attempted to do prosaic justice to these
"seens of visionary inchantment." Even if their spelling was better,
none of them topped Lewis, the poet-explorer. Bob Singer has
brought along copies of Bodmer's paintings of the White Cliffs,
which we pass among ourselves as we sit and listen to Ambrose's
reading. One of the scenes can be seen just downstream from us,
looking exactly as it did when Bodmer painted it in 1833. I find

myself looking up to see nature imitating art and, like Lewis, mistakenly reversing my analogies.

The reading of Lewis's description, the soft sound of the riffling waters of the Missouri, and the silent appearance of the rising moon cast a spell that settles over us with the gentle blanket of twilight. A beaver swims by the campsite, his nose and head barely visible, cutting a wedgelike wake in the river. Prairie falcons are circling the nests they have made in the rock crevices across from us. My small group of Lewis and Clark buffs, our shoulders beginning to stiffen from the exertion of paddling, sits speechless as each one of us savors the gifts nature freely provides only when she has been left alone: a sense of timelessness, a feeling of awe, a moment of communion with those who have been here before and proceeded on.

We are nearly two centuries behind the footsteps of Lewis and Clark on a trail many others have followed. They were the first; at this precise moment, we are the last. Others will follow us. But the magic of this landscape is that all of us see it through the fresh eyes of the first explorers, and each one of us is thinking the same thing. *This* is where they camped, *this* is what they saw, *this* is how they must have felt.

The thing I've never liked much about camping is the logistics involved in finding a campsite and, most of all, the cooking. I enjoy all the other parts—the hiking, the paddling, the satisfaction that comes from being in remote places accessible only to those who are willing to sweat and toil. Left to my own devices, however, my sleeping bag ends up being unrolled when it's too dark to see whether the spot happens to be in the midst of poison ivy or prickly pears; dinner usually is a can of tuna fish or a bare hot dog cooked on a stick. Outfitted wilderness trips, it turns out, were designed with people like me in mind.

During the time the rest of us have been caught in reverie with the scenery, Bob Singer and Larry Cook have prepared dinner. And what a dinner it is: juicy steaks, chicken-fried rice, fresh salad, and French bread—enough for seconds on everything, even the steaks. Life imitates art again, if beer commercials can be considered art. I want to turn to someone and say, "It doesn't get any better than this."

Late into the night, after the others have retreated to their tents,

I sit by the fire with Singer, Cook, Ambrose, and Jim Wimmer, my canoe partner who is on the tour with his two teenage sons. We share the remains of my bottle of B. J. Holladay's Private Keep, appreciating its link to the Lewis and Clark expedition (and the fact that we empty the bottle not all that far from where the expedition finished its supply) as much as its musky flavor.

The full moon, like a lantern in the deep sky, gives off enough light to cast a reflection of the chalky cliffs across from us onto the river surface. A few coyotes can be heard on the bluffs, talking of the day's exploits, as we are, with the moon as the moderator.

Singer, a wiry, weathered man, grew up in Jordan, Montana, but was drawn to Fort Benton by his interest in its history and his love of the river. "Fort Benton always seemed like the most romantic place I'd heard of," he says. He speaks wistfully about the steamboat days on the Upper Missouri, his voice tinged with regret that he was born too late to see one come rounding a bend and get the chance to talk to a pilot about the challenges of the changing river.

Cook, in his mid-thirties, like Singer a former teacher but about twenty years younger, describes himself as a "river rat." He also runs a flat-bottomed barge for tours on the river, but the recent low water conditions have closed him down, so he's helping Singer—in effect, Cook's competitor and mentor—with canoe trips as they both try to survive the drought. "Nobody knows this river, the land around it, its history, like Bob," he tells me. "At low water, like now, you have to know the bottom of the river. Bob's teaching me that."

"It's a tough racket, but it's fun," Singer says. "I never get tired of this river."

"There isn't a better place to work," Cook agrees.

Warmed by the fire and the firewater, we watch the river flow by and listen to the sounds of night. Far to the south, the sky brightens and darkens from the alternating current of heat lightning, noiseless and mesmerizing as an aurora borealis. Even the coyotes have gone quiet.

"Yup," Singer says, extinguishing the fire, "this sure is the life."

Early the next morning, John Tubbs and I climb the bluffs across the river to reach the Needle's Eye, a large sandstone arch two hundred feet above the Missouri. Curly, a golden retriever that John and Stephenie have brought along—the modern equivalent of Lewis's Newfoundland dog—accompanies us.

John's father, Bob Tubbs, until recently operated tour boats in the Gates of the Rockies part of the Missouri, just north of Helena. During one summer, while John was working for his father, he met Stephenie Ambrose, who was accompanying her father on one of the family trips along the explorers' route. A few years later the two children of Lewis and Clark buffs were married on the decks of the Tubbs excursion boat, the *Sacajawea*. During the ceremony, Steve Ambrose read the portion of Lewis's journal that described the Gates of the Rockies and gave the region its name. To the many far-reaching consequences of the Lewis and Clark expedition, add one more: bringing John and Stephenie together.

A half hour's climb up soft sandstone crevices and among ancient juniper trees, much of it spent pulling, lifting, pushing, and coaxing Curly, brings us to the Needle's Eye, where I proclaim Curly the first dog to reach this spot. *Well . . .* The first retriever.

A computer dating service couldn't have picked a better canoe partner for me than Jim Wimmer. Broad-shouldered and easygoing—two important traits to look for if you're going to spend three days in a canoe with someone—Wimmer shares many of my interests. We both enjoy politics (Wimmer was once a chief assistant to a governor of Wisconsin, as I was to a New Hampshire governor), sports, history (he tells me about famous battles from the Zulu wars to Gallipoli; I tell him about famous people unfortunate enough to be buried along the Missouri), cotton khaki shirts, and John Ford movies. Our only disagreement of substance is about the relative merits of bourbon (my favorite) and Scotch (his). Conversation flows as easily as the Missouri current carrying us through fantastic scenery on a clear, hot day.

To combat the heat, we institute a schedule of pulling over every half hour and taking a short dip in the cool river. We invent the concept of a "pleasurometer" to measure various experiences, and decide that what we're doing is a nine on a scale of ten, missing only a case of iced beer in the gunwales of the canoe and two expensive cigars to push it to the top.

Wimmer's sons, Jonathan and Chris, paddle up next to our

canoe. Chris smiles at his father and says, "By Godfrey, but this is fun!" (Wimmer has an enthusiasm for Teddy Roosevelt that he has instilled in the boys.)

At midday, we stop for lunch. Then Steve Ambrose, the three Wimmers, John Tubbs, and I take a strenuous one-hour hike to the Hole-in-the-Wall, an opening at the tip of a high bluff jutting out over the river. Curly suffers through the heat to tag along, becoming the first retriever ever to have visited the Hole-in-the-Wall *and* Needle's Eye in the same day. We are intent on making history as well as following it.

Back in the canoes, Ambrose tells me the story behind his interest in Lewis and Clark. "It was 1975," he says. "I was given a number of books to read, including one about Lewis and Clark. I'm ashamed to admit it, but here I was, a Ph.D. from one of the best American history departments in the nation, and I didn't know a thing about them. Starting at paragraph one, sentence one, I got hooked."

"Hooked" doesn't quite describe his condition. This is his sixth trip through the White Cliffs; he has retraced the entire expedition trail three times. He has traveled the Lolo Trail in the Bitterroots of Idaho by truck and by backpack, with groups and with just his wife. Hooked? He decided the best place to celebrate the nation's bicentennial on the Fourth of July 1976 was at Lemhi Pass, where Lewis became the first American to cross the Continental Divide. Hooked? He once slept in a truck next to Lewis's grave in Tennessee. When a policeman stopped to move him along, Ambrose said, "Officer, you've got to understand; I'm in love with this man." The cop let him stay. And, of course, he must be one of the few men alive to have read from the Lewis and Clark journals at a daughter's wedding. No, "hooked" is too mild a word. A fish that's been hooked doesn't keep coming back for more bait.

The Ambroses paddle off. Moira turns to me from the bow of their vessel to add a postscript to the story:

"If I hear him say 'scenes of visionary enchantment' one more time, I may tip the canoe over."

We float past formations with names like Citadel Rock, the Cathedral, the Seven Sisters, and Steamboat Rock; past groupings that look like sandstone calliopes, chess figures, guards on a castle's battlements, cobra heads, mosques, anything else you can imagine; past walls of dark, reddish lava rock that descend the hills to the river shore, disappear under the water and emerge on the other side to climb again, walls that nature made as straight—and that seem as startlingly out of place in this barren wilderness—as the stone walls built by colonial settlers that can still be found deep in the forests of New England. We see ospreys, owls, Canada geese, a solitary eagle soaring in one canyon, pelicans, blue herons, and a few mule deer. Only the buffalo and the feared grizzly are missing.

Twenty-two miles from where we started this morning, we pull in for our second night. This spot is a rare one in the history of the Lewis and Clark expedition, because it is one of the few campsites used on both the westward and eastward journeys. Lewis and some of the men camped here on the return trip, moving hurriedly after a near-disastrous fight with some Blackfoot Indians near the upper Marias River in which two of the Indians were killed.

The night the explorers camped here on their way west was also the end of an adventurous day for the Corps of Discovery, and as Lewis sat down on this spot on May 29, 1805, he had much to put in his journal. A buffalo bull had careened into the previous night's camp, nearly trampling the heads of some of the sleeping men; Lewis credits his dog with alerting the camp and chasing the beast away. The mouth of a "handsome" river had been passed, and Clark named it the Judith River in honor of Miss Julia (Judy) Hancock of Virginia, who in the years following the expedition would become Mrs. William Clark.

Just before reaching this campsite, the explorers had encountered a grisly scene: an Indian "buffalo jump." In order to "distroy vast herds of buffaloe at a stroke," Lewis writes, the Indians would sneak up on a herd and stampede them over the precipice of a river bluff. To decoy the frightened animals to the cliff, one Indian, disguised in a buffalo robe, would run in front of the herd like the lead bull, and then try to jump into a safe crevice while tons of animals crashed to their death hundreds of feet below. In one of his greatest understatements, Lewis notes that "the part of the decoy I am informed is extreamly dangerous." At the bottom of the jump, the expedition saw "the fragments of at least a hundred carcases they created a most horrid stench." Wolves were feeding on the remains; Clark speared one with his espontoon. A small river near the site of this carnage was named Slaughter River (it now has the less compelling name of Arrow River). The men were

rewarded for the day's tough pull against the river's current with
a ration of liquor, which made them "all very merry."

As if they had been listening and decided to perform a modern
reenactment of the journals as soon as the reading is completed,
four black Angus cattle—Wimmer's sons have been calling cows
"twentieth-century bison" during the day—amble into our camp.
Curly responds on cue to chase them until they're a quarter mile
away.

Dinner tonight, a mile upstream from Slaughter River, is buffalo
roast, cole slaw, green beans, mashed potatoes and gravy, and
French bread. Bob Singer tells some more river stories. Jim Wimmer opens his bottle of Scotch, which makes us all very merry.
We all go to bed early, tired but satisfied.

This has been a delicious day, the kind whose taste lingers long
after it ends, whose memory even months later activates all your
senses. Good food, good conversation, spectacular scenery, and
vivid experiences. The hot sun to warm your back, a cool river to
escape into, and the luxury to enjoy them both. Simple pleasures.
Trails to explore, mountains to climb, vistas to view, and good
companions to share them with you. A day, like the surroundings,
that will remain frozen in time.

The last day on the river is an easy ten-mile run to the Judith
Landing, where the tour bus picks up Ambrose's group and where
Singer's truck and canoe trailer are waiting. Our expedition is
ending long before any of us wishes it to.

"I've got one last suggestion," Wimmer tells me after lunch just
above the landing.

"What's that?"

"Let's swim our canoe to the landing. There's cold beer and
some cigars in the bus when we get there."

"My pleasurometer will be broken forever."

The drive from Great Falls to Helena is eighty-nine miles of interstate, a violation of the Road Rules justified by the fact that it's
the only practicable route and mitigated by the dramatic change
in scenery. Goodbye plains, hello mountains. With the Big Belt
range on the east and the Rockies on the west, the river and the
interstate twine and cross each other like vines climbing a trellis
and using one another for added strength. Glistening rock peaks

replace eroded bluffs, ponderosa pines replace cottonwoods, and the Missouri itself is a new river, fresher, clearer, faster.

Just beyond a deer-crossing sign, the carcass of a dead mule deer lies on the interstate shoulder. It certainly drives the point home, and makes me more alert to my duties as pilot of the *Discovery*. Somebody else could have used Deputy Sheriff Ron Rowton's driving tips last night.

At the Gates of the Rockies, I stop to meet Bob Tubbs for a quick tour. He has sold his excursion-boat business and retired, so he takes me out in a small power boat. Holter Dam has raised the river's water level twenty feet, but the towering limestone canyon walls still look as magnificent as they did when Lewis described them as "the most remarkable clifts that we have yet seen."

Tubbs shows me where his son, John, and Stephenie Ambrose were married. A shaggy, white Rocky Moutain goat looks down on the site from a perch on the cliff face; not far away a small herd of bighorn sheep graze on the riverbank. Both species have been reintroduced to the area in the last twenty-five years. Like the osprey and bald eagles that Tubbs and I see in an hour's tour, the sheep and goats are surviving thanks to the successful efforts to protect most of the Gates from development. The choice boiled down to second homes on the waterfront for humans vs. permanent homes for rare animals.

"It was a real struggle for a number of years," he says, involving state and federal agencies and conservation-minded landowners and individuals like Tubbs. "The Gates are protected now from the entrance up fifteen miles on both sides, otherwise the wildlife would probably disappear."

One of the ninety-passenger excursion boats, the *Perogue,* glides past us. The new owner-guide waves to Tubbs.

"This is where I always quoted the journals," he says, and goes on to describe Lewis's lines by memory, his ice-blue eyes sparkling when he reaches the conclusion: "From the singular appearance of this place I called it the *gates of the rocky mountains*."

Over the span of twenty-five years Tubbs has taken this trip thousands of times, he says, some summers bringing up to thirty thousand people with him to give them a "little taste of one of the greatest journeys anyone ever took, as far as I'm concerned." With the exception of a higher water mark along the canyon walls, the scene is "pretty much the same as when they saw it," he says. "I never get tired of it. It should remain like this forever for people to enjoy."

A bald eagle, its head as snowy white as Tubbs's, its eyes as clear and piercing, lands on a limb of a pine tree and watches us turn back downriver. We pass a pictograph drawn on a canyon wall thousands of years ago, a mark of man telling a story long forgotten except to say that someone was here who wished his presence remembered, just as Clark often carved his name and the date into large trees and rocks along the expedition's route. In the ageless story of man struggling to change and subdue nature and leave his mark on the land, and in the accompanying struggle between men over whose mark will be left, Bob Tubbs's struggle has been to preserve one small spot of earth from too much human touching.

These days, sometimes a man's mark on the land is found by the relative absence of the marks of man.

15

Somewhere
Between
Boom and Bust

this evening we entered much the most remarkable clifts that we have yet seen. . . . the tow[er]ing and projecting rocks in many places seem ready to tumble on us. the river appears to have forced it's way through this immence body of solid rock for the distance of 5¾ Miles and where it makes it's exit below has th[r]own on either side vast collumns of rocks mountains high . . . from the singular appearance of this place I called it the gates of the rocky mountains.

From Meriwether Lewis's journal
Gates of the Mountains
July 19, 1805

Helena, Montana (population 23,938), sits a good ten miles from the river, in the foothills of the Elkhorn Mountains and at the southern end of a huge bowl-like basin. Unlike Great Falls, it was founded by accident instead of by plan, and its history is linked to the mountains instead of the Missouri.

Four unsuccessful prospectors were returning to Georgia from the mining camps of Idaho in 1864 when they decided to take one last stab at fortune in the Prickly Pear Valley. The gold they found in "Last Chance Gulch" touched off a rush of miners that turned the gulch into a wild mining camp, which in turn became the town of Helena, which in 1894 became the capital of Montana. (There are two stories on the pronunciation of HELL'-a-na: that it was named for Helen of Troy, or that the prospectors thought the accent should be on the "hell.")

In his history of the state, *Montana: An Uncommon Land,* K. Ross Toole makes the argument that Montana developed as a "colonial economy" whose major industries—furs, silver, copper, gold, cattle, and lumber (and now oil and coal)—have all been extractive. The immense amounts of capital for these empires, by necessity, had to come from the East and, he writes, "as Eastern capital flowed westward, control and the bulk of the wealth flowed eastward. . . . The economic picture has often been one of exploitation, overexpansion, boom, and bust."

While gold and then silver were important enough to be the two minerals mentioned in the state's motto, *Oro y Plata,* copper soon became king. It was the copper mines and copper smelters that created the jobs that at their peak employed three out of five working Montanans, copper that created the smelters' demand for wood and prompted the unrestrained cutting of the forests, copper that created the need for the railroads, copper that left an open pit in Butte as big as the town itself and that poisoned the plant life of Anaconda with arsenic dust from the world's largest smelter, copper that owned all of Montana's major newspapers into recent times. It was a feud between two of the copper kings that led to $1.3 million being spent in the 1894 referendum (more than twice the amount spent in the 1984 gubernatorial election) over whether the state capital would be in Anaconda or Helena.

Copper, not gold or silver, covers the dome of the state capitol building, even though the copper boom, big as it was, has gone bust. Coal and oil are the latest booms. No one has yet suggested using them to gild the dome.

"There is little or nothing moderate about the story of Montana," Toole writes in his history. "It has ricocheted violently down the corridor of possibilities. What is good in reasonable measure is often bad in full measure, and Montana has been a place of full measure." The beaver were trapped until they nearly disappeared; the buffalo were hunted until they were on the brink of extinction; mines were dug until the claims played out; the open ranges spawned cattle empires that prospered until the grass was gone and the brutal winter of 1886–87 decimated the herds; the early home-steaders tried to make the thin and arid soil yield what it was not suited to produce, until eleven thousand farm failures in the early 1900s left some communities vacant.

The big land inspired big dreams, dreams predicated on a notion of limitless resources that stampeded blindly ahead until they reached the line on the far horizon that turned out to be the limit of those resources. And then, like a herd of buffalo, the big dreams crossed over that line, plunged over the cliff, and piled up like dashed carcasses. "Montana's growth," Toole writes, "in one sense has been a series of traumas."

The land is still just as big, but there is a sense of limits these days in Helena, where the government—the state government, the federal agencies, and the courts—has become the arbiter of con-flicting dreams. Demand (the dreams) exceeds supply (the re-sources), and government struggles to bring the two into balance.

Oil deposits are discovered in the "overthrust" region along the eastern face of the Rockies, but unrestrained development would endanger the pristine wilderness areas that are one of the few remaining habitats of the dwindling grizzly-bear population. Ranchers and timber cutters seek to use the federal lands that others want to see protected. Miners seek to dig pits and erect smokestacks that others say pollute the ground and the air. Tourists wish to hike, camp, and hunt in places ranchers wish to ranch, lumbermen wish to lumber, developers wish to develop, and preservationists wish to preserve.

Each has been guaranteed the unalienable right to pursue his own happiness, to follow his own dream, but with the once limitless frontier closed these individual pursuits keep colliding with each other. And so the government that made the guarantee becomes a manufacturer inundated with consumer complaints about the warranty on their dreams. Montana's story is America's story, compressed in time and space.

Water being one of the most vital resources of the West, the Missouri River itself, the great western river, is at the center of many competing dreams and the search for balance.

Some of the conflicts reach across state boundaries. The main stem of the Missouri is 2,315 miles long, and the vast basin it and its tributaries drain covers one sixth of the land mass of the lower forty-eight states. As it travels from the mountains, across the High Plains, and into the heart of the nation on its way to St. Louis, the Missouri represents different things to the different regions. States on the lower end, where rainfall is plentiful, want enough water for commercial navigation but not so much as to flood the river cities and the rich farmland. Their big cities and factories want water for municipal and industrial uses. The semiarid upstream states, where rainfall is scarce, want water for irrigation and hydropower. Large numbers of people want to fish and enjoy the water—but some want to catch trout and raft on fast-flowing waters, others want to catch big pike and sail or water ski on lake waters behind the dams. The Indian tribes want their flooded lands back, or at least compensation for their loss. South Dakota wanted to make a killing by diverting water in its reservoirs all the way to the coal fields of Wyoming, where it would be used as a coal slurry stretching to Arkansas and Louisiana; downstream states took the issue to court.

Even in normal years, many of these demands are mutually exclusive. In the drought of the summer I am in Montana, almost all of them are. Because of the lack of rain, the ranchers need even more water for irrigation from reservoirs and streams that have less water to give. The Montana Power Company is concerned about having enough water for its turbines. The Montana tourist industry and the state's fish managers are worried that the ranchers and the power company are not leaving enough free-flowing water in the streambeds for the trout to survive and the rafts to float.

The papers are filled with stories of groups clamoring for their share, while the dry sky shines big and blue and indifferent to it all.

The story of Lowell Hildreth's fence across the Beaverhead River, as it's told by Hildreth, the rancher who put up the fence, and by Mark O'Keefe, who helped have it taken down, is the story of conflicting demands on the water, of different versions of the pursuit of happiness and the American dream.

The facts are these: in the years following completion of the Clark Canyon Dam on the Beaverhead, one of the headwater tributaries of the Missouri in southwestern Montana, recreational use of the small river began increasing. The regulated flows from the dam provided better conditions for both trout and rafts. Hildreth raises about a thousand cattle on the 6,000 deeded acres he owns (and 14,000 acres he leases from the federal government) downstream from the dam; the Beaverhead, a small but swift stream at this point, cuts through his property, and his deed includes ownership of the streambed. In the fall of 1980, he put a fence across the water—he says to keep his cattle from getting into a hayfield, although it was equally effective against rafters—and the Montana Coalition for Stream Access took him to court, arguing that state law gives the public the right for recreational use of the river. Hildreth's fence, the coalition argued, infringed on that right. Hildreth argued that the Beaverhead is not a navigable river, and to buttress his point used excerpts from the Lewis and Clark journals in which the men complain about the extreme difficulty of pulling their canoes upstream.

The courts, in an interpretation broadening the definition of "navigable" rivers, ruled for the coalition, and Hildreth had to remove his fence. The legislature then enacted a complicated law to put the ruling into wider practice.

I meet Mark O'Keefe, a wilderness outfitter and environmental activist and member of the coalition, in Helena. In the world of environmentalists, O'Keefe, a gregarious and energetic man, would not be counted among the radicals. He hunts and fishes, and his business, located primarily in Glacier National Park, is based on enjoying nature by being in it and using it. He is a believer in the public management of resources and is now involved in a project trying to bring Upper Missouri River states together for a coordinated water policy.

"This is a new era for the Missouri," he says, "an era of accommodation. The days of doing whatever we want—building dams, appropriating water, diverting streams—and thinking of the consequences later are over. We don't have that luxury anymore."

Lowell Hildreth, whom I visit at his ranch south of Dillon, sees it in different terms. While he is philosophical about losing his fence, it nettles him that the court case was decided without a jury and that the ruling did not consider the public use designation a land-taking that would require compensation to the landowner.

"It's something I didn't believe could ever happen, that they could come on your land and take it without at least a jury," he says. "These are things you think are yours because that's the American way—that's what distinguishes us from Russia, is the ownership of private property—and then they come in and say 'Well, you have to let people *play* on it.' "

Hildreth has experience with the concept of eminent domain and public land-taking. Interstate 15 is being widened to include a good portion of his front yard. But he differentiates that from the stream issue.

"This isn't a matter like when a road goes through your place, and you tried to stop somebody from reachin' his destination, or stop him from reachin' his land. This isn't that; this is just for people who want to play. To me that's a lot different than the concept of public necessity for a public way. There are some legitimate reasons. This isn't one."

Hildreth is a big, strong man, with an aura of quiet friendliness. He takes me on a tour of his ranch, past the site of the famous fence, up to a point of land for a view of the dam, the Beaverhead, and the interstate construction.

"Considerable changes," he says. "Maybe they're what you call progress. Overall for the nation they might be considered good, but as far as this little valley . . ." He shakes his head.

When I get back to Helena I tell O'Keefe that if he and Hildreth met each other on a hunting or fishing trip, instead of in a courtroom, they'd probably be best buddies.

Hap's Bar sits across the street from the Burlington Northern freight yards on the northeast side of town. I go there with Jim Robbins, a freelance writer who has become my unofficial guide to the area, because I tell him I'd like to meet a hobo and learn about riding the rails. Hap's, I figure, is the place to go.

I like it the moment I enter—a long wooden bar, old pictures of trains on the walls, a jukebox, and a pool table. Nothing fancy, just a good beer joint. It reminds me of Kelly's Westport Inn in Kansas City. To my dismay, when we arrive, however, the crowd is changing from businessmen in suits who stopped on their way home from work to young people just starting their night on the town. Neither group is what I'm looking for, but we stay for a beer, even though we're now the oldest people in Hap's by about fifteen years and the jukebox is blaring New Wave music.

"I would have staked my reputation that there'd be some hoboes here," I shout to Robbins over the tumult of music and loud talk. "All my instincts tell me this is the place." I explain my theories about bars being the best place to meet people on the road and about the signs a modern traveler should look for. His smile as he listens is the smile of someone humoring a person who is expounding some crackpot theory of why there might be life on Mars, figuring it's no use arguing, just let this lunatic jabber away.

At that moment, an old man walks in wearing bib overalls with a chain looping to his watch pocket, a bushy white goatee, a crumpled hat, and thick work boots. He takes the spot next to me at the bar and orders a beer. Guessing him to be a rail worker getting off a shift, I ask if he just got in from a train, and he nods.

"Work for the Burlington Northern, do you?" I ask.

He takes a deep pull on his beer and looks at me.

"I'm Fry Pan Jack," he says. "King of the Hoboes. On my way to the Hobo Convention in Britt, Iowa."

Robbins, who has been listening, becomes an immediate convert to the Road Rules.

ROAD RULE 15: Trust your instincts. When they're wrong, you can blame it on bad luck. But when they're right, you can take the credit.

I buy him a second beer, and we try to talk over the noise, but the latest hits by the Eurythmics and the Pretenders are just too loud. We agree to meet the next morning, when he'll give me any advice I want about becoming a hobo.

In a small park next to the train station, across the street from Hap's and its companion cafe, Next to Hap's, I find the King of the Hoboes for my royal appointment. He's getting up from a bench where he's been sleeping. He remembers my questions from last night, and before I can ask one this morning, he has a question for me. Or maybe a comment: "You don't know much about railroads and hoboes, do you?"

ROAD RULE 16: People are more willing to talk to travelers if you feign ignorance about their particular field of interest.

FIRST COROLLARY: Feigning ignorance is easier if you don't know anything about the subject matter.

For more than an hour he talks, slowly, in a wheezing, low voice with cinders in it, pausing to take a chew of tobacco or to spit, talking on and on, answering questions I don't even ask (in an hour, I ask only six), his thoughts stopping and changing direction like a long train unhitching some boxcars at one depot, leaving them empty, and hitching up some new, full ones to take farther down the line.

Fry Pan Jack became a hobo in 1928, he says, beginning a lifetime of travel for the sake of traveling. His pursuit of happiness for more than half a century has been un-American in its rejection of the dream of material gain and progress, yet typically American in its restless, constant movement; its definition of freedom being a light pack of belongings, a freight train's whistle, and a track into the unknown. He was fourteen years old when he hit the road.

"I went out for a loaf of bread for my sister. Freight train came through, I reach up and grab a handful of it. Nine years later she met me in Seattle, tapped me on the shoulder. I says, 'Hi Sis, how are ya?' 'Don't Hi me, I want my damn loaf of bread.' She ain't got it to this day either. Never did get that loaf for her, nope.

"But I had a good life. Those days you could get off in any town, go to work for a farmer, go to loadin' trucks by hand. You could get a spot job anywhere. You'd work a while 'n' go a while.

"In the old times, I broke in under Three Day Whitey as a young kid. He told me to keep clean, go to a house and ask for some work to do, somethin' to eat, which paid off. We slept on the tracks down there, what you call jungles. General rule, we'd try to find a little place got a crick, runnin' water, build us a nice little camp which is cleaner'n most homes. Drive nails in a tree, we'd hang our fryin' pans on the trees, stretch a wire for a clothesline across, and build our own little fireplace there and everything was kept clean. You wash your supper, you put it away, and everybody shared.

"You went uptown and one guy goes to a butcher shop, another one goes to a grocery store over there—we'd sweep up the store, break down his boxes and stuff. End of the day, he'd say, 'How many?' We'd always tell him five—that's six with you—and you get enough groceries for six guys. It was his way of helping the old tramp on the road, which was good."

He pauses to take a wad of tobacco and put it in his mouth, one boxcar of the past emptied, a boxcar of the present is hitched, and he chugs and spits along.

"Today, we have a different setup altogether. In '48 it went out, after the Second World War. They got to stealin' among themselves. They got food stamps, they're on welfare, most of 'em, and they won't share with a guy. It's a shame.

"And you look at your trains that you see today. How much stuff they got to ride on today? It's all this piggyback that you see . . ." and he keeps on rolling, crossing the present and returning to the past, telling it all in his fashion, the stories speeding up on the straightaways and slowing down on difficult grades.

His real name is John Fisk, and he's gone by Cucumber Kid, Yogi the Bear, and Run Shorty Run, changing names with the seasons, until his fellow hoboes made him a Grand Duke fourteen years ago, and he needed a steady name to go with his exalted status. Steam Train Maury named him Fry Pan Jack for the fourteen-inch frying pan he carried carefully wrapped in a paper sack to keep its black grease from soiling the rest of his grip.

Being a Grand Duke is a greater honor than being Hobo King, he says, because the Dukes are chosen only by fellow, card-carrying hoboes. The Hobo King and Hobo Queen are selected by the votes of nonhobo tourists at the annual convention in Britt, Iowa. He's been King for four years and is returning to Britt to turn in his title. The demands on his time for royal appearances at train-buff meetings and such are wearing him down, and it's time someone else took over the duties. He'll be content to be just a Duke again.

He talks about riding the rods: putting a board, called a "ticket," between the metal rods underneath a train car and lying on it until the next stop. Like many of the changes he bemoans in hobo life over the last fifty years, riding the rods is no longer a good idea. The trains go too fast, the steel's not as good, too much debris gets kicked up, "so only an idiot will crawl under a thing like that, which there are plenty of."

Weaving through Fry Pan's hour-long discourse are nuggets of advice for a would-be hobo—in effect, Road Rules he has developed in more than a half century of his particular variety of exploration and travel:

1. Don't ride loaded coal cars. "That coal just blows like sand on the road. You get chewed to pieces."
2. "Stay off'n lumber as much as possible. It'll shift. And iron pipes—they'll shift, cut you right in the middle."
3. Don't ride cars carrying automobiles, because "they get in there, they steal batteries, try to steal tires off'n 'em, and that just makes it hot for the railroad and the railroad bulls."
4. If you're on the outside end of a boxcar—some have a nice little platform to sit or lie down on, he says—be on the front end, not the tail end. If you're on the tail end and fall, the next car will be right on top of you; if you fall from the front end, you at least have the whole length of the boxcar to try to roll out of the way of the wheels.
5. "Lots of kids make a mistake, they ride in the grain cars, they stand up, they fool around, they lean way out the door. He [the engineer] jars that air hose too hard—what they call Big Six, and sometimes he has to, especially at street crossings, some people gonna beat that goddamn train across the track, you've seen 'em do it—he can throw you out or throw you the full length of that car."
6. Don't stand, or sit, in the doorway, "stickin' your head out—stay away from that. People do throw rocks at you. Most oldtimers stay away from that door. They can look out, but they're far enough back. They can see, but they're sittin' down."
7. "Spike" the boxcar door open—Fry Pan carries small, wooden wedges, so it doesn't close and lock him in. And remove the spikes when you get out.
8. "Never build a fire in a boxcar. You don't know what was in that boxcar—could be gas, oil on that floor, and once that's on fire, there's no way to put it out."

9. If you're sleeping in a boxcar, sleep with your side toward the end. If there's a sudden stop or jolt, you'll roll instead of banging your head in a tumble.

10. "Never, gettin' off'n a train, carry your bag 'n' step off. Drop your bag, then when you get to the other side of it, then step down. You see, that way, it don't get tangled up with your feet and you fall over it. But never step off carryin' that thing in your hand." He doesn't like big backpacks; they're too heavy.

11. "I try to tell the kids not to go to back doors of homes now, not to bother home people. Cause they're workin'. There's nobody home. They see you messin' round the house, in the yards, in 'n' out, it ain't long ol' John Law is down there, 'What the hell you think you're doin'? Get the hell out of town.' You can't blame John Law, because they're breakin' into the homes and stealin' stuff these days. So he's got to put the run on you, which is no more than right. Sometimes, you're takin' the goat for someone else. And like these railroad bulls here, the average one of 'em, you speak to the man right, he'll talk to you 'n' tell you to stay out of his yard if it's a little bit hot right now or somethin'. "

Fry Pan Jack is ready to move on now. Unloading boxcars of memories and advice has him itching to hit the rails again. He's got plenty of time to get to Iowa to turn in his kingship, but he hasn't decided which route he'll be taking. Maybe straight east, maybe north first to the High Line near the Canadian border; he's leaning toward the High Line.

He fishes into his pack and gives me a card good for a free bowl of his Mulligan stew at the Hobo Convention, if I can attend. Since I'm heading the other direction, he tells me the secret of his stew: "Everything you got, whatever comes in, goes in the pot. Bring it to a boil good, then kick the fire out'n it and just simmer it, covered up. All that juice cooks into your cabbage, your potatoes, everything. Then you've got a good stew. It has to cook six to seven hours before I let anyone eat it; it's even better the next day."

He gathers up his bag, his stick, his crumpled hat, and we walk to the trainyards.

"Would you do it all again?" I ask.

All the miles he's traveled, all the trains he's ridden since 1928 rumble through his mind in a minute.

"I believe I'd do the same things over," he says. "I've had a good life at it. I'm still ridin'."

For how much longer, I ask.

"Till they bury me. Until a boxcar buries me."

He steps down from the depot platform and heads toward a line of freights being coupled to an engine. My audience with a king is over.

For four days I linger in Helena, using the time to rest myself from my travels, to clean the thick accretion of dust from the *Discovery* and get its engine oil changed, to learn more about the history of Montana, and to try to put my finger on what it is I like so much about its capital city.

At breakfast one morning with Jim Robbins a waitress places my order of huevos rancheros in front of me. Resting atop the casserole dish of eggs, fiery peppers, and cheese is something I've never seen before on huevos rancheros: a large garnish of bean sprouts. When I order coffee, she asks me if I want espresso, cappuccino, or regular coffee. Helena, I tell Robbins, must be the only town in the West where huevos rancheros have been transformed into a health food served with gourmet coffee.

Even though I don't care for sprouts, and remove them from the dish, the notion of the mixture seems to me the key to Helena and its appeal. Small yet cosmopolitan, active but with a laid-back sophistication, Helena seems at peace with itself, so unlike Great Falls and its stifled yearning for big-city status. Many of the people in Helena have come from somewhere else—often to escape the big cities that Great Falls is striving so hard to emulate. They like being close to the mountains, the forests, the rivers, close to the plains and the big sky. They like the fact that Helena is more town than city. But they also want to be able to see the latest foreign films.

Against the backdrop of the big booms and the big busts of Montana, in the wide gap between East and West, and between the disparities separating urban and rural life styles, Helena appears to have achieved a balance. Not that the result is without its contradictions and odd mixtures, readily apparent to an eastern traveler who has just arrived from the Dakotas and the lonely stretches of the High Plains. Posters in the historic Last Chance Gulch (a refreshing change from the number-for-name streets of Great Falls) announce a jazz festival, theater groups, film societies, astrology seminars, and transcendental-meditation lessons. A Catholic priest has gained notoriety by opening a pornography shop; the civic center is a former Shriner mosque with a minaret poking over the skyline. At one restaurant the waiters are predominantly gay; in one bar my waitress tells me she wrote a master's thesis on postrevolutionary fertility among women in Cuba, and in another the folk singer is interrupted by rock music from the "ghetto blaster" at the table of some drunken Indians. The maître d' of another restaurant, dressed in a fashion more fitting for Manhattan than Montana, turns out to be recovering from a wilderness mauling by a grizzly bear.

At the state capitol, where a Charley Russell mural of the Lewis and Clark expedition lines one wall of the House chamber, are two statues. One shows Thomas Francis Meagher, a Civil War brigadier and territorial governor renowned for his impetuous belligerence, sitting astride a charging horse with his saber drawn; the other is of Jeannette Rankin, the first woman ever elected to Congress and the only U.S. Representative to have voted against America's entry into both World War I and World War II.

And of course there is Hap's, the place I like best in a town I like a lot, where the day's clientele ranges from young folks full of boisterous exuberance to old men seeking solace in the bottoms of their beer glasses, from businessmen tied down by debits and credits to hoboes fettered by nothing heavier than a fourteen-inch fry pan.

It's mix and variety that defines Helena. Like the Gates of the Mountains just to the north that Lewis called "singular" and "remarkable," Helena has gone through the traumatic upheavals of Montana's history and emerged singular in its own way, through compromise and balance. Kind of like sprouts on Mexican food.

16

Mountain Men

. . . the country opens suddonly to extensive and bea[u]tifull plains and meadows which appear to be surrounded in every direction with distant and lofty mountains. . . . beleiving this to be an essential point in the geography of this western part of the Continent I determined to remain at all events untill I obtained the necessary data for fixing it's latitude Longitude &c.

From Meriwether Lewis's journal
Three Forks of the Missouri
July 27, 1805

Jack Schilla's small living room in Helena teems with wildlife. Mounted on the walls are six stuffed game fish, including a twenty-one-pound trout, a grouse, a duck, the skins of an otter and a bobcat, and the heads of a shaggy Rocky Mountain goat, a bighorn sheep, an elk, and a bull moose. Schilla and Phil Walsh are sitting in the room, telling me about modern hunting and trapping. The animals crowded around our shoulders seem to be listening intently but politely. I keep expecting one of them—probably the moose, he's the biggest and the most likely spokesman for the others—to cough deferentially and then enter the conversation.

They're an odd couple, Schilla and Walsh. Schilla, thin and wiry and taut with energy, is the businessman of the two, making his living by outfitting elk hunts into the mountains in the fall, trapping in the other seasons just to be outdoors. Walsh, burly and slow-going, tries to scrape an existence from trapping—"If it's worth more than a quarter, I'll trap it," he says—prospecting, and finding odd jobs when those endeavors aren't enough, which is most times.

And yet Schilla, the businessman with mortgage payments to make and a family to support, is the one who talks poetically of his experiences. He says things like, "I love the mountains. I love just lookin' at 'em. It's like lookin' at my heart." Or, "I trap for the experience of being alone in God's country. There's a solace in it."

A typical conversation with the wisecracking Walsh, on the other hand, goes more like this:

"Sometimes I spend five months alone in the mountains."

"Why?"

"Just to walk around."

"What do you do?"

"Walk around."

Schilla suggests that the three of us take his inflatable raft to the Three Forks of the Missouri, where they trap beaver when it's in season, so I can get a better feel for the country—more or less the equivalent of a businessman saying, "Let's go down to the office and I'll show you where I work." I accept gladly. I'd like to see the scenery, and we can probably talk more freely without all these animals eavesdropping.

The Corps of Discovery reached the Three Forks in late July 1805, recognizing it instantly as "an essential point in the geography of this western part of the Continent." Three rivers meet here to form the Missouri, and the explorers named them the Gallatin (for Treasury Secretary Albert Gallatin), the Madison (for James Madison, then secretary of state and later president), and the Jefferson ("in honor of that illustrious personage Thomas Jefferson"). The Gallatin and Madison flow from the mountains to the southeast, in Yellowstone National Park. The Jefferson approaches from the southwest, where it is formed by its own three forks of the Beaverhead, Big Hole, and Ruby rivers. At each juncture, the expedition chose the correct stream to follow in the search for the Shoshonis and horses to take them to the Columbia waters: the Jefferson, then the Beaverhead.

Because of its abundance of otter, beaver, and other game, and because just beyond its broad basin lay the prime buffalo hunting grounds, the Three Forks area was fiercely disputed by the neighboring tribes of Blackfoot, Shoshoni, Flathead, and Hidatsa. Sacagawea, now beginning to enter territory she recognized, showed the men the site where a Hidatsa raiding party had abducted her from the Shoshonis five years earlier.

In the years following the expedition, the Three Forks would also figure prominently in western history. The first in the succession of financial empires established in this new part of the United States was based on trading and trapping furs. Mining, buffalo hunting, cattle and sheep grazing, and, finally, homesteading would create their own booms and rushes, but the first stampede of fortune seekers into this vast and remote section of the country was touched off by the expedition's reports of mountain streams choked and dammed by a big rodent with a shiny pelt. The mountain men came for the beaver, and one of the prime locations was the Three Forks.

Three members of the Corps of Discovery would return here to trap beaver, two also to meet their deaths. John Potts, a private in the expedition, was killed by the Blackfeet here in 1809. A year later George Drouillard (also called Drewyer), the man Lewis and

Clark valued most as a hunter and interpreter, was scalped and decapitated; the state boat access where Schilla and Walsh and I unload our raft on the Jefferson is named in his honor.

John Colter's is the most fantastic story, and it has a happier ending. On the return trip from the Pacific coast in 1806, the Lewis and Clark expedition met a pair of westbound trappers at the Mandan villages. They were looking for someone who could show them the best places to find beaver, so Colter joined them and headed back into the wilderness while the others returned to St. Louis. At the Platte River, on his way back to civilization a year later, he met Drouillard, Potts, and some others who were headed upriver to the Yellowstone to build a trading post with Manuel Lisa; and again Colter decided St. Louis could wait. From the fort at the mouth of the Big Horn, Lisa sent Colter west to find the Blackfeet and encourage them to trade. In his wanderings, he became the first American to cross the Great Divide since the expedition, he saw thermal springs that were later dubbed "Colter's Hell" by doubting listeners, and he was the first white man to enter the mountainous plateaus of what is now Yellowstone National Park. He joined with a party of Crows and Flatheads and with them participated in a Three Forks battle with the Blackfeet, which some historians blame for the fierce hatred the Blackfeet harbored against American trappers for years afterward. The next year, he was with Potts at the Three Forks when they encountered some more Blackfeet. Potts was killed right off, but the Indians had other things in mind for John Colter. He was stripped naked, given a short head start, and then pursued across the prickly pears to be caught and murdered for sport. But Colter outran all of them, except one, whom he managed to kill, and then he kept running, blood streaming from his mouth and nose, until, five miles later, he jumped into the Gallatin and hid among the driftwood. The enraged Indians searched but couldn't find him. That night, he slipped downriver and then started overland—stark naked, but scalp intact—for the two-hundred-mile trip to the fort and safety. Over a week later, he arrived at the fort with more fabulous stories to tell.

Colter finally retired from the life of a mountain man and returned to St. Louis in May 1810, a full six years after he had first left with Lewis and Clark. He settled near Daniel Boone's farm in La Charette, Missouri, and died three years later.

"They're the ones who amaze me, the mountain men, the Colters and the Drewyers," Schilla says as we push off from Drewyer's landing and begin floating toward the Three Forks. "What they had to put up with! I wish I could have entered this country with them for the first time, I really wish I could. That would have been something to see."

Myself, I'm perfectly content to be here 180 years later. The scenery is the only thing I need to worry about taking my breath away.

The Jefferson is swift, clean, cold, and dark blue, speckled with white over the rapids. Rocks and boulders in the shallow riverbed rub against the rubber bottom of the raft like large cats arching their backs against your hand. As we float along, Walsh talks about the scent glands he uses for bait (beavor castor smells good, he says; mink glands stink worse than a skunk); about modern game management ("You've got to manage your fur just like a cattleman manages his herd; you've got to have a breeding stock left for your next season"); about the difference between an elk's bugle call and its grunt (Walsh gives his imitation of the latter, which sounds like a pig snorting); and about being alone for days in the mountains ("You can't believe the silence," he says. "That's what scares people more than anything else").

Prices for pelts and furs have been dropping recently. Foreign countries are still the principal markets, and the strong dollar has weakened exports. Coyote skins that brought $125 a few years ago are now worth $40 to $50; otter has fallen from $90 to $50; and while beaver pelts commanded up to $75 apiece thirty years ago, the average now is $10. On a good day, two men can get twenty pelts, but each pelt takes two to three hours to skin.

"When the prices go up, *everybody* is trapping," Schilla says. "But now it's mostly government trappers financed by stockmen groups for control, kids, and a few diehards like us. No one makes their living solely off trapping."

A pair of mink scamper from the shore into the water; later some otter. Ospreys and blue herons fly overhead, and we get a brief glimpse of a bald eagle. Walsh points out signs of beaver: smooth mud slides along the riverbanks, some willows and small cottonwoods recently gnawed down. "Obviously, as much beaver as we took out of here, we didn't take them all," he says.

In every direction are mountain ranges—the Madisons, Gallatins, Bridgers, Big Belts, and Tobacco Roots—with shining, snow-capped peaks. The roll and sweep of the Plains have been replaced by an equally awesome, even more majestic panorama. Schilla, for whom this spectacle is nothing new, seems to read my thoughts and finally breaks the silent reverie. "You're looking at 90 percent of the paycheck," he says. "It gets in your blood and stays there."

The era of the mountain man was as brief as it was colorful and romanticized. Within about thirty years it was over. The market collapsed when beaver hats went out of fashion in Europe, which was just as well; the beaver had nearly vanished from overtrapping. In that short span of years, people like John Jacob Astor, Manuel Lisa, and Pierre Chouteau had amassed their fortunes; forts had been built, and many abandoned; the vast terrain of the High Plains and mountains, while not settled, had been probed and wandered over by men willing to brave the elements and risk their scalps, and the geographical information they had acquired would aid those who would follow with pickaxes, buffalo guns, cattle herds, and covered wagons. Colter's exploits made him a legendary figure, as would those of Jim Bridger, Kit Carson, Jedediah Smith, Thomas Fitzpatrick, and the other mountain men who entered the wilderness as mortals and emerged as mythic heroes.

Trapping and hunting, like mining or the use of water in the West, are now regulated, the government attempting to keep a balance in nature that otherwise would be tipped precariously far past equilibrium. This is the new reality. Without the regulations, without the restrictions on what a man can do in the mountains, hunters would soon have nothing to hunt, trappers nothing to trap, and would-be mountain men nothing to do except tell tales of a mythic past.

But a myth encountering a new reality is like a surging river that hits an impediment—a manmade dam or just a beaver's structure of mud and twigs. On the surface, the river may appear to have been stopped, tamed, and controlled. Underneath, however, the current is still strong, and it forever seeks new channels to keep moving.

The myth can be diverted into acceptable channels, as it has been in the case of Jack Schilla and Phil Walsh: poetic words and the steadfast adherence to regulations they willingly follow for the privilege of "being alone in God's country."

Or, as in the case of Don and Dan Nichols, the myth can churn and roil in a man's mind, until it breaks out, perverted into a channel of horror.

Donald Boone Nichols always preferred the wilderness to society. Over long periods of time alone in the mountains of Montana and Wyoming, he developed his own "mountain policy," a wilderness code that rejected the rules of society. In the fall of 1983, he and his son, Dan, moved permanently into the wild, roaming throughout the Rockies and living off what game they could kill and wild plants they could find. As their code formed in their minds, it rejected more and more of the laws of the civilization which, from their vantage point on mountain peaks, was literally and figuratively beneath them. They hunted game out of season. Sometimes when game was scarce they poached cattle for meat. They decided they needed a woman for their wilderness home, and that the way to get a bride was to capture one. As far back as 1978, Don had bought a chain for the purpose.

And so, on July 15, 1984, they were ready when twenty-three-year-old Kari Swenson, a world-class biathlete of stunning beauty wearing a T-shirt that read "John Colter Mountain Man Run," jogged around a mountain trail in the Spanish Peaks of Gallatin National Forest and into their grasp. The father and son, one in his fifties and the other just twenty, with long hair and unkempt beards and army fatigues stained with animal blood and soot from their year in the wilderness, grabbed her wrists and dragged her to their campsite, where they chained her to a log. They told her their plan was to keep her chained until she got to know them well enough to remain with them willingly.

The next morning, two young men who were part of a larger search party came upon the camp. In the ensuing confrontation Kari Swenson was shot—mistakenly, according to later testimony—and wounded by young Dan Nichols. Alan Goldstein, one of the rescuers, who was holding a pistol, was killed by a single, well-aimed, deliberate rifle shot from Don Nichols. The Nicholses fled the scene. Swenson was later found by the search party; she recovered. In December 1984, Don and Dan Nichols were finally captured in the mountains, and in the summer of 1985 they are being brought to trial.

Dan Nichols's case has already been tried when I arrive in Virginia City for a few days of the father's trial with Jim Robbins, who is covering it for several eastern publications. Much to the disgust of people like Jack Schilla, the case, which is receiving national attention, is being called the "mountain man" trial.

Virginia City was another Montana boom town. After gold was discovered in Alder Gulch in 1863, it grew to a population of 35,000, but today fewer than two hundred people live there year round. It is a ghost town turned tourist town. One of the favorite tourist stops along Main Street is a small wooden shack where the Virginia City vigilantes once dispensed frontier justice. In the wild days of the gold rush, outlaws were robbing and killing miners and merchants with impunity; even the local sheriff was part of the gang. In the face of this lawlessness, the secret vigilante society was formed. Community leaders banded together, and in the secrecy of the night they would round up one of the road agents, bring him to the shack, stand him on a box, and slip a rope over a crossbeam and around his neck. Just before the box was kicked away, James Williams, the commander of the vigilantes, would intone the words, "Men, do your duty." Arrest, trial, sentence, and punishment were over before dawn.

The process is considerably different these days. Although the trial of Don Nichols is held just across the street from the vigilante shack, in Madison County Courthouse, it is conducted in daylight and in public—there are even television cameras in the court-room—and it is expected to last at least a week. Merely selecting a jury takes one full day.

As the prospective jurors are being publicly interrogated by the lawyers, it becomes clear that Don Nichols's defense attorney is trying to get his client off on three arguments.

The first is the contention that Don Nichols can't get a fair trial in Virginia City. During his son's trial, Don Nichols testified to shooting and killing Alan Goldstein. (Based primarily on the father's admission, the son was acquitted of murder but convicted of kidnapping.) Don Nichols's lawyer is arguing that Madison County residents followed the news reports of the son's trial, and therefore have already made up their mind about the father's guilt. This is the most striking contrast to the vigilante system. In the old days in Virginia City, the justification for a vigilante trial and hanging was that everybody knew the suspect was guilty even if he didn't admit it. A hundred years later, the fact that everyone has already heard the admission is considered possible grounds for a mistrial.

A second argument will be that since Goldstein was pointing a pistol at him, Don Nichols fired in self-defense. The third will be that a person's attitude toward the rules of civilization understandably changes during extended stays in the wilderness.

Nichols's lawyer asks the twenty-seven prospective jurors, divided nearly equally between men and women, a number of questions, a poll of sorts which reveals that differences still exist between the ways people live in different parts of America. Half of them ride horses regularly. A majority have camped in the wilderness for longer than a weekend. All twenty-seven have handled and fired guns; only seven *haven't* used one within the last year. Membership in the National Rifle Association outnumbers regular church attendance five to four. Honesty is the principle most of them would like to pass on to their children.

During the polling, the lawyer asks the jurors follow-up questions, the answers to which will be part of the defense strategy. Wouldn't you agree that your state of mind changes when you've been in the wilderness a long time? he asks one man. He gets agreement. What's the first thing you're taught when you learn about guns? he asks several jurors. Never point it at a person unless you intend to use it, they answer.

These answers and the statistics from the courtroom "poll" prompt a lot of speculation among the reporters during breaks in the trial. Some say the jury is comfortable with firearms and may accept the self-defense argument. Some believe the previous publicity will guarantee a successful appeal for a mistrial. Others think Nichols's life style and strict adherence to his own principles may elicit a tinge of respect from the jurors. Still others argue that people who have themselves been alone in the wilderness may sympathize with a defendant who claims that his years in the mountains changed his view of society's laws. Two days into the trial, a consensus is forming that Don Nichols may be found innocent of the murder he has already, in effect, confessed to have committed.

I can't stay for the entire trial. By the time it is concluding, I am riding a horse with a pack train deep in the Elkhorn Mountains on my way with Jack Schilla to his remote elk-hunting camp. We will be out of contact with civilization for five days.

"Here's a mountain man, not them," Schilla says, touching his chest as we ride. "They're just criminals. When you spend a long

time in the wilderness, you get attuned to laws—nature's laws—
but it also makes you more mellow, not more violent. These guys
and the neo-Nazis with their automatic weapons and camouflage
caps are just outcasts and misfits. Wackos. They were breaking
every law, every rule of hunting—shooting game out of season,
poaching, shooting cattle. Who or what gave them the right to do
that?"

Just getting to the borders of this wilderness has been a time-
consuming and often frustrating logistical exercise, which has given
me a deeper respect for the work that outfitters do and a better
understanding that while life in the mountains can have a refreshing simplicity, the preparations for getting there can be very complicated.

We loaded up Schilla's truck/camper with food, saddles, packs,
fishing gear, and a mountain of other equipment, then drove to
the Deer Lodge area to pick up his six horses. Catching and coaxing
them into the horse trailers was an adventure in itself. Then we
had to recross the MacDonald Pass—where the intense heat and
the large load made Schilla nervous about his truck brakes—only
to have a flat tire back in Helena on our way south to Elkhorn.
We stopped to get me a fishing license and stopped again for some
last-minute groceries, including a bottle of Lewis and Clark bourbon. By the time the horses and hay were unloaded and our base
camp established near Elkhorn, a mining ghost town next to a
small creek, the best part of a day had been chewed up.

The next morning we prepare to take the pack train to Hidden
Lake, a high and isolated body of water in the crater of an extinct
volcano.

Larry Hogan, a young man from Kansas who has just graduated
from an outfitting school in Victor, Montana, is along; Schilla is
trying him out for a possible job during the fall hunting season.
As I try to help him wrap hay bales in tarp and balance them on
the packhorses, Hogan tells me his story. He was born and raised
in southeastern Kansas, where he learned to ride horses and hunt
raccoon, possum, and coyote. But he dreamed of bigger things:
bigger game ("Back home, deer was considered big game; out here,
nobody even bothers talking about them"), bigger mountains, bigger spaces between himself and towns and cities and other people.
He hopes someday to have his own outfitting company, or maybe
a ranch. In pursuit of his dream, Hogan went to outfitting school

to learn the finer points of shoeing horses, handling mules, repairing tack and canvas, wrapping and balancing packs, cooking, taking compass readings, fishing, marksmanship, and handling questions from greenhorns like myself without making them feel completely stupid. From the way he's working this morning, he seems to be well trained, although he admits he almost failed cooking: his flapjacks tasted all right, he says, but they had irregular shapes. Good food, well presented, is an important source of pride among outfitters.

Schilla assigns me Brandy, a bay gelding with short legs and an easy temperament. We get a late start and run into occasional delays in climbing the road through Elkhorn and into the mountains. By noon, Hidden Lake is still nearly three hours away by horseback, and we're running behind time if we're to get there and get back. I seem to be the only one concerned about it.

"The mountains keep you off a rigid schedule," Schilla says as we eat lunch. The road/trail keeps getting steeper, rockier, and smaller. With the rising altitude, the surroundings change. Lodgepole pine gives way to shorter, whitebark pine. Huckleberry, purple lupines, bluebells, yellow and white daisies, delicate, pink elephant heads, and the brasher orange and red Indian paintbrushes provide splashes of color which the sagebrush in the valley must envy. No reason to hurry, they seem to say.

The pace is slow, and for a little while longer the trail is wide enough for Schilla to ride next to me and talk. These horses have the trail memorized from their many trips over it, he says; they're surefooted enough to do it in the dark if you let them. The only thing to worry about is something unusual—a hiker, a deer jumping across the trail, an elk snorting. Then one spooked horse can cause the whole pack train to "blow up"; then it's "rodeo time." I pat Brandy on the neck to reassure him. The horse has already figured out that he knows more about this than I do.

We have passed some gouges in the mountainside from a miner's bulldozer, which prompts a short explanation from Schilla about outfitters, hunters, and environmentalists allying themselves against the corporations that want to drill, dig, and erect power lines in the wilderness. "Greed has always been the biggest enemy of the wilderness," he says.

He talks about life in his hunting camps, of being in the mountains for weeks at a time. It brings out the poetry in him. "I remember some scenes," he says. "There was this one morning. I was leading the pack train as the sun was just coming up. There was a low cloud cover, and our trail was just above it—nothing but clear sky and mountain peaks above, the clouds right under us. It was like we were riding on the clouds. You almost got the feeling that you were a king or a god or something. I didn't have a camera, but that picture's right up here [he taps his head] forever. You don't get rich here. What you see, the way you live, that's the richness."

We pass the site of his fall hunting camp, a small wooded plateau with a corral. The horses stop out of habit until we urge them on toward Hidden Lake. The trail narrows to a dirt path, a mere line along the northern face of the mountain barely wide enough for the horses' feet as they plod single file. For a half-mile stretch, the mountainside drops vertically about four hundred feet from the trail. Not even enough room for flowers to grow between the dust and the drop. The pointed tops of pine trees far below look like skewers waiting for meat. "A lot of people don't like to look down here," Schilla says. "Trust your horse. Enjoy the scenery."

The north and northwest panorama stretches across the Helena basin to the Gates of the Mountains and the Garnet Range nearly forty miles away. We are corkscrewing around Elkhorn Peak, several hundred feet below its 9,381-foot summit.

The trail descends back into the forest, runs across some mountain meadows where we see elk tracks, turns and climbs again, passes some small alpine lakes dimpled by rising trout, and then, after a particularly steep and rocky climb, emerges into a basin. Stony cliffs littered by rock slides form a three-quarter circle around and above us; we are on the quarter side where the top of the mountain erupted who knows how many years ago to expose the crater. Hidden Lake.

Hogan and I unload the hay bales, stash them under some pines, and water the horses in the creek that trickles down from the lake. It's 5:30 P.M. Hogan and I figure we're going to start our return immediately, to avoid night riding in the mountains.

Schilla, however, has something else in mind.

"Isn't this something?" he says. "We may see some goats in those cliffs, or at least hear the rocks when they move. Let's do some fishing."

This is a modern mountain man in every sense. Hidden Lake is a prime trout lake, and he'll be damned if he's going to ride all the way up here and not do some fishing. But because of the drought conditions, open fires have been temporarily banned in national forests; Schilla isn't going to violate the restriction. The only place we can legally have a fire—and therefore fry any fish—is on the cook stove in his truck/camper. That's back at our base camp, four hours' ride from the lake. The mountain man principles require fishing when there are fish to be caught, and eating fish if you catch any. The *modern* mountain man principles require obeying regulations, especially those aimed at preventing the mountains from burning. This means we will fish, ride back to the camper, and have our supper.

Spending the night up here without a fire is not the problem; frying the fish is the issue. Mountain men, even modern mountain men, don't eat sushi.

Schilla gets out the rods and lures, and we follow him to the lake shore, a jumble of rocks and boulders around the clear, blue-green water. He gives me a few tips on casting, then moves around to the far side of the lake. He gets a strike on his first cast.

The secret of casting is in releasing the line at the right moment, he has told me—not too soon, not too late. My initial attempts alternate between a short, direct toss of the spinner straight down into the water at my feet (releasing too late), or a loft, like some space shot, straight above me that lasts thirty seconds and then drops into the water at my feet (releasing too soon). After a half hour, I've got the arm movement, rhythm, and release coordinated to the point where I can toss the lure in an arc sixty feet from the shore. The only sounds are the faint whizz of the line as the cast reels out, the soft plunk of lure against water, the slow whir of reeling it in. Occasionally, the basin echoes with rocks tumbling—goats heard but not seen.

The shadows from the cliffs behind us lengthen across Hidden Lake, and the fish start biting. I shout when I bring in a trout. Then another and another. Hogan and Schilla are equally busy. The excitement takes my mind off the fact that the long shadows mean the sun is getting lower. When we've caught a total of fourteen trout, Schilla calls off the fishing, cleans our catch, and we go back to the horses.

Earlier in the day, Schilla had told me that when Brandy trots
to keep up with the other horses, I should stand in my stirrups to
make things easier on my rear end.

"Get ready to stand in your stirrups," he says when we saddle
up to retrace our trail. "I intend to make time getting back." It's
eight-forty-five. Sunset is an hour away.

Down the trail we go, trotting and cantering in the flat parts,
walking in the steeper parts. In silence we ride, each of us with
his own thoughts. Mine are riveted on the cliff face we have to
cross, those pine skewers, and whether there will be any light at
all when we reach it. The sunset has begun behind the trees directly
in front of us, a broad band of slowly changing colors: oranges,
pinks, reds, purples, gray, and mauve. We slow to a walk as we
begin approaching the cliff face. The silence is punctuated only by
the noises of the horses. Swishing tails, horseshoes scuffling dust
and occasionally clopping against a stone, leather saddles creaking,
snorts and bursts of hard breathing from the front ends of our
mounts, *pffffffts* and plops from the other ends—this is the music
of our ride.

Then we are at the cliff, and the sky opens before and below
us. The sun is below the horizon, but has left a sliver of color on
the horizon, as if some minimalist artist had plucked one of the
Indian paintbrushes and made a few quick strokes of orange, ember
red, and purple along the bottom of a huge, dark slate canvas.
The lights of Helena are already twinkling in the deepening darkness, distant, like a constellation of stars, yet *underneath* us. It
seems as if we are no longer earthbound, but moving though the
sky itself, riding literally into the smoldering remnants of this sunset, suspended in time and space.

When we reach the trees at the far end of the cliff trail, at Schilla's
hunting camp, the color is gone, not even a hint of color or light,
only the remembrance of the color and the moment. This must be
what Schilla meant earlier when he talked about riding over the
clouds one sunrise: feeling like a king or a god, experiencing a
moment of richness that your mind will hold forever.

Of course, there's still a lot of riding ahead of us, and now it's
pitch dark. I can hear the other horses and can see a faint outline
of the white rump of Hogan's horse, the darker outlines of the
trees, a few sparks from hooves now that the trail is all rocks, but
that is all. The descent gets steeper. "Trust your horse," I keep

telling myself, chanting it like a soothing mantra. I hold the reins with one hand and take the saddle horn in a tight clench with the other. Brandy seems unconcerned and plods on.

TRAIL RULE 1: Trust your horse.

We arrive at the truck and base camp shortly before 1 A.M. I help Hogan unsaddle and water and feed the horses, while Schilla starts frying the fish.

Given the time of night and how tired and hungry we all are—we haven't eaten in over twelve hours—Schilla doesn't bother with a fancy outfitter's meal: just some bread, cold beer, and all fourteen trout, rolled in flour and fried in butter. It tastes just as good as any five-course dinner I've had.

We unwind with a burst of talk, as if we hadn't seen each other for some time and have a lot to tell each other about the day we've been through. I tell Schilla about my worries during the night ride, and how his earlier advice helped get me through it. This starts him on more mountain stories: hunters getting lost during an unexpected snowstorm, panicking, and running wildly and getting even more lost; helping search parties for children who wandered off into the woods and never returned; accidents during "blowups" on the trail; a horse foundering in snow so deep Schilla's saddle got hooked on the top of a small tree. Mules are better pack animals than horses, he says, because they don't spook so easily. "You can sense the moment when a horse realizes it might die," he says. "They can die of sheer panic." I'm glad I didn't hear these stories this morning.

I break out the bottle of Lewis and Clark bourbon, we toast the day, and Schilla talks about his dream of finding a ranch near some good hunting grounds, getting more horses, maybe some mules, and moving out of Helena so that in the off season he can walk out the door of his house and trap three days a week.

The talk dwindles as our tired bodies and stiffening muscles assert themselves. We've been up for more than nineteen hours.

Larry Hogan, a quiet young man to begin with, hasn't said much during dinner or afterward. This is his first summer in the West. His two days in the mountains so far can't be what he had imagined. He's had to deal with the logistics and aggravations of an outfitter: the delays and hard work of preparing a camp, the guidance from

Schilla about an outfitter's first duty being to the client (I caught more fish than Larry at Hidden Lake; he had to take time out to unsnarl my line). He's had to face the realization that being free in the wilderness these days can include relaxing with a smoke under the metal roof of a camper instead of the big sky, doing without an outdoor cookfire, or making sure your horses aren't tethered within polluting distance of a clear lake.

I'm wondering how it all squares with the dreams he had in Kansas. Just after we turn out the lights to go to sleep, he speaks his thoughts.

"I was just thinkin'," he says. "That was the purtiest scenery I ever saw."

My thought is that, in addition to seeing the prettiest sunset of my life, I've just witnessed the birth of a new mountain man.

We spend three more days and two more nights in the Elkhorns. We return to Hidden Lake, surviving a "blowup" along the trail that sends an electric current of tension through the animals, and camp there for a night. We catch some more fish, but eat cold cuts and elk sausage and huddle around a battery-powered lantern, swapping stories.

When we ride back down to base camp the last day, as we pass across the cliff face in broad daylight, I can still see that sunset glowing in my mind. One of the pack mules temporarily loses its footing but doesn't panic.

Late that night, in my motel room in Helena, I have the first chance to look at myself in a mirror. I haven't shaved, showered, or changed clothes, for that matter, in five days. I look different, and I feel different.

The radio is on, and the news says the jury in Virginia City deliberated for five hours and then found Don Nichols guilty on all the counts of kidnapping, aggravated assault, and homicide. Kari Swenson, both Nicholses, and the sheriff who finally captured the "mountain men" are all reportedly negotiating the book or movie rights for their life stories.

Don Nichols's defense lawyer is quoted as saying it's too bad Don Nichols wasn't born a hundred years ago, but I'm not sure that's historically accurate. Colter, the first mountain man, spent six straight years in the wilderness, yet he was able to return and adjust to civilization. Somehow, somewhere in the mountains of the Three Forks area, in the pursuit of his dream of being a modern mountain man, Don Nichols had lost his bearings, and unlike Lewis he didn't stop at this "essential point" to regain them.

In an additional sense, Nichols is lucky this isn't a hundred years ago: if he'd abducted a woman and shot a rescuer back then, my guess is that his Virginia City trial would have been a lot shorter, and his punishment more than eighty-five years in prison.

Being in the mountains for a long time can work changes on a person, I've learned, but you're still responsible for who you are underneath. I shave off my stubble and shower off five days' worth of dust and sweat, turn off the radio, and go to bed.

17

Passage

at the distance of 4 miles further the road took us to the most distant fountain of the waters of the Mighty Missouri in surch of which we have spent so many toilsome days and wristless nights. thus far I had accomplished one of those great objects on which my mind has been unalterably fixed for many years, judge then of the pleasure I felt in all[a]ying my thirst with this pure and ice-cold water which issues from the base of a low mountain . . . we proceeded on to the top of the dividing ridge from which I discovered immence ranges of high mountains still to the West of us with their tops partially covered with snow. I now decended the mountain about ³/₄ of a mile which I found much steeper than on the opposite side, to a handsome bold runing Creek of cold Clear water. here I first tasted the water of the great Columbia river.

From Meriwether Lewis's journal
The Continental Divide
August 12, 1805

The far-reaching significance for
America of Lewis and Clark's expedition is difficult to summarize.
Their discoveries were so many and so varied, their journey so
epic in its scope, that entire books have been written on single
aspects of their exploits without exhausting the material in the
mother lode of their journals. The saga of these white men (and a
black slave, an Indian woman, an infant, and a Newfoundland
dog) is unparalleled in the annals of exploration in its multiple
facets of scientific discovery, sociological commentary, wilderness
acumen and competence, bravery, and sheer human drama. As
explorers, military men, diplomats, naturalists, ethnologists, even
herbal healers, they expanded the nation's knowledge just as they
expanded its territorial horizons.

The important symbiosis between the East and the West, each
exerting influence on the other, began in earnest with the expedition. While passing out presents and peace medals to the Indian
tribes they met along their trail, the captains communicated to the
natives that representatives from the new "White Father" would
be following in their footsteps to trade and barter. With few exceptions, as the first harbingers of Manifest Destiny, their arguments and their respectful conduct convinced the Indians that the
United States's intentions were peaceful and potentially beneficial
to both sides. The redheaded Clark would be particularly remembered and highly respected by western tribes, even throughout his
later career as an Indian agent.

Conversely, the explorers brought back to the East news of
animal and plant life never known before to exist. The detailed
information the expedition provided about the terrain, the inhabitants, and the commercial possibilities of the West proved invaluable in the expansion of America's empire. Their descent of the
Columbia to the Pacific coast helped stake the nation's claim for
ownership of the rich Oregon territory in its later dispute with
England.

Equally important—and equally remarkable—was the simple
fact that for the first time a group of Americans had crossed the
continent, survived, and returned. They were "firsts" themselves,

and their reports were filled with more "firsts," "biggests," "fiercests," "longests," and other superlatives. In a nation that celebrates superlatives, the captains became national heroes and their stories further fired the imaginations of a restless people.

Understandably, then, it is often forgotten that the expedition failed in its principal objective: to find the Northwest Passage, the "direct & practicable water communication across this continent for the purposes of commerce."

The notion of a Northwest Passage—a series of straits, or a river, or a series of rivers across the continent that would provide an easy trade route to the Orient—was nearly as old as the discovery of America itself. British exploration of Canada, including Alexander Mackenzie's historic transcontinental journey in 1793, had failed to find it. The Spanish had not located it in the Southwest. Now the Americans set out to discover the Passage, and claim it and all the wealth that would accrue to the nation controlling it.

The Missouri and the Columbia were considered the two keys to the puzzle. The Missouri River had been explored as far as the Mandan villages, where the Indians said it flowed from the western mountains. The mouth of the Columbia River had been discovered by ships on the Pacific, where it entered the ocean almost within sight of a large mountain range, possibly, it was thought, the same mountains the North Dakota Indians described. All that remained was for someone to trace the Missouri to its source, and then take the Columbia to the sea.

Perhaps the Missouri cut through a gap in the western mountains—that was the experience of the Blue Ridge range. At worst, if no such gap existed, a one-day portage of about twenty miles over the mountain divide would no doubt bring you from the Missouri's waters to the Columbia's—that was the experience of the Alleghenies. Whichever was the case, the Northwest Passage was sure to exist, because for the three hundred years leading up to the Lewis and Clark expedition so many people *wanted* it to exist. Dreams of the fortunes to be made from a better trade route created the desire for a Passage. And desire created the myth of the Passage's existence.

With the advantage of having never actually seen the Rockies, eastern cartographers had drawn their maps showing a single mountain range about a hundred miles from the Pacific and running parallel to the coast. It looked good on paper, and conformed to the myth of an easy Passage. What Lewis and Clark were about to discover, however, as they proceeded up the Jefferson River from the Three Forks, is that the Rocky Mountains are not a neatly ordered single range of eastern-sized mountains but a broad and unruly series of immense ranges, each one of which would dwarf those east of the Mississippi. Nor are they within a hundred miles of the coast. That range is the Cascades, west of the Rockies and high and daunting in their own right. There is no Northwest Passage and never was.

Lewis and Clark, of course, knew none of this while they were still on the Jefferson River. Nevertheless, some doubts about the accuracy of information from the Hidatsa Indians the previous winter and the eastern conception of western geography were forming in their minds.

The Missouri was supposed to be a navigable river that penetrated the mountains. But the arduous portage of the Great Falls had already taken longer than the theoretical portage between the Missouri and Columbia. And following the river had brought them southeast instead of west for a great distance. They stopped to take astronomical observations at the Three Forks. It was three hundred miles farther east than they had conjectured at Fort Mandan— they were three hundred miles farther from the coast than they had expected to be at this point. From the Three Forks they turned west along the Jefferson, then southwest along the Beaverhead. At last they were moving again toward the mountains and their goal, but the travel was getting harder. These rivers were smaller, shallower, and swifter, or alternately clogged with beaver dams. The men were complaining about the effort of dragging the canoes up the current. Mosquitoes were even more troublesome.

The captains became alarmed at their situation. Time was running out. Earlier hopes of reaching the coast and returning to the Mandan villages by winter had long since been abandoned. Now, they might have trouble crossing the mountains and reaching the ocean before winter's onset. Worse, they had yet to meet any Shoshonis, whose horses they would need for the mountain portage. There had been signs of Indians, but no Indians themselves.

On August 8, 1805, with the expedition a few miles south of present-day Twin Bridges, Montana, Sacagawea pointed up the river to a large rock bluff she recognized from her youth and assured the men that they had entered the land of her people. It was welcome news. The same day, Lewis decided to take three men and set out ahead of the main party to search for the Shoshonis, even if it meant passing over the mountains and took a month. For without the Indians there would be no horses, and without horses, Lewis feared for the fate of the entire expedition.

Leaving Clark and the others behind with the slower task of pulling the heavy canoes, Lewis and his three men (Drouillard, John Shields, and Hugh McNeal) followed an Indian trail to a fork in the Beaverhead, where they headed toward the mountains along the western branch, Horse Prairie Creek.

The suspicion that an easy water route might not exist was growing in Lewis's thoughts, but his hopes had not yet expired. In the journal entry of August 10, 1805, he concedes that "it would be vain to attempt the navigation . . . any further," but later counterbalances this with comments praising the navigability of the Missouri and Jefferson in the mountainous country. "[I]f the Columbia furnishes us such another example, a communication across the continent by water will be practicable and safe," he writes, admitting at the same time that this may be wishful thinking.

The next day, the eleventh, Lewis and his men saw an Indian on horseback two miles ahead, the first they had seen since they left the Mandan villages four months earlier. Despite their attempts to coax the horsemen to allow them to approach and parley, he rode away and disappeared. Profoundly disappointed, and drenched by a heavy rain and hail shower, Lewis continued ascending the creek valley until nightfall.

The twelfth of August was a momentous day. A major Indian trail was found and followed along Trail Creek, and then west into the mountains. A few miles below Lemhi Pass, McNeal "exultingly stood with a foot on each side of this little rivulet and thanked his god that he had lived to bestride the mighty & heretofore deemed endless Missouri." At a spring near the summit, Lewis himself exulted as he kneeled and drank from a spring he considered the source of the Missouri.

From the spring to the pass itself is a short distance, an easy, uphill walk for legs already hardened to exercise and propelled by the energy of great expectation. With each step, Lewis and his men knew, they were approaching history. No Americans had ever crossed the Continental Divide. None had ever found the Passage. Just over the rise would be the watershed of the Columbia River, where the waters flow west. Maybe they would see the river itself, or a broad plain stretching toward the sea. Maybe they would also see the Shoshoni Indians and herds of much-needed horses.

Lemhi Pass is a shallow saddle of a ridge running north and south, affording vistas to the east and west. When Lewis finally reached it, he probably didn't bother looking back east. He had already covered it by foot. The view out west was what he was after. He had dreamed of this historic moment and had crossed the vastness of the newly acquired Louisiana Territory to achieve it.

Cresting the rise, he expected to see comfirmation of the Passage. Instead, he saw . . . more mountains. No sweeping plain, no mighty river, not even a descending tier of foothills, but mountains: "immence ranges of high mountains still to the West of us with tops partially covered with snow." Here, as geographer and author John Logan Allen describes it, "the distinction between the geography of hope and the geography of reality" was finally made.

Myths, if they die at all, die slowly, stubbornly, clinging tenaciously to life even in the face of incontrovertible facts. The myth of the Northwest Passage—the principal myth of North American geography for hundreds of years—was simply too powerful to be killed outright, even by the intimidating vista confronting Lewis at Lemhi Pass.

This was not the Passage Lewis had been sent to find, that much seemed clear. But a Passage might still exist, and maybe he would yet discover it. Myths die hard. This one had just suffered a near fatal blow, but it had some life left in it.

Lewis proceeded on, descending the western slope of the pass and thereby stepping from U.S. territory into land that was not only unknown, but unowned by any nation. He drank from a mountain stream whose waters were bound eventually for the Pacific—another historic sip on this historic day. His journal entry, however, notes this matter-of-factly, in stark contrast to his soaring emotions at the fountain only a short distance away but on the other side of the Divide that separated myth from reality.

Lewis covered twenty miles this day. His pace, once quickened by hope and expectation, did not slacken on the west side of the pass. Determination and urgency now moved his feet. His mind had shifted focus from finding the Passage to finding the Shoshonis.

The definition of success had narrowed to a more immediate concern: simple survival. The battered dream of the Passage could be tended to later. He had to keep moving forward.

The same shift of objective became a recurring national characteristic in the years following the Lewis and Clark expedition. When the truth became clear that no Northwest Passage existed, it no longer mattered. New dreams, new desires, new myths were born whenever an older one died.

Within the journals of the Corps of Discovery was the disappointing news about the Passage. But, as Bernard DeVoto explains in his edition of the journals, overshadowing the disappointment was "the first report on the West, on the United States over the hill and beyond the sunset, on the province of the American future . . . It satisfied desire and it created desire: the desire of a westering nation."

There was no Northwest Passage, but there were beaver in the mountain streams, and, it was said, an easy fortune to be made in trapping them. The beaver trade dwindled, but tales filtered back of gold lining the riverbanks, waiting for anyone to come West, bend over, and stuff his pockets. And so the cycle kept repeating itself. The buffalo herds were said to be inexhaustible and a source of quick, steady profit. When they disappeared, the grasslands left behind were supposed to provide ranges where unfenced cattle could graze and fatten for the market.

Most of all there was the land, cheap land and good land, land that reportedly responded to the plow and seed with stupendous crops, a land of plenty beckoning to be settled by anyone with enough grit and energy and sense of will and adventure to pit his dreams against the big land.

Dream, desire, myth. Once the seed of a dream was planted in a person's mind, it grew—to desire, desire to myth—until reality intervened and cut it down, only to have the seed of another dream take its place: a crop rotation of hopes.

Like other famous searches by New World explorers—for an El Dorado, for a Fountain of Youth—the search for the Passage was, in the end, a search for a mirage of the imagination. Lewis and Clark couldn't find it because it never existed in the first place. That it turned out to be pure myth, however, does not diminish its importance. Pursuit of the mirage lured them West and kept them moving forward. Failing to find the Passage, they found other things instead, which ultimately turned out to be more important.

The westering nation followed the same path. Myth after myth lured more and more people into the new territory, all of them full of fresh hope, pursuing new dreams. If the reality they discovered didn't square with the dreams that brought them there, they moved on. Sometimes moving on meant adjusting to a new dream. Sometimes it simply meant moving on, picking up their dreams, and heading a little farther west, where the rainbow's end surely waited for them.

The act of settling this expanding frontier became a regenerative act. Successive generations would venture West to relearn and reexperience the frontier, reinforcing an emerging national identity of optimism, restlessness, and spunky determination to push onward. In the semiarid West, the nation found its own fountain of youth.

I pull into Dillon, Montana (population 3,976), with my own worries, different from those of Lewis and Clark when they were here. Chief among them is whether the *Discovery* can get me over Lemhi Pass. It's early June; there's still snow in the higher mountain elevations. I've heard there's a dirt road over the pass, at elevation 7,373 feet, but I don't know what kind of condition it's in. Despite the drought, there are rain clouds in the southwest skies, in the direction of my destination. My concern is not whether and where the Passage might exist; I know it doesn't. I just want to know whether attempting the route in a Volkswagen camper with low road clearance, two-wheel drive, and a small engine is a fool's errand.

Like Lewis and Clark, who often received contradictory or hazy directions from the tribes they met, I get mixed signals from the locals on my chances. The National Forest Service office in Dillon has a detailed map identifying the roads to take, but the clerk isn't sure whether the pass is, well, passable. A gas station attendant says it's "no sweat" getting through. A woman at the Beaverhead County Historical Museum has profound doubts. None of them has ever taken the trip. The person to see, I'm told, is Elfreda Woodside.

When I enter her room in a Dillon nursing home, Elfreda Woodside has just finished watching a baseball game on TV, an intense interest she acquired, she tells me, when she was dating a baseball player in high school. She follows the sport every day on television and in the papers, and we spend the first minutes of my visit talking about the season. (The Atlanta Braves have become her favorite team, thanks to a satellite dish bringing in every game, but she thinks they've traded away too many good players to be a contender this year.) Her love of Lewis and Clark lore is even stronger ("I was in St. Louis once and passed up a chance to see a Cardinals game in order to visit Clark's grave," she confides), and she's happy to talk about the expedition. She wishes she could go with me to camp near Lemhi Pass tonight, but she can't. Elfreda Woodside is eighty-eight years old.

We talk at length about the expedition, especially its journey through this area. She has the incidents, the dates, portions of the journal descriptions memorized. The best place to view Beaverhead Rock, she says, is from the river, north of the outcropping. "It doesn't look like a beaver from the highway," she says. "It's hard to convince people." (In fact, most locals call it Point of Rocks; a different bluff farther south, which Lewis called Rattlesnake Cliffs, is what they refer to as Beaverhead Rock. It can get confusing.) Elfreda was instrumental in getting Lemhi Pass set aside as a park in the 1930s. Now she is working to get another landmark, called Clark's Lookout, designated as a historic park.

"If you're looking for it, don't ask people how to find Clark's Lookout. They won't know. Ask them where Lover's Leap is," she says with a contagious laugh.

I ask Elfreda what she thinks the significance of the expedition was, and she gives me the best, most succinct answer I will hear: "Well, it was the opening of the West. Thomas Jefferson wanted them to come out here and see what he had bought."

She has been to Lemhi Pass more than fifty times, she says, and describes the trail, the view, and Lewis's spring in precise and loving detail. Which brings me to my reason for visiting Elfreda Woodside in the first place.

"Can I make it there this time of year in a Volkswagen camper?" I ask, waiting for her words of wisdom.

She looks at me with her bright, young eyes, and laughs again. "You won't know unless you try," she says.

ROAD RULE 17: Travelers and explorers in unfamiliar territory should expect conflicting advice from the natives about what direction to take, in fact about whether they should even proceed on.

WOODSIDE'S COROLLARY: Proceed on. You won't know anything unless you try.

My place to spend the night before crossing the Divide will be the site of the explorers' Camp Fortunate, just south of Lowell Hildreth's ranch.

The day after he crossed the Great Divide, along the Lemhi River in what is now Idaho, Lewis finally encountered a village of Shoshonis with a herd of 700 horses. They had never seen any white men before, and their reaction to the explorers was a mixture of hospitality and wariness.

Through a combination of diplomacy, cajolery, and promises of trade goods, Lewis convinced the band's reluctant chief, Cameahwait, to recross the pass to meet Clark and the rest of the expedition. On August 17, 1805, the groups were reunited at the point where Horse Prairie and Red Rock Creeks form the Beaverhead. The captains named the spot Camp Fortunate, for here Cameahwait learned that the Indian woman with the expedition was, incredibly, his sister, who had been kidnapped by the Hidatsas several years before. And here, after the usual ceremonies of peace medals, speeches, and displays of York and the air gun, Cameahwait agreed to provide horses and guides to his new white friends.

Camp Fortunate is now under the waters of Clark Canyon Dam's reservoir. When I arrive at the Horse Prairie campground on the lake's north shore, there are no Shoshonis in sight, but there are eleven Winnebagos. I drive on to the West Cameahwait campground, which is better sheltered from the cold, brisk wind sweeping down from the mountains, and park the *Discovery* near the lake shore next to several truck/campers. A fierce storm has built up in the west. Dark clouds, occasionally brightened by lightning bolts, are expending their fury on the peaks. Now I know how the farmers east of the Divide must feel when they stand in their parched fields and watch the mountains steal the rain. The mountains don't need the moisture, I do, they must think, shaking their heads at the unfairness and worrying about tomorrow. Let the farmers have it, I say to the clouds; the dirt trail I want to take doesn't need it. I'm worrying about tomorrow too.

Night falls quickly on the lee side of the mountains. Inside the camper, I read the journals again. Clark estimated that Camp Fortunate was 3,096 miles from their starting point at Camp Wood; the *Discovery*'s odometer shows I've traveled 4,293 since I left St. Louis. They had been gone sixteen months by this point; I've been on the road for just over a month.

Lewis made a journal entry here on August 18, 1805, that has always haunted historians intrigued by his personality. He had crossed and returned across the Divide by this point, had witnessed the improbable reunion of Cameahwait and Sacagawea, and had just finished describing his successful trade of a uniform coat, a pair of leggings, a few handkerchiefs, and other articles, "the whole of which did not cost more than about 20$ in the U' States," for three much needed horses. Then his journal writing turns darkly introspective:

> This day I completed my thirty first year, and conceived that I had in all human probability now existed about half the period which I am to remain in this Sublunary world. I reflected that I had as yet done but little, very little, indeed, to further the hapiness of the human race or to advance the information of the succeeding generation. I viewed with regret the many hours I have spent in indolence, and now soarly feel the want of that information which those hours would have given me had they been judiciously expended. but since they are past and cannot be recalled, I dash from me the gloomy thought, and resolved in future, to redouble my exertions and at least indeavour to promote those two primary objects of human existence, by giving them the aid of that portion of talents which nature and fortune have bestoed on me; or in future, to live for *mankind,* as I have heretofore lived *for myself.*

"Gloomy thoughts" indeed, and they start infecting my own. A full month traveling by myself has subtly changed the front-seat "conversations" between me and my vehicle from offhand comments on the scenery outside to more inwardly directed questions tinged with self-doubt. What, if anything, have I discovered so far on my journey? What, more precisely, am I looking for?

In the last few days, it's been increasingly hard for me to stop and strike up conversations with total strangers. They've been generous and open, but more and more I've felt like an intruder, an outsider forcing himself into their lives, like the artist Karl Bodmer capturing an Indian's spirit on canvas and taking it away for my own purposes.

I'm worried about tomorrow's attempt at crossing Lemhi Pass. Worried that I'll fail and won't make it. At the same time, I'm worried about a greater failure. Worried that, in the mood that now grips me, I will make it over the Divide but just keep driving to the coast nonstop, without pausing to meet any more people, accept their hospitality, listen to their stories, collect their dreams, and pass on, leaving nothing of my own spirit behind.

Lewis's self-assessment only diminishes my own self-evaluation. At this same spot he took stock of his life. He was thirty-one and felt he hadn't accomplished much of note. Already he had been the personal secretary to one of the nation's greatest presidents; already compiled more descriptions of previously unknown animals, plants, terrains, waterfalls, and Indian tribes than most explorers in any succeeding generation would ever encounter; already become the first American to straddle the Continental Divide; already entered territory never before trod by members of his race. Yet he felt he hadn't adequately applied his talents.

Where does that leave me? I have arrived at the same point 180 years later, not breaking new ground but merely following his footsteps. Not even following his footsteps, but riding in comfort, secure in the knowledge that my maps, unlike his, are at least accurate. He was driven by a dream; I am driven by an engine in the back of the *Discovery*.

The 20/20 vision of historical hindsight makes the comparison worse, not better. I have the advantage of knowing Lewis's self-assessment was wrong. By his thirty-first birthday, he had already done much, very much, to advance the information and further the potential happiness of the next generations. In the years following the expedition, he became a national hero and governor of the Louisiana Territory.

Lewis was also wrong on a second count. His thirty-first birthday did not mark the halfway point of his life. On October 11, 1809, when he was thirty-five—my age—Meriwether Lewis was dead, most probably by suicide.

Hoping a walk in the brisk night air will shake these gloomy thoughts, I pace the shoreline of the lake that entombs Camp Fortunate. A couple from Darby, Montana, is fishing on the bank, near a small fire. We talk briefly. They've never heard of Lemhi Pass and have no idea if I'll be able to cross it in the morning. They ask me where I'm from. I tell them, already knowing their response, which they say in unison: "You're a long way from home."

And that's how I feel when I climb into my sleeping bag in the top of the *Discovery*—alone and a long way from home.

Elfreda Woodside's words return: there are things you won't know until you try. They focus my thoughts on tomorrow rather than the past. The memory of her laughter and her spry spirit at the ripe age of eighty-eight is what gets me through the night.

The morning is partly sunny. Or partly cloudly, depending on your disposition. A few dark clouds are still clinging to the western peaks, but most of the big sky has been partitioned into a checkerboard of white and blue. I get up early and depart for Lemhi Pass by seven-thirty. The large, broad valley of Horse Prairie Creek is active with the new day. A badger waddles up a side hill, too intent on his own route to look back to the road when I honk. Where Route 324, the paved road I'm on, turns south toward Bannack Pass, I go straight instead, along a gravel road into the center of the lush intervale formed by Horse Prairie Creek and Trail Creek. Three people on horseback, with the help of two dogs, are driving a herd of about fifty cattle across the road from one pasture to another. The people smile and wave as I pass. The dogs keep their attention on the cattle.

Along the road, a golden eagle stares at the *Discovery* from a fencepost. When I stop, it flaps its impressive wings as a salute and then flies off. A little farther, another eagle on a telephone pole, then a big red hawk. Plump little gophers crisscross the road. The hawk and eagles are watching for gophers, the gophers watching for eagles and hawks. They've got their business, I've got mine. There are signs of last night's rain: puddles in the road ditches, glistening green grass in these high meadows, the fresh smell of dampened sage.

I look in the rearview mirror. No clouds of dust behind me. And no troubling thoughts clouding my mind; yesterday's worries have been cleaned away by today's sense of adventure. Even though she is still in her nursing-home room in Dillon, Elfreda Woodside is with me on the way to Lemhi Pass. The morning is partly sunny, not partly cloudy.

The intervale narrows into a valley, a hundred to two hundred yards wide, bordered by high hills on both sides and cut through the middle by a winding, willow-bordered creek. The road roughens, passes the last house (no telephone or electricity lines extend past it), and roughens some more. All this time I have been climbing gently, almost imperceptibly. As the valley opens into a wide swale, I can see the ridge of the Divide several miles in front of me, and notice for the first time that along the northwest slopes there are snow patches at the same elevation as the road.

A big puddle blocks my path, forcing me to stop and wonder if the two bulldozers in the yard of the last house were a portent. Probing the puddle's bottom with a stick, I can tell the roadbed is firm enough underneath to get through. Another badger, basking in the morning sun, supervises the fording. A second puddle, larger this time, prompts the same procedure. By the time I reach a third, and then a fourth, I am too riveted on reaching the ridge to bother stopping; the *Discovery* splashes through them both.

At the bottom of the ridge, a small rivulet passes underneath the road. This is where McNeal "thanked his god that he had lived to bestride the mighty & heretofore deemed endless Missouri," and this is where I stop to do the same. In my excitement, I jump ahead of history by two miles and taste the cold, clear water. Lewis's spring is still ahead, up the steep ascent of the ridge, but I figure I'm playing it safe by drinking here, in case the climb is too much for the *Discovery*.

By now the clouds have moved east, leaving an azure sky that beckons me up the switchbacks to the spring below the Divide. The Forest Service has erected three signs to read when I stop at the spring, which gurgles out near some pines. Two of them are quotations from Lewis's journal of August 12, 1805—about McNeal's exultation at the creek below, and about Lewis's pleasure in "all[a]ying my thirst with this pure and ice-cold water." The other sign says: "Warning: Water Unsafe to Drink."

I had expected to be alone at Lemhi Pass, but when I reach it, my presence pushes the number of people to six—two more than when the first Americans stood here 180 years ago.

A big truck from the Lemhi County (Idaho) Highway Department is parked next to a late-model Buick with a rental trailer behind it. The driver of the car, standing with his wife and small child, tells me he started up the Idaho side six hours ago, got stalled when the car couldn't pull the trailer up the grade, and luckily two men in the highway truck showed up to tow him the rest of the way. Dreams of an easy Passage apparently have never been totally vanquished. He's moving to Colorado, he says. A "friend"—he says this with the quotes around the word—told him this was a shortcut over the Divide. The highway workers shrug and head back down the steep western road.

The man asks anxiously about the east side of the pass, and I reassure him that after the switchbacks, the descent is gradual and the puddles are all easily forded.

Some things have changed since Lewis stood here and first saw the mountains he never expected to see. A wooden fence runs along the saddle of the ridge, with a sign that says this is both the Continental Divide and the border between Montana and Idaho; in Lewis's time, there was no sign, and the ridge separated United States territory from the unowned. A nearby pine tree has a dark streak of charcoal down its side; its top is blasted off—punishment from a lightning bolt for trapping rain clouds headed to expectant farmers.

But the mountains are still there, still immense, their tops still partially covered with snow. Toward the west as far as the eye can see, the peaks poke toward the sun, each one another spike puncturing the myth of the Passage. As exhilarating and simultaneously sobering as the sight was for Lewis, he did not tarry here for long. His mission was to reach the Pacific coast, even though the western view told him that getting there would not be as easy as he once dreamed. Mountains or not, he had to proceed on. So must I.

The man in the Buick has started his car and is ready to head east. Before he leaves, I ask him if there's anything I need to know about going down the west side.

"I sure hope you've got good brakes," he says, and drives off.

18

Myths Die Hard

we have not as yet seen one of these anamals, tho' their tracks are so abundant and recent. the men as well as ourselves are anxious to meet with some of these bear. From Meriwether Lewis's journal
April 13, 1805

the Indians may well fear this anamal . . . but in the hands of skillfull riflemen they are by no means as formidable or dangerous as they have been represented. From Meriwether Lewis's journal
April 29, 1805

I find that the curiossity of our party is pretty well satisfyed with rispect to this anamal. From Meriwether Lewis's journal
May 6, 1805

Having obtained horses from Cameahwait's band of Shoshonis, the Corps of Discovery cached their canoes and a few supplies at Camp Fortunate and began the overland search for a navigable river that could take them to the Pacific. The first river they came upon—the Lemhi—had salmon in it, a confirmation that they had indeed crossed the Divide and were in the Columbia River watershed. The north-flowing Lemhi soon joined a bigger river (Clark named it the Lewis River, in honor of his co-captain; its present name is the Salmon), which curved and headed due west. Maybe this wasn't going to be so difficult after all, despite the unexected, formidable mountains between the explorers and the sea.

But the Indians told them the river was impassable, and Clark's brief reconnaissance convinced him they were correct. The Salmon, churning between steep mountain slopes, would be impossible to follow, by water or by land. Clark's guide told him of an Indian tribe to the north and west, the Nez Perce, who took a trail through the Bitterroots each year on their way east to hunt buffalo. The captains decided they would have to take this route and headed their pack train north.

For several days they labored, cutting their own trail toward a mountain pass. It snowed and sleeted. Some of the horses slipped and fell; a few were crippled and gave out. The whiskey had been finished at the Great Falls more than a month earlier; now the supply of salt pork was exhausted. In early September 1805, they descended the pass, back into what is now the portion of Montana west of the Divide. A broad river (Lewis returned the favor and named it after Clark; it is now the Bitterroot River) flowed north through a gentle valley. Here the expedition met another tribe of Indians who had never seen white men before.

These were the Ootlashoots of the Tushepaw nation. The captains apparently misinterpreted the sign language for the tribe's name, and called them the Flatheads, even though these Indians did not engage in the practice of squeezing their infants' heads between boards to flatten their foreheads as a mark of distinction. (Tribes they would meet later, however, did.) Nonetheless, Flatheads they were called in the journals, and Flatheads they are called to this day.

They spoke a Salish dialect which Clark describes as "a gugling kind of language spoken much thro the throat." The strange language, combined with the lighter complexions of the Indians, briefly ignited the hope that the explorers had finally discovered the much-rumored Welsh Indians.

This myth was as old as the myth of the Northwest Passage, and as firmly established in the imaginations of easterners and Europeans. Jefferson himself hoped his pet expedition would at last find them. According to the legend, which became current in 1583, a Welsh prince named Madoc discovered America in the year 1170, more than three hundred years before Columbus. The story of Madoc and his three thousand colonists took many forms. They were given credit for the ancient mounds discovered near the Ohio and Mississippi rivers; they created the Mayan civilization; they founded the Aztec and Inca empires; they fought an Armageddon-like battle with their enemies in which only a few survived. Remnants of Madoc's descendants were rumored to still exist, fair-skinned, highly civilized, and speaking Welsh or at least a Welsh variant.

Like the Passage itself, their existence was not in question, only their precise location: somewhere just a little farther west, along some as yet unexplored river or just over the latest line of the frontier. As civilization pushed westward, each new Indian tribe that was heard about, but not yet fully known, became the likeliest candidate. In all, thirteen tribes at one time or another were initially believed to be Madoc's Welsh Indians—including the Delawares, Tuscaroras, Comanches, Pawnees, and Mandans. And now, for a couple of days at least, the Flatheads.

"[W]e take these Savages to be the Welch Indians if their be any Such from the Language," Private Whitehouse notes in the Flathead encampment. "So Capt. Lewis took down the names of everry thing in their Language, in order that it may be found out whether they are or whether they Sprang or origenated first from the welch or not."

They weren't. Their language was strange, but it wasn't Celtic. Not only were the Flatheads not flat-headed, they were no more Welsh than was York. Another myth was dealt a fatal blow.

The expedition moved north again, to where Lolo Creek de-

scends from the western mountains to join the Bitterroot, about
10 miles south of modern-day Missoula, Montana. The expedition
paused here at a camp they called "Traveller's Rest." While the
travelers rested, the badly wounded Passage myth also momen-
tarily revived.

The captains were given two important pieces of geographic
information by the Indians. From this spot, they were told, the
trail west was rugged and there was little game along it, but a five-
day journey over the Bitterroot Mountains would bring them to
the Nez Perce villages, food, and a river big enough and smooth
enough to resume traveling by canoe. The second bit of information
was that from Traveller's Rest a shortcut existed eastward across
broad valleys and a pass in the Rockies to the Missouri River.
Four days' travel overland would bring them to a point on the
river just north of the Gates of the Mountains.

The Corps of Discovery had obviously not taken this four-day
shortcut from the Gates of the Mountains to Traveller's Rest. They
had followed the Missouri to its source, up the Jefferson and Beaverhead, over the Great Divide, north over another mountain pass
and along the Bitterroot. It had taken them fifty-two days instead
of four.

If both parts of this new information were correct, a trip from
the Missouri River to a navigable western river in the land of the
Nez Perce could be covered in a little more than a week. Maybe
there was a Passage after all.

Keeping a foot on the brake and the *Discovery* in first gear, I start
my descent from Lemhi Pass, stopping only to taste the water in
the first creek I come to (if the water is unsafe on both sides of the
Divide, it's already too late for me to worry about it). By late
morning I am in the Lemhi River valley. Within about twenty
miles, the Lemhi joins the Salmon, a rolling stream with rocky
banks and gravel bars that moves north in a big hurry.

Salmon, Idaho (population 3,308), is a tourist town that seems
to specialize in outfitted canoe and raft trips. If only Cameahwait's
people had started this business before 1805, Lewis and Clark could
have saved themselves a lot of time and trouble. The lead story in
the local paper is filled with complaints from the Idaho Steelhead
and Salmon Unlimited group that Indian fishing along the Colum-

bia is preventing the fish from reaching the higher streams of Idaho. "The pussy-footing with this 'fish war' has to come to an end," the group says in a letter to Idaho's governor and Congressional delegation. "It's time to play hardball."

U.S. 93, which pretty much traces Lewis and Clark's route north from Salmon to the Traveller's Rest campsite near Lolo, Montana, follows the river to where it bends west at North Fork. A small road turns off the highway to hug the Salmon River. I take it about as far as Clark went on his reconnoiter of the river, to Shoup, which consists of a gas station/post office/general store and one house. The mountains by this time have closed in on the river, which boils and surges over boulders, angrily seeking passage west. No question, Clark made the right decision here and turned back. To have attempted taking the river west—on its waters or along its steep banks—would almost certainly have led the expedition to disaster. I'm not sure I'd even want to try the river with a well-equipped outfitter. Just past Shoup the small road ends; any further travel is by water and all one-way. Even today, they call this "The River of No Return."

Back on U.S. 93, the highway north of North Forks begins the switchbacks to Lost Trail Pass, so named because of the explorers' difficulties in the area. This is the only major road across the mountains between Interstate 15 and U.S. 12, both more than a hundred miles away in either direction. Traffic is heavy with lumber trucks and RVs groaning toward the pass. Still, I can't complain about the slow going. Often having to blaze their own trail in miserable weather, the expedition toiled for more than two days over what Clark calls "some of the worst roads that ever horses passed" before reaching the top. I've got clear skies and dry pavement. The *Discovery*'s been on much worse roads than this. Even with the trucks and campers slowing me down, it takes only half an hour to make the climb. Suddenly I'm back in Montana and down into the lovely Bitterroot Valley.

As river valleys go, the Bitterroot's is hard to beat. The glacial valley is U-shaped, not V-shaped, making it appear much broader than it actually is. Rich farmland lines both sides of the river. The humped Sapphire Mountains line the east side, a gentle contrast to the western Bitterroots, whose sharp-pointed, snow-topped peaks look like turbulent white caps on a fast-frozen ocean. The river itself flows north through the valley's center, swift and clear and rock-bottomed like the Salmon, but not as angry. The climate is dry, although not as dry as the country on the east side of the Divide; warm Chinook winds occasionally curl into the valley during winter to moderate the coldness.

Through the first part of this century, the valley was busy with apple orchards, with farms growing sugar beets and raising cattle and hogs and sheep, and with lumber companies and some prospecting in the Sapphires. Today, most of that has given way to tourism, second homes, bedroom communities near Missoula, and a string of companies that specialize in preparing log houses to be shipped in pieces and erected thoughout the West.

It's Bitterroot Day at the Ravalli County Museum in Hamilton (population 2,661), so I stop to celebrate with the other tourists. The old building is festooned inside with the pink and white flowers, or pictures of the pink and white bitterroot flowers.

Lewis had noticed the Shoshonis digging the plant's root, boiling it, and eating it. Because enemy tribes had guns and they didn't, the Shoshonis only occasionally ventured out onto the Plains to hunt buffalo—a risky business, as Sacagawea's abduction by the Hidatsas at the Three Forks attested. Most of the year, they remained in their mountain stronghold, "sometimes living for weeks without meat and only a little fish roots and berries," according to Lewis's journal. "[B]ut this added Cameahwait, with his ferce eyes and lank jaws grown meager for the want of food, would not be the case if we had guns, we could then live in the country of buffaloe and eat as our enemies do and not be compelled to hide ourselves in these mountains and live on roots and berries as the bear do."

When Lewis tasted some roots, he found out for himself why Cameahwait was so gaunt and so eager for American weapons to hunt buffalo and defend his tribe. The roots, Lewis reports, "had a very bitter taste, which was naucious to my pallate, and I transfered them to the Indians. . . ."

On his return trip, Lewis collected a few specimens of the flower and brought them back East where, six years later, a botanist gave the bitterroot its scientific name, *Lewisia rediviva,* in honor of the man who couldn't stomach it.

Tasty or not, the bitterroot is beautiful enough to have a majestic mountain range and sparkling river named after it; and it is Montana's state flower.

Inside the museum's foyer, two women are serving boiled bitterroots out of a bean pot, lifting them carefully from the hot water with tongs and placing them on small paper plates. Paper napkins adorned with a picture of the flower complete the presentation.

The woman serving me advises that in preparing the bitterroot it's important to peel the root first, then boil it for at least thirty-five minutes.

"Most people like them with sugar and cream," she says, motioning to a supply of both on the table.

Not me. I try the first root, a small sliver about the size of a child's little finger, Shoshoni-style, with no condiments. One hundred and eighty years have not improved their taste from Lewis's very accurate description. The woman notices my grimace.

"I also make them with beef broth," she says. "I served them to some Indians once; they seemed to prefer it with sugar and cream." No kidding. They also preferred buffalo roast when they could get it without getting killed or kidnapped.

I dab the second one with sugar and cream. It's only a little better: a sugar-and-cream paste, with a slightly bitter aftertaste.

A woman behind me takes her turn, chewing the root slowly and pondering her opinion like a connoisseur at a wine tasting.

"It'll never replace the cheeseburger," she says.

In Stevensville (population 1,207), I visit St. Mary's Mission, the first church built in Montana. Its history proves that in the interplay between whites and Indians, misconceptions and myth creation existed on both sides of the cultural divide.

The British and Canadian trappers of the last century often employed Iroquois Indians to teach western Indians "modern" trapping techniques. The Iroquois had been converted to Catholicism by the Jesuits near Montreal, and so when four of them arrived to live with the Flatheads of Montana in the early 1820s, they passed on stories of the Black Robes and their mysterious powers. The Flatheads became intrigued. They and their friends, the Nez Perce, sent four separate delegations—in 1831, 1835, 1837, and 1839— to St. Louis asking for someone to return to the mountains with them to bring the "White Man's Book of Heaven."

The news reports of their first visit aroused the missionary zeal of various denominations, particularly the Methodists and Presbyterians, who quickly dispatched ministers to the West. These, however, were not the Black Robes the Flatheads had heard about. The Protestants settled farther west with other tribes; the Flatheads headed again for St. Louis. And again, and again. Finally, in 1840, a young Jesuit, Father Pierre-Jean DeSmet, was sent to the Bitterroot Valley. He started construction of the St. Mary's Mission in 1841.

DeSmet later went on to play an important role throughout the West as one of the few white men the Indian tribes trusted, but his instruction of the Flatheads was not one of his great successes. As it turned out, the Flatheads saw the Black Robes and their religious practices not in metaphysical terms, but in practical ones. They believed the Black Robes would provide powerful "medicine" to help them against the Blackfeet and other Plains tribes who had pushed them (and the Shoshonis) out of the buffalo grounds and into the mountains, where they had to eat things like the bitterroot. Anxious for conversions, whatever the source, Father DeSmet did not attempt to dissuade them of this notion.

The early years went well. On the Flathead side, the hunting was good and they won some skirmishes with the Blackfeet, which they attributed to the devotions the Black Robes taught them. For their part, the Fathers were happy: the Flatheads were saying prayers, wearing crucifixes, and observing the Sabbath. Then, during a buffalo hunt in the summer of 1846, Father DeSmet told his flock he was going to continue on to St. Louis, but on his way he was going to visit the Blackfeet and try to Christianize them.

The Flatheads considered this the equivalent of turning the secret of the A-bomb over to the Russians. When they returned to St. Mary's (DeSmet was on his way east), Father Ravalli noticed that the Flatheads were now cool toward the priests, were again practicing older tribal ceremonies, and had returned to, as he put it, "savage obscenity and shameless excesses of the flesh." Relations seesawed for several years, but by 1850 they had worsened to the point that the Jesuits leased the mission grounds for a fort and left the valley.

The old log mission still stands. Services, however, are held next door in a modern church, where the congregation appears to be all white. The stained-glass windows portray scenes of the Fathers ministering to the Indians. The Flatheads themselves, however, were long ago removed to a reservation north of Missoula.

Sometimes myths turn out to be based on fact, not fantasy. Such was the case of the grizzly bear.

The Indians at Fort Mandan had warned Lewis and Clark about this beast, but the captains discounted much of it as tall tales told around an earth-lodge fire. The explorers could believe in a North-west Passage or the existence of Welsh Indians, but the idea of a bear so big, so ferocious, and so tough to kill was simply beyond belief, obviously a concoction of overly fertile imaginations.

Near the mouth of the Yellowstone, as they entered what is now Montana, the Corps of Discovery started seeing the bears' tracks. They were big, all right, but they only heightened the men's eagerness to see the animal itself. On April 29, 1805, Lewis finally met one. This myth came in the form of three hundred pounds of yellow-brown fur, with sharp claws and snarling teeth. He wounded it with one shot, was pursued by the maddened animal, but got the chance to recharge his muzzleloader and killed the bear with a second round. While previous explorers had reported sightings of grizzly bears, Lewis's description in his journal that day was the world's first detailed notation of its size, color, and anatomy.

Flushed with his success, Lewis notes: "the Indians may well fear this anamal equiped as they generally are with their bows and arrows or indifferent fuzees, but in the hands of skillfull riflemen they are by no means as formidable or dangerous as they have been represented."

About a week later the expedition encountered its second grizzly. It took ten slugs, five of them through the bear's lungs, to bring the grizzly down; even so, the bear swam across the river before expiring on a sandbar.

Myths die hard, especially when they're well earned.

After seeing a third grizzly the next day, Lewis, somewhat chastened after his earlier braggadocio, writes: "I find that the curiossity of our party is pretty well satisfyed with rispect to this anamal."

Satisfied or not, they saw a lot more of these "monsters" through-out Montana. Men were chased across the prairies, chased up trees, and chased over bluffs into the Missouri by grizzlies. Lewis's dog was reduced to "a constant state of alarm with these bear and keeps barking all night," according to the captain. By the end of June he decided that the grizzlies were "so troublesome that I do not think it prudent to send one man alone on an errand of any kind."

The captains called this animal by various names—white bear, grey bear, yellow bear, brown bear—before settling on "grisley" or "grizly." Years later, it would receive the scientific name of *Ursus horribilis* and common name of grizzly. (Teddy Roosevelt preferred "grisly," because it means ghastly, over "grizzly," which refers to the look of its fur.) Whatever, before he left Montana soil, Lewis had been impressed enough by its strength and ferocity to say he "had reather fight two Indians than one bear."

One hundred and eighty years later, I have covered more than 1,500 miles within Montana's borders along the expedition's route without seeing a single grizzly. Not that I'm abjectly disappointed. I'd rather not fight an Indian *or* a grizzly bear. But before leaving Montana, I stop in Missoula (population 33,388) and talk to Charles Jonkel, a biologist and grizzly expert associated with the University of Montana, to find out what happened.

The story of the grizzly has many of the same elements as the stories of other species in the years after Lewis and Clark encountered them during the Voyage of Discovery. The beaver were overtrapped. Whooping cranes and bald eagles were killed and poisoned to the brink of extinction. Passenger pigeons disappeared entirely in 1914. Wolves have all but vanished. Pronghorn sheep and Rocky Mountain goats are scarce. The elk that formerly grazed the open plains have retreated to the mountains. The buffalo, once too many to count, survive now only in protected parks and private ranches.

No one knows how many grizzlies once lived in the American West, but reports of early travelers starting with Lewis and Clark certainly show they were common sights. Estimates range up to the tens of thousands. Compared to the Indians with their bows and arrows, the men of the expedition had an easier, albeit still difficult, time killing the grizzly with their single-shot muzzleloaders. Later, settlers armed with high-powered repeating rifles found *Ursus horribilis* even less *horribilis*. The bears had existed for centuries without encountering a predator. They were therefore unprepared for the influx of man and rifle. Since they didn't run and hide, they were relatively easy pickings as long as the hunter's shot was true. Intelligent though they may be, they still did not learn to fear humans. By the end of the 1970s, they were listed as a threatened species and placed under federal protection. No one knows for sure how many remain in the American West—estimates put their numbers at fewer than a thousand.

The grizzly's story has one big difference from that of, say, the now extinct passenger pigeon. It is this difference that both continues to threaten their survival and attracts a lot of attention: grizzly bears still kill people on occasion. Usually it occurs when they feel provoked or threatened near their cubs or near their feeding grounds. In their ceaseless search to find enough protein to survive their winter hibernation, they will eat anything from roots and insects to moose and elk. A sheep also provides a good meal.

"It's different to live with grizzlies than being just concerned about them in New Orleans," Jonkel says. "It's a different thing if you live in Baltimore and want to save the grizzly bear than if you live on the east front of the Rockies [one of the bears' last refuges]. City people don't understand the problem, the way we don't understand why they can't stop crime in the cities."

The rub comes, he says, in the fact that "good grizzly habitat is good people habitat." Places with clean water, good fishing, good soil for plants and grazing, and even nice scenery are the places grizzlies like. They're also the places for things like ski resorts, second-home developments, cattle ranches, and even oil exploration.

Jonkel compares the grizzlies' plight to that of the Indians: "The bear has to be where the land is rich. We've taken all of that, given them some of the leftovers, and told them to survive."

Depending on the availability of food sources, the home range of one male grizzly can be anywhere from 189 to 387 square miles. Female "sows" and their cubs roam around in smaller ranges. Not surprisingly, then, despite their dwindling numbers and increasingly remote refuges, grizzlies still keep running into their principal obstacles for survival: man and his ever expanding home range. And so Jonkel is among the handful of biologists and environmentalists trying to educate people on how to live with bears, and bears on how to live with people.

Jonkel heads a project aimed at teaching "problem" bears— bears that have caused trouble in human settlements—to fear humans. The hope is that this "aversive training," combined with the grizzlies' natural intelligence, will result in a wariness that can be passed on to the remnants of the species. Captured bears are deliberately provoked, and when they charge across their cage toward the provoker, they're sprayed in the face with an acrid concoction of red pepper. As the training is repeated, the bear is supposed to start associating humans with unpleasant experiences.

The harder task is teaching humans to leave grizzlies alone. Not that long ago, tourist areas near Yellowstone National Park set their garbage out for the grizzlies to feed on in view of people who had paid to sit on specially erected bleachers and see the West in all its wildness. (Unfortunately, despite advice to the contrary, when the dumps were finally closed it was done so rapidly that the grizzlies, reacting to this "cold turkey" treatment, fanned out to campgrounds and other remaining sources of garbage. Nearly two hundred bears, suddenly "problem" bears, had to be killed.)

In addition to developers and oil drillers who encroach on the bears' dwindling refuges, the "problem" people these days are often hikers and campers who are careless with their food in grizzly territory. (In Glacier, more than two million people—about eleven thousand humans for each grizzly—passed through the park in 1983.) The bears learn that the easiest source of protein is where people are; the next campers encounter a hungry grizzly; complaints are lodged; grizzly is killed.

Jonkel has prepared lists of advice for people in grizzly land. The precautions include having the good sense to avoid places posted by park personnel warning off hikers; keeping campgrounds clean and your food stored in containers away from where you sleep; wearing bells on your boots to prevent your surprising a grizzly on a turn in the trail; and knowing how to react in a confrontation.

"There's no precise formula on how to act if you meet a grizzly," he says. Don't turn and run; it often encourages the bear to chase you. Break eye contact and back away, seeking a tree or rock to hide behind; the bear often accepts this as a signal that you're not challenging its territory and don't want trouble any more than it does. While they can climb trees, grizzlies sometimes accept your climbing as a submissive act and will leave you alone. If the bear's on top of you, playing dead sometimes defuses the situation; if all else fails, fight for your life—both have worked, Jonkel says.

Reports of grizzlies' killing people (about one a year) are over-sensationalized, he says. More people die each year being struck by lightning, more children simply disappear or are murdered by their parents.

"If you're going to be done in this summer, it's probably going to be on the highway or by a friend with a butcher knife," Jonkel tells me. "You should be a lot more frightened of Highway 93 than you are of grizzly bears." I've had experience with the highway, so I understand that threat; I'm not sure my friends would appreciate the comparison.

I also have doubts about playing dead beneath a grizzly, I tell him. Seems like playing it might lead to the reality of it. But Jonkel knows several people who have done it and survived. One couple he knows was surprised by a grizzly in their campsite. They both played dead. The grizzly sniffed their bodies and nudged them a couple of times. Then it squatted over the man, defecated on him, and walked off.

"How'd the guy feel?" I ask, seeking some sort of greater symbol in the act, perhaps a grand comment from one species to another.

"He accepted it," Jonkel says. "Better that than being eaten."

Before leaving Missoula, I stop to visit Richard Steffel, an air-quality specialist. I've been told he has an update on the Northwest Passage. Lewis and Clark weren't the only ones who had a hard time getting around these mountains. The same thing happens to the air in this part of the Big Sky State.

The high mountains on both sides of the Bitterroot River that make the valley so scenic also have the habit of trapping air movement, creating inversions, that are "just like putting a lid on the valley," he says.

In the middle part of this century, pulp and paper mills in the Missoula area emitted stinking exhausts that hung in the valley air like very bad breath in a cramped elevator. Federal and state environmental regulations cleared up the problem by requiring stricter emission controls. The new standards have greatly improved things, and now the smell is more like cabbage cooking in the kitchen instead of the sulfurous stench that mill workers once called "the smell of money."

In the late 1970s, the combination of rising oil prices and a higher environmental awareness brought about a switch by many Missoula residents to wood heat. Steffel estimates that half the homes in town now have wood stoves—a total of nearly fourteen thousand stoves. The result was that on some particularly cold, windless winter days, you couldn't see the scenic mountains, the sun, or the forests for the smoke.

Missoula has responded with an "air stagnation plan." It's a procedure that squares with the romantic view of freedom in the West about as well as the idea of wearing jangling bells on your feet when you hike in the wilderness. If air-inversion and wood-smoke conditions reach a certain point, an "alert" is called. Unless they have special exemptions, people have three hours to extinguish the fires in their stoves or they are liable for fines of up to $100.

The new regulations provoked controversy and resistance that was complicated by ambivalence, Steffel says: "It was easy back fifteen years ago to look at some of the industries and say, '*They're* the problem, make *them* clean it up.' But now that the problem is *us,* it's a little bit stickier."

The officials entrusted with enforcing the law are called "smoke sheriffs" locally. Steffel says compliance has been good during the last few winters—fewer than a couple of hundred warnings and only two fines have been issued. Nonetheless, he adds, the "smoke sheriffs" only knock on doors during the day. They think it might be too risky after dark.

If you're looking for evidence that the frontier is closed and the mythical days of the "Wild West" have passed, Missoula offers the proof. Grizzly bears are enrolled for "training" at the university; the modern vigilantes operate during the day, not the night; and instead of picking up and moving farther west whenever they can see smoke from a neighbor's chimney, the modern pioneers' solution is to ask the neighbor to put out his fire.

Have things changed since the days of Lewis and Clark? The rejoinder was going to be: does a bear shit in the woods? Then again, there might be something new between it and the forest floor.

A late-afternoon storm is brewing over the jagged peaks of the Bitterroots when I reach the site of Traveller's Rest, just south of Missoula. On the west side of the mountains, many of them over 8,000 feet high, the clouds are dumping rain—or snow. A strong wind bends the cottonwoods in this valley, but there is no rain here. Every so often, a piece of gray cloud rips loose from the

Bitterroot peaks like a hunk of rank meat and sweeps across to be speared again by the Sapphires.

The explorers lingered in this area to prepare themselves for yet another mountain passage. On the one hand, they were disheartened by the Indian information about the shortcut they had missed from the Gates of the Mountains to Traveller's Rest. They could have saved a month and a half by taking it instead of the tortuous route they had followed. September was already two weeks old. The Bitterroots were getting whiter with snow.

On the other hand, the information was hopeful: four days from the Missouri to Traveller's Rest, five days from Traveller's Rest to the Nez Perce and a navigable river to the sea. Not a half-day portage, to be sure, but a Northwest Passage of sorts.

The Indians had been right about the grizzly; their descriptions of the beast turned out to be highly accurate, not exaggerations. They had been right about the Salmon River; it was impassable. And the Indians were right about the shortcut to the Missouri River; Lewis would take it on the return trip. But their estimate of a five-day journey over the Lolo Trail was wishful thinking. Five days would become eleven—days of bitter cold, rain, sleet, and heavy snow, days of struggling to find and follow a faint trace through dense timber on high mountains, days of air too thin to breathe and little or no food to eat. Eleven days over what Sergeant Patrick Gass called "the most terrible mountains I ever beheld."

The Bitterroot crossing would be the expedition's severest test. During the eleven-day ordeal, the entire group would nearly perish and vanish in this blank spot on their maps, this place where mountains were not supposed to exist. But they would make it through. Exhausted, seriously weakened, and on the brink of starvation, the explorers would finally stumble out the other end of the Lolo Trail and survive.

The same can not be said of the Passage myth. Somewhere in the Bitterroot Mountains, already crippled by the view from Lemhi Pass and unable to keep up with the Corps of Discovery, it would be left behind to fend for itself. Alone in those terrible mountains, the myth died.

I will linger near Traveller's Rest as well. I'm not worried about the mountains. I have a good map, and U.S. 12 is a good road.

It can get me to Lewiston, Idaho, and Clarkston, Washington, in less than a day. I have the supplies I need, and I'm not burdened with the baggage of the myth of a Northwest Passage.

I intend to stay here for a few days to wrap myself in the glow of another myth, a younger one—one that Lewis and Clark never knew because, unlike me, they didn't grow up with Saturday movie matinees and prime-time television—but a myth just as powerful. I'm going to spend a few days with some cowboys.

19

Cowboys

those people possess ellegant horses.
From William Clark's journal
Bitterroot Valley
September 5, 1805

From the porch of his ranch house, Lee Hames can look across U.S. 93 to the lush, subirrigated meadows near the confluence of Lolo Creek and Bitterroot River, where the Corps of Discovery camped on its way west and on its homebound journey. Hames was born and raised near Traveller's Rest. Within the context of the comparatively short history of white settlement in the Bitterroot Valley, where the local version of the Pilgrims arrived just before the Civil War, his roots are deep. His mother's ancestors settled here in 1858, six years before Montana was organized as a territory; his father's in 1889, the year of statehood. To Hames and his kin, Traveller's Rest has been more than a pleasant stopping place on the way to someplace else. It is home. Three sets of his great-grandparents are buried in Stevensville.

Hames is sixty-six years old, his head capped with white like the mountains, a mustache angling across his rugged face like a snowbank at lower elevations. His body, taut and corded as a lariat, bends slightly in the middle as he walks, as if some of the many horses he's broken kicked him in the gut; but he's spry enough to climb a fence easily so he can unlock the gate to let the *Discovery* into the meadows. When we walk the last two hundred yards to the mouth of Lolo Creek, I have trouble keeping up with him, even though I'm half his age. Hames pumps his arms as he walks and talks about the expedition.

"They missed the trails [from the Missouri] into this valley," he says. "Sacajawea led them to her home, not to the Columbia. They'da been here fifty days earlier otherwise. Instead of bein' here in September, they'da been here in July. And they'da gone over these mountains at just about exactly the right time. You see, the mountains hold snow until about the Fourth of July. July, August, that's the best time. Before that, or later than that, you're gambling on snow."

Hames knows what he's talking about. The road paralleling the Lolo Trail through Idaho wasn't completed until 1960. Until then, traffic from Missoula to Lewiston had to detour up to Spokane and then down, the equivalent of going from Boston to New York City by way of Albany. In the late 1920s, when he was still a boy,

Hames accompanied an uncle and cousin in herding 150 horses over the Lolo Trail to Washington. There were decent roads at both ends of the route, but the middle portion was essentially the same as when Lewis and Clark had traveled it more than a hundred years earlier. They did it at the right time of year, to avoid the chance of snow. Even so, it took them a week each way.

The Lolo Trail was the path the Nez Perce took each year from their homeland west of the Bitterroots to the buffalo territory on the Plains. It was also the route Chief Joseph and eight hundred of his tribe followed in 1877 in their ill-fated flight from the U.S. Army. When the tattered band of Indians emerged from the mountains and headed south along the Bitterroot, they crossed what is now Hames's ranch. One of his great-grandmothers stood on a battlement of Fort Owens in Stevensville and tried to count the Nez Perce horses—more than two thousand of them. The national Appaloosa association, which claims that the Nez Perce were the first to breed Appaloosas, each year retraces a different two hundred miles of Chief Joseph's long trek over the Bitterroots, down this valley, through the Big Hole basin, across Yellowstone National Park, and then north to the Bear Paw Mountains, where Joseph surrendered four months and 1,700 miles after he had left his reservation in Idaho. Hames has led the Appaloosa group through this section of the trail. Showing polite Western hospitality, he didn't tell them that his great-grandmother confirmed what the Nez Perce themselves contend: there weren't any Appaloosas to speak of. Unlike most Indian tribes, the Nez Perce did practice selective breeding to improve their horse herds, but distinctive coloring was not their goal. Myths die hard.

Hames spent his younger days ranching, logging, and riding in the rodeo—the first out of preference as an occupation, the second out of occasional necessity, and the last out of sheer enjoyment. You can tell this because most of his complaints about changing times deal with ranching, and most of his favorite stories are about rodeos. He doesn't talk much about logging.

In Hames's day, rodeo cowboys were ranch hands who spent their weekends at nearby rodeos trying to earn a few bucks roping steers and calves and riding mean-spirited broncs. In other words, doing what they'd been doing the rest of the week. Hames's father, uncle, and cousins all competed. Hames's event was saddle bronc riding. "I wasn't heavy enough to bulldog," he says. "And I was a good roper on the range, but never fast enough getting off a horse to tie a calf; out here on the ranch, though, if you had to rope a calf or a horse, well, I was considered good enough." Riding saddle broncs was just like breaking horses at the ranch. Hames was good at it.

Rodeo and ranch; the two formed Hames's life. The money won from one helped supplement the earnings from the other. Workday skills were simply brought in from the range and applied to the arena. Saddle, rope, horse, cattle—these defined both of his worlds.

During World War II, while he was waiting in Burma to lead a mule train into China, Hames watched in amazement as natives led big Brahmas around for milking. Milking!? He thought they were supposed to be ridden. He ordered his men to cut a small clearing in the jungle, got together some of the mules and a few horses, some of the local cattle, and put on what was probably Burma's first rodeo. Since Hames was an officer, General Stilwell wouldn't let him compete against the enlisted men, so he ended up being a judge instead of a rider. "The natives stayed back," he says. "They did quite a bit of yelling at us, didn't like us very much. Cows are sacred over there."

Back home after the war, older now but still a skilled horseman, he switched events again to stay active in rodeo. Rather than riding broncs for prize money, he was the one who picked up the contestants at the end of their rides. It turned out to be steadier money and kept him in the arena for a good number of more years. Now he just watches.

Modern rodeos are different, he says. The purses are bigger, the circuit is highly organized, the finals have been moved to Las Vegas, and the rodeo cowboys are specialized athletes instead of ranch hands. "They wouldn't know one end of a horse or a cow from another if they saw it out here in an open field," Hames says. "They don't know stock. Don't have to. They've been trained just like another boy has been trained to throw a basketball. They're lost when they get out on the hills in a ranch. They don't have any idea what a ranch is all about. They're strictly a trained athlete."

Still, Hames has a soft spot for anyone willing to try to ride a bull or a horse that has been bred specifically for its mean streak. "There's an element of danger in rodeo they like," he says, "and any man I've ever known who's worth a darn always had an idea that he had to prove himself some way."

While rodeos have changed toward bigger purses, ranching has gone the other direction in Hames's lifetime. Like any farmer I've ever met, Hames can remember the prices he paid and received for nearly everything in his past. In 1950, for instance, he says, when an average hourly union wage was a dollar fifty, calves brought twenty-five cents a pound; a new pickup cost a thousand dollars. Now, he says, the wages are around fifteen dollars an hour, the pickup goes for $11,000, and calves bring only fifty cents a pound.

"You just can't make it on a small ranch anymore," he says. The ranches are being bought up by the only two groups who can afford the high land prices that they themselves have fostered: developers who cut them into small parcels for house lots and big corporations that can write off the ranch losses against their other profits.

Hames looks down the valley at the housing developments and at the busy traffic on U.S. 93. "You can't ride a saddle horse across that road safely anymore," he says. "You can't hardly walk across it safely anymore. Where are they goin' in such a hurry? Just a few miles, to the next coffee shop. We used to cross with four hundred to five hundred head of cattle. Today you'd get fifty head killed and fifty lawsuits against you." (Unless the area is marked as an open range, Hames says, the rancher is legally liable for any accidents involving cars and cattle.)

Hames still has a small horse herd on his ranch, but he's gotten out of the cattle business. Instead, he runs a bar on U.S. 93. "It's like milking cows," he says of his new business, a hard admission for a cowboy to make. "It's a confining job."

During our morning travels, Hames leans forward in his seat with a conspiratorial look and asks me a question as if someone might be listening through the open windows.

"You've studied this matter. What do you think Lewis and Clark's most important discovery was while they were in Montana?" He watches intently as I ponder my answer.

"That the best route across the Rockies from the Missouri was the shortcut they didn't take on their way west," I say.

Hames slaps his knee. "That's exactly what I'd say."

It isn't until we're back in his kitchen drinking coffee that I begin to understand that his question is going to lead me on a treasure hunt. He brings out a yellowed newspaper clipping of a story in the Missoula paper in 1981. Summarized, it tells this tale: as part of a promotional campaign, a man from a New York advertising company came to Montana in 1980 and buried a case of Canadian Club whiskey somewhere along the Lewis and Clark trail. Ads for the whiskey then began appearing in national magazines, giving a few clues about where the case might be found and challenging people to try to find it. (Other cases had been hidden in other adventurous places, from the Yukon to Loch Ness, as part of the campaign.)

Hames has the Lewis and Clark clue underlined:

We retraced Lewis & Clark's historic expedition up the Missouri River into Montana. And where they found their roughest going, we hid a case of the smoothest. Canadian Club. Where Lewis and Clark had floated the unspoiled river, Canadian Club's rafts followed. We tested our nerves, as the explorers had, on the wild rapids of the Clark's Fork. As we explored those historic streams, we buried our case of Canadian Club overlooking the site of one of the expedition's most important sightings. One clue: Neither Lewis nor Clark made it.

The ad includes a picture of people rafting through a gorge of Clark's Fork west of Missoula.

Lee Hames knows his Lewis and Clark lore, so he knows (and the newspaper article points out) that the expedition was never on the waters of Clark's Fork. But he also knows that the captains sent two men north from Traveller's Rest to reconnoiter the river's existence. That fact has led him many times to searching in vain for the whiskey where the Hellgate River meets Clark's Fork at Missoula.

"Have you covered it pretty thoroughly?" I ask him.

"Some people claim I've rechanneled the river," he says.

I tell Hames I think the clues point to a different location. It seems to me there are three conditions to meet in the clue: rough going; a crucial *sighting,* which is different from a discovery; and the sighting was made by someone other than Lewis or Clark. The mentioning of Clark's Fork is probably just advertising hype, bad history, or both.

"Beaverhead Rock," I tell him. "That's where the whiskey is. It meets all three conditions. The men were complaining about how hard it was to bring the canoes up the river. Sacagawea was the one who saw the rock. And it was her information that they had now entered the land of her people that prompted Lewis to form the advance party that led him over Lemhi Pass to find the Shoshonis."

Lolo, Montana, is about two hundred miles from Beaverhead Rock. I figure that's the end of this topic. The riddle is solved in theory.

"When do you want to go?" Hames asks.

You don't say no to a man who once turned sacred cows into rodeo stock. We agree to make the search on my return trip. It'll give me something to look forward to.

When Joel Bernstein was in the fourth grade at P.S. 144 in Forest Hills, New York, a homework assignment about New Mexico changed his life. It got him interested in horses. His father enrolled him in English-riding lessons at one of the city's parks, but young Joel's comments after the first lesson presaged that his interest was in more than just horses. "I want cowboy boots," he told his father.

The trail that brought Bernstein to the Palo Verde Ranch he owns near Traveller's Rest was as long and winding as that of the explorers. An athlete and a scholar, Bernstein earned graduate-school money one winter as a ski instructor in the Rockies, where he met some rodeo cowboys who offered to exchange lessons. Bernstein taught them how to schuss; they taught him bareback bronc riding. By the time he was back on the coast teaching American studies, he was spending his weekends at rodeos on the Eastern circuit. He even kept a Wyoming address for his rodeo entries and a "Cowboy State" license plate for his car; he thought it fit with his dreams better than Virginia.

Since permanently settling in the West more than twenty years ago, Bernstein has been a college professor, art agent, museum director, publishing-company editor, national director of a traveling art exhibition called "Indian Pride on the Move," and author of *Families That Take in Friends,* an informal history of dude ranches. But during this summer, as if everything else had just been preparation, he is nearing age fifty and finally doing what he always dreamed about: being a cowboy for a cattle ranch in the Big Hole.

It's a long way and a long time since he first asked his father for cowboy boots, but Bernstein seems content, especially when he can put them up on the coffee table in his living room, put on a record by Marty Robbins, Ian Tyson, or the Sons of the Pioneers, and talk about the West. In this setting, he delivers what might once have been a lecture to an American Studies 101 course at an Eastern college:

"The West, as an American symbol, has always been a place of freedom, where Americans can be themselves, free from the superficial demands placed on them by society," he says. "The existence of a western frontier and the concept of Manifest Destiny is what separates the United States from the experiences of all other countries. It created our view of ourselves, and other nations' views of us—did you know there are more than a hundred Western clubs in Munich?

"There was adventure out on the frontier. And there was opportunity. I think that's the key thing. The frontier provided opportunity, and it was for anybody. Color, national origin, wealth didn't matter. And it didn't even matter whether you actually went to the frontier or not. Psychologically, you knew it was an option for your life, an escape valve.

"Manifest Destiny evolved into more than a concept of coast-to-coast settlement. It grew to include a belief in unlimited resources—forests, farms, oil, minerals—to be developed. Americans have the notion that if it *can* be done, it *should* be done, which derives from Manifest Destiny. That's not necessarily always a good notion—the atom bomb is an example—but it's an American notion.

"We're only realizing now that there are limits. The frontier is closed. Resources aren't inexhaustible. We've learned there are some things we can't do, and there are some things we can do that we shouldn't do. Today I think a lot of people feel really trapped. A lot of people aren't happy with their life style but they don't know what to do and don't know where to go."

The lecture breaks off so Bernstein can have me listen to Ian Tyson's song in honor of Will James, the cowboy-artist-writer whose books Bernstein read as a youngster in Queens. This steers the conversation to cowboys.

If the West has become a symbol of America's identity, Bernstein says, then the cowboy is the human symbol of the West and imbued with as many romantic myths. "The cowboy era was short—from the end of the Civil War until roughly 1890—and there were never more than about forty thousand of them, total," he says. "His life wasn't romantic, it was hard and lonely, but the myth has captivated Americans since the first dime novels. Sure it's been romanticized, but there's nothing wrong with that. I don't know why people are ashamed or afraid of that."

Bernstein certainly isn't. His academic life has been spent exploring (and sometimes exploding) the myths of the West; but his personal life has been spent in pursuit of becoming like its central character. If there's a contradiction in this—or in Bernstein's mixed apparel of blue jeans, boots, a properly soiled Stetson, and a Brooks Brothers button-down shirt—it doesn't bother him. It was the dream, the myth of the cowboys and the West that pulled him from New York to the Bitterroots, and it is the dream he now intends to live. He feels lucky to be living it.

> She eases the silver barrette
> from her palomino hair,
> one long strand still clinging,
> and hands it to me
> for good luck. I've tried everything
> from striped socks to homespun prayer,
> even had the lining in my hat signed
> by a famous country singer
> cooing in her long southern drawl,
> "hold it real tight now." Still
> those broncs keep dumping me,
> Stetson-first, into arena
> after arena dirt and fences.
> Somebody up there loves bucking
> horses more than me, and nothing
> but nothing's going to change that—unless
> maybe this silver barrette
> from a girl raised with a mustang
> Montana wind in her mane.

Paul Zarzyski, who wrote that poem, was born and raised in a logging and mining town near Lake Superior in Wisconsin. It wasn't any romantic dream that brought him West, it was a teaching assistant's job at the University of Montana in Missoula, where he could study, earn a master's degree, and make a little money so he could continue writing poetry. What Zarzyski didn't know until he got to Montana was that he had always been a cowboy at heart. He didn't know much about horses, he had never seen a rodeo, he was already in his mid-twenties, and his frame was husky and muscle-bound. In short, just about everything was wrong for starting out to ride bareback broncs, an event that favors younger, slimmer, more experienced men.

Zarzyski is thirty-four years old now, still riding the rodeo circuit in the summer, still writing free-verse poetry, still not making money at either. You'd be hard pressed to find someone who has deliberately chosen two vocations so virtually guaranteed to keep a person in poverty.

He has trouble explaining why he does these things. "There isn't any 'why,' there isn't any reason," he says. "It's just something I love. It's become an obsession. I don't make a living at either one. Part of it may be the need to take on what seems to be an impossible task. There's no reason, just an obsession. Maybe obsession is another word for love. I don't know."

He talks about the friends he's made in the rodeo, the thrill of pitting himself not against another rider but against the horse. "You love the people, you love the animals, and you love the risk," he says, and then he makes a remark that reminds me of Lee Hames, who was born a cowboy.

"Anything that's real hard is worth pursuing," Zarzyski says. Maybe that's why the title of his poem about getting dumped by broncs is "Call Me Lucky."

"A cowboy is a hopeless romantic livin' in a diminishin' way of life," Tom Bryant tells me. "That's his whole heartache: tryin' to hold on to a way of life that's diminishin'."

By the time little Joel Bernstein came back from his English-riding lesson in New York and asked his father for cowboy boots, little Tom Bryant had already decided he wanted to be a cowboy too. Like Bernstein, who helps him at his job at the McDowell Ranch in the Big Hole, Bryant has lived his half century to reach the point where he can earn twenty-five dollars a day on a horse chasing cows. He was born in southern Georgia, where his father was a sharecropper, but a neighbor had some beef cows and taught Bryant about cattle and horses.

"I learned at the age of about five or six that it was a hell of a lot more fun to be up on a horse heppin' him with those beef cattle than it was followin' along lookin' at the ass end of a mule all day," he says. He has held other jobs to make money—as a Pinkerton agent, recreation director for Missoula, running a campground— but he's always considered himself a cowboy.

His feelings about farming in southern Georgia have only been deepened by the cowboys' traditional contempt for farmers. ("The West is still a great country, but the picture and the story part of it has been plowed under by the farmer," wrote Charley Russell, the cowboy-artist whose gallery in Great Falls is more Montana shrine than a museum.) Bryant puts it this way: "A cowboy is a man a' horseback. And all down through history people have always looked up to a man on horseback. A farmer is a man a' foot. And anybody a' foot is somebody to be looked down on. I hope I never live long enough to go that route."

Spending long days alone on the range tends to harden a man's opinions. Bryant has similar thoughts about "urban cowboys" and the notion that truckers are modern-day cowboys.

On the movie: "I thought *Urban Cowboy* drove up the price of cowboy clothes so goddamned bad that a workin' man couldn't hardly afford to buy a pair of blue jeans. I'm damn glad that phase is over."

On truckers as cowboys: "A trucker is a teamster, doing what they did in the old days deliverin' goods with a team. They wear a Western hat and Western boots, but they're a hell of a long way from a cowboy."

Which leads him to his definition of a cowboy:

"A cowboy, number one, right up front, has got to be a stockman. That's what a cowboy is. There's a 'cow' in 'cowboy.' You gotta be able to look at a cow and know if she's healthy. You gotta be able to look at her coat, her hide, and tell if she's on good feed. You gotta be able to look in her eyes and tell if she's in trouble of any kind. You gotta be able to look at a calf and tell if that calf has sucked today or if he's lost his mother.

"Ridin' a horse is basic. You ride a horse to git from one place to another. And you gotta be able to rope. That's an important thing. Movies emphasize gunplay, but a rope is the most important tool to a cowboy. I use a rope twenty times a day; I've used a gun twice, to put a cow out of her misery.

"The ability of man to ride a horse, use a rope, and know stock—that's what makes a cowboy. It ain't nothin' else."

He tells me about the calving season that took place in April. As a "contract" cowboy (he doesn't live on the ranch, and doesn't do any ranch chores; he's paid to ride), he was assigned one thousand cows in two square-mile sections. Each day he would ride out to make sure there were as many live births as possible. Each calf was tagged and inoculated. If a mother was having trouble with a calf coming out backward or upside down, he would help in the delivery. One calf had turned sideways in the birth canal and died; Bryant had to reach in, cut the carcass into quarters, and extract it, while saving the cow. Temperatures in the Big Hole, a broad basin at an elevation of 6,000 feet, were often ten or twelve degrees below zero in the morning. Bryant spent fourteen to sixteen hours a day in the saddle. "It's hard, hard, hard work," he says. Risky too. In the last five years, he's been in the hospital five times from "wrecks."

"What's romantic about that?" I ask. I don't remember any of the scenes he's just described in the Saturday matinees.

"Waaall," Bryant starts, taking in a deep breath. I wonder if I've just brought his whole life's dream into question and now he's reconsidering it. He isn't. He's just taking a deep breath.

"I'm out, I'm doing what I wanna do," he explains. "I'm not locked up in an office. I'm not takin' a lot of shit from a lot of people. The job that I do, they give me to do and then they get the hell out of the way and let me alone to do it.

"The rewards are intrinsic. Out in the open, I see the sun come up, see the first robins when they git here, see the Canada geese when they git here, see the moose calves and elk wander around. See eagles, hawks, coyotes and baby coyotes followin'. That's what I see. No telephones ringin', car horns blowin', people cussin' and screamin' and bein' uptight. I see the moon come up and shine on the mountains."

Bryant walks the same way as Lee Hames, a little bent, a little gingerly. It comes from so many hours in the saddle, just as a farmer's shoulders round into a concave curve from the years hunched over a tractor's steering wheel. And it comes, as he says, from all the "wrecks" he's been in.

"Cowboyin' is a rough son-of-a-bitchin' way of life, I'll tell ya," he says. "It's a hard way to make a dollar. I've had my leg broke,

I've had my hand broke, I've had my foot broke, I've been kicked, and I've been run over by bad cows. But when I fall, as long as I still bounce like a young man, I guess I can ride like one too."

He doesn't think cowboys are obsolete. In the big outfits of the West, at least, he says, there are still places accessible only to a man who can ride a horse, knows stock, and uses a rope.

"There ain't nothing that can do the job of a man and a horse. They cain't do it," he says. "There's still a need, and I'm damn glad of it."

And there's the moon coming up and shining on the mountains. It sure beats the back end of a mule.

Joel Bernstein is my host and part-time guide during my stay along the Bitterroot. With the calving and branding season completed, and the cattle already moved to their ranges for the summer, there isn't much contract cowboy work for him or Tom Bryant. Bernstein keeps himself afloat by organizing a lecture series and leading trail rides for a hotel in Missoula; he has time to show me around.

He takes me to Glen's Cafe in Florence, which has the greatest selection of great pies—thirteen varieties on some days—this side of Lynch, Nebraska. The chance for some pie at another of his favorites, Skeets Cafe in Dillon in the Beaverhead Rock area, adds him to the prospective Canadian Club search party. Not to be outdone by his friends, Paul Zarzyski the cowboy-poet, Tom Bryant the hopeless romantic, and Lee Hames the cowboy–treasure hunter, Bernstein gives me his own nugget of cowboy philosophy: "A pie without a good crust is like a horse without good hooves," he says. "Useless."

A day is spent in the Big Hole, the high basin rimmed by the Bitterroot, Pioneer, and Anaconda ranges. We visit Big Hole National Battlefield, where 182 men under Col. John Gibbon ambushed Chief Joseph's immigrant village of eight hundred Nez Perce (including only 125 warriors) before the dawn of August 9, 1877. The surprise attack killed a number of women and children, but the Nez Perce warriors quickly regrouped and soon had the Army pinned on a small, wooded rise. The Indian siege lasted a few days, while the village buried and mourned its dead and then packed up to continue the long flight toward Canada. Near the end, the Army force was being kept immobile by about a dozen braves, who later crept away to join their tribe. Nevertheless, the

Army claimed victory. The officers were given promotions; seven Congressional Medals of Honor were handed out.

We also stop by the McDowell Ranch, where Jock and Kathy McDowell invite us to supper with them and their ranch hands. One of the men rode a horse all the way from Iowa to be in the West; he has just married the ranch cook. Another young hand is from the West Coast, spending his first summer on a ranch. He's decided to enter the bull-riding event at the Hamilton rodeo and is getting a healthy combination of advice and kidding from Joel and Tom. Jock, who was raised on this ranch and was the National Intercollegiate Rodeo Association saddle bronc champion for 1972 and 1973, seems to be caught between amusement at the prospect and concern that he might lose a ranch hand to injury. Their daughter Jamie has already been riding horses for three years, and even though she's only six, Joel claims he'd rather have her along on a cattle drive than some of the other hands.

On my last full day near Traveller's Rest, Bernstein and I take a trail ride from his ranch into the foothills of the Bitterroots. As he saddles up Winsome (his black mare) and Sugar Lips (my sorrel), I ask if there's anything special I need to know.

"If she starts going too fast, hold on," he says.

We move out of the corral and west along a dusty road. The sky is a clear, robin's-egg blue; the absence of any wind intensifies the heat in the valley. We turn onto an old logging road, then again onto a smaller trail, each turn accompanied by a steeper incline. Bernstein's two dogs are with us. Bouncer follows the back left heel of Joel's horse, just out of kicking range. Gray is the one who bounces. She is chasing squirrels out ahead of us, leaping and bounding in the tall grass. After another turn, another increase in the slope, a rushing creek appears below us, its roar a sudden intrusion on the silence, like a noisy child bursting into a quiet study. Behind us the Bitterroot Valley has dropped and receded into a miniature version of itself. Bernstein turns in his saddle and gestures toward the panorama.

"In the West, *this* is what is important: what's outside, not inside," he says. "In the East, people spend their time and energy on decorating their homes and apartments. Out here, life is defined by the land. *This* is a reality the rest of America has lost touch with."

Still climbing, we follow the creek into thicker timber of straight and tall ponderosa pine, yellow and brown trunks with high, green branches that shade us from the sun. The temperature drops and the noise hits a crescendo when we cross the creek on a log bridge, then we round a ridge and the sound of the water is gone as quickly as it first reached us. Indian paintbrush and lupine begin decorating the trail in the pines. Through the occasional breaks in the trees, the snow-capped mountain peaks tower above us—white substitutes for the clouds that are missing. A narrow irrigation ditch courses next to our path. Not many hours ago, its clear water was snow being melted by the hot sun on the southeast mountain faces.

The horses stop to slurp the irrigation water. Bernstein says we'll leave the trail here to angle over to a high meadow a half hour away. He and Winsome turn down the steep side of the ditch and disappear into the ponderosas; Sugar Lips is still slurping. After several kicks in her side, I wheel her around to follow down the embankment.

What happens next is a blur in my memory, recalled in sensations of color, sound, and motion, and then pain. As soon as Sugar Lips reaches the bottom of the embankment, her ears go straight back and she lunges into a full gallop. Not a trot, not a canter. A full-steam gallop through the trees. These things I remember: pulling the reins and saying "Whoa" to no effect; gold shafts of sunlight and dark green shade; lighter green branches slapping my face; Joel's voice shouting something unintelligible as Sugar Lips and I pass him and Winsome at careening, full tilt; losing my Stetson to the force of rushing air, a branch, a bounce, something; and the yellow-brown trunks of ponderosas, particularly those tree trunks, telescoping to the size of brick columns as we weave through them until it seems we're running through a solid maze of yellow-brown. Somewhere along this route, I fall off Sugar Lips's left side, spread-eagling and turning, my arm and face scraping dry pine from the ground cover. My right knee strikes something hard, sending a pulse of bright color through my mind. I roll two or three times and come to a stop next to a tree. It's a yellow and brown ponderosa.

Joel trots up, carrying my hat. He sees I'm alive and trots on through the trees. A few minutes later he reappears with Sugar Lips in tow. Horse and hat are uninjured.

"Can you stand up?" he asks, handing me my hat.

My knee is throbbing, and the pain or shock sends waves of

nausea through me with each throb. I can stand up, but it's hard
to walk. I tell Bernstein *what* happened, but seek from him a reason
why. He quotes the late Spike Van Cleve, who ran a dude ranch
in the Crazy Mountains and wrote several books about life in
Montana: "Who knows what ghosts a horse sees in its mind?"
Thanks a lot, Spike.

TRAIL RULE 2: Never trust your horse.

Everyone, I guess, knows the adage about getting right back up
on a horse that has just thrown you to the ground. It's supposed
to imply grit, determination, overcoming defeat and adversity,
maybe even a little courage. I'd like to be able to say those are my
motives for climbing back up on Sugar Lips there in the piney
slopes of the Bitterroots. But the truth is, we're two hours by horse
from Bernstein's ranch. It's much too far for someone with a knee
swelling to the size of a ripe cantaloupe to hobble.

The long ride back gives me plenty of time to reconsider any
romantic notions about selling my house in New Hampshire to
sign on as a contract cowboy for twenty-five dollars a day at the
McDowell Ranch. I figure that by nightfall, the tale of me being
unable to handle Sugar Lips will have replaced the idea of the
young ranch hand's wanting to ride a Brahma bull as the main
joke from the Bitterroot to the Big Hole. In the motion picture
Western of my fantasies, I am now trying out roles other than the
lead cowboy. Editor of the frontier newspaper? Bartender or piano
player at the Longbranch? Sodbuster? Shop clerk?

Two good things, however, result from my "wreck," although
I wouldn't recommend deliberately dismounting from a galloping
horse in the mountains to learn them.

The first, easing the physical pain, is the discovery of the treatment. After applying ice to my knee, which by the time we reach
his ranch is straining the seams of my jeans, Bernstein drives me
to the Sleeping Child Hot Springs near Hamilton, Montana, to
relax in the warm waters. For the remainder of my journey, long
after my knee has healed, stopping at natural hot springs becomes
as automatic as stopping at historic markers.

The second discovery soothes the psychological injury to my
cowboy fantasies. Joel treats the incident not as the result of an
Eastern dude's stupidity, but as the kind of "wreck" that is part

of any cowboy's existence. Tom Bryant's question when he hears of it is whether I bounced like a young man and whether I walked or rode home. Obviously, Lee Hames and Paul Zarzyski don't see anything unusual in a man getting bucked from a horse; that's what they've done for sport. The dream, like my knee, recovers. Call me lucky.

20

Give and Take on the Lolo Trail

I have been wet and as cold in every part as I ever was in my life. . . . Killed a Second Colt which we all Suped hartily on and thought it fine meat. From William Clark's journal
Lolo Trail
September 16, 1805

Just beyond the crest of Lolo Pass, just past the signs that welcome me to Idaho and remind me to turn my clock back an hour for the Pacific Time Zone, at the point where U.S. 12 begins a downhill descent that continues to the state of Washington, a highway sign warns me what to expect of this route: WINDING ROAD NEXT 77 MILES.

The world is different here. Topographical lines are vertical, not horizontal. The pines and cedars and firs reach heavenward like giant crusaders' jousting lances, gently tapering to their points. Colors are defined in gradations of green, not brown. Once it has plummeted to the Lochsa River valley, the highway bends with the curves of the river. The trees and the steep slopes offer few openings to the blue sky and fewer glimpses of mountain peaks. And no horizons. Froth on the Lochsa provides the only glistenings of white.

The expedition struggled to survive this area. September snows were falling. Nights were cold and wet. Their guide led them by mistake from the Indian trail on the high ridges down to the river, wasting at least a day. Accidents with the pack animals were daily occurrences in the rough, choked terrain. The captains wanted to get through here as fast as possible and reach a navigable river to the Pacific, but the five days the Indians had told them the trip would require stretched into eleven. There was no game for food, so the explorers ate some of their horses for strength. When it emerged on the Weippe Prairie east of modern-day Orofino, Idaho, the entire troupe was on the brink of starvation.

I, on the other hand, am in no rush. I could easily make the 180-odd miles to Lewiston this June afternoon, but I don't want to. This is one of the prettiest roads I've been on, and I intend to enjoy it.

I pause first at the Bernard DeVoto Memorial Cedar Grove, named in honor of the great historian and Lewis and Clark scholar who often camped in the stillness of the giant cedars when he was editing the journals. His ashes, according to his wishes, were scattered from a plane flying over the Bitterroots. My visit is brief but reverential, like walking from a sunlit plaza into the dim light and coolness of a cathedral.

On the condition that I not reveal its location, Richard Steffel has told me where to find a secluded hot spring on a creek feeding into the Lochsa. The well-marked Jerry Johnson hot springs—the site the salesman in Great Falls had recommended as a prime place to meet women—are also in this area, but I'm more inclined to soak my still-tender knee in solitude than in firing up any more Road Fevers. Finding the trail Steffel described, I follow it up a small, clear stream for twenty minutes. Two small basins rimmed by a halo of yellow buttercups sit on a side hill about forty feet above the creek. The basins, formed by natural depressions in the hillside, are shallow pools about seven feet in diameter and eighteen inches deep. Hot water from a thermal spring dribbles down the hillside and collects in the basins before tumbling on into the creek. The water is about 100 degrees, hot enough to make me ease in slowly, cool enough to allow me to soak for an hour, interrupted by one plunge into the frigid, snow-fed stream. From my perch in the hot pools, I can look up the creek to a sunny clearing where two mule deer are browsing.

Cedars are all around me, and I bask in their mute majesty. They were here before Lewis and Clark hurried through; they were here when Chief Joseph led his flight across the mountains. They must have wondered what all the rush was about. They were here for DeVoto, they're here for me, and they'll be here for who knows how much longer. Their stolid presence seems better attuned to solace than suffering, but then again, they're not talking to those of us who measure life in years instead of centuries.

This epiphany, like the others on my trip so far, occurs not because I was seeking it, but precisely because I wasn't. Like a cat that doesn't come when it's called, this kind of special moment sneaks up on you when you're not looking, rubs against your leg, and begins purring for attention.

I suppose an argument could be made that hiking along a rough trail twenty minutes in, twenty minutes out, is an odd treatment for a sore knee, but the hot waters and the cedars have worked their wonders by the time I get back to the *Discovery* and head for the campground near the Powell Ranger Station. The campground is about half full. There is no problem finding a spot near the Lochsa, a river whose name means "rough water," as it winds through the thick walls of pines. A few pines slant from one bank toward the other like half-raised toll gates. I see two more deer while I set up camp. Supper is made from some groceries I bought in Missoula, a simple but satisfying meal of cold cuts, fresh bread, some fruit, and a piece of Glen's Cafe pie.

The Lochsa Lodge—a restaurant/lodge/bar/gas station, the only one of any of those four modern conveniences in the ninety-mile stretch of U.S. 12 between Lolo Hot Springs and Syringa, Idaho— is close to the campground. After supper, I walk over to check out its breakfast menu and have a beer before bed. The building is a former hunting lodge, and its high-ceilinged main room is adorned with trophies of moose, elk, deer, and mountain-goat heads, and rack after rack of antlers. A jukebox, video game, and pool table dominate the bar section. The bartender says the lodge cabins are filled this week with people planting trees in the mountains, an odd notion for me to ponder since I haven't seen anything *but* trees since cresting the Lolo Pass. A woman at the bar, a member of the Flathead reservation in Montana, is working with the tree- planters in areas of the national forest that have been clear-cut by lumber companies. Her job is to place a small covering on the south side of the seedlings to shade them from the harsh sun until they're strong enough to survive on their own. It's hard work, she says (she shades between 1,200 and 1,600 seedlings a day), but good money (up to $200 a day, depending on how many trees she shades). Most of her fellow workers are Indians.

Back at the *Discovery,* I light a small campfire, relax with a pipeful of tobacco, and read the journals by the light of a lantern and to the whispers of the Lochsa. This is the only spot where U.S. 12 and the Lewis and Clark route along the Lolo Trail cross each other. The ridge trail itself was no picnic, but it was a better route in those days than this rough valley that resisted any road until the last quarter century. On their fourth day in the Bitterroots, after their guide had become confused and directed them down the steep mountainsides to the river, the explorers reached this point. Their horses had stumbled and stalled among the fallen timber. The men were already out of meat, so they killed one of the colts in their pack train and ate it. To commemorate the meal, Clark named the creek that joins another to form the Lochsa at this campsite "Colt Killed Creek."

With the exception of the White Cliffs of the Missouri, the Lolo Trail area of the Lewis and Clark trail is probably the least changed since their journey across the continent. The river is still untamed, "Swift and Stoney," as Clark described it, the mountains still formidable, the pockets of cedars still hold their ancient secrets. The sparks from my campfire rise up through the canopy of evergreens and float between the treetops pointing toward the Big Dipper, just as they must have when the Corps of Discovery huddled around their cookfire on a cold September night in 1805.

And yet, just as the modern road and the expedition's broken trail intersect only briefly here before going their own ways, my experience here only brushes with theirs. This is an intersection of settings, but not of time or circumstance. For the explorers, this was a grim, nearly fatal passage—snow, cold, wet, no game, no food; terrible in its isolation from any comforts greater than fresh horse meat and a small fire. For me, the area's seeming remoteness from civilization is the very source of its pleasure.

Other differences are evident. This evening I've seen deer where they found none. Tomorrow, I can gas up my camper and eat a hearty breakfast before continuing down this lovely highway. Trucks from Montana will be traveling down this modern passage, hauling grain. People will already be swarming over the mountainsides, planting the kinds of trees that obstructed the explorers' path. Isolated as this area still is, it is not untouched by man.

Their journals speak of deprivation and hard going here, and not at all of the area's beauty; mine are filled with notes of sensual and spiritual delight. It seems appropriate that the name of Colt Killed Creek has been changed to White Sand Creek. Same water, same rocks, many of the same trees. Different times, different names, reflecting different experiences.

ROAD RULE 18: One explorer's misery can be another's joy; one traveler's near defeat can be another's epiphany; one man's place to fear untimely death can be another's chosen spot to have his ashes spread.

COLT KILLED CREEK COROLLARY: One man's meat can be another man's horse.

Mornings come early in the camper. By 6 A.M., I am up and splashing cold Lochsa water on my face. Breakfast at the lodge (eggs, hash browns, a big torpedo of Polish sausage, four pieces of toast, an unending cup of coffee) is eaten in the presence of the trophy heads of all the game animals the starving explorers never saw in this neck of the country.

Highway 12 is as pretty today as it was yesterday. Its gentle curves along the riverbanks keep offering new variations of sparkling river, tall trees, steep slopes, and cascading creeks. The *Discovery* steps along happily. The road surface is smooth and unobstructed, the going is still all downhill. I inadvertently introduce two potential elements of danger into this pleasure cruise. One is the tendency to rubberneck at the scenery instead of watching for grain trucks or other gawking explorers in their cars. The second is my habit of trying to fill, tamp, and light my pipe on the move, a complicated maneuver if you're also steering a vehicle along a mountain stream. The Road Spirit is with me today. The *Discovery* and I proceed on without incident.

The Lochsa eventually joins the Selway to form the Middle Fork of the Clearwater, a broader, darker river, which in turn meets the South Fork at Kooskia to become the Clearwater proper, running north now toward Orofino. New colors: gold and yellow flowers crowding the highway shoulder, red clover, purple vetch, and mountain bluebirds, the Idaho state bird. Signs of civilization: clusters of houses, more traffic, some open farm fields where Appaloosas, the white-rumped horses the Nez Perce never bred, graze in the sunshine. And Pepsi signs, Pepsi signs everywhere, the logo used for advertising everything from gas stations to insurance agencies.

At Greer, Idaho (population 30), I turn off Highway 12 and take a state road up severe switchbacks to reach the uplands of Weippe Prairie. The traffic is heavy with lumber trucks, empties climbing with me, full ones with straight fir and cedar logs descending. On top of the plateau are rolling wheatfields that briefly rekindle memories of Nebraska, except the white peaks of the Bitterroots are looming in the distance, and a turn in the road exposes precipices to the wooded Clearwater valley.

Clark and six men had pushed ahead of the main party on September 18, 1805, in a desperate search for food and friendly Indians. On the nineteenth, they came upon a stray horse, a doubly good omen. It meant Indians were nearby; and it provided them their third meal of horseflesh. On the twentieth, Clark and his men rode out of the woods and onto the Weippe Prairie, where they met some Nez Perce Indians.

Like the Flatheads and Shoshoni before them, the Nez Perce had never seen white men. Tribal legend holds that some Nez Perce members wanted to kill the explorers, which would have been an easy task, given the men's small numbers and fatigued condition. An old woman in the camp, however, convinced her fellow tribesmen to befriend the strangers—an act of life-saving generosity toward this first probe of Manifest Destiny that was later repaid by the U.S. government with the same treachery visited on all the other tribes whose assistance was crucial to the expedition's ultimate success.

During their eleven-day ordeal in the Bitterroots, the men had been reduced to eating anything they could get their hands on—a few grouse, a coyote, a raven, some small crawfish found in a stream, an ill-tasting "portable soup" in their provisions, bear oil, twenty pounds of their candles. Horse meat was a stomach-filling delicacy in comparison. Pvt. Joseph Whitehouse's journal entry that "the most of the party is weak and feeble Suffering with hunger" summarizes their plight, as do the various names given to their camps: Colt Killed Creek, Lonesome Cove, Hungery Creek, Portable Soup Camp, Hearty Meal Stop (where the Lewis party discovered the butchered horse meat left by Clark), Full Stomach Camp, and Pheasant Camp.

The Nez Perce gave the explorers dried salmon and camas roots to eat, and a supply of food was sent back to the main party, which joined the advance group several days later. The famished men gorged themselves on the new Indian food. This created its own ordeal: acute diarrhea and stomach pains. Accustomed as they had become across the Plains to an essentially all-meat diet of buffalo, deer, and elk, the sudden change to oily fish and camas debilitated the whole group. Rush's powerful "thunderbolts" and every other diuretic and emetic in their medical arsenal were administered, but what seemed to work best in their slow recovery was buying a few Nez Perce dogs and roasting them for supper. From here to the Pacific coast and then back until they crossed the Bitterroots again, as they traveled along one of the world's richest salmon and steelhead waterways, the expedition dined instead on dogs. The men traded for them in quantities of up to forty a time from the bemused natives. Lewis grew to prefer dog meat to lean venison or elk; Clark never did acquire a taste for it. No one knows how long it took the Columbia River system's dog population to recover.

WEIPPE COROLLARY: One man's delicacy can be another man's bellyache; one man's pet can be another man's pâté.

Although Lewis mentions seeing some Indians with pierced noses among the host tribe, it is a matter of continuing controversy whether they were native tribal members or visitors from neighboring areas. Regardless, the name Nez Perce that the explorers gave the tribe stuck just as firmly to the Chopunnish as Flathead did to the Ootlashoots.

Among all the tribes they encountered across the continent, the Nez Perce would be the most fondly remembered by the expedition for their magnanimous assistance in the Corps of Discovery's greatest time of need. On the return trip, when the Nez Perce gave the expedition some horses to eat, Lewis called it "a much greater act of hospitality than we have witnessed from any nation or tribe since we have passed the Rocky mountains. in short be it spoken to their immortal honor it is the only act which deserves the appellation of hospitallity which we have witnessed in this quarter." Clark described the tribe as "much more clenly in their persons and habitations than any nation we have seen sence we left the Illinois."

My experience in one of the cafes of Weippe (pronounced WEE-ipe, population 828) raises the question of whether a contingent of haggard and alien-looking strangers would be greeted with such open arms here today. I'm not that hungry, even though it's past noon. The Lochsa Lodge breakfast, particularly the sausage, is still very much with me. But a piece of pie would get me through to supper.

The main lunch crowd has dispersed when I sit down at the counter. The waitress and the four patrons, all at separate tables and spaced as far away from each other as possible in the room, are hashing over the ills of the world. This issues forum is conducted at full voice, so it's not exactly as if I'm eavesdropping. Or interrupting. My presence is ignored, like that of a lone child at an adults' dinner party.

The waitress and one woman are dissecting the billing clerks and credit companies that apparently annoy them like so many insects. The problem seems to be that all clerks are incompetent. My cup of coffee is poured while the waitress recounts one particularly triumphant moment in which she gave a clerk a good tongue-lashing.

Talk switches to taxes. The waitress moves over to the serving window by the kitchen, the maximum distance from everyone, thus assuring that this topic can be discussed at the decibel level it deserves. A second woman explains how her trailer home is overtaxed, and how she has challenged the tax collector either to buy it at the assessed value or lower the appraisal. The waitress likes that approach, but has a better story of her own, which again deals with putting an incompetent bureaucrat in his rightful place. She walks toward me while telling it and pauses in mid-story to lean forward, smile sweetly, and ask, "Decide what kind of pie you want?" I order cherry, and she resumes her account, back at full volume now, as she goes to the kitchen and puts a piece in the microwave. This requires a third woman to use a near-shout in order to convey her story about a tax appraisal problem with some land she owns.

After my pie has been properly irradiated and placed on the counter, the waitress brings up welfare. Here is a topic everyone has an opinion about. The fourth patron, a man, joins in now, and the whole cafe resounds with the chorus of five voices. Welfare is what's primarily wrong with the country, according to the waitress, prompting unanimous agreement among the participants, each with his or her own horror story of unbelievable giveaways to listless but sly recipients.

"This world would be all right if they just got rid of that welfare," the waitress opines, concluding this section of the agenda.

Schools—or rather how lazy and bad and overpaid most teachers are—are next on the list. They chew on the issue; I chew on my cherry pie. All of us now are getting different types of indigestion. History is repeating itself.

I fight back the temptation to bring up the subject of pie abuse and microwaves, something I feel strongly about, and instead finish my coffee without speaking. As I pay my bill, bureaucrats have been dragged out again for another bashing. California requires citizens to get appointments to apply for driver's licenses just to

accommodate the clerks, the waitress reveals. The group is reacting
with appropriate outrage when I walk out the door, relieved that
I hadn't entered as the modern equivalent of Lewis and Clark.
After all, they were employees of the federal government.

Back on U.S. 12, just beyond Orofino, I pass the Lewis & Clark
Trail Cafe and Sacajawea's House of Gifts, which advertises ten-
cent coffee, and wish I hadn't made the side trip to Weippe. This
would have been a better stop, I bet. Across from the site where
the expedition hewed out its canoes, the North Fork of the Clearwater enters. A high concrete dam on the fork and a federal fish
hatchery are the principal sights.

Farther downstream along the broad Clearwater, the mountains
and forests begin gradually to relinquish their dominance of the
terrain. The valley sides aren't as steep; the hilltops are rounded,
not pointed; a thin layer of light green grass, through which red
soil and rock is evident, replaces the evergreens. The topography
is pleasingly familiar in its scale—New England without the trees,
or a crumpled Iowa. Both make me think of home.

At the Nez Perce National Historic Park visitor center in Lapwai, I meet Albert Barros, a young park ranger and an enrolled
member of the tribe. He agrees to show me around, and in keeping
with Nez Perce tradition, offers me a place to stay during my visit.

Dating from the time of Lewis and Clark to 1877, the Nez Perce
were peaceably inclined toward whites. Henry and Eliza Spalding,
Presbyterian missionaries who came to the West after the reports
of the desire of the Flathead and Nez Perce for conversion, arrived
here in 1836 to preach the dual gospels of Bible and civilization to
the Nez Perce. Near their preserved mission is a plaque from the
Idaho Daughters of the American Revolution honoring the Spaldings. It is attached to a seven-foot basaltic rock that, in ancient
Nez Perce lore, represented a medicine man turned to stone for
religious offenses.

Other tribal shrines have survived in better shape. Coyote, an
important figure in Nez Perce mythology, had a habit of turning
living things to stone. He saw Ant and Yellow Jacket arguing, and
when they refused to settle their grievances as he suggested, Coyote
transformed them into rock, locked in frozen, eternal struggle on
the banks of the Clearwater. Black Bear interrupted his fishing
one day, so Coyote flung his fishnet and the bear onto the hillside,

where they can still be seen in rock form. A monster lived near modern-day East Kamiah. Coyote killed him and tossed his dismembered parts in all directions. Where they landed, Indian tribes sprang up—the Flatheads, Cayuse, Crow, Sioux, Blackfeet, Pend Oreilles, and others. At the battle site itself, Coyote squeezed the remaining heart of the beast, and the drops of blood mingled with the rich soil to create Nee-me-poo ("the people"), the Nez Perce, his most favored humans. The rock mound, Heart of the Monster, marks the spot.

A treaty in 1855, when Idaho and western Montana were part of the Washington Territory, reserved seven million acres for the proud and powerful tribe, although the Nez Perce permitted some white settlements on their land. Then gold was discovered in 1860. From the squeezing of this different kind of rock sprang a different kind of people. Wild mining towns like Pierce and Orofino were settled in blatant violation of the treaty. Rather than enforcing the existing treaty, the government solution to the problem was to propose a new treaty, reducing the Nez Perce land to 757,000 acres.

The tribe divided over acceptance of the proposal between "treaty" and "nontreaty" Indians—a division that also roughly paralleled the split between those who had converted to Christianity and those who remained true to Coyote. The government claimed that the "treaty" Indians signed for the entire tribe. "Nontreaty" Nez Perce compared it to a village neighbor selling someone else's horse and refused to move onto the shrunken reservation.

By 1877 the Army was on the scene to respond to settlers' demands for action. Chief Joseph's and the other "nontreaty" bands were told to relocate peacefully or the soldiers would move them by force. An old chief was thrown in jail for extra persuasion, and the bands were given thirty days to get their belongings together, locate their scattered horse and cattle herds, say goodbye to the land that had been theirs from time immemorial, and get across the flood-swollen Snake River to the reservation. Reluctantly, they began complying. During the exodus, however, a hotheaded young warrior slipped away from camp with two companions to avenge the murder of his father two years earlier by a white man. They killed four whites, all known for hostility toward the Indians; the next day they were joined by some more Nez Perce on a two-day spree that left about fifteen more whites dead.

What followed next is a saga of struggle and, finally, tragedy.

On June 17, 1877, an Army and volunteer force of more than a hundred men tried to surprise the "nontreaty" village in White Bird Canyon, but were defeated by about seventy poorly equipped warriors. The Nez Perce suffered no casualties; thirty-four whites died on the open ground. Any hopes Chief Joseph harbored of remaining in the area and settling the issue through negotiation vanished. General O. O. Howard, under national pressure because of the Army's humiliation at White Bird Canyon, amassed more troops. A two-day battle on the Clearwater in July resulted in a draw.

Like salmon spawning against the strong river currents of their native land, reversing the nation's historic westerly movement in pursuit of life, liberty, and happiness, the Nez Perce began their flight east, hoping for refuge with the Crows near the Yellowstone. They crossed the Lolo Trail, went up the Bitterroot, fought the battle of the Big Hole, escaped to the Yellowstone, were refused help by the Crows, and headed for Canada, where they intended to join Sitting Bull in exile.

By now, the bulk of the U.S. Army in the West was converging on them from all directions. A contingent of six hundred men led by Col. Nelson Miles surprised the exhausted village-on-the-move on a cold morning in late September near the Bear Paw Mountains, ninety miles from the Canadian border. Five days of inconclusive fighting ensued. Joseph was lured across Army lines for a parley, then seized and arrested, but later released in exchange for one of Miles's officers. Howard arrived with reinforcements and sent word that if Joseph and his chiefs surrendered, they could return honorably to Lapwai. With many of his top war chiefs dead and the women and children starving in an early snowstorm, Joseph rode out and handed his rifle to Miles. Having helped lead his band in what military historians still consider one of the most remarkable combinations of battles and running retreats with a civilian population in tow, Joseph uttered these words into the bitter Montana wind:

> Tell General Howard I know his heart. What he told me before I have in my heart. I am tired of fighting. . . . It is cold and we have no blankets. The little children are freezing to death. My people, some of them, have run away to the hills, and have no blankets, no food; no one knows where

they are—perhaps freezing to death. I want to have time to
look for my children and see how many I can find. Maybe I
shall find them among the dead. Hear me, my chiefs. I am
tired; my heart is sick and sad. From where the sun now
stands, I will fight no more forever.

Joseph and 480 of his followers surrendered. Promises to the
contrary, they were shipped to Indian Territory in Oklahoma,
where many of them died in the hot, humid, alien country. In 1885
Joseph and the survivors were moved to the Colville Reservation
in northeast Washington. New treaties, new laws were passed.
The Nez Perce lands shrank again—to less than 90,000 acres, a
little over a tenth of the area encompassed by the 1855 treaty
boundaries. The promises made to Joseph in Montana were given
the same honor as the treaties. He died in Washington in 1904,
still waiting to be allowed to go home.

My visit to the Nez Perce reservation is well timed. The seventeenth
of June is a doubly historic day. In 1806, the Lewis and Clark
expedition was stopped by deep snows while attempting an eastbound crossing of the Lolo Trail on their way home. On the same
day in 1877, the battle of White Bird Canyon was fought, setting
Chief Joseph's flight toward Canada in motion. The reservation is
holding a weekend powwow on the fifteenth and sixteenth to honor
their ancestors' tribulations. Albert Barros has the day off on the
seventeenth and offers to take me up the remote gravel road the
government has built along the Lolo Trail. The Road Spirit is still
smiling upon me.

Barros sends me to a communal dinner at the tribal headquarters
with a warning the men of the expedition would have appreciated
before they gorged themselves sick on salmon and camas root:
"Don't overindulge yourself." I eat a moderate meal of salmon loaf,
potato salad, fried bread, and Kool-Aid, then drive off for my own
tour of White Bird Canyon and the Spalding Mission before meeting Barros to attend the evening dance ceremonies.

We arrive after 10 P.M., but the dancing is still going strong.
This is no sock hop from my personal past, even if it is being held
in a school gymnasium. Five separate drum-and-chant groups alternate in starting an insistent beat on their bass drums and singing
traditional chants, each one building in a wailing crescendo. The

dancers, some of whom have come from other tribes in the West, are arrayed in colorful regalia: flowing headdresses of eagle and owl feathers, bright quills and beads, copper or ribbon armbands, buckskin leggings and moccasins, bells around their ankles to accentuate the rhythm of their footsteps. Prior to modern times, women weren't allowed on the dance floor, Barros tells me; they could stand on the edges and rock back and forth to the drum beats, but the floor was an all-male domain. Tonight, a male dance is followed by a female dance, and children's dances are interspersed with adult dances. "Honor" dances and "flag" dances are occasionally announced, during which the crowds in the bleachers stand and the men remove their cowboy hats while they watch.

Needless to say, I don't recognize any of the songs, except to note their similarity to the Hidatsa chants Gerard Baker sang to me in North Dakota and to the Sioux ceremonies at Sitting Bull's South Dakota grave. The male dancers move individually around the gym, dipping their heads and shoulders sharply and stiffly like plumed birds searching for feed on the hardwood floor. Their jangling steps to the tom-toms strike the floor ball first, then the heel on the off beat. The women's dance style, with the exception of the dervishlike "shawl" dances, is a more sedate shuffle in a circling line.

Shortly before midnight, when Barros and I leave, the dancing shows no sign of ending soon. An oldtimer has just donated five dollars to each chanter from one of the groups because they made him think of the days of his youth. A group of boys, some hardly five years old but already accomplished dancers, has taken the floor.

We stop at a bar in the ironically named town of Culdesac (population 261), where Indian couples are dancing to the music of a country-rock band. The attire here is jeans, Western shirts, and cowboy hats. When the bar closes, the entire group drives to a field near Lapwai to continue the celebration around a bonfire. Cars and pickups encircle the site, all pointing toward the center. Old pallets, crackling yellow in the heart of the pyre, give off a heat intense enough to warm our faces through the windsheld when we drive up. Small groups gather in the warmth, each one forming its own smaller circle around a beer cooler. Some bald tires are thrown on the fire, creating a green flame and sending a tendril of dark smoke toward the stars. This is a cultural activity I recognize

from my own experience. It reminds me of a homecoming celebration, and, in essence, that's what it is.

My journey so far has made me a connoisseur of Western sunsets.
I have given names to different varieties. A Charley Russell Sunset,
like the ones I witnessed in the White Cliffs of the Missouri, is
painted in soft pastels, muted colors of pink and mauve, with white
clouds spotting the canvas. A thicker cloud cover, with golden rays
radiating to prove the hidden sun's existence, is a Revealed Hand
of God Sunset. When the sinking sun sets the western horizon on
fire in deepening hues of crimson—the one I saw on horseback in
the Elkhorn Mountains is the standard against which these are
judged—it is a Valhalla Sunset. On rare occasions, the sun goes
down in a background of eggwhite and blue, a Once in a Blue
Moon Sunset. During this dry summer, the most common occurrence is a red sky at night, a Traveler's Delight, appreciated by
landbound voyagers in their wheeled vessels but a scourge to farmers waiting for oceans of rain.

Dawn, when it creeps in to join us at the bonfire around four-
thirty, is a new experience. The cone of firelight no longer defines
our world. Our view slowly expands toward the rolling hillsides
in ever lightening colors of green, tan, and brown. Fences, trees,
weeds, houses, horses and cattle in the fields, the reality of the
present steps forward through the waning veil of darkness to assume form. The fire itself loses its color and its mesmerizing pull
on our gaze until, like the pale morning star, it too extinguishes in
the sun's yellow light. Birds begin chirping. Our group disperses
and quietly sets about the individual business of the day.

Following a morning sleep, I go to today's tribal event, a noon
meal and ceremony for the descendants of the "nontreaty" Nez
Perce. The emcee calls it a "memorial to the chiefs and warriors
who died for their land they were chased away from." A special
flag song, termed the "Nez Perce national anthem," is chanted to
the slow beat of the drums. The blood descendants of those who
fled with Chief Joseph march across the gym floor. The rest of us
stand in the bleachers, hats off in respect. Albert Watters, a solid
man with gray, braided hair, and his family hold a memorial
ceremony for their ancestor Chief Ollokot, a renowned warrior and
buffalo hunter who was Joseph's younger brother. Joseph, like his
Sioux counterpart Sitting Bull, was more of a spiritual leader than

war chief. Just as Sitting Bull did not ride with the warriors battling Custer, Joseph was not the military leader of the Nez Perce; both, however, are the figures who dominate the white versions of their conflicts. Chiefs like Ollokot, Looking Glass, Five Wounds, and Rainbow were the Nez Perce counterparts to Crazy Horse and Gall, who defeated Custer. Ollokot was a leader in the battle of White Bird Canyon and the other fights and skirmishes in the long trek that ended near the Bear Paw Mountains, where he was killed in the final battle with Miles.

Watters and his clan spread a large quilt on the gymnasium floor and bring out an array of gifts: blankets, scarves, a headdress, ribbons, a mirror, a quill-and-feather dance bustle, shirts, shawls, baskets filled with smaller items. Some people are called by name from the audience to receive a gift (a descendant of Looking Glass gets a brass ring). Others are called by category—boys visiting from other tribes, a couple from Alaska, girls who participated in last night's shawl dance. All receive a handshake from the male descendants of Ollokot, a kiss and a hug from the women. Family members fan out to the chairs where elder tribal members sit and give them gifts as well. A gift of one hundred dollars is announced for the men who sang and drummed the honor song to start the ceremony. Watters offers two colts to anyone who will take care of them properly.

He speaks in the native tongue and the emcee translates it to English: "The feeling is good because they have done this. The memory of their loved ones will continue and go on. The ones who received the gifts will remember it. Those who witnessed it will also remember."

I have already learned my own lesson in this custom of generosity from Albert Barros, who is giving me a place to sleep during my visit. Yesterday, when I told him how much I admired the rattlesnake headband on his cowboy hat, he removed it and handed it to me, despite my protests. He also offered a lapel pin with a cattle head on it, which I at first refused, until he explained the protocol. Declining a gift is a great offense; offering one is a great honor. Openly admiring a Nez Perce's possession often makes him feel compelled to give it to you. The maple syrup I embarrassedly offer in return seems paltry in comparison, yet oddly apropos: the history of his tribe is one of giving much more than they ever received.

—

A different powwow is in progress in Lewiston. About five hundred RVs, camper/trailers, and truck/campers have gathered at the fairground for the Idaho State "Samboree." Chapters of the Good Sam Club, an organization with an international membership of 500,000, have arrived from around the state and nation to encamp for the weekend.

While touring America in the 1830s, Alexis de Tocqueville was struck by several phenomena he described as uniquely American. One was the propensity to form groups for nearly every possible purpose. "Americans of all ages, all conditions, and all dispositions, constantly form associations," he wrote in *Democracy in America*. "As soon as several of the inhabitants of the United States have taken up an opinion or a feeling which they wish to promote in the world, they look out for mutual assistance; and as soon as they have found each other out, they combine."

The Good Sams I meet in Lewiston are de Tocqueville's Americans. The self-powered RVs and big trailers are lined up in neat rows, forming their own streets and avenues on the asphalt parking lot. Most of the members are retired couples ("I'm spending my children's inheritance" is a popular bumper sticker) who consume much of the year in the typically American custom of restless travel. By forming club chapters, however, they have imposed purpose on their restlessness; in organizing themselves, they have given structure to the loose freedom of the road; in gathering at designated points across the land, they have created community, mobile mini-cities on rubber wheels.

Large maps of the nation are painted on the sides of their vehicles, with each state they have visited colored in. American flags fly over their awnings, with Good Sam pennants and other insignia fluttering in the brisk wind. Nearly all of the Good Sams I talk to are wearing special vests festooned with badges and medals from past Samborees and tourist sites; they also wear name tags displaying their name, their hometown or home chapter, and their role (the husband is usually the "RV Pilot" and the wife an "RV Co-Pilot"). They are universally friendly to me as I wander through their encampment. It seems to be a trait the club encourages.

Several people give me tours of their "rigs." De Tocqueville characteristics are on display again. He found Americans to be openly generous yet also single-minded in their pursuit of material wealth. Inside one RV, a woman shows me their double bed, four-burner stove, microwave, toilet and shower, large and well-stocked refrigerator, new CB radio, and color TV. She insists on giving me a cup of coffee and some pastries, and while we chat at the kitchen table she reveals that they're hoping to trade this 23-foot rig in for a 27-footer next year. When I point toward the *Discovery,* which is parked nearby and looks as if one of these other rigs has been put into a clothes dryer after a rainstorm and shrunk five sizes, her eyes fill with tender sympathy.

Some sections are filled with people from the same small towns; they travel in caravans on weekends and park together at the events, an act of moving entire neighborhoods to new parking lots around the nation. Each chapter has a "wagonmaster," whose duty it is to have scouted ahead to make sure the next stopping place has enough electricity and water hookups and—this is essential—facilities to dump the contents of the toilets. ("The only thing that would cause me to stop RV-ing is when I have to empty the holding tanks," one man tells me.)

In another section of the maze of vehicles, two women tell me they met and became friends at a Samboree two years ago and now try to plan three or four rendezvous a season. Their husbands arrive from what one describes as "the most excellent propane seminar I ever attended." The women are preparing to attend a crafts workshop later in the day. Each couple has a cat with them and they're hoping to win some ribbons in the pet show.

I recommend Highway 12 to them, since they're planning to go next to Montana, but they're worried about the grade of the road and have already decided to take the traditional route to Spokane and across on the interstate. Our ways of travel, our notions of discovery are as different as the sizes of our rigs, but I leave the parking lot, which today is Idaho's fiftieth largest town, feeling, like de Tocqueville, charmed by its citizens. I've made some new friends.

It's mid-morning on the seventeenth before Albert Barros and Brian Castaldi, also a park ranger, and I are organized to attempt the Lolo Trail. Into the back of Barros's Datsun 4 × 4 pickup (named the *Blue Nose*) we pack: three sleeping bags, two shovels, an ax, my camera equipment, binoculars, a manual winch, and two ice coolers with food and refreshments. We're not sure how far we'll be able to get, or where we'll spend the night.

Albert's decision to take the scenic route from Lapwai to Orofino delays us even further. At the Lewis & Clark Trail Cafe and Sacajawea Gift Shop, where we had originally planned to have breakfast, all three of us order "Wilderness Burgers" at eleven-thirty. The day is sunny, clear, and very hot—about 90 degrees.

We stop for gas at Weippe and stop again at Musselshell Meadows, where Barros shows us the blue camas plants that once were a regular part of his people's diet. The gravel road we're on is busy with gravel and logging trucks until we reach the site of Pheasant Camp and turn onto the Lolo Motorway, a narrower road built by the Civilian Conservation Corps in the 1930s either on or near the ancient trail the Nez Perce and the Corps of Discovery took toward Montana. No sooner have we said that we won't be meeting any more traffic than the *Blue Nose* nearly collides with a vehicle on a sharp bend. It's a van with California plates coming down from the ridges. The driver, a man in his fifties, tells us he was turned back by snow on the road; three dogs are barking in the back of his van.

"I'm surprised," Albert says as we proceed on toward the ridges.

"At what?" I ask.

"That you didn't try to buy one of his dogs for dinner. He had more than he needs." Nez Perce joke.

The road climbs and winds, seeking the ridges through the dense growth of trees. We pass two more Lewis and Clark campsites and reach a fork in the road. Our map shows that one fork follows the explorers' trail for about four miles before coming to a dead end; the other, the motorway, loops north until it rejoins the historic trail at Horse Sweat Pass. We take the motorway, which weaves over to the north face of the ridges. Patches of snow begin appearing, remnants of winter hugging the road's cuts into the sidehills to escape the sun. The *Blue Nose* plows through.

The patches get deeper and wider. Finally, a snowbank three feet deep and forty yards wide blocks our path. Castaldi and I get out with the shovels to carve two wheel tracks across the top. We're shirtless and in summer shorts, sweating from our effort; the *Blue Nose* sinks up to its wheel wells in snow when it tries to follow us. Albert stops and backs up to drier ground. We're at an elevation of 5,000 feet, and the motorway climbs to a height of nearly 7,000 feet before it reaches Lolo Pass. Each thousand feet, Albert says, equals another week of lingering winter. Things will only get worse if we try to go on. Defeated, we head back to the fork.

The dead-end road follows Hungery Creek past two more campsites before it stops. We climb Boundary Peak for a look around. The terrain in all directions is a tangle of valleys, mountains, ravines, and nothing but trees. The peaks of the Bitterroots on the Montana border are eighty miles to the east, but they look close enough that we might be able to reach out and grab a handful of snow off their white tops.

Not since the White Cliffs have I felt this way: I am seeing what *they* saw, virtually unchanged; I am experiencing the same sense of defeat *they* must have felt, for the same reasons.

There is solace in the journals. On this day in 1806, Clark writes, the expedition and its horses encountered snow drifts of up to fifteen feet. The horses could walk on the crust, but the deep snow made recognizing the right trail through this forbidding landscape impossible without a guide. They decided to turn back, hire some Nez Perce guides, and try again.

"[T]he party were a good deal dejected, tho' not as much so as I had apprehended they would have been," Clark notes, "this is the first time since we have been on this tour that we have ever been compelled to retreat or make a retragrade march." They set off again on the twenty-fourth, and reached Traveller's Rest on the thirtieth.

Following their wisdom, we turn the *Blue Nose* toward Lapwai and the home of the Nez Perce. On the trail back we pass lumber camps, more lumber trucks, several gravel pits, and more gravel trucks—reminders of something else de Tocqueville said about Americans: "They will habitually prefer the useful to the beautiful, and they will require that the beautiful should be useful."

On my way out of this area the next day, the Lolo Trail serves up some final ironies. In Lewiston, Idaho (population 27,986), the larger of the twin cities named for the explorers (Clarkston, Washington, has 6,903 residents), I stop at the offices of the city's port.

Lewiston and Clarkston are now official *sea*ports. The extensive damming of the Columbia and Snake systems allows deep-draft barges to bring ocean cargo here from the Pacific. The Northwest Passage turned out to be a myth. These Western mountains were too high and too broad, and there were too many of them. Getting from where they had cached their canoes on the Beaverhead to where they climbed into their new dugouts on the Clearwater had taken the expedition two months overland, during which they had nearly died of exhaustion, starvation, and finally diarrhea. But if nothing could be done about those mountains, the water opening to the Orient has at least been moved inland more than four hundred miles. Jefferson would have liked that.

Jefferson, whose dream of an American-dominated trade with China was one of the main reasons for sending the Corps of Discovery into the unknown, would also have appreciated what the port director tells me. Much of the grain that comes over the Lolo Pass to Lewiston is bound for the Orient, he says; and one of the loads of trade goods disgorged from the barges that arrive to pick up the grain is fireworks—from China.

The other irony, here where the explorers switched from horses to dogs as their main diet, is the sign for the Lewis & Clark Animal Shelter. A quarter of the sign is filled by a Pepsi logo.

21

Déjà-Vu and Something New

we purchased all the dogs we could, the fish being out of season and dieing in great numbers in the river, we did not think proper to use them. From William Clark's journal
Columbia River
October 17, 1805

After their overland ordeal across the Bitterroots, the Corps of Discovery was happy to be traveling by water again when they pushed their canoes into the Clearwater River on October 7, 1805, and headed toward the sea.

Lewis and Clark were in a hurry to reach the mouth of the Columbia and build quarters before winter. The wild waters of the Clearwater, Snake, and Columbia sped them along. The captains gambled by shooting through many rapids which Clark admitted would have been portaged "if the season was not so far advanced and time precious with us."

Being waterborne was a familiar experience, but floating downstream instead of battling a big river's current was new to the expedition; so, too, the trip from the land of the Nez Perce toward the coast was both reminiscent of the journey up the Missouri yet full of strangeness.

The changes in landscape and climate were a condensed *déjà-vu* of what they had experienced between St. Louis and the Great Divide. In the three hundred and fifty miles to the Columbia Gorge, they left a wooded terrain to cross an arid, treeless plateau along a mighty river, and encountered another dramatic range of mountains. Traversing that kind of climatic and topographic change east of the Divide had taken them fifteen months; on this side, it took three weeks.

At Celilo Falls and the Long and Short Narrows of the Dalles, the expedition again came upon a great intertribal trading market, a Columbian version of the mid-Missouri, where tribes from the plateaus and coast mingled to barter their specialties: buffalo robes from one in exchange for dried salmon from the other. Particularly in the desertlike regions, the men relied again on local Indian tribes to survive. With little game for food, or even trees for firewood, they traded for roots, dried salmon, and dogs to eat, for sticks of wood for their campfires, and for assistance in transporting their belongings when the rapids and waterfalls required portages.

At one point wood was so scarce that, Clark notes, "We were obliged for the first time to take the property of the Indians without the consent or approbation of the owner." Some vacant dwellings were raided and dismantled for their timbers. (Another reminder of their earlier journey: Clark mentions the structures as being "the first wooden houses in which Indians have lived Since we left those in the vicinity of the Illinois.")

The natives themselves were different from the Plains and plateau Indians the expedition had grown accustomed to, and often fond of. Their clucking Sahaptian and Chinookan tongues were foreign to the explorers' ears, and communication was increasingly difficult. Some of them were "flatheads" in the real sense: children's heads were gently and persistently squeezed between boards to achieve a sloping forehead that was a sign of honor. Clark noted that their teeth were bad and worn to the gum—which he attributed to their diet of unwashed roots and sandy salmon—in contrast to the strong and white incisors of the Plains tribes. The houses and their inhabitants were infested with fleas and lice, which spread to the expedition.

Most disconcerting, however, was a change in attitude toward the Americans. Accustomed as they had become to Indian generosity and to trading prices skewed in the expedition's favor, the explorers were ill prepared for the hard bargaining of the Columbian tribes. Even worse, items left unwatched started disappearing. The men didn't like these tribes, and the journals are filled with complaints about theft, high prices, chilly relations, and declining cleanliness. Some expedition members seemed "well disposed to kill a few of them," but were prevented from it by the captains.

At Celilo Falls, an Indian was seen wearing a sailor's jacket, and as the expedition progressed toward the sea, more manufactured goods appeared among the possessions of the coastal tribes. Vessels seeking otter pelts for the China trade had been plying the northwest coast for years. DeVoto believed that the higher prices, thievery, and higher incidence of venereal disease were as much evidence of the Indians' contact with maritime traders who "treated them with appalling brutality" as were the European clothes the men began noticing on the natives. A Clark journal entry seems to support this: "They ask high prices for what they Sell and Say that the white people below give great prices for everything." James Ronda, in his book *Lewis and Clark Among the Indians,* contends that "in pilfering small objects from the Americans, they [the Indians] sought Lewis and Clark's acknowledgement of their importance. Taking an axe was done to remind the white men of the need to offer respect and attention to the trading lords of the Columbia."

Instead, the explorers grew increasingly annoyed. In their pecking order of esteem for the continent's first inhabitants, they assigned the coastal tribes to the bottom rung.

Equally new to the Corps of Discovery were the fish. They appeared in mind-numbing quantities. The rivers were "crouded with salmon," Clark notes, and "the number of dead Salmon on the Shores & floating in the river is incrediable to say." At one village, he estimated that 10,000 pounds of salmon were drying on scaffolds. Unfamiliar with the life cycle of the Pacific salmon—an anadromous fish that leaves its freshwater breeding grounds for several years in the ocean, then returns to its home rivers to spawn and die—the men were as leery of the dead fish as they were astounded by their quantities. Dog meat continued as the meal of preference for all except Clark.

In one sense, the trip from the Clearwater to the Cascades brought the Corps of Discovery from a blank space on existing maps back to the edge of the known world. Beyond the mountains, the mouth of the Columbia had been discovered, mapped, and explored by seagoing adventurers, whose reports Lewis and Clark had already read. An American, Robert Gray, had discovered the mouth of the river in 1792, naming it for his vessel. The same year, the British captain George Vancouver sent one of his men up the river to a point just below the Columbia Gorge; Mount Hood and Mount St. Helens were named for a British admiral and statesman, respectively, and were included on maps in the two American captains' possession.

Because of their rush to reach the sea and the disquietingly strange river life they encountered, no feeling of either exhilaration or comfortable satisfaction radiates from the journal entries for this section of their westerly quest. Instead, uneasiness, annoyance, an almost irritated sense of being hurried and harried mark the pages.

A hundred miles past the Cascades, they would at last see ocean swells lapping the shores, breathe salt air, and feel some satisfaction at their accomplishment. Here, though, their experience was a disturbing mixture of newness and the already known, a distortion of the familiar, as if seen through a prism or backward in a faulty mirror, and not quite right.

Eastern Washington has an element of otherworldliness. Five miles out of Clarkston on U.S. 12, I find myself thinking I've been beamed back to the Badlands by some spaceship. Red rocks and tan sage are the only sight, except for the Snake River, which here is just a sluggish, green-tinted canal with no current discernible to the naked eye. (Snake Lake would be a better name.) The sun is baking hot, and the rush of air through the *Discovery*'s front window feels like dragon's breath on the left side of my face. Small tributaries of sweat descend from my shoulders and flow undammed down the ridge of my spine. The temperature is almost 100 degrees.

A one-hour drive east would bring me back to the rushing waters of the Clearwater, the cool shade of spruce and pine, the fields and flowers, even patches of snow in the higher elevations. Instead, I am westbound, moving along about 5 mph over the speed limit, and getting a first-class sunburn on my left forearm crooked on the window ledge.

Rock ledges give way to rounded hills as Highway 12 and then Highway 261 leave the river to carve a straighter route. Small towns are again presaged by the sight of grain elevators and water towers. Outside Starbuck, Washington (population 234), a freight train of grain cars strings along the highway for 2.2 miles. With a little smoothing, this could be eastern Nebraska or Kansas.

The terrain is composed of huge, inverted bowls, all of them cultivated in curving strips of green and tan, as if a braided rug had been thrown over them. This is the southern end of the Palouse, two million mounded acres of rich volcanic ash, where 10 percent of the nation's white winter wheat is grown. Specially designed bulldozer/tractors wheel around the steep grades, raising columns of dust devils that can be seen swirling in every direction. People might farm this way on Mars.

Approaching the Tri-Cities of Pasco, Kennewick, and Richland, where the land has flattened in the Columbia plateau, dramatic displays of the possibilities of water on desert soil begin. Lines of irrigation sprinklers, linked by pipe to the Snake, spray streams of river water into the arid air and onto the ground, darkening it to the color of midwestern soil. (As I drive near them, the pores of my forearm and baked face drink in the mistlike moisture over the highway.) Emerald-green rows of corn and beans are sprouting in these fields. Next to them, in fields untouched by irrigation, the soil is parched and supports only prickly pears and a paltry crop of sagebrush. Arizona and Illinois alternate within the same section of land.

The Snake River joins the southbound Columbia here, just before the Great River of the West turns in that direction toward the coast. Lewis and Clark reached this point, 3,714 miles and seventeen months from Camp Wood, on October 16, 1805. In *Passage Through the Garden,* geographer-historian John Logan Allen notes that "the journals which recorded the event were singularly unemotional, and it is obvious that for the members of the expedition, and particularly for its commanders, the final discovery of the river that had existed so long in fable was an anticlimax. . . . The Columbia was not close to the Missouri and the route between the two master components of western geography was not easy."

Still, it was significant enough for them to camp for several days on the site where the modern Sacajawea State Park stands, reconnoiter the area, and take celestial readings.

From that day in 1805 to 1943, things didn't change all that much around here. Wheat farmers and cattlemen moved in, the Indians were moved out, but the treeless desert plain just above the confluence of the Yakima and Columbia rivers couldn't support much more than the four-hundred-person town of Hanford.

Suddenly, in early 1943, the government announced that 700 square miles had been condemned. Residents were given ninety days to get out. By spring, 51,000 construction workers were living in barracks and makeshift housing—making Hanford the fourth largest city in Washington overnight. The largest bus system north of Los Angeles was transporting workers out to the construction sites, where large, long buildings and strange equipment were being built. Outside of a handful of between thirty and fifty people, no one knew what they were building. After three big buildings were erected, 24,000 workers were laid off in March 1945, the largest overnight layoff in history. The remaining thousands of workers went each day to the plants, where they knew they were producing something, but not what it was, or what it was for.

In late summer of 1945, they found out. An atom bomb was dropped on Nagasaki, Japan. Hanford had produced the plutonium. (The workers also learned that they had made the plutonium for the world's first atomic detonation, a highly secret blast on July 16, 1945, near Alamogordo, New Mexico. A Hanford supervisor had taken the plutonium by car to Portland and then by train to southern California and across to the test site.)

The years following World War II were busy. Five more reactors were added to the existing three to produce weapons-grade plutonium. A ninth was built, but with the added ability to produce steam to generate electricity—the nation's only dual-purpose reactor. The Washington Public Power Supply System (known as "Whoops" more recently, when its overly ambitious nuclear-power dreams grew out of control and set off a disastrous financial chain reaction) built a generating plant on the site in the 1960s. Arms-control agreements led to the closing of the first eight reactors and more layoffs.

Life in the Tri-Cities still revolves around the atom. The government and its research contractors employ 13,500 of the residents. The three cities claim to have the highest density of scientists in the nation. The Fast Flux Test Facility, the world's largest liquid-metal breeder reactor, tests fuels and materials for breeder reactors, which create more nuclear fuel than they consume. Weapons-grade plutonium and steam are still produced at the dual reactor; the WPPSS plant is still going, but work on additional nuclear stations has been halted. High school athletic teams are nicknamed the "Bombers."

About 40 million gallons of waste from the plutonium production is stored in large underground steel tanks; the state operates one of the nation's three commercial low-level radioactive waste dumps on the site. Basalt rock formations underlying Hanford are being studied for their potential for deep holes to store high-level waste for tens of thousands of years. On the day of my arrival, the local paper is announcing that, despite protests from some peace groups, state politicians and the Tri-City Industrial Development Council are endorsing Hanford as the best place to make and test what will be the nation's first reactor in space, part of the "Star Wars" program.

"The nuclear industry is here to stay," the manager of the Hanford Science Center tells me, amidst the displays and hands-on exhibits that make it seem like a miniature Disneyland of the Atom. "New technology tends to bring concerns that last for a generation. Then the next generation looks at it differently."

Small glass marbles, turned amber brown from exposure to gamma radiation from cobalt 60, are on sale for ten cents. I buy a couple and walk out, getting lost in the mathematics of counting how many generations there are in 10,000 years, the amount of time required before the waste proposed for storage in the basalt holes will be safe. Undoubtedly those generations will see it differently. The thermometer outside says the temperature has reached 101 degrees.

At a local senior-citizen center, I ask around for anyone who worked on the secret project during World War II and am introduced to Angelus Janos, age seventy-one. Janos, it turns out, was one of the few people who knew what was being made. An engineer, he arrived at Hanford from Oak Ridge, Tennessee, where he was part of the Manhattan Project, and was made supervisor of the "B" reactor, the one whose plutonium fueled the Nagasaki bomb. Rumors were rampant among the plant workers, he says. "One man was going around saying we were making baby diapers," he remembers. "I don't know why. I think just because he didn't know *what* we were making."

The day after the bomb was dropped, the reaction in Hanford was quite a bit of talk, some celebration, a lot of handshaking. Stores closed until noon. The Richland paper, under a thick headline that said IT'S ATOMIC BOMBS, reported that "disbelief was soon followed by enthusiasm. Everyone had the same reaction: 'It's nice to know what the project is all about' and 'Maybe the war will end promptly.' " Under a blurb entitled "What Is Atomic Bomb?" the paper described its awesome destructive ability, speculated that "the source of its power is said to be coal, oil, and power produced by the great dams of the Northwest and Tennessee," and concluded that "it is the greatest force ever harnessed—and may change the entire course of civilization." They were wrong about the power source, but correct about its implications.

"We looked at it as a way of ending the war without too much loss of life, American lives," Janos says, although "many of us felt we should have dropped the bomb for observation instead of in the middle of a city." He went to work for WPPSS after the war, but believes that they, like the rest of the nuclear-power industry, tried to build too much too fast, and that the public no longer accepts the industry's safety promises.

Janos wheezes as he talks. He apologizes and then shows me the scar on his neck from an operation for thyroid cancer. Caused by radiation exposure, I ask him? He shrugs. No way of telling. A sister of his also had the same problem, and she never worked on nukes.

I drive out to the sprawling site, called the Hanford Nuclear Reservation. Modern buildings rise from the desert sand, where even the sage is sparse. The mothballed WPPSS plants, with their signature reactor domes, shimmer eerily in the heat waves like giant, concrete barrel cactuses. The breeder reactor, several miles away, has its own, smaller dome. Guard gates (SAC headquarters *déjà-vu*) block the road to the eight retired plutonium plants, the waste sites, and the dual reactor on the banks of the Columbia. The nuclear site does hold some secrets. In 1949, for reasons the government still refuses to disclose, 5,500 curies of radioactive iodine—nearly five hundred times as much as escaped into the atmosphere at Three Mile Island—were deliberately released at Hanford. I wheel the *Discovery* around to return to Richland. A cop car follows me until I reach the city limits.

The Hanford Nuclear Reservation, it seems, is an ultramodern, mutant version of all the other reservations of the West. It is a parcel of land chosen for its desolation. Large numbers of people were moved here for purposes they didn't understand. Its inhabitants, most of them subsidized by the federal government, worship the elemental forces of nature and feel that those on the outside don't understand or appreciate their religion. And it is surrounded by a general public worried that what's inside the reservation will escape its boundaries once again.

South of the Tri-Cities, U.S. 395 crosses the mouth of the Walla Walla River and bends west to follow the Columbia River to Umatilla. Answering the pleas from the Nez Perce and Flatheads for the "White Man's Book of Heaven," Protestant missionaries Marcus Whitman and Henry Harmon Spalding reached this area in the fall of 1836. Their wives, Narcissa Whitman and Eliza Spalding, had made history on the Fourth of July of that year, when they ascended South Pass in Wyoming and became the first white women to cross the Continental Divide. The Whitmans established a mission among the Cayuse Indians about thirty miles up the Walla Walla; their daughter, Alice Clarissa, was delivered there on March 14, 1837, the first white child born west of the Divide. The Spaldings went on to found their mission among the Nez Perce in Lapwai. The Whitmans' glowing letters home to a great extent helped spur the wagon trains of the Oregon Trail in the 1840s.

"The missionaries were vortices of force thrown out in advance by the force to the eastward that was making west," DeVoto wrote in *Across the Wide Missouri*. "They thought that they came to bring Christ but in thinking so they were deceived. They were agents of a historical energy and what they brought was the United States. The Indians had no chance. If it looked like religion it was nevertheless Manifest Destiny."

The memory of the stern Spaldings is still controversial among the Nez Perce, who point to the split the missionaries' presence created in the tribe. The Cayuse, their population cut in half by a measles epidemic brought to their territory by the flood of Oregon emigrants, reacted more violently than the peaceful Nez Perce. They massacred Whitman, his wife, and twelve other whites at the mission in November 1847.

To avoid Interstate 84, which hugs the southern, Oregon shore of the Columbia River, I cross back into Washington at Umatilla and take Highway 14 along the north shore. The gas stations at Patterson (population unlisted) are closed, but the Desert House is open and I buy three cold sodas to combat the parching heat. A sign inside says "Don't Insult an Alligator Until You've Crossed the River"; a sign outside on Highway 14 says NEXT GAS 66 MILES. The gas gauge is just below a quarter full. Montana *déjà-vu*. (A mirror *déjà-vu:* This is one of the few stretches of my trip that follows the same road taken by William Least Heat Moon in *Blue Highways*. Traveling east instead of west here, he nearly ran out of gas on Highway 14, but found fuel in Patterson.)

This tends to rivet my attention on making it to the next chance to cross the river, at Biggs, Oregon, where the alligator interstate will surely provide fuel if I apologize for the insult. The lakelike Columbia is an oasis of water in this desolate stretch. A barge plies its waters, and another long freight train bearing wood chips, new cars, and subway vehicles creeps westward between me and the river. On the far shore, Interstate 84 is busy with truck traffic.

A ferocious headwind stiff-arms the flat front of the *Discovery*. I can watch the gas gauge dropping from the resistance. Fingers of wind curl through my window, frisk the far corners of the camper until they find the paper-towel dispenser hanging behind me, and start rolling out flapping sheets of paper. The towel becomes like a bored, disobedient child in the backseat: it reaches around and taps my right shoulder, rests, then slaps my left cheek and pokes out the window, then returns to its rightful place, unfurls some more, and begins pestering me again.

Do I stop to discipline it and secure it against these distractions? Do I consider turning back, to take advantage of a tailwind and the shorter distance to a gas station? Do I slow down to take the wind, the chance of running out of gas, the possibility of driving a two-lane with a paper-towel blindfold into account?

Do you remember Road Rules 1 and 5? I reach over, grab my pipe, and light it in between blasts of wind and swats at the towel. And of course I speed up.

Near the John Day Dam (named for a member of the Astor party who went insane here in 1813), the highway climbs to the high terraces overlooking the river and bends slightly to offer a view to the southwest. Staring me in the face, floating like a mirage in the dusty, late-afternoon air, is the white cone of Mount Hood.

Mount Hood and the other volcanoes spaced out at regular intervals along the Cascade Range, all about a hundred miles from the coast, are responsible for the singularity of this area. Lava floods from them and other, earlier, fissures in the earth created the basalt plateaus. It was their volcanic ash that formed the rich loess of the Palouse. It is their forbidding heights that refuse eastward passage to moisture from the Pacific. East of the Cascades, the Columbia plateau receives an average yearly rainfall of six inches; on the other side, moist air currents from the ocean drop more than sixty inches a year.

One catastrophe was answered with another: as the last Ice Age receded, pent-up seas of water covering vast areas as big as western Montana broke their ice dams and raced west, scouring the Columbia's path through the Cascades. Mount Hood has seen fire, and it's seen ice. Little wonder that today its snowy peak is unimpressed by my comparatively puny crisis of an ebbing flow of gasoline from fuel tank to engine.

Shifting to neutral, I coast down the other side of the rise, all

the way to the bridge, where I go back to full power, cross into
Oregon, and reach a truck stop. The *Discovery* drinks 13.7 gallons
of gas into its 14-gallon tank. Jack's Cafe rewards me for following
Road Rule 7 with a good oyster stew, a chocolate malt, and a piece
of boysenberry pie.

Both refreshed, we cross back to the Washington side and camp
at the Maryhill State Recreation Area. The wind blows all night,
forming small sea swells running counter to what once was the
Columbia's current. The waves remind me of the lakes covering
what once was the Missouri.

22

Colliding
Forces

accordingly I deturmined to pass through this place notwithstanding the horrid appearance of this agitated gut swelling, boiling & whorling in every direction. From William Clark's journal
Entering the Columbia Gorge
October 24, 1805

Sam Hill left his eccentric mark on history in the indifferent shadow of Mount Hood. Near the beginning of this century Hill, a road builder and railroad tycoon, decided that the region just east of the Cascades had the right ingredients for an agricultural paradise, a "hole in the mountains where the rain of the west and the sunshine of the east meet."

He platted a town and invited Belgian Quakers to settle and till the soil. He began construction of a palatial mansion for himself and his wife, Mary. The farmers soon realized that the promise of sunshine and rain was only half right, and left the parched soil. Despite the impressive mansion, even despite its name of Maryhill, Hill's wife was equally disenchanted: She never moved in. The mansion is now a stately museum, and its collection of Rodin sculpture, international chess sets, native American artifacts, seventeenth-century Flemish paintings, and the donated clothing from a queen of Romania is as strikingly eclectic as the sight of this palace on the dry plateau.

Hill's other legacy is a concrete replica of Stonehenge, built to honor the men from Klickitat County who died in World War I. A Quaker himself, he had visited England and the original Stonehenge and had been told it was used for human sacrifices to pagan gods.

"After all our civilization," he said, in a quotation inscribed on a bronze plaque on the concrete monoliths, "the flower of humanity still is being sacrificed to the god of war on fields of battle." A quarter century later, on its way to "change the entire course of history," the packet of plutonium from Hanford would have passed between the twin monuments to destruction, Sam Hill's Stonehenge and the Mount Hood volcano.

The plaque also gives instructions on how to calculate the summer and winter solstices by where the sun rises and sets between the pillars. With Mount Hood peeking over my shoulder, I line up the interstices to confirm that this midsummer's day is dawning at the proper time and place. In a region like this, a veritable breeding ground of natural and manmade cataclysms, you seek any reassurance of changeless certainty you can find.

A glint of yellow appears, and the sun begins its highest climb of the year. Behind me, the snowfields on the dormant peak glisten in reflection. Below, the Columbia's water sparkles, even if it doesn't move anymore. The song of greeting from some morning birds mingles with the distant whine of truck tires on the interstate across the river.

ROAD RULE 19: Change is the only certainty. Whether it is measured in the life of a volcano, a nation, one person, or one split atom, the passage of time is change's passage.

MARYHILL COROLLARY: This Road Rule is as sure as the sun's coming up in the morning.

At Sam Hill's Stonehenge I make a bargain with the Road Spirit: allow me a few miles on Interstate 84, so I can be on the Oregon side for a while; in return, I'll follow every other Road Rule. I will shun franchises, eat at a first-name cafe, trust my instincts, admit ignorance to strangers, and stop wherever it's required—at historic markers, unusual sights, places offering interesting experiences, and, even though my knee is healthy now, any hot spring I can find.

The sun has begun its longest day of the year. Keeping my end of the deal will turn this into my longest day as well. I won't be back in bed for nearly twenty-four hours. With all the required stops, however, I will cover only fifty miles. In a place like this, you don't break a promise to the Road Spirit.

The Dalles, Oregon (population 10,820), is the only town in America with a "The" in its name. Lewis and Clark called the rapids here the Long and Short Narrows, but later French voyageurs called it Les Dalles ("the flagstones") because of the basalt layers that terrace the river banks. It's just as well. The dam here has inundated the narrows, as well as the Indian fishing grounds of Celilo Falls upriver. The Columbia river/lake is as wide here as anywhere else. "Narrows," long or short, wouldn't make sense anymore.

Keeping my end of the bargain with the Road Spirit, I avoid the Shamrock ("Chinese/American Cuisine"). Johnny's Cafe serves me a hearty breakfast and enough coffee to keep me alert for the rest of the day. In return, the interstate yields a scenic loop to the cliffs above Rowena, where Mount Adams, another snow-capped volcanic cone, can be seen in its hiding spot on the Washington side.

Between The Dalles and Hood River (population 4,329) I would suggest they erect a sign that says: RESUME GREEN. The treeless, rectangular red-and-black rock bluffs end as abruptly as they began. Pine-covered mountains take over, and the land sprouts flowers, shrubs, and lush grasses along fast, clear streams.

As I cross the bridge to Washington and Highway 14, the water is dotted with windsurfers, colorful petals blowing back and forth on the surface. The wind tunnel of the Columbia Gorge has made this one of the best inland windsurfing spots in the country. Wind speeds of 25 mph blow eastward, creating three-foot swells on the water, which is good news if you've got a bright sail and a surfboard and the day off.

The effect is considerably different if you're trying to coax a bulky camper west on a two-lane. Gusts ricochet off the hillsides, blindsiding the *Discovery* and bringing Larry Weiskopf's words about accidents and Volkswagens vividly back to me with each logging truck I meet. Obituary headline: *Writer Pursues Northwest Passage to Grill of Mack Truck.*

Smack in the middle of the Gorge is the site of the Columbia's defeat. The river that in prehistoric times had the force to break two-thousand-foot ice dams, cut through a high plateau of lava rock, and become the only river to carve its way west through the barrier of the Cascades, the river that propelled the canoes of the Corps of Discovery over terrifying cataracts and seething rapids to their rendezvous with history, this river that drains an area of 258,000 square miles and carries twice as much water as the Nile— the Great River of the West stops. The Bonneville Dam was built here in the 1930s, followed in quick succession by eighteen more farther upstream along the main stems of the Snake and Columbia. The river seen by Lewis and Clark disappeared forever.

From Bonneville stretching back to near the Canadian border, the Columbia is a placid, currentless pool, bearing as much resemblance to its former self as an Oregon Trail ox did to a wild buffalo. Like the ox, it has been domesticated, harnessed to do man's work, and allowed to move along only at his bidding. The Columbia contains 40 percent of the nation's potential for hydropower generation. By the time its water is released through Bonneville's turbines and the Columbia is permitted to become a river once again for its final hundred miles, nearly all of that potential has been squeezed from it. Some of the power system's 29,000 megawatts run air conditioners in Los Angeles. A high-voltage line to Phoenix is contemplated.

Captain Dale Jones is bringing the towboat *Tyee* and five barges, three with wheat, one with wood chips, one with peas, through the Bonneville lock on their way from Pasco to Vancouver. He lets me ride with him in its passage, the modern equivalent of Lewis and Clark lowering their canoes by rope through the Cascade rapids that were drowned when the dam was built. The Tyee pushes two barges past the upstream gate and into the lock. The gate closes behind us, valves are opened to release water downstream, and we begin lowering slowly inside the lock's walls, as if on a descending elevator. Twenty-seven minutes later, sixty-four feet deeper, the downstream gate opens, and we push onto the river.

Jones has been working boats on the Columbia for twenty-nine years. Even within his lifetime, some of the excitement has gone out of the business, as new dams and their reservoirs inundated shallow rapids he once had to run. He once lost his share of barges. "If you ran rapids, you had accidents," he says. "These"—he motions to the dams—"knock the fun out of it, that's for sure."

He noses his load toward the three barges waiting to be coupled. Unlike the river upstream, there is a current here; the front of his lead barge is two football fields from the pilot's chair and Jones has to nestle it next to the others. His CB crackles with signals from a deck hand on the lead barge. Jones adjusts the throttle and rudder controls. The two loads join without a bump.

In a darkened room below the water level of the Bonneville Dam, a young woman sits watching an illuminated window. The audio portion of a television soap opera plays in the background. A steelhead trout, working its way up the terraced fish ladder built beside the dam, swims past the thick glass. *Click*. The woman presses a counter. A dozen lampreys have attached themselves to the water side of the window, resting against the fish ladder's current by sucking their oval mouths against the glass. Their slimy, snakey bodies flutter downstream like small pennants in the wind.

No clicks. Lampreys aren't counted. Some more steelheads struggle past. *Click. Click. Click.* A carp. *Click.* A sturgeon, big and scaly, prehistoric looking, as if it was here before Mount Hood, lumbers by. *Click.* Silvery sockeye salmon swim past. *Click. Click.* Then one is forced backward by the current. A different click. It passes again. *Click.*

The dams made it possible for big boats and big loads to reach Lewiston, Idaho, more than four hundred miles from the sea, and they made it possible for people in the deserts of eastern Washington and Oregon, even southern California, to make ice in their refrigerators. They turned Hood River into the windsurfing capital of the Northwest, and they allowed corn and beans to grow where once only sagebrush and prickly pears lived. But they played holy hell with the fish.

Before the dam-building began in the 1930s, large-scale commercial fisheries on the rivers and at sea had already started to take their toll on the fish population. But the dams blocked the salmon, shad, and steelhead from migrating to the sea and back, and the reservoirs inundated many of the natural breeding grounds and hatcheries.

Fish ladders were constructed to allow mature fish to return upstream from the sea to spawn in their natal streams. This helped some, but not enough. Yearling smolts had to get *down*stream to the sea, if there were to be any adults to return *up*stream two to five years later. The dams were a problem.

What once had been a two-week ride down the rolling waters for the young fish changed to an arduous journey that only a small percentage survived. In low-water years, when power administrators were stingy with releasing water over the spillways, the main route from one side of a dam to the other was through the turbines. A considerable number were churned into kilowatts; another portion survived but emerged stunned from the spin and became easy prey for predators in the downstream pools. Even with the spillways operating, the shifting pressures from quiet reservoirs to spillways formed gas bubbles—the fish version of the bends—inside the fingerlings, and more died or were seriously weakened.

Each new manmade threat to the fish's survival has been followed by attempts at manmade solutions, or at least mitigations of the devastation. The fish ladders provide passage for the spawning adults. Upstream, they are captured and artificially spawned by stripping the females' eggs and mixing them with sperm for fertilization. Eggs are kept in trays until the fry are hatched, and then the young are fed a special diet in the hatchery pools. Much of the downstream migration is done by man. Most of the fingerlings are trucked from hatcheries and catchment basins at the upper dams to a point below Bonneville and dumped back into the river; some of them are barged downriver through the locks. This program, called Operation Fish Run, transported 8.3 million fingerlings in 1981.

If all that seems complicated and convoluted, it is nothing compared to the regulations on *catching* the fish. Salmon and steelhead are to the Pacific Northwest what water is to the arid Plains: a limited but highly coveted commodity. There are myriad competing interests and claims on the fish: oceangoing commercial vessels from our country and others; ocean sports fishermen; commercial fishing interests on the lower Columbia; sports fishermen ranging all the way from the river's mouth to the angry groups in Idaho; and the Columbia-basin Indian tribes, who have solemn treaties from the government preserving their fishing rights in exchange for the land we took from their ancestors. Regulations cover each group, and more regulations and agreements and international treaties govern how each group, all suspicious and jealous of the others, interacts with the rest.

Down in the fish-counting room at the Bonneville Dam, two sockeye swim past. *Click. Click.* Like the soap opera playing in the background, bad as things have gotten, the fish have survived for the next show. Things are now improving. *Click. Click. Click.* A sockeye, two steelhead.

Nature's balance has been unalterably tipped by the hand of man and nothing short of blowing up the dams and putting most of the West Coast into a blackout could restore it. So a new, more delicate balance is being maintained artificially. Here where Lewis and Clark said the salmon existed in numbers beyond calculation, counting the fish is now not only possible, it is essential for decision-making. The struggle of breeding, birth, and life is being scripted entirely by humans. The soap opera climaxes in an organ swell of tension and suspense. The lampreys flutter in the current and some more fish swim across the screen on cue. *Click. Click.*

—

Kathryn Brigham is fishing at the old Cascade Locks, just upstream from the Bonneville Dam, when we meet. From a small platform built on the side of the now defunct locks, she dips a long pole attached to a large, hooped net into the water and waits for a steelhead or salmon to pass. Kathryn is a Cayuse Indian, short, with a square, friendly face and gentle features. She is also an articulate and knowledgeable woman, characteristics that serve her well as her tribe's representative on the Columbia River Inter-Tribal Fish Commission, a group that provides technical and legal advice on fish management and treaty provisions to the Yakima, Warm Springs, Nez Perce, and Umatilla reservations.

Indian fishing is a controversial issue along the Columbia. Court rulings on the tribes' treaties allow them to fish at times of the year and in methods forbidden to non-Indians. Following the letter and spirit of an Indian treaty and actually providing native Americans with what they were promised a hundred years ago is a relatively modern notion. Clauses like "for as long as the sun shines and the grass grows" and words like "forever" have usually been considered as fine print written in disappearing ink. So it was not uncommon for descendants of the men who built the dams and the deep-sea trawlers to blame the Indians when the salmon and steelhead started to vanish.

Statistics show that, compared to the commercial and sports-fishing harvests in the Pacific, even compared to the salmon caught by whites in the river itself, Indian harvests are a tiny fraction. Still, try to explain that to a white fisherman driving down the river in the off-season who sees a tribal member out laying gill nets in the water.

"We used to go to meetings and see pickets saying DOWN WITH TREATIES, or SAVE A SALMON, CAN AN INDIAN, or SEND THEM HOME," Brigham says. "SEND THEM HOME. We used to get a charge out of that one. Now it's gotten so we can sit together, talk together, because we all have one common goal: we all wanna have fish."

Among the reservations, where the poverty level is staggeringly high (the per capita income of the Nez Perce is $1,531 a year), catching salmon not only fulfills ancient ceremonial purposes, it is important for subsistence. Brigham and her husband provide for their family's food by hunting and fishing; surplus fish and game are sold or bartered for other goods.

"A number of people fail to realize that the tribes see fish as a great importance to them today *and* tomorrow," she says. Tribal regulations technically allow ceremonial or subsistence fishing year-round, but sometimes even subsistence catches are called off if the fish counts are too low. "I have a granddaughter who's one year old. I want her, when she gets big, to be able to go fishing. And I want her to be able to teach *her* children. That's my goal."

Brigham is cautiously optimistic about the future of the fish. If Lewis and Clark reappeared on their two-hundredth anniversary in the year 2005, she thinks they would find more and healthier fish than exist today. Not as many as they saw in 1805, certainly— "They couldn't walk across the river on the fish's backs," she says— but a better crop than now.

"I'll tell you another thing they wouldn't have seen before, was women fishing," she adds. Until recently, fishing was an all-male activity among her tribe, and some men still consider it bad luck to fish with women, she says. Her three children are all girls, and they've already been taught how to fish and hunt.

Kathryn Brigham dips her net back into the Columbia, reenacting a scene as old as her tribe yet as modern as the women's movement. Nothing has been caught during my brief visit, but she is patient. "Things are looking up," she says.

BRIGHAM'S COROLLARY: The river of time is change's passage, but it doesn't always have to flow downhill.

On a hunting trip in 1876, Isadore St. Martin discovered a hot spring near Carson, Washington. He brought his wife back a few years later, and the hot mineral water seemed to help her neuralgia. By the turn of the century, he had erected the Hotel St. Martin, and not long after that a bathhouse for the growing numbers of patrons who came seeking cures for everything from poison oak to arthritis. A certain Robert Brown visited in March 1910 and quarreled with St. Martin about the spring's efficacy. The next day's paper reported that "this was always a tender spot with the old gentleman who, though he was of a quiet, industrious disposition, was always ready to scrap with anyone who made disparaging remarks about the quality of water in these celebrated springs." The argument ended when Brown stabbed the sixty-eight-year-old St. Martin to death.

The Hotel St. Martin hasn't changed much since then, except for new coats of white paint and the addition of a pay telephone near its front door, not that anybody would complain, given its history. Even the prices seem at least a half century behind the times: a bath in the spring water and a room for the night goes for twenty dollars. Arriving before supper, I figure a bath and massage might take the kinks out of my neck from battling the Gorge's winds and refresh me for the night's activities still ahead.

The bathhouse is two large, darkened rooms with institutional green walls. A dozen cots line the perimeter of the main room. On one, a man lies wrapped cocoonlike in flannel sheets, a towel draped across his forehead. A faint scent of sulfur floats in the silent air. An attendant dressed in white cotton emerges from the other room. He tells me to pick any cot I want and disappears. Confused, I sit down, thinking I may be in some Victorian sanitarium.

He returns and tells me my bath is ready, so I disrobe and walk into another dimly lit room containing a dozen old iron tubs, and ease into the one the attendant has filled. He tells me the water is naturally 126 degrees, so they mix cold water from a nearby stream to make it tolerable.

A sign on the wall informs me the water has a pH of 8.2, powerfully alkaline, and, in parts per million, the following minerals: potassium, 6.6; sodium, 300; calcium, 50; magnesium, 4.0; sulfate, 12.6 (the smell); ammonia, 0.2; phosphate, 0.044; nitrite, less than 0.001; and silver, less than 0.010. I'm not enough of a chemist to know whether the sign is a boast or a warning. The attendant hands me a paper cup.

"What's this for?" I ask. Maybe this is a hospital ward, not a sanitarium.

"Drink some of the hot mineral water," he says. Careful not to start any argument, I give him a look that would translate into something like "You must be kidding."

"It's what helps you sweat," he says, and leaves me.

I'm still staring at my empty cup, trying to remember whether the guy on the cot in the other room was breathing, when an older man hobbles in, climbs into another tub, holds his cup under the spigot and takes two long drinks before leaning back in the water. He notices my stare.

"Been comin' here for forty years," he says and goes on to tell me a string of stories. His father, who started bringing him to

Carson in the 1930s, was a heavy smoker; after a bath and a drink of the waters, his old man's sheets in the sweating room would get stained from the nicotine coming out of his pores. A World War I veteran, gassed at Ypres, came here for lengthy stays, until he had sweated out the poison from his lungs and recovered. Kids have been cured of poison oak by the treatment. Himself, he's a retired bookkeeper who's been replaced by computers. Both hips have been operated on, and the water soothes his aches and pains. He takes gallons of mineral water home with him when he leaves after each visit.

Somewhere in the middle of the story about the gassed veteran, I am converted enough to fill my cup and drink. This is not something I'd recommend sipping, like a fine wine. Gulping is a better method, unless you have a fondness for the bouquet of sulfur.

After I've spent twenty minutes in the tub, the attendant appears and tells me it's time to get out. Lying down on the cot with my arms against my sides, I get wrapped with flannel. A towel is placed over my head, leaving only my eyes, nose, and mouth exposed. The sweating begins immediately and continues for the next forty minutes. Dust from as far back as North Dakota works its way out onto the sheets.

Following a cold shower, I enter the massage room, where the masseur slowly kneads out every kink and knot between my toes and head. A supper of salmon and Washington State wine, a piece of French apple pie with a great crumb crust, and a cup of coffee that prevents me from collapsing in my chair from exquisite relaxation, and I walk out the front door of the hotel, feeling fresher than I did at Stonehenge Jr. fourteen hours ago. It's seven o'clock, the sun's still high in the sky, and I have two more stops to make before I can come back to my room.

The Columbia Gorge's history is the story of the collision of competing forces. Fire vs. ice, water vs. lava, desert vs. rain forest, river vs. mountain range, wind vs. rock, salmon vs. kilowatts, riverboats vs. rapids, culture vs. culture—conflict, catastrophe, and traumatic change are told in every turn of the river and echoed in the canyon walls. Like some epic poem passed on by word of mouth from the beginnings of time, new stanzas have been added by each succeeding generation. From the time the volcanoes were worshiped as angry gods to the day in 1980 when Mount St.

Helens's eruption was described in scientific terms like harmonic tremor and pyroclastic flow, from the moment Lewis and Clark worried about too many salmon to the present when the problem is too few fish, the Gorge has been a battleground.

The battle going on now is between two groups calling themselves Friends of the Columbia Gorge and Columbia Gorge United. Both groups' declared purpose is "saving" the Gorge. The conflict arises in the question of what "saving" means, and the fight, while perhaps not on the same scale as an Ice Age flood trying to scour its way through a basalt plateau, is nonetheless high-pitched.

The Friends of the Columbia Gorge organized in 1980 to seek federal legislation designating the eighty-three-mile stretch of the Columbia as a "national scenic area." According to the view of its members—shared now by the country's principal environmental organizations and a majority of the two states' political leaders—the spectacular scenic beauty and historic significance of the Gorge can be protected only by placing the area under a complex management plan supervised by the National Park Service. Restrictions on development and land use would be imposed, and some "critical" properties not in federal ownership (the Corps of Engineers and Forest Service are already the major landowners) would be purchased or taken by eminent domain; existing incorporated areas would be exempted. As a staff member of the group, based in Portland, explains it, the Gorge is an "area of national value, and they [the local residents] aren't maintaining it as well as it could be."

Many of the local residents, particularly those in Skamania County, Washington, the focal point of the conflict, don't agree. At an evening meeting of Columbia Gorge United in Stevenson (population 1,172), Ed McLarney, editor and publisher of the *Skamania County Pioneer,* summarizes their feelings: "This is a prime example of elitist thinking by environmentalists who think they know better than we do, on the false premise that local people have not, cannot, and will not take care of this national treasure." The proposed legislation, he says, would "take away our property rights, our rights as Americans, our way of life." The administration of a federal scenic area would "have us disenfranchised, it would have us live literally under a federal reservation," he says, casting the battle as one between well-financed, well-connected "so-called environmentalists with fat calves" from outside the area against those who "represent the best that rural small-town life has to offer."

McLarney's group contends that most of the damage to the Gorge has been done by the federal government and its dams; most of the preservation has been accomplished by private citizens who have protected the area because they live there. The other side points to lax zoning regulations in Skamania County and development pressures from Portland as dire threats to the Gorge's future.

In this most modern conflict of the Gorge, where each side employs computers for mailing lists and the battle is waged through newsletters and television interviews, one of the striking things is how the pattern of Manifest Destiny has come full circle. A painting of Sitting Bull hangs in McLarney's office, a reminder of how the local residents identify with the Indians in their fight against a "reservation." (When I ask one resident what Lewis and Clark would discover if they returned two hundred years after their first visit, he says: "What they found before, a population wondering what the Great White Father back in Washington is going to do with their lives.") Yet in the Indians' case, tribal lands and customs were fractured in the name of private ownership of property; for the Gorge, the issue is whether private-property rights should be subjugated to communal needs. And if Manifest Destiny in all its permutations has been the story of Americans attempting to control land and impose manmade change on nature, sometimes simply to prove man's dominance, here in the Gorge the current conflict is not over creating change but preventing it.

Each group seeks to keep things the way they are, but differs on what that means and how it can be accomplished.

GORGE COROLLARY: Resistance to change is as certain as change itself. Building dams across the river of time involves many construction crews, each with its own set of designs.

The graveyard shift at the Bonneville Dam is on duty when I visit the control room at midnight. In a solitary chair surrounded by huge banks of gauges, levers, meters, computer screens, buttons, graphs, and multicolored lights, the operator is sipping a cup of coffee.

A dull vibration from the turbines far beneath us pulses through the concrete. As surely as the needles on the gauges, the faint rumble is evidence that things are right with his world. The standing joke is that if the turbines stop and the reservoir begins building up behind the dam, the first order of business is moving your car to higher ground.

The operator tells me about tailrace, head, turbine torque, and the other terms that translate into the ability of people up and down the West Coast to flick a switch so they can watch Johnny Carson on television. His business being to generate electricity, he adds some complaints about being prohibited from operating some new, additional turbines until the spring smolt run is completed.

Ross Johnson, the lock keeper, reports in and invites me to help a barge make a late-night passage. Out in the gatehouse, I push two buttons, the lock fills with water, and the upstream gate opens. The *Sara Brix,* pushing a barge with 14,000 salmon, steelhead, and sockeye fingerlings in its hold, enters the lock. Ross hands me the day's paper for the crew, and I climb onto the towboat's deck.

We sink inside the lock's canyon until our elevation and the lower Columbia's is the same. The downstream gate opens, and we head out onto the river. The captain's face is intent on the radar screen and the searchlight's beam on the portside shore. Several miles downstream, the rugged outline of Beacon Rock rises eight hundred feet out of the water. Clark, who gave the landmark its name, noted that when the explorers passed the final gauntlet of the Cascade rapids and reached this rock, the ebb and flow of coastal tides was first evident here.

Out on the flat deck of the barge, I watch a biologist and deck hand signal the captain to reverse his engines, keeping the boat's propellers upstream so the fingerlings that have been so painstakingly transported from the upstream dams don't get chewed to silver ribbons. They turn big wheels to open the bottoms of the barge, and we look down into the hold as the swarm of small fish, safe now from the dams' turbines, empty into the river and continue their voyage to the sea unescorted.

It's nearly 3 A.M. when the gate clangs and echoes behind us back in the Bonneville lock. We rise slowly, and when I get off at the gatehouse the crew is talking about a poker game during the upstream ride for the next load of fish.

Climbing back into the *Discovery,* bone tired from my long day, I am reminded of my first day on the trail, when in my excitement

I combined destination travel with discovery travel and ended up spending eighteen hours crossing the entire width of Missouri. I have been up longer than that already today, although I've covered 370 fewer miles. But my bargain with the Road Spirit has been kept, and to make up for the offense of retracing my route to the Hotel St. Martin, I make a final stop at a historic marker near the bridge that will take me to the Washington side.

The marker recounts the legend of the Bridge of the Gods, which is also the name of the modern, steel structure. Chief Ka'nax courted two princesses, one at Mount Hood and the other across the river at Mount Adams, using a natural stone bridge here in his romances. But the gods of the two volcanoes became angry at his duplicity and destroyed the bridge. The scientific explanation of the legend says that about eight hundred years ago, the mountains on the north side collapsed into the Columbia, shoving the river a mile south and forming a two-hundred-foot-high rock dam just upstream from where the seventy-foot-high Bonneville Dam now stands. The river backed up until it finally washed away the impediment and created the treacherous Cascade rapids.

There's more, although it's not included on the marker. While the natural bridge lasted, the tribes that controlled it charged tolls to other tribes seeking passage across the river. By the time Lewis and Clark arrived, when there were rapids but no bridge, they paid a charge to the tribes to transport their goods during the portage. The flood of settlers bound along the Oregon Trail to the Willamette Valley paid tolls to the Indians to get their belongings through here, until the white men realized there was big money to be made and took over. They built a road, then a railroad, and then the old Cascade Locks—all with tolls attached.

Between me and a warm bed is this newer bridge. The sun will be up soon. Tomorrow, or more precisely, later today, I'll sleep late and treat myself to another mineral bath, sweat, and massage before heading downriver.

Repeating an ancient custom of the Gorge, I pull the *Discovery* onto the approach of the Bridge of the Gods, pay my toll, and cross.

BRIDGE OF THE GODS COROLLARY: The more some things change, the more they stay the same.

23

To the Coast

Ocian in view! O! the joy.

> From William Clark's notebook
> November 7, 1805

In the spring of 1843 nearly a thousand people gathered their covered wagons in Independence and Westport, Missouri, waiting for good traveling weather. The tier of states between the Mississippi and Missouri rivers was already filling with settlers. Expansion into the Plains was out of the question: It was popularly known as the American Desert on the maps, and besides, it was still reserved for the Indians.

Oregon—far beyond the Missouri, far beyond the Rockies— was the new escape valve and magnet for the restless nation. Reports to the East from Marcus Whitman and other early visitors to the Columbia region had described fertile soil and a mild climate with a long growing season, particularly along the Willamette River. Narcissa Whitman and Eliza Spalding had already proved that the West was not the exclusive domain of mountain men; women— white women—could survive and raise families. The government was eager to settle Oregon as a way of resolving the northwest boundary question with Britain in the United States's favor. The promise of free land and new opportunity hung redolent in the spring air as the wagons left Missouri. The Great Migration had begun.

Nothing like this had been done before. Expeditions like Lewis and Clark's had covered this distance, but they had been military-exploratory parties whose purpose was to venture west and return. Mountain men and gangs of fur traders had formed impromptu communities in the wilderness with their yearly rendezvous, but those were only as permanent as a campfire and the whites who showed up were exclusively male. Smatterings of missionaries had gone west, a few with wives and families in tow, but their numbers were minuscule. This wagon train of 1843 was something new. It would traverse two thousand land miles not for exploration but for emigration; its goal was not trapping or proselytizing but settling permanently in a new land. It was comprised primarily of families. There were more milk cows than people, and many of the people were women and children.

When the wagon train arrived at what now is The Dalles, the prairie schooners had to be abandoned for real boats to reach Fort

Vancouver by river. From there, the emigrants moved up the Willamette River to a point south of modern Portland and selected homesites. Their arrival doubled the American population in Oregon.

The mighty engine of Manifest Destiny was fueled by many sources as it jumped the nation's boundaries over the Rockies and to the far West before turning back to settle the open stretches of the Plains. Land fever drew the wagons along the Platte River and over South Pass into Oregon, which became a state in 1859, thirty years before Montana and the two Dakotas were admitted to the Union. California was grabbed from Mexico in the war of 1846; the Gold Rush of '49 turned the stream of westbound settlers into a flood, and what had been Mexican territory only four years earlier became the thirty-first state in 1850. Meanwhile, the Mormons were also heading west along the opposite shore of the Platte, seeking neither gold nor land for its own sake but as much distance as possible between them and the mob that had murdered their martyr, Joseph Smith, in Illinois. Zion was reestablished in the basin of the Great Salt Lake. Only after the mountains had been conquered and the western coast populated did settlers begin filling the vast portion of America first explored by Lewis and Clark. The frontier collapsed upon itself, and in 1890 the Census Bureau declared it officially closed.

Most of the migrations since that time have been from the land of the pioneers to the gleaming cities. Jefferson's dream of a nation of small farmers has become a country of service-industry employees clustered in suburbs. The descendants of people who crossed half the continent in an ox-drawn wagon for the chance at 640 acres of free land now define space in terms of front lawns or so many square feet in a condominium complex. Their favored outlet for restlessness is cheap airfare to a vacation spot on the Mexican coast, or maybe a trip to Yellowstone to watch the bears feed at the garbage dumps.

Sucked into the vortex of rush-hour traffic as I approach Portland (population 366,383) and the mouth of the river valley that was the Promised Land for the Great Migration, the *Discovery* becomes just one more small fish in the school of cascading metal and rubber. For the first time since Omaha and Kansas City the big-city tension grips my body. Which exit from the six-lane thruway should I take? Which lane should I be in? Am I the only traveler unfamiliar with this city, uncertain of his route, unfocused in this hurried race between work and home?

Never fond of metropolises to begin with, I find my preference for small towns and open spaces has only been reinforced by this trail. Towns like Hermann, Missouri; Lynch, Nebraska; Watford City, North Dakota; Dillon, Montana; Lapwai, Idaho; Stevenson, Washington; even all of Harrison County, Iowa—they could be lumped together and moved to a city and still not make a suburb big enough to warrant its own exit. But obviously I'm out of step. Most of those towns are, in fact, picking up and moving piecemeal from country to city. Within my own brief lifetime, nearly 80 percent of the 23 million Americans living on farms have moved, most of them to cities. Census Bureau statistics show that in the same thirty-five years, the percentage of Americans in nonmetropolitan areas has declined from nearly a third to less than a quarter of the population.

Not that Portland is a bad place, as big cities go. It's cleaner than most, either because of civic pride or the heavy coastal rains or both. It feels both vibrant and laid back—a West Coast city with all the urban bustle but without the hard edge of, say, Los Angeles or any Eastern city you can name. (On the day of my visit, the major news is that city officials have become concerned about the growing population of hoboes and bums living in the freight yards under the interstate cloverleafs. But, in a spirit that Fry Pan Jack would appreciate, the city has decided to warn the transients in advance before dispatching the police to sweep the area; most of them will be offered temporary shelter by charities or the city government.) The city center has tree-lined boulevards and flowery parks; the big harbor is a working port, unmarked by the empty buildings or upscale boutiques that characterize the former commercial centers of too many other cities.

So many people: well-dressed professionals walking purposefully along the streets, the women wearing sneakers and bouncing as they stroll; teenagers displaying this year's fashion rebellion with their orange- and purple-tinted spikes of hair; hoboes on street benches, adjusting to the ambiance in the polite way they panhandle; and, proving that Jefferson's vision of the importance of interchange with the Orient has not been abandoned, a heavy mixture of Asian-Americans. (Just as every Missouri town from St. Louis to Weston claims to be the Gateway to the West, every town on the Columbia from Portland to the river's mouth calls itself the Gateway to the Pacific Rim.)

So many stores and shops: asking about a camera store to buy supplies, I am directed to three within a two-block area. I pass one cafe, bigger and busier than most I have eaten in for the last two months, that specializes just in cookies and coffee; on one street corner, enough newspaper boxes to provide papers for the entire population of a small town.

I find supper at a Thai restaurant, my first "non-American" meal since an ill-conceived visit to a Chinese restaurant in Bismarck; here, at least, the cuisine and personnel share the same heritage, and the meal is savory proof that the axiom "When in Rome, etc." has a lot of wisdom in it and should be remembered whenever you visit cities named after Prussian chancellors. Western hospitality isn't necessarily confined to small towns: one of the people I interview in Portland lets me sleep on a mattress in a spare room.

And so, despite my biases, I find myself liking Portland. Or at least not disliking Portland. One of the reasons I prefer smaller communities is brought back into focus on the day I leave and find myself again in the midst of the twice-daily, twentieth-century version of the Great Migration. One of the best local views of Mount Hood is from the interstate bridge crossing the Columbia River. When I turn for a final look at the volcano's cone, I inadvertently slow down to something approaching the legal speed limit and am nearly run over by the crush of vehicles intent on shaving four minutes off their three-mile trip.

ROAD RULE 20: Prejudices are like heavy furniture in a Conestoga wagon on the Oregon Trail. In order to keep moving forward, sometimes you have to toss them out, even if they are family heirlooms.

More than fifty years ago, when Bob Lange was a young Boy Scout in Oregon, he went off to a summer camp named Camp Meriwether in honor of Captain Lewis. One of the camp activities was a mini-pageant in which the Corps of Discovery's historic journey was reenacted. The Scouts would walk forest trails, stop at small replicas of Mandan lodges, walk some more, stop at a miniature version of Fort Clatsop (the expedition's winter quarters on the

Oregon coast), and learn about the explorers on the way. As he grew older and started traveling the state for an electrical-supplies distributor, Lange would stop at libraries and check out books about the expedition. At night, in a motel room, he began reading the first of the eight-volume edition of the journals. He hasn't stopped reading them since.

Retired now at age seventy, Lange spends about five hours every day in his study, literally surrounded by Lewis and Clark. As he sits at his desk, portraits of the captains are at his right shoulder. The rest of his study includes additional paintings and pictures of the expedition, framed maps, figurines and whiskey bottles commemorating individual expedition members, a rock from the site in northern Montana where Lewis fought and killed two Blackfeet Indians, looseleaf notebooks systematically arranged with material about every aspect of the trail, and, of course, an edition of the journals that is his own, lined up on a rack within an arm's reach of his typewriter.

It is safe to say that, with the possible exception of professional historians who have studied it for a living, Bob Lange is the most knowledgeable living American on the topic of Lewis and Clark. He has visited every spot along the long trail not once, but several times. In addition to the captains' journals, he has read and reread those of Sergeants Patrick Gass and John Ordway and Private Joseph Whitehouse, and the abbreviated journal of Sergeant Charles Floyd, whose last entry was made shortly before he died near Sioux City. Lange's name crops up in the acknowledgments of most modern books written about the expedition, because he is as important a source as a library.

He is one of the leading lights of the Lewis and Clark Trail Heritage Foundation Inc., a nonprofit organization devoted to keeping the expedition's memory alive. The foundation has about a thousand members—schoolteachers, secretaries, business executives, farmers, lawyers, housewives—whose common interest is the Corps of Discovery. Lange served as president during its early years; his wife, Ruth, keeps the membership rolls.

Lange's labor of love is being editor of *We Proceeded On,* the group's quarterly magazine that takes its name from the most repeated phrase in the journals. In its pages, scholars and amateurs alike explore various aspects of the expedition, from sweeping topics such as the role of Clark's maps in American settlement of the

West to the details of what happened to the plant specimens Lewis brought back to Jefferson; from Lewis and Clark as ethnologists to a description of how the air gun they used to impress the Indians actually worked. An edition devoted solely to Lewis's Newfoundland dog has gone into three printings.

He and I have lunch with Irving Anderson, whose specialty is the Charbonneau family: the French trapper-interpreter so often maligned in the journals, his infant son, Jean Baptiste, and of course Mrs. Charbonneau, the more-famous Sacagawea. If uniformity in the place names, statues, parks, and descriptions devoted to the Indian woman is ever achieved, it will be credited to Anderson's messianic mission to correct what he considers "false history."

A former documents specialist for the Bureau of Land Management, Anderson is a stickler for documentation. His persistence helped confirm the site near Danner, Oregon, where Jean Baptiste died in 1866. Anderson's self-imposed task of correcting the mistaken popular image of the Indian woman's name, her actual role in the expedition, and how and where her life ended is more daunting. Too many people have read the novels about her and accepted them as fact.

In any case, it is a pleasant afternoon with Lange and Anderson, swapping stories about the American epic as if we'd been along on it and had gotten together today in a reunion of the last three surviving members. We inspect the snowberry bush that grows outside the Lange home, a species Lewis discovered in the Bitterroots. It needs pruning, but Lange shakes his head. "You can't cut down Lewis's plant," he says. Ruth Lange serves a good meal and sits in on the conversation. Private George Shannon, the youngest member of the expedition, the one who seemed to have the habit of getting lost all the time, is her favorite, she says. Lange is one of the few Lewis and Clark buffs who doesn't have a favorite character or episode; he revels in it all.

At the urging of the Langes and Irving Anderson, I stop in Longview, Washington (population 30,950), to see Hazel Bain, a former president of the Lewis and Clark Trail Heritage Foundation. Her living room is a scaled-down version of Lange's study, filled with Lewis and Clark paintings, plates, bottles, placemats, postcards, and books. She takes me to the high, arched bridge that I need to cross to get back to U.S. 30 for the final drive to the coast. It used to be called the Longview Columbia River Bridge. In 1980, on the 175th anniversary of the explorers' passage, Hazel Bain was one of the dignitaries at the ceremony renaming it the Lewis and Clark Bridge. As testimony to her efforts in promoting the legislation necessary for the new name, among the memorabilia in Hazel's living room is the pen Washington's governor used to sign the bill.

Driving west toward the Coast Range you understand where all the "moisture" is that doesn't make it past the Cascades and Bitterroots and Rockies, and where all the trees grow that are missing from the Dakotas and Nebraska. The town names tell the story: Forest Grove, Woodland, Timber, Mist. The thick growth of conifers is one of the few examples of a true rain forest outside of the tropics. A lumber truck passes, fully loaded with just four trunk sections of a pine whose diameter is wider than the height of the burr oaks along the Missouri. The forests are so dense here that you wonder where the first tree is supposed to fall when a cutting operation begins; the air is so damp that an explorer without a razor would probably grow moss instead of a beard.

"Disagreeable" is the word that replaced "we proceeded on" as most used in the expedition's journal entries here. It rained constantly. On November 7, 1805, Clark reports "Great joy in camp we are in view of the Ocian, this great Pacific Octean which we been so long anxious to See. and the roreing or noise made by the waves brakeing on the rockey Shores (as I suppose) may be heard disti[n]ctly." In truth, it was Gray's Bay near the broad mouth of the Columbia, not the Pacific itself, they were seeing and hearing. Wind, rain, and waves pinned the group on the lee side of Ellice's Point for five days until a break in the rough seas allowed them to round the point and make camp on the western side, where Clark decided this "would be the extent of our journey by water, as the waves were too high at any stage for our Canoes to proceed further down." Nine more "disagreeable" days were spent here in the rain while the men's buckskin clothing continued to rot on their soaked bodies. They were out of salt, flour, and meat, and survived on pounded salmon. Clark estimated that from the mouth of the Missouri to this "land's end," the Corps of Discovery had traveled 4,162 miles.

Small parties reconnoitered the area surrounding the promontory of Cape Disappointment (named such by Captain John Meares, who erroneously but understandably concluded in 1788 that the bay behind was not the mouth of the Great River of the West), hoping in vain to encounter a white trading vessel. Camping here for the winter was out of the question. Game was scarce, and the flea-infested Chinook tribes were bothersome. Told that elk were abundant on the southern, Oregon side of the river's mouth, the captains proposed moving across or returning to a site back up the Columbia. The issue was put to a vote, and in a ceremony that would predate the exercise of democracy in the United States by sixty-five and one hundred and fifteen years, respectively, York (a black slave) and Sacagawea (a woman and an Indian) were allowed to participate. The vote was overwhelming for wintering on the Oregon side if game could be found there. Elk was needed for food and for hides to replace the moldy clothing; the climate would be more moderate than farther upriver; salt would be available from the sea; and remaining near the coast was important because they still harbored the hope that a trading vessel would appear to replenish their supplies and take the journals and collected botanical specimens back to civilization. (The idea of returning the whole expedition by sea was apparently never contemplated.)

On November 26, 1805, a break in the weather allowed them to cross the fifteen-mile-wide river to a spot near modern-day Astoria. The weather was still miserable. "This is our present situation!" Clark notes, now using exclamation points more often in his entries, "Truly disagreeable." Lewis and a small group scouted the area. Before Lewis returned with the welcome news that a small rise several miles up what is now Lewis and Clark River would be a good spot for winter quarters, Clark, the inveterate graffiti artist, carved the following into the side of a spruce tree: "Capt William Clark December 3rd 1805. By land. U. States in 1804–1805." The expedition moved to Lewis's selected spot and began building a small fort on December 8. By the thirtieth, the finishing touches were made to Fort Clatsop, where they would remain for four wet, disagreeable months.

Chasing one more sunset, I spur the *Discovery* down U.S. 30 along the dense canyons of spruce and fir. There is no sky. A gray cloud cover rests on the treetops. Astoria, Oregon (population 10,000), appears on the hilly banks of the river mouth, the oldest town in the Pacific Northwest, founded in 1811 as part of John Jacob Astor's ill-fated attempt at a continental fur monopoly. Crossing the river on another toll bridge, I make a hurried visit to the Lewis and Clark Interpretative Center atop Cape Disappointment, an impressive display of the expedition's history on a site with an impressive view of the treacherous bar that had deceived and disappointed so many seagoing explorers until Gray sailed through to stake America's claim to the Columbia. The odometer on the *Discovery* says we've traveled 6,156 miles since we left Wood River, Illinois, a little shy of two months ago.

Back in Astoria, I stop for supplies. The Park Service has kindly agreed that tomorrow night, once the tourists leave, I can sleep in the reconstruction of Fort Clatsop. At a Scandinavian festival, I buy some Norwegian dark bread in honor of my grandmother's heritage. At a smokehouse, I purchase some salmon jerky, some smoked winter chinook salmon, and a bag of chocolate-covered huckleberries. No need to go overboard in trying to relive the expedition's experience. Like Clark, I'll take salmon over dog meat; but I'll also have bread where they didn't, and a dessert. (I've also got a bottle of Lewis and Clark bourbon from Montana, something the men would have killed for at this point.)

The chocolate-covered huckleberries and my inability to save them all for tomorrow night at Fort Clatsop almost bring my trip to a tragicomic end. Pulling up to a red light at the intersection of Highways 30 and 101, I pop a huckleberry in my mouth, chew it too quickly, and swallow in mid-breath. A big gob of chocolate and berry lodges in my windpipe. No air.

Lewis and Clark, I am pleased to report, were not the only explorers in American history who knew how to practice emergency folk medicine on the trail. In the time it takes to construct the headline *Failure to Find Passage Results in Corpse of Discovery* I am out the front door, put my doubled fists just below my rib cage, and run myself three times into the flat front of the camper. This is called a self-administered Heimlich Maneuver, a handy thing to know if you breathe through your mouth. The pressure on my diaphragm blows the ball of food up and out of the windpipe, and I can start rewriting the headline in the fresh, salt air. Climbing back into the front seat, I make a mental note to put the huckleberries in the cooler so the chocolate won't melt before tomorrow night. The light changes, and I proceed on. The guy in the car behind the *Discovery* is still sitting at the intersection with a stunned look on his face.

ROAD RULE 21: Always carry a first-aid kit in your vehicle. Indians and non-Indians often require "medicine" in their travels.

FIRST COROLLARY: Sometimes your vehicle itself is a first-aid tool. This is called "Big Medicine."

My last westbound sunset occurs in Seaside, Oregon (population 5,193), a honky-tonk resort community already bustling with summer tourists. For the first and only time on my journey, I have to stop at four motels before I can find one with a vacancy. The restaurant I visit for a supper of fresh razor clams is jammed with people, and there is a long wait for a table. History repeats itself: prices for room and board are almost double what I have grown used to farther inland. At least there aren't any fleas.

During their winter at Fort Clatsop, a small contingent from the expedition established a camp here to boil seawater and make salt for the return trip. The salt cairn has been preserved, thanks primarily to Olin Wheeler, a historian who retraced the Lewis and Clark trail and wrote of the changes along the route on the centennial of the expedition. It rests in a small lot between two houses in the residential section of Seaside.

Farther south on the coast, Clark led an excursion in January to view a whale that the Indians reported had been washed ashore. Sacagawea pleaded to go along. "She observed that She had traveled a long way with us to See the great waters," Clark writes, "and that now that monstrous fish was also to be Seen, She thought it verry hard that She could not be permitted to See either (She had never yet been to the Ocian)." Indians had already picked the whale carcass clean by the time Clark's party, including Sacagawea, arrived. The captain bought three hundred pounds of blubbery meat and a few gallons of rendered oil, measured the 105-foot skeleton, and returned to the fort. At a campsite in what is now Ecola State Park, Clark "beheld the grandest and most pleasing prospect which my eyes ever surveyed, in my frount a boundless Ocean; to the N. and N.E. the coast as far as my sight could be extended, the Seas rageing with emence waves and breaking with great force." Cannon Beach, a more restrained and pleasant resort community than Seaside, sits along the sandy shore where the whale was beached; the waves still crash against Haystack Rock as spectacularly as they did when Clark and the astonished Indian woman surveyed the scene.

In Seaside, the main street, Broadway, runs due west past salt-water taffy shops, caramel stands, T-shirt emporiums, a bumper-car and video arcade, a one-hour photo business, more gift shops and cafes (one is named the Dog House, a place the expedition undoubtedly would have patronized), and a hotel before it reaches the Lewis and Clark Turnaround. A marker says that the Oregon legislature has declared this the official end of the Lewis and Clark trail and the westernmost point where the expedition camped. *Well* . . . Not quite on either count.

But it's as good a spot as any to sit and watch the sun sink into the water, a Farewell Sunset. The ocean, at low tide, hisses rather than roars. A thick mist clings to the hills to the south. Cloud banks out to sea look like yet another mountain range across a liquid plain. On Broadway, the traffic is heavy. Most of it is comprised of young kids, driving Jeeps and rumbling cars with their windows down and their tape decks blaring rock music. Westward they roll, one behind the other in an unending line, restless and impatient and exuberant in the summer of their youth. One by one the vehicles noisily, eagerly approach the "official end" of America's probe west. Each one sends a fragment of loud music, an insistent bass heartbeat of life pulsing out its window. Then they pass the marker and its flagpole, arc around the circle, catch one brief glimpse of the sun that can be pursued no farther, and head east down the same street.

The gold sun has touched the horizon now, distorting like a hot egg yolk dropped on water. It lingers for a moment, allowing one last look from the continent it has crossed in a day, and sinks from sight.

24

Homesick at Fort Clatsop

our repast of this day tho' better than that of Christmass, consisted principally in the anticipation of the 1st day of January 1807, when in the bosom of our friends we hope to participate in the mirth and hilarity of the day, and when with zest given by the recollection of the present, we shall completely, both mentally and corporally, enjoy the repast which the hand of civilization has prepared for us. at present we were content with eating our boiled Elk and wappetoe, and solacing our thirst with our only beverage pure water.

> From Meriwether Lewis's journal
> Fort Clatsop
> January 1, 1806

In a small clearing in a grove of towering Sitka spruce a young man tends an iron kettle over an open fire. He is wearing a coonskin cap, a rough-cotton shirt, elkskin leggings, and moccasins. The fat in his kettle boils slowly, rendering into tallow over the burning sticks of alder. When it's boiled long enough, the young man pours the mixture into a leaden mold, four cylinders with wicks dangling down their centers.

"And that's how the expedition made their candles," says Dan Dattilio, a Park Service ranger at the Fort Clatsop National Memorial and leader of its "living history" program. He passes some cooled candles to the ring of tourists gathered around the fire. They ask a few questions and wander off to another clearing on the banks of Lewis and Clark River to watch some other park employees, also dressed in period attire, hewing a giant log with an adze. A dugout canoe's outline is beginning to take form. A little later, after an outdoor lecture in which the audience participates in bartering beaver pelts for beads, Dattilio and another ranger begin pouring black powder into a muzzleloader. The crowd gathers behind them. Before raising the rifle to his shoulder, Dattilio puts small plugs in his ears. This wasn't part of the explorers' routine, he explains, but it's a new government regulation. He points the rifle toward the river and pulls the trigger. A flash, and a crashing boom rocks the clearing. The crowd applauds, particularly the children.

An announcement is made that the park will close in fifteen minutes, and most of the people head for the gift shop. Dattilio leads me to the fort to show me my room for the night and give me some final instructions.

Based on a rough sketch Clark made of its floor plan on the elkskin cover of his field book, Fort Clatsop was reconstructed on its original site in 1955, the sesquicentennial of the Corps of Discovery's arrival at the Columbia's mouth. It is a log stockade, fifty feet by fifty feet, with a small parade ground separating the two rows of rooms, four rooms in one row, three in the other. Palisades and gates are at each end of the parade ground, closing the square.

My room is on the three-room side, where the enlisted men slept.

The rooms across the parade ground were for the captains, York and an orderly, Charbonneau and his wife and infant son, and the fourth to smoke and store meat. My room is sixteen by fifteen feet, with a window and door opening to the parade ground. A small hearth is against the back wall. Four bunk beds, a small table, and a chair, all rough-cut from local trees, are the only furniture. The bedding consists of elk hides and a few buffalo robes. A small stack of cedar slabs and dry alder logs are next to the hearth; two elkhorn candle stands sit on the table. Dattilio hands me some tallow candles from today's rendering.

"Keep your fire next to the back wall or your room will fill with smoke," he tells me, citing both the journals and his own experience for authority. "And don't build the fire too big; the chimney's made of cedar." He lugs in a fire extinguisher, just in case.

The other members of the living-history program have gathered in the parade ground. One of them brings down the American flag—it has seventeen stars, as it did when the expedition camped here, hundreds of miles west of the United States boundary, so many years ago—and folds it carefully. Their day of playing Lewis and Clark is over, and soon they'll be out of their buckskins and into more modern clothing. They seem mildly amused that I'm going to sleep in the vacant fort and complete the reenactment cycle that they started this morning.

"Maybe we should have put some fleas in the bedding to make the experience completely authentic," one of them tells Dattilio as they walk to the parking lot, leaving me alone with the ghosts of the explorers.

Fleas were a bother for the men during their coastal winter at Fort Clatsop—Clark grumbles in his journal about losing several nights' sleep around Christmas because of them—but they weren't the only problem. From November 4, 1805, to March 23, 1806, it rained every day except twelve, and only half of those had clear skies.

The men suffered from colds and rheumatism because of the gloomy dampness. Game, while available in the area, was not abundant, and as the winter wore on could be found only at increasing distances from the fort. In all, they killed 131 elk, twenty deer, one raccoon, and a few beaver and otter—hardly sufficient for a contingent of thirty-three people for four months. Dogs were still a staple of the diet, when they could be purchased from neighboring tribes. Most of the newly made salt had to be saved for the return trip; the wood was often too wet to make good fires for smoking the meat. Whatever elk or deer were killed had to be eaten quickly before the meat spoiled in the dank climate. For Christmas 1806, Clark reports, "our Diner concisted of pore Elk, so much Spoiled that we eate it thro' mear necessity, Some Spoiled pounded fish and a fiew roots."

Having already run out of whiskey at the Great Falls on the previous Fourth of July, the men saw their remaining luxury of tobacco start to disappear. The captains divided half of the remaining supply among the smokers for Christmas (the nonsmokers received handkerchiefs as gifts); all of the tobacco was gone by the end of March. The candle supply gave out in mid-January, but Lewis's foresight was proven again by the extra wicks and the molds he had brought along. They made their own candles, the same way Dan Dattilio made mine.

With the exception of the field trip to see the whale, the winter routine was as monotonous as the weather. Instead of "we proceeded on," a new phrase, "not any occurrence today worthy of notice," becomes a refrain repeated again and again in the journals. The men were occupied with making new clothes from the elk and deer hides, a task they considered woman's work compared to the adventures they had gone through to get here. They made 338 pairs of moccasins—about ten per person—for the return journey.

The neighboring Clatsops were friendly and helpful, even though they brought fleas into the palisades just about every time the explorers had vanquished the last infestation. Chinooks from the other side of the Columbia were another matter, becoming enough of a pest themselves that the password at the fort's gate was "No Chinook." Apparently, however, they weren't always unwelcome: a number of Chinook women visited often enough to leave cases of syphilis behind. (Commenting that "the captains simply accepted sexual relations as part of frontier life and were worried only if they endangered the expedition's health or security," historian James Ronda has pointed out that venereal disease was such a common complaint during the twenty-eight-month exploration that "it is probably safe to say that 'Louis Veneris' was an unpaid, unenlisted, but ever-present member of the Corps of Discovery throughout its long voyage.")

While it is unclear whether the social diseases were introduced to the region by the maritime traders, other signs clearly showed the impact of whites along the coast. Some of the women sported tattoos with sailors' names; the captains reported that some Indians' vocabulary included phrases like "sun of a pitch &c."

The captains were busy throughout the winter. Lewis filled reams of paper with details about animals, plants, and Indian customs of the Northwest, while Clark compiled a master map of the region from Fort Mandan to the Pacific and other more detailed maps of the country west of the Great Falls.

The commanders decided upon a new wrinkle for the return trip. The expedition would divide at Traveller's Rest. Clark and his party would go south to Camp Fortunate and then overland to explore the Yellowstone River. Lewis and his group would take the shortcut eastward from Traveller's Rest to the Great Falls to confirm the Indian information. Lewis would also lead a small exploration of the upper reaches of the Marias River to determine the northern limit of the Louisiana Territory. The entire expedition would regroup at the mouth of the Yellowstone.

Jefferson had written a special letter of credit for Lewis to carry, in case they met a trading vessel along the Pacific. The letter guaranteed payment from the U.S. government and was to be used in buying supplies and paying for return passage of copies of the journals, the growing collection of specimens, and, perhaps, a few of the men. While the captains compiled lists of vessels the coastal tribes told them often stopped in the area, no ship was seen during the winter. The brig *Lydia* from Boston traded along the Columbia's mouth in November 1805, but neither its captain nor Lewis and Clark learned of the twin American presence in the territory.

When the expedition abandoned Fort Clatsop on March 23, 1806, they left behind several copies of a memorandum briefly chronicling their achievement, the names of the Corps of Discovery members, and a sketchy map showing the relationship of the Columbia and Missouri River watersheds. One copy was tacked to the door of the captains' room, the others given to neighboring tribes. The captains turned the fort over to the Clatsop tribe for whom it had been named and began their homeward journey. When the *Lydia* returned to trade in the spring of 1806, its skipper was given one of the notices, as well as some medals the captains had distributed. By the time the memorandum made its way back to an Eastern port in January 1807, the expedition had already reached St. Louis and personally delivered the news of their discoveries to an amazed nation.

My supper this evening in Fort Clatsop is a quarter pound of Chinook salmon, rich, oily, and flavorful; a quarter loaf of the dark Norwegian bread; an apple; and a can of cold beer. Even though it is still light outside at 7:30 P.M., the trees crowding the fort are casting long shadows from the lowering sun, and my room's window faces east, not west. The fire in the hearth wards off the onset of the twilight's chill; most of its smoke goes up and out the chimney, although a small portion lingers in the corners of the room.

Two candles provide the light for reading the journals. Lewis's entry in March that "the leafing of the huckleberry riminds us of Spring" reminds me of my dessert. Two chocolate-covered huckleberries are consumed without any threat to my life.

Emotions new to my journey gather round me like the lengthening shadows outside, closing in to surround and finally overwhelm the sense of satisfaction of having reached the sea. The confinement of the trees, the smallness of the darkening room redirect thoughts inward. The sea, though several miles away, is a presence, a barrier against any farther westward dreams, turning the mind in a new direction: east. The salt air makes me acutely aware that an entire continent separates me from my home. Home. *You're a long way from home,* I tell myself. Homesickness, one of the historical maladies of Fort Clatsop, washes over me, and it is harder to treat than the other diseases that have infected the fort's inhabitants.

There's nowhere else to go now, except *back*. Each day's goal will no longer be an unknown spot where the sun sets on the horizon, but back, all the way back across the already known to the starting point, the well known. Once the mind is settled on that goal, the journey is no longer discovery travel but destination travel.

The idea that merely reaching this spot would be the crowning accomplishment is now exposed as a delusion. This is not the final point of the journey, it is the halfway point. And it is halfway with a difference. There's less anticipation in going back to what you already left behind. On the way out, the act of going was as much the purpose as where you were headed. The joy of discovery, of seeing something for the first time, of having literally no idea what was just beyond the horizon—the innocence and much of its excitement are gone, and gone forever. Whatever anticipation remains is of getting home, the destination, rather than the discovery.

So it must have been for the members of the expedition as they sat in these small rooms during that wet and gloomy winter. As if the rain, the fleas, the spoiled meat, the lack of liquor and tobacco were not reason enough, no wonder they were cranky, bored, dispirited, and increasingly homesick here. They were explorers, first and foremost, the Corps of *Discovery* as they called themselves. For nearly two years, their life had been one of movement, not staying put. And the movement had been in one direction, literally and mentally: west, into the unknown, where no one had gone before, often mapless with the racing sun's path the only marker to follow.

With the exception of the side explorations they planned for Montana, what lay ahead from Fort Clatsop was not so much adventure as obstacles to a safe return. Consider the Bitterroots. On the westward trek, these mountains where no mountains were supposed to exist had nearly killed them in a crossing that had lasted twice as long as their Indian guides had promised. They would have to be crossed again. Only this time the explorers *knew* just how formidable the dense tangle of peaks would be.

Their mission had been to trace the Missouri to its source, cross the mountains, and descend to the ocean. They had done all that, and along the way seen sights unbelievable to Eastern thought—animals and plants new to civilization; semiarid plains that stretched as far as the eye could see and tested a man's conception of space; waterfalls and cascades unheard of in their scale; mountains so high, broad, and majestic that the Alleghenies and Blue Ridges would forever seem puny in comparison. All this they had discovered, and, equally remarkably, had survived with only a single, unavoidable casualty. But none of it could be known unless and until they returned. If any of the obstacles they now knew existed between them and St. Louis defeated their homeward journey, if they and their journals perished somewhere along the way, it would be as though they hadn't gone out West in the first place.

Without question, the expedition was eager to leave the miserable winter quarters and be on the move once more. But proceeding on from this point meant going back. It meant knowing what lay ahead, and knowing exactly just how far they were from the destination that now dominated their thoughts. The last half of the journey would be different, requiring a new determination to replace the innocence of discovery.

And so it has been for the nation that followed their footsteps west. It has been the pursuit of the goal, the getting there, the quest for the unreachable, the proving of the unproven that stirs us. "Biggests" and "firsts" and "newests" have been our fascination. Always in a hurry, often without a map, we have pushed on.

The Corps of Discovery was the first American journey across the continent, and the vast area they crossed, at the time just an embryo of a nation, was to become the ground where everything that defines America would grow: the equation of progress with literal mobility; the preference for the simpler values of the small town over the tangled complexities of the big cities; a brashly commercial and pragmatic character that simultaneously sees itself in romantic and idealistic terms; an uneasy suspicion of the strictures of society; the idea of footloose freedom associated with cowboys and mountain men; the promise of having your own piece of land and a fresh start simply by packing up and moving to the frontier farther west; the presence of wide-open spaces that breeds a feeling of almost naive optimism as expansive as the horizon; and the concept, derived from Manifest Destiny, that if it *can* be done, Americans *should,* and *will,* do it.

And now, nearly two hundred years after the Lewis and Clark expedition and nearly one hundred years after the frontier closed, we are still trying to come to grips with the realization that the journey out gets us only halfway to a final destination. The vehicle of Manifest Destiny left some litter behind as it propelled us along, and the debris lines the return route. We built the Bomb because we thought we had to, and we were proud to be first; then we tamed the atom to more peaceful purposes. But now we must face the quagmire of nuclear negotiations and of storing deadly wastes that survive for ten thousand years. We dammed the rivers so we could save the floodlands, generate electricity, provide water for irrigation, and create playgrounds for fishing and boating. But now we have people displaced by the reservoirs, an oversupply of food in a hungry world that is throwing farmers off their land, and barges and complicated programs to transport the fish around the dams we built. In the need to provide land for "American" farmers, in the need to dig for gold and silver, in the need to offer space for a growing nation—in the name of progress we displaced the nation's first inhabitants, confined them to reservations, and shattered a society based on harmony with the land. But in the name of progress, another land-based society, the rural life centered on family farms, is now being shattered and displaced. As de Tocqueville noted, the American impulse has been to use the beautiful, and our land and its natural resources are where the beauty resides. But there are different definitions of its best use—from preservation to conservation to recreation to exploitation—and not enough of it available to satisfy everyone.

We have pushed forward relentlessly, with great things to accomplish and in a rush to get there and do them. Our national Road Rule has been to proceed on, to keep moving and never stop unless there was no alternative. For a while, whenever things bogged down and seemed too complicated or strained, we could pick up and go out West to new territory and leave our troubles behind. Then we hit the coast, the frontier closed. We had to turn back, and turning back is a new and different national experience. Success and progress have been defined by moving on; turning back was failure. Myths die hard. Like the teenagers in Seaside, our energy has been restless and youthful, and we keep heading west up Broadway to test whether the turnaround is still there at the ocean's edge.

Some birds caw from the branches of the conifers outside Fort Clatsop, signaling the end of another day. There is still enough daylight in the sky for a walk to the canoe landing near Lewis and Clark River. A veil of clouds turns the twilight gray as I inspect the progress on the dugout. The growth of trees and bushes is dense along the trail back to my night's quarters, obstructing any view of the Park Service visitor center or the parking lot where my modern vessel waits for tomorrow's start toward home.

Inside my room, I add some logs to the fire, pile the hides and robes onto a lower bunk to be ready for the night, and sit down near the candles to read some more from the journals. Sergeant John Ordway, Christmas Day, 1805, in a room just like this one: "they divided out the last of their tobacco among the men that used [it] and the rest they gave each a Silk handkerchief, as a

Christmast gift, to keep us in remembrance of it as we have no ardent Spirits." Times change. I light my pipe, pour a small shot of Lewis and Clark bourbon into my cup, and raise a silent salute to other kinds of spirits: theirs, and the Road Spirit.

The faint light through the window says that the sun is setting, but my usual compulsion to go outside and watch it is gone. There are too many trees for a good view, and besides, my thoughts have turned toward the other direction. From here, out West, everything is back East.

25

Homeward

The object of this list is, that through the medium of some civilized
person who may see the same, it may be made known to the in-
formed world, that the party consisting of the persons whose names
are hereunto annexed, and who were sent out by the government of
the U'States in May 1804. to explore the interior of the continent
of North America, did penetrate the same by way of the Missouri
and Columbia Rivers, to the discharge of the latter into the Pacific
Ocean, where they arrived on the 14th of November 1805, and
from whence they departed the [blank] day of March 1806 on their
return to the United States by the same rout they had come out.

> Memorandum left by Lewis and Clark
> Fort Clatsop
> March 23, 1806

ROAD RULE 22: The trip home is a reverse image of the outward
journey, like looking at the negative of a photograph you took
not too long ago. Looking forward is looking back; each new
sight is something seen before only from the opposite direction;
counting mileage is a subtraction, not an addition, of the
distance from home; memory is an image fading in the rearview mirror.

The *Discovery* balks against starting in the damp morning of Fort Clatsop, as if turning back were against its nature and the act of retracing a trail might strip it of its name and identity. Finally it starts and we turn eastward, toward the rising sun and a new routine. Mornings, not afternoons, are seen through sunglasses. My left arm resting on the window ledge is now in the northern shade of the camper's shadow. The strange tan I have grown—a reddish brown from elbow to wristwatch, wristwatch to fingers; sunbleached hairs on the left arm, dark hairs on the right—withers with each day. The prevailing wind is at our back, hastening us along.

I stop at familiar places and see familiar people: enjoy a bath, sweat, and massage at Carson Hot Springs; watch the *Sara Brix* going up the Columbia for another load of salmon fingerlings; buy a four-pound salmon from Kathryn Brigham in the Gorge and eat it that night with Albert Barros in Lapwai. The snows are melted enough on the Lolo Trail to permit a detour from U.S. 12 to follow the high ridges of the motorway and camp one night near the rock piles called the Indian Post Office. A spectacular Valhalla Sunset climaxes the day—bands of crimson and purple and orange and yellow slowly squeezed by the weight of the darkening sky; a sliver of a crescent moon tilting above. Forest-fire fighters, not tree planters, crowd the Lochsa Lodge at breakfast; most of them, as in my westward journey, are Indians. At the Jerry Johnson Hot Springs I meet (instead of the girls the salesman from Seattle had promised) two young men who are bicycling from California to Montana. One of them is from Maine and I fight back the urge to tell him, "You're a long way from home."

Montana's drought has deepened when I recross the Divide. Grasshoppers swarm across the highways. The *Discovery* slaughters hundreds of them as we speed along and they pelt the camper like a hailstorm. The news in the papers during breakfast at Next to Hap's Cafe in Helena includes stories about forest fires in the Rockies, the growing list of farm counties being named disaster areas, more disputes over the dwindling supplies of water, and how a sow grizzly and her cubs keep returning to raid beehives in

western Montana after being airlifted by helicopter back into the
wilderness.

I don't stop at historic markers. I already know what they say
and can pass them by without offending the Road Spirit.

ROAD RULE 23: You know you've explored a state correctly
when you start anticipating the historic markers.

There are, however, several new sights. I criss-cross Montana,
trying to cover the same terrain the expedition did when, on its
return journey, it split into separate parts at Traveller's Rest to
explore the Marias and Yellowstone watersheds. Retracing Lewis's
shortcut toward the Great Falls, I hike to the crest of Lewis and
Clark Pass, named for both explorers even though Clark never
saw it. Not far from the saddle of the pass, the coldest official
temperature ever recorded in the continental United States was hit
on January 20, 1954: minus 70 degrees. The day I labor up the
mountainside, the temperature is 165 degrees warmer than that.

Wilbur Werner, a man who hitchhiked from the Midwest to
Cut Bank, Montana (population 3,688), to set up a law practice,
gives me a hand-drawn map to find the spot on the Two Medicine
River where Lewis and three of his men fought with eight Piegan
Blackfeet after the Indians tried to steal the explorers' guns and
horses. Two of the Blackfeet were killed in the skirmish—the only
gunplay and only loss of life through hostile action during the entire
expedition. My visit is briefer than Lewis's, and more enjoyable.
The river is swift, clean, and cold, and taking a dip in it on a hot
afternoon is irresistible. I sit on the shallow, stony bottom and stare
out toward the west, where the peaks of the Rockies look like
shards of broken blue glass planted in the Plains to puncture the
tires of anyone who might dare to pass. An osprey wheels overhead.
The pleasurometer climbs into the high nines.

I pick up Clark's eastbound trail at the Three Forks, and follow
it across Bozeman Pass to the Yellowstone Valley. This takes me to
Billings (population 66,842), Montana's biggest city. It reminds me
of Great Falls, the city it surpassed when the coal and oil boom rumbled down the valley: tall buildings along dust-blown pavement,
a river and trainyards, high mountains in the distance across rolling
plains, the sense that Montana should pass a law restricting cities

to population caps of 30,000. Dejected by my farewell to the mountains, I console myself by going to a Clint Eastwood cowboy movie.

East of Billings is Pompeys Pillar, a singular two-hundred-foot sandstone bluff which Clark named in honor of the infant son of Charbonneau and Sacagawea (whom the captain had dubbed "Little Pomp"). On one side of the outcropping is the only remaining physical evidence of the Corps of Discovery along the entire route. Clark had carved his name and the date, July 25, 1806, in the soft yellow stone. It is still there, surrounded by graffiti dating from Custer and the 7th Cavalry to the other tourists who are there the same day I am.

I skip North Dakota entirely, saving time by heading straight for Pierre. The sun has already set behind me when I reach the D & E Cafe, where the food is still good, the prices still unbelievably low, the place still busy. I am tempted to buy a year's supply of food to cut costs for the next twelve months.

Cabool Chambers lets me park the *Discovery* in his front yard in Lynch, Nebraska. The big news is that the town of Gross has been sold. A family of four is moving in to take over the Nebrask-Inn and make Gross the fastest-growing town in America. *Well* . . . By percentage, anyway.

At the Harrison County fair in Iowa, the talk is that the crops are good, but prices too low. The livestock events have fewer entries than past years, and some of the farmers look anxiously at each other, probably wondering which ones won't be around for next year's fair. A satellite dish sits on display with the cultivators and tractors.

Near Omaha, the trees reappear, giving off a sultry haze in the moist summer heat. Like the mountains, the High Plains become merely a memory. A rain squall hits on the road to Kansas City, and I realize that while droughts may be the scourge of farmers, ranchers, rafters, hydropower engineers, fishermen, and forest-fire wardens, they're not bad for explorers with a cooler full of liquid refreshments.

My friends in Kansas City have a fresh bottle of B. J. Holladay Private Keep waiting for me. We stay up late sipping its musky warmth while they listen to the story of my favorite adventure of the return journey—perhaps my only real adventure, the one I deliberately saved for the trip home, just as Lewis and Clark had decided to explore the Marias and Yellowstone Rivers on their way back East. I tell the tale of trying to find a case of buried whiskey in Montana. Telling it is like going through it all again.

The Canadian Club search team gathered at Skeets Cafe in Dillon, Montana: Lee Hames, cowboy, rancher, Lewis and Clark buff, the man who organized Burma's first rodeo, the man who has already dredged a good part of Clark's Fork and the Hellgate River confluence looking for the buried treasure; Joel Bernstein, cowboy, former American-studies professor, Lewis and Clark buff, a man who says he "once thought Pittsburgh was the frontier"; Don Keysser, a young investment banker on vacation from Minneapolis I met during my horseback camping trip in the Elkhorns, a man who says he knows next to nothing about Lewis and Clark but likes the idea of trying to find a case of whiskey; and myself, a Lewis and Clark buff, would-be explorer and cowboy. None of us likes Canadian Club; we're in this because, well, it's there.

We reviewed the three critical clues from the advertisement: "We buried our case of Canadian Club overlooking the site of one of the expedition's most important sightings"; the going was rough; and neither Lewis nor Clark made the discovery. We had some additional information since Lee Hames and I first decided to explore the Beaverhead Rock region. I had called the advertising man who buried the whiskey, learning only that the case was buried in the ground, it has no nails or other metal that would make a metal detector of any help, and he relied on DeVoto's edition of the journals for his information. (He also said he is distantly related to William Bratton, one of the expedition members.) Hames had talked to the outfitter who showed the advertising man from New York around southwestern Montana's rivers for a couple of weeks in 1980. The Beaverhead was one of the rivers they rafted, he was told. Also, the adman left Missoula by car, alone except for his case of whiskey, and returned a day later without it—it would take about that amount of time for someone to get to the Dillon area, bury some treasure, spend the night, and get back to Missoula.

I had a Forest Service map of the area, which shows roads and streams in greater detail than a highway map. Hames and Bernstein brought spades and shovels from their ranches. Keysser, already caught up in the adventure, stopped at an Army surplus store to buy a camper's shovel.

Our difficulties began immediately, before we even left the cafe. If my premise was correct that the "important sighting" was when Sacagawea saw Beaverhead Rock, then how did you narrow it down to the point "overlooking the site"? You can see Beaverhead Rock from just about anywhere in Beaverhead County. We needed either an Army Corps of Engineers bulldozing crew or a coherent system. Poring over the Forest Service map, I suggested that the whiskey should be buried on public, not private land—easier access, fewer legal problems for the whiskey company, a better way to keep a secret than asking a rancher if you can dig a hole on his range. Bernstein suggested that it's probably near a road: no one, particularly someone from Madison Avenue, would want to lug a case of whiskey very far.

Now we were getting somewhere. There's a historic marker on Highway 41 on the upstream side of Beaverhead Rock, I told them. As Elfreda Woodside had explained, it's the wrong side of the landmark (the expedition first saw the giant bluff coming south from the Three Forks), but it's on public land with the easiest access by car. Hames liked this theory because of his serious doubts about the historical knowledge of anyone foolish enough to live in New York City. We took off, Keysser and me in the *Discovery*, Hames and Bernstein in Joel's car.

At the marker's turnoff, we got out and scouted around the small parking lot, looking for any signs that the land had been tampered with. On the north side was a small depression, which on closer inspection, we decided, looks about the size of a case of whiskey. Bernstein dug in with his shovel, and it clanged after about a foot. Our collective pulse quickened, and we all dug in. A rock.

Two tourists pulled up to read the historic marker. They tried not to stare at the four of us roaming the area, shouting to one another to come over and inspect various spots that don't have any grass cover. What will we tell the state trooper when he arrives to arrest us? I wondered. Hames spotted a little hump of soil that looked like a four-foot trench that has been filled in. We started digging again. The tourists were staring at us instead of the marker. Nothing.

Next theory. DeVoto's editorial comments say the expedition campsite where Lewis wrote about Sacagawea's sighting is "about twenty miles north of Dillon." We mounted our vehicles and headed up the highway, counting off the mile markers on the shoulder. Along the way, we passed Point of Rocks Cemetery, just north of Beaverhead Rock.

"What about the cemetery?" Keysser said.

"No one would be that twisted," I answered, pulling the *Discovery* over at the twenty-mile marker. Bernstein's car pulled up.

"I'll bet it's in the cemetery," Joel said as he got out.

I began getting a better understanding of gold fever.

We searched both rights-of-way next to the highway. No marks of disturbed soil, just various forms of litter.

I checked the detailed map again. A gravel road crosses the Beaverhead several miles from the highway, roughly near the spot where the expedition must have camped. A man with a car and a case of whiskey to bury could get there easily. It must be the spot, we all agreed, quickly getting into the habit of adjusting our convictions as soon as we had a new theory. The two-car convoy set out for the bridge.

It's worth remembering here that the *Discovery* has Texas license plates. I bring this up only because of the way a rancher and his wife looked out their picture window at two vehicles, one with a Montana plate and the other with a Texas plate, that pulled up across the river from their home and disgorged four men who started swarming around the area, digging exploratory holes up and down the riverbank and gesturing wildly with their arms. Over dinner that night, I'm sure they began planning how to spend their oil royalties.

Nothing again. We sat on the riverbank and reassessed. Our problem is not so much finding exactly where Sacagawea first pointed to Beaverhead Rock, but figuring out where the advertising man *thought* she saw it, I reiterated.

"Let's try to put ourselves in his mind," I suggested.

Joel still wanted to check out the cemetery.

"Well, boys," Hames said—he starts most of his sentences that way: "Well, boys . . ." or "Now, boys . . ."—"What's the *one* place that would overlook any site where Beaverhead Rock could be sighted?" We chewed on it a while, then admitted we were stumped.

"Why, the top of ol' Beaverhead Rock itself!" he said. "That's where she'll be, I'm bettin'."

Beaverhead Rock is, first of all, solid rock. Second, the reason it can be seen from great distances is that it rises about three hundred feet up out of the Beaverhead River floodplain. The midday temperature was climbing over 90 degrees.

"Let's check the cemetery," I said. As I followed Bernstein's car I could see Lee Hames talking a blue streak and pointing at the top of the landmark.

We drove through the cemetery, seeing only tombstones with epitaphs like "Alone" or "At Peace" chiseled in the stone. Even Joel agreed: no one would be that twisted to bury a case of whiskey here. Hames was still pointing at the top of Beaverhead Rock. We took off again.

At the base of the rock, we parked the cars and got out, craning our necks to look up. The cliff face is vertical on the river side, but sloped enough to climb on the back end. Three of us expressed severe doubts about a man climbing this with a heavy case of booze.

"Well, boys," Hames said, *"I'm* going to have a look." He and Bernstein, both in cowboy boots, started hiking toward a gentler slope.

Hames is the one who told me he never knew a man worth a darn who didn't have to prove himself some way. I wasn't about to stay behind and let a man nearly twice my age climb a bluff. Keysser felt the same way. He and I began a direct ascent up the side. Twenty minutes later, when we reached the summit, panting and sweating heavily, we surveyed the view: to the southwest the Beaverhead Mountains and the Continental Divide, the Pioneer Mountains on the west, the Tobacco Root and Gravelly ranges to the east; at our feet, the river curling through the valley. Far below were Bernstein's car and the *Discovery,* where Bernstein and Hames were sitting down in the camper's shadow. They waved to us from the shade.

Keysser and I scouted around the huge, humpback top of Beaverhead Rock, finding a small hole covered with a flat rock. We started digging. Nothing. My hands began to blister. Another depression in the soil, more digging, more blisters, more nothing. Just as we were about to give up, we came across a very intriguing spot: a few stones resting over a place with loose soil on the edges. We removed the stones and I shoved my spade into the soil. It was soft, real soft. As if it had been dug before.

When Clark's division of the eastbound expedition arrived at

the Camp Fortunate caches on the Beaverhead in July 1806, they
had been without tobacco for three months. Their craving for
nicotine is underscored by Clark's journal entry that many of the
men had already dismantled their tomahawk-pipes to chew the
tobacco-soaked wood in the stems. There was a supply of tobacco
in the Camp Fortunate caches, and when Clark's group got there,
he reports, the men leapt from their horses and scrambled to get
at it.

Keysser and I dug at the soft soil in probably much the same
way: crazed with anticipation. The hole got deeper. More blisters.
We took turns at the sweaty work. Three feet down we hit bedrock.

On the hike back down to the cars we scared up a coyote, who
scampered away, constantly looking over his shoulder in seeming
disbelief that any humans would be here. Keysser and I were
already talking about giving up the search and returning to Dillon
for cold beers.

When we reached Hames and Bernstein, however, they already
had a fresh theory. Near the Highway 41 bridge over the river,
next to the vertical face of Beaverhead Rock, there's a small river-
access turnoff, slightly hidden from the road by willows. A fella
could bury a case of whiskey there without being spied by passing
traffic, they had decided. Besides, they said, no one would climb
that bluff with a heavy load.

During the excavation of several holes in the riprap near the
bridge, the thought of a Montana state trooper kept recurring, and
I rehearsed my explanation about how a person with a New Hampshire driver's license and a camper with Texas plates could be
innocently digging holes in Montana and not need a psychiatric
examination before sentencing. A trout fisherman on the opposite
bank was watching us as we piled rocks back into a deep trench
we had dug. His look was suspicious. Hames didn't help matters.
With a mischievous look in his eyes, and in a voice loud enough
to carry across the water, he said, "This'll teach her for talkin'
back." Keysser lowered his head and made the sign of the cross.
*Really, officer, we weren't burying anyone, actually we were search-
ing for a case of Canadian Club; you see, our theory is this . . . No,
I don't think handcuffs are necessary.*

Back in Dillon, still clinging to the hope that our theories were
at least based on the right premise, we checked some motels to see
if the advertising man stayed there for a night five years ago. The

clerks gave us a look like the coyote's at Beaverhead Rock and explained they didn't keep their records that long.

Hames had one final idea: "Let's invite the guy out here, get us a rope, drape it over a beam and just sort of stretch him enough to make him talkative."

We ate a late lunch (Bernstein and I both had pieces of pie) and I asked them to return to the historic marker for a picture of our exploration. As I lined them up with their digging tools, Beaverhead Rock in the background, Hames turned to Bernstein.

"The West has gone to hell," he said. "Even the cowboys of Montana have shovels."

The same can probably be said for modern exploration of the West. We've come from searching for a Northwest Passage to an adman's gimmick, from caches of canoes and tobacco to cases of Canadian Club.

I snapped the photos, we said our goodbyes, and headed in opposite directions.

ROAD RULE 24: Always save some adventure for your return trip. It takes your mind off your destination.

FIRST COROLLARY: If you're going to dig for things on the way back, your chances for success are a lot higher if you're the one who buried the cache.*

Destination travel, rather than discovery travel, overtakes me when I leave Kansas City, and I switch to Interstate 70 for the final miles to St. Louis. It's just as well. The corn is growing tall in the humidity of August and it blocks any views from the two-lane roads; the broad right-of-way for the interstate offers the only thing approaching the expansive vistas I yearn for.

*A year after our quest, Bernstein sent me a clipping from the Missoula paper. The mystery had been partially solved. Two men searching in the vicinity of Beaverhead Rock (at least our theories had been right) dug up the lid to the whiskey case on July 4, 1986. But the whiskey itself was missing. A note on the lid said: "Nov. 8, 1981 No Whiskey Here Wendy Lowell Ribish." According to the paper, no one knows who Wendy Lowell Ribish is, or how she could have known to dig up a case of booze half a year before the first advertisement appeared saying it had been buried.

The monotony of the road sends my mind along its own travels.
The first stop is unresolved questions:

1. Where are the demarcation lines separating caps from cowboy hats, bags from sacks, supper from dinner, ranches from
   farms, rain from moisture, pop from soda, drafts of beer
   from draws, toothpicks in individual wrappers from plain
   toothpicks?
2. What other effects did the Texas plates on the *Discovery*
   have on the people who saw me drive up? What if the plates
   had been from New Jersey or California?
3. Is the fact that the local Rotary meets at a small-town cafe
   a good sign or a bad sign?
4. The change of roadside vandalism marks the transition from
   city (spray-painted graffiti) to country (bullet holes in the
   signs). Why do you feel safer in the places with the bullet
   holes?
5. Is a road sign that says END CONSTRUCTION a marker or a
   political statement?
6. Why are there "Western wear" stores in every region of the
   nation, but no "Eastern wear" or "Southern wear" stores in
   any region?
7. Which tribe—the Mandan and Hidatsas or the Nez Perce—
   would Lewis and Clark think got the rawest deal from the
   "White Father"?
8. Now that the coal and oil boom of the West seems about
   to go bust, what will the next boom be?
9. Why, with the exception of the first homesteading on the
   frontier, have there been no sustained farming booms, but
   instead a steady decline marked only by periodical drops
   into new busts?
10. How many miles of fence are there in Montana?
11. Why do the television commercials that are meant to make
    us feel good about America and buy the product being hawked
    usually highlight scenes of farmers, cowboys, small towns,
    Indians, and other endangered species?
12. Is the fact that I remember the good times of my expedition
    more vividly than the bad times an individual version of a
    nation's myth-making?

The smell of a dead skunk seeps into the *Discovery,* prompting another unresolved question: "Why do you smell a skunk carcass after you've passed it but not before?"

Then the other smells of the trip come wafting back in memory: the steamy, industrial smell of St. Louis; fresh-cut hay and a tinge of manure in the Farm Belt, startlingly sweet and brief; the Omaha stockyards, overpowering on a hot day; the musty, claustrophobic air of the SAC bunker, like a tomb; smoke in an earth lodge; buffalo, which smells like, well, buffalo; dust caking your nose on a back road in Montana; sage pungent after a rain and even the air cleansed by lightning; horse sweat, a smell *and* a feel, rank and sticky; trout frying in a pan, a smell *and* a sound, as is an open campfire; snow and pine and cedar in the Bitterroots; sulfur from hot springs; the permeating scent from a pulp mill that makes you wrinkle your nose and look to see if someone else is in the passenger seat; baked air on the Columbia plateau desert; fish and seaweed in the bays near Astoria, fresh and stagnant at the same time.

The interstate crosses the Missouri River halfway to St. Louis, and near Rocheport is a sign for the Lewis and Clark 24-Hour Wrecking Service. Another question: What would the captains make of all the namesakes left in their wake? Not the rivers, hills, streams, or landmarks they named in their own and the other members' honor. Not the towns, national forests, counties, schools, colleges, cafes, motels, and tourist shops that bear their names. What would they think of places like the Lewis-Clark Chiropractic Information Bureau in Clarkston, the Lewis and Clark Search and Rescue Association in Montana, the Lewis and Clark Distillery a few miles from where they ran out of whiskey, the animal shelter with a Pepsi logo, or, given Lewis's moodiness, the Lewis and Clark Mental Health Center in Yankton?

The interstate stretches out in a straight line. Road Rule 11 is fully activated now. The faster the *Discovery* moves forward, the farther back in time it sends my thoughts—back to the final leg of the Corps of Discovery's return journey.

The expedition's intense desire to get home had not taken the snows of the Bitterroots into account. They arrived in the land of the Nez Perce in early May and had to remain there until the last week of June, when they finally ascended the mountain barrier and reached Traveller's Rest. Their trade goods virtually gone, the explorers used coat buttons, empty phials, and tin boxes to exchange for roots and dogs to eat. Clark's medical treatments became the expedition's main source of barter for supplies, and across the West he left behind a reputation as a great healer.

Nez Perce oral history indicates he left something else behind, as well. When Chief Joseph's band surrendered to the Army in 1877, the officers were shown a redheaded Nez Perce prisoner the Indians said was the son of Captain Clark. Whether Clark took part in the same cross-cultural practices as the men throughout the journey is impossible to verify, other than this one piece of tribal lore. While the journals mention sexual liaisons between the rest of the expedition and the natives—although often circumspectly—they include nothing about Lewis or Clark's nighttime activities.

ROAD RULE 25: Keep a journal of your travels. It is an invaluable tool to remind you of your trip, and the details within it are important for recounting history and the mark you leave upon it.

CLARK'S COROLLARY: If traveling with other people, always volunteer to be the journal writer. That way, yours will be the version of history that is recorded.

At Traveller's Rest, the expedition divided. Lewis headed east to follow the shortcut to Great Falls, and then took a smaller party north to explore the Marias River. After the fight with the Blackfeet, his group proceeded down the Missouri to rejoin Clark's. In western North Dakota, while hunting elk with Pierre Cruzatte (an expert boatman and good fiddle player, but a poor marksman because of his one eye), Lewis was severely wounded when Cruzatte mistook him for their quarry and fired a round that ripped his left thigh and sliced through his right buttock. Lewis didn't recover until a month later.

Clark went southeast from Traveller's Rest to the cache of canoes and supplies at Camp Fortunate. At the Three Forks, his group also divided: part went by canoe down the Missouri to join Lewis's party; Clark went east to the Yellowstone. (At one point on the return trip, the expedition was split into five separate groups across Montana.)

The Corps of Discovery reunited between the mouth of the Yellowstone and the Mandan villages. Charbonneau, Sacagawea, and the infant remained at the villages; the interpreter was paid $500.33⅓ for his work. Colter left the expedition here and went out West with some trappers, destined later to discover "Colter's Hell" and write his own colorful pages of history. A Mandan chief was persuaded to accompany the captains back to Washington to meet Jefferson.

Heading downriver, the explorers encountered a band of Teton Sioux in South Dakota, exchanged unpleasantries from canoe to riverbank, and proceeded on. They visited Floyd's Bluff and repaired the sergeant's damaged grave. Two days later, on September 6, 1806, they met a trading boat and purchased a gallon of whiskey, the first the men had tasted in fourteen months.

More and more trading expeditions started appearing below the mouth of the Platte. The captains traded information of their journey into the unknown for news from home: Zebulon Pike had already left on America's second major exploration of the West; Aaron Burr had killed Alexander Hamilton in a duel; tensions between the United States and England were rising; the Corps of Discovery, having not sent a courier back from the Great Falls the previous summer as they had promised Jefferson in a letter from the winter quarters at Fort Mandan, "had been long Since given out [up] by the people of the U S Generaly and almost forgotten, the President of the ,U. States had yet hopes of us."

Propelled by their own destination travel and the Missouri's strong current, they sometimes covered seventy to eighty miles a day. As they neared St. Charles, they saw a few new settlements farther west than any had been in 1804.

On September 21, a Sunday, they pulled their canoes into St. Charles, saluting the village with "three rounds from our blunderbuts and the Small arms of the party." They stayed a second day to celebrate, buy supplies, and wait for the rains to stop. After an early breakfast on the twenty-third (a "wet disagreeable morning," according to Ordway), they proceeded on as an expedition for the last time. The Corps of Discovery canoed to the mouth of the Missouri, paddled across for a brief visit to Camp Wood, which they had left twenty-eight months earlier, and then floated down the Mississippi to a triumphant greeting at the docks of St. Louis.

The men were given double pay and 320 acres of land for their part in the expedition. Except for a few, little is known about the later years of this contingent that made history. Colter became a mountain-man legend. Drouillard and John Potts were killed by Blackfeet at the Three Forks on trapping expeditions. Some of the men reenlisted and served in the War of 1812. Nathaniel Pryor led the first attempt to return the Mandan chief to North Dakota, but was turned back by hostile Arikaras and Sioux; young Shannon was wounded in the battle and had to have a leg amputated. Pryor later married an Osage woman and lived with the tribe in Oklahoma (where a town is named for him). Shannon went on to become a legislator in Kentucky, then a state senator and U.S. attorney in Missouri. Patrick Gass published his journal in 1807 and outlived the rest of the party, dying in 1870 at the age of ninety-nine.

The fate of Clark's slave, York, is somewhat of a mystery. Accounts differ on when, and under what circumstances, Clark gave him his freedom, as well as what York did with it. Most believe he went into the freighting business with a team and wagon, failed at the business, and died of cholera at an unknown date sometime before 1832 in Tennessee. One legend holds that "Big Medicine" returned to the West, where he lived out his life among the Crow Indians.

According to statements by Clark and the trader at Fort Manuel in South Dakota, Sacagawea died there in December 1812; the Sacajawea of the novels lived until 1884, dying in Wyoming near the age of one hundred. "Little Pomp" was educated by Clark in St. Louis, toured Europe, roamed the West as a mountain man, dug for gold in the California Rush of '49, returned to the "great waters" he had visited as a year-old infant, and died in Oregon in 1866. Charbonneau stayed among the Mandans and Hidatsas, taking more Indian wives into his dotage, and died in either 1839 or 1840.

Clark married Julia Hancock, for whom he had named the Judith River, in 1808 and made St. Louis his home. His reward for his historic effort was 1,600 acres of land and being made Indian Agent for the Louisiana Territory. During his later career, he remained as head of Indian affairs for the western tribes, who fondly referred to him as the "Red-Headed Chief" and considered him an advocate on their behalf; served as the first appointed governor of the Missouri Territory, once Louisiana was made a state (he was reappointed three times until Missouri became a state in 1821, when he lost the election for governor); profited as a business partner in fur companies; and, as a respected source of information on the geography and people of the West, was consulted by anyone passing through St. Louis on the way to the new land he had first explored.

His last journal entry on the historic expedition, on September 26, 1806, was brief: "a fine morning we commenced wrighting &c." In 1838, at the age of sixty-nine, he died in St. Louis at the home of his eldest son, Meriwether Lewis Clark.

When the expedition arrived back in St. Louis, Lewis immediately wrote a letter to Jefferson, opening with the "pleasure" of announcing the safe return of himself and his party and stating that "In obedience to your orders we have penitrated the Continent of North America to the Pacific Ocean" and found "the most practicable rout" to the western sea. Then came the bad news: the long-desired passage from the Missouri to the Columbia (the shortcut Lewis had taken on the return trip) was no one-day portage but 340 miles from the Great Falls to the Clearwater River. "The passage by land of 340 miles . . . is the most formidable part of the tract proposed across the Continent; of this distance 200 miles along a good road, and 140 over tremendious mountains which for 60 mls. are covered with eternal snows." It was passable, but would not replace a sea route as the best way to the Orient.

Nonetheless, Lewis wrote his president, the Missouri and its tributaries abounded "more in beaver and Common Otter, than any other stream on earth." A profitable empire was there for the United States, "if the government will only aid, even in a very limited manner, the enterprize of her Citizens . . . and in the course of ten or twelve years a tour across the Continent by the rout mentioned will be undertaken by individuals with as little concern as a voyage across the Atlantic is at present."

Lewis was appointed governor of the Louisiana Territory and awarded 1,600 acres of land. The following years, leading up to his untimely death at age thirty-five in 1809, were troubled times for the explorer-turned-bureaucrat. As settlers and merchants began populating the new territory, problems multiplied and piled up on his desk: rival trading companies seeking concessions; squabbles over land titles; squatters on federal and Indian lands; friction between the tribes and the traders and settlers. Lewis and his assistant bickered openly over policy. A change in administration in Washington ended Jefferson's imprimatur on the leader of his dream-project, and the new people in power began questioning Lewis's supervision of America's expanding frontier. Expenditures, especially one made to return the Mandan chief to his home on the Upper Missouri, were challenged. Lewis's personal debts rose, and work on publication of his and Clark's journals bogged down as the two men focused on their new duties.

In September 1809, Lewis decided to go back East to settle his differences with officials in Washington and hasten along the long-delayed publication of the journals. He gave Clark the authority to sell his property, packed up the journals, and set off down the Mississippi. A week later, he made out his last will and testament. A commander at Memphis noted that Lewis was in a "state of mental derangement" and after learning from the boat crew that they had twice prevented the governor from committing suicide, he temporarily detained Lewis and guarded the valuable journals. When Lewis seemed to recover, the journey was resumed, but because of increased naval tensions with England he decided to make the trip to Washington overland, instead of by sea.

On October 10, he arrived at Grinder's Stand, a small inn on the Natchez Trace in Tennessee. Turning down Mrs. Grinder's offer of a bed, Meriwether Lewis spent the last night of his life on the bearskins and buffalo robes he had brought along and spread on the floor. At 3 A.M. on the eleventh, Mrs. Grinder was awakened by two gunshots in Lewis's room. She and the servants found him with a wound in the head and breast. He died within a few hours, just as the sun was rising. They buried him nearby the same day. (The grave site, which I visit on my way home, is marked by a solitary column, broken at the top to symbolize Lewis's early death. The base includes an inscription paraphrasing Jefferson's words about the explorer: "His courage was undaunted; his firmness and perseverance yielded to nothing but impossibilities; a rigid disci-

plinarian yet tender as a father of those committed to his charge;
honest, disinterested, liberal, with a sound understanding and a
scrupulous fidelity to truth.")

Whether Lewis took his own life or was murdered has never
been proven. In the late 1800s, the popular notion was that he was
killed during a robbery. The Natchez Trace was a notoriously
dangerous road, and the murder theory was easier for people to
accept than the thought that a national hero would do himself in
at so young an age. Opinion is still divided, although many scholars
believe the circumstantial evidence points to suicide. In this, they
agree with Clark and Jefferson. The president wrote that Lewis
had exhibited "hypochondriac affections" and "sensible depressions
of mind" while serving as his private secretary, traits Jefferson said
were common in Lewis's kin. When Clark learned his fellow explorer was dead, he exclaimed, "I fear O! I fear the weight of his
mind has overcome him."

Sixteen of the expedition's members were dead by 1828, an
unusual number of premature deaths for a group that had survived
such adversity. Not counting Floyd's, only six undisputed grave
sites, including Lewis's and Clark's, can still be found where their
remains now lie. All that can be hoped is that as each member of
the Corps of Discovery embarked on his final voyage, he found
the Passage and proceeded on.

The cackle of the CB brings my thoughts back to the present and
to navigating the *Discovery* into St. Louis. A trucker is trying to
sell his radar detector; hookers and drug pushers are making deals;
another trucker is complaining about the four-wheelers in his way
on the fast lane.

A convoy is forming and one truck is lagging behind.

"Cain't you go move it up some?"

"My big ol' truck won't go that fast."

"It's not your truck that's the problem."

"Pedal won't go no farther than the floor, will it?"

"Oh, it'll go farther than the floor. When you feel your toenails
scratching on the road, you got her all the way down."

Another truck pulls out to pass the convoy and is invited to join
a space in the group.

"Just pull 'er on over now."

"No thankee. Ah got a long way to go and a short time to git there."
"Ah heard that."

When I pull into my hotel, the *Discovery*'s odometer registers 15,585 miles since we left Wood River three months ago.

I had departed from this area with a camper loaded with sup- plies, a stack of blank notebooks and tape cassettes, an American itch to travel west toward the setting sun, and, depite my modern maps and my history books, only the vaguest notions of what I would discover. Excitement and undefined expectations were packed along with the other essential baggage for my journey.

If it was adventure I was after, I'd had a few. Skinned two buffalo bulls, slept in an earth lodge, rode a horse down a moun- tainside in total darkness, took a raft and a canoe along some untamed stretches of rushing river. I had learned the pleasures of mineral baths, hot springs, and sweat lodges; had suffered the pain of a "wreck" on a horse trail. Survived an encounter with a dan- gerous chocolate-covered huckleberry.

If my purpose was sightseeing, I had seen my share. Eleven states, comprising more than a quarter of the continental United States's landmass, had been touched. The corners and boundaries of some were all I had seen, but a few had been covered extensively and I had driven through the heart of many. At various times I had been within short distances of the population center and geo- graphic center of America. It was not just the heart of some states, but the heart of the nation I had visited. Along the way, I had witnessed majesty in the land: purple mountains and spacious skies and fruited plains and amber waves of grain. Things worthy of song. And sunsets, oh so many sunsets, that stop you in your travels, force you to drink in their colors and replenish your spirit with their richness so you are eager to follow the sun once more when it heads west again the next morning.

History? I had bumped into it and its constant companion, myth, at every stop. They twine together and grow on the roadside, like the bramble and the rose, increasingly hard to separate. Jesse James and Joseph Smith, Custer and Sitting Bull, mountain men and cowboys—they and many others existed once in fact; they live on in myth, exerting as much or more influence on *our* present as they did on their own. The myth industry is the only one that has always boomed and never gone bust.

At three places—the White Cliffs, the Bitterroots, and Fort Clatsop—the sights and experiences had seemed to closely approximate the explorers'. Four, if you count tasting an unsweetened, boiled bitterroot.

I suppose one of my expectations had been the hope of "finding America"—one single individual, a particular place on the map, some illuminating moment or situation that might explain a nation and its history. Unloading the contents of the *Discovery* in the hotel parking lot, I find that such a souvenir is not among my possessions. I have instead a Stetson hat with a rattlesnake band, a secondhand guitar, the remnant of a medicinal root, a pair of cowboy boots that are now well broken in and dusty, pamphlets and brochures and town histories—and a menu from the D & E Cafe—and a stack of filled notebooks, rolls of exposed film, and tapes with the voices of many people. These are things I didn't have when I first set off. They are things I can keep—trophies I can display at home like the stuffed animals and plant specimens Lewis presented to Jefferson for Monticello. Treasured as they are, however, they are only tokens of my journey, lifeless artifacts that bear the same relationship to my total experience as a mounted buffalo head does to a whole living and breathing buffalo.

But I can put the hat on my head, rest my boots on a table, and lean back to let my mind wander up the long reach of the Missouri River in search of a Passage. There will be sights and sounds and smells I will remember, and snippets of history and myth. But most of all I will remember the people I met. Some became friends. A few didn't like me, nor I them. I spent weeks with some, a couple of minutes with others. From Amish farmer to SAC captain, barge pilot to Indian fisherwoman, buffalo hunter to grizzly specialist, big-city businessman to small-town resident or hobo king, from those fighting to hold on to their land to those who already lost theirs—each one had his or her own personal dream to follow and definition of happiness to pursue. Taken together, and mixed with the vast landscape they inhabit and the history they share, they were not necessarily what I began searching for, but they are what I found.

Lewis and Clark went out West looking for the Northwest Passage and returned instead with information about geography, plants, animals, and people. Those who followed went seeking other things—furs, minerals, homesteads, fame, and fortune, to name a few. Most didn't find what they thought they wanted, but many didn't regret that they went.

I had left the Rainbow Arch and gone out West with less specific goals in mind, intent on merely traveling an old trail and happy to have the freedom to pursue it. The only thing I actively *searched* for, a hidden case of Canadian Club, proved as elusive to me as the Northwest Passage was to the Corps of Discovery. Like the explorers before me, I have learned something in my travels.

ROAD RULE 26: The final value of any expedition is not what you failed to discover but what you found in its place; the important thing is not so much the dream you pursued but the fact that you pursued it. Looking back on your journey, what you remember most is not what you were searching for, but the search itself.

Along with members of the Lewis and Clark Trail Heritage Foundation, I immerse myself in three days of expedition lore during their annual meeting in St. Louis. We tour museums, take field trips to Camp Wood, explore the Arch, and listen to lectures. We buzz with excitement over the latest in the controversies over names in the expedition: Donald Jackson has a story in *We Proceeded On* arguing with authority that Lewis's Newfoundland dog was named Seaman, not Scannon as previously believed. Most of the time, as at any convention, we socialize. Always, the topic returns to the Corps of Discovery.

Elfreda Woodside couldn't come from her nursing home in Montana. It's too bad. The day we visit Clark's grave there's a one-day baseball strike, so she wouldn't have had to choose between the Cardinals and the captain. Clark's burial site is on a hill looking west toward the Missouri, with a tall obelisk graced with a bust of the explorer at its base. Unlike Lewis's grave, so sadly solitary in a confined opening in the Tennessee woods, Clark's remains are in a large cemetery, surrounded by the plots of his family, friends, and servants. At one corner of the monument is a quotation from Deuteronomy: "Behold, the Lord thy God hath set the land before thee: go up and possess it." His epitaph includes words with special meaning for the captain who carved his name in so many trees and stones throughout the West: "Soldier, explorer, statesman and patriot. His life is written in the history of his country."

On my last night in St. Louis, the foundation charters the paddle-wheeler *Huck Finn* for a dinner cruise on the Mississippi. While most everyone else is below decks singing popular songs with lyrics rewritten to fit the expedition (to the tune of "Row, Row, Row Your Boat": "Row, row, row your boat; row in agony; mosquito bites and sunburnt eyes; why did they leave St. Louie?"), I go to the stern deck for some fresh air.

William Clark Adreon is standing there. His face bears a strong resemblance to the bust at Captain Clark's grave. We chat for a few minutes, until another member comes up and asks for his autograph. Like his ancestor, always willing to leave his name marked on something, he takes the piece of paper and scrawls across it, "Great-Great-Grandson, Wm. Clark Adreon, Nothing Better Than the West," and then goes below to join the singing.

The *Huck Finn* churns into its dock, not far from where the Corps of Discovery beached their canoes for the last time in 1806, after following one dream out West and returning to plant the seeds for many more. The sun has already set. A beacon light at the top of the Rainbow Arch shines in the night.

Acknowledgments

Conversations across fences, interviews over coffee in someone's kitchen, offers of meals and places to spend the night, little kindnesses that a lonesome traveler learns to savor and treasure—all these things were given freely to me with no expectation of something in return, and by more people than can be recounted in this space. Whether they have been mentioned in this book or not, my hope is that those who befriended me will consider themselves in some small way repaid for their generosity by whatever worth they find in these pages.

Several Lewis and Clark scholars have been unselfish in their time and guidance and helpfulness. James Ronda, John Logan Allen, and Joseph Porter, upon whose knowledge and published works I have relied heavily, were kind enough to read the manuscript with an eye for historical accuracy. I have nothing to offer in return except my deep thanks. Gary Moulton, who is in charge of a new edition of the Lewis and Clark journals in progress at the University of Nebraska, was of greater assistance than he knew during several brief encounters at the annual meeting of the Lewis and Clark Trail Heritage Foundation in St. Louis, when he patiently and readily answered questions I peppered him with during long tour-bus rides. Those who have read the insightful works of Paul Cutright, Donald Jackson, and the late Bernard DeVoto will see their influence on the historical sections of this book; their books were as important as road maps.

Out and back on the long trail, whenever I needed encouragement or assistance in their locale, members of the Lewis and Clark Heritage Foundation were there to help in any way they could. In particular, Elfreda Woodside's spirit was an inspiration, E. G. Chuinard's enthusiasm infectious, and Wilbur Werner's handwritten map invaluable. Marilyn Clark and Patti Thomsen loaned me books that I could not find elsewhere. John Foote gave me a tour of Pompeys Pillar; Bob Saindon provided an alternative view of Sacagawea's name. Roy Craft treated me to dinner and some good stories about the Columbia River. Bob Lange deserves special

[417]

recognition for plugging me into this remarkable network. If this book has whetted anyone's appetite for more about Lewis and Clark's expedition, I urge them to join the foundation by writing for a membership application, and the group's periodical, *We Proceeded On,* at 5054 S.W. 26th Place, Portland, Oregon 97201. Annual meetings are more like family reunions than conferences and a joy to attend.

The New Hampshire State Library, and especially Stella J. Scheckter, the director of the library's reference and loan division, deserve thanks for trusting me with their eight-volume edition of the journals on my trips, and for allowing me to monopolize their other Lewis and Clark books at home during the writing of this book. Various employees of the National Park Service made my research not only fruitful but enjoyable, and they taught me a greater respect for the professionalism of the people entrusted with our nation's treasure of parks.

For those who gave me a bed or couch or place to park my camper for a night, I wish to add my thanks to the small bottle of New Hampshire maple syrup I left behind: Peter and Kate Goelz, Joseph Porter, Dennis Hastings, Cabool Chambers, Steve Holen, Gerard and Mary Kay Baker, Bob Buzzas, Jim Robbins, Jyl Hoyt, Joel Bernstein, Albert Barros, and Marie Pampush.

Michael Larkin and Ande Zellman of the *Boston Globe Magazine* made my first trip in pursuit of Lewis and Clark's trail possible, and their faith in the idea and publication of my first recounting of the journey is something for which I will always be grateful. Similarly, Chuck Verrill, my editor at Viking Penguin, provided not only much-needed editorial guidance but friendly encouragement.

Finally, family and friends were an important part of this effort. Don Mitchell, Peter Goelz, and Ernest Hebert are traveling companions of mine of long standing; conversations, observations, and theories dating from past journeys with them have worked their way into this book. Ernest Hebert, who writes better than I can ever hope to, read this manuscript as it was being written and offered gentle criticism, as did Bob Trebilcock, Joel Bernstein, Ben Fisher, and Charles Kenney. My sister, Dawn Duncan, and her husband, William Kendall, made the contribution of their Volkswagen camper (and permitted me to rename it for the purposes of my expedition); 16,000 miles later, I returned it with nothing more than brotherly love for repayment. Throughout the long and sometimes lonely stretches of my travels, and during the stresses and strains of putting the experience onto paper, Dianne Kearns has been either in my thoughts or at my side. Had I been Lewis or Clark, I would have named a river for her. Instead, she has had to settle for my off-and-on presence, one lovely sunset in the Bitterroot Mountains, and putting up with all the troubles of associating with a would-be author whose second love is the open road.

Bibliography

The works of John Allen, Paul Cutright, E. G. Chuinard, Donald Jackson, and James Ronda, as well as the DeVoto and Thwaites editions of the journals, are specifically mentioned in the text because of their importance in preparing this book. They were indispensable for me. However, if someone were to ask me what *one* book to get to learn about the Lewis and Clark expedition, I would recommend Roy Appleman's; the first half of his book contains a thorough yet succinct narrative of the expedition, and the second half locates and describes modern sites along the trail for those who wish to follow the explorers.

In addition to the sources listed below, much of the historical information in this book came from pamphlets and museum programs available from local and state historical societies and national parks. *We Proceeded On,* the periodical published by the Lewis and Clark Trail Heritage Foundation Inc., was also a valuable source.

Allen, John L. *Passage through the Garden: Lewis and Clark and the Image of the American Northwest.* Urbana: University of Illinois Press, 1975.

Appleman, Roy E. *Lewis and Clark: Historic Places Associated with their Transcontinental Exploration.* Washington, D.C.: National Park Service, 1975.

Bakeless, John. *Lewis and Clark: Partners in Discovery.* New York: William Morrow, 1947.

Betts, Robert B. *In Search of York: The Slave Who Went to the Pacific with Lewis and Clark.* Boulder: Colorado Associated University Press, 1985.

Billington, Roy Allen. *The Westward Movement in the United States.* Princeton: D. Van Nostrand, 1959.

Chuinard, Eldon G. *Only One Man Died: The Medical Aspects of the Lewis and Clark Expedition.* Glendale: Arthur H. Clark Co., 1979.

Connell, Evan S. *Son of the Morning Star: Custer and the Little Bighorn.* San Francisco: North Point Press, 1984.

Coues, Elliott, ed. *History of the Expedition under the Command of Lewis and Clark.* 4 vols. in 3. 1893. Reprint. New York: Dover Publications, 1964.

Cutright, Paul R. *Lewis and Clark: Pioneering Naturalists.* Urbana: University of Illinois Press, 1969.

DeVoto, Bernard, ed. *The Journals of Lewis and Clark*. Boston: Houghton Mifflin, 1953.

———. *Across the Wide Missouri*. Boston: Houghton Mifflin, 1947.

———. *The Course of Empire*. Boston: Houghton Mifflin, 1952.

Dillon, Richard. *Meriwether Lewis: A Biography*. New York: Coward McCann, 1965.

Gass, Patrick. *A Journal of the Voyages and Travels of a Corps of Discovery*. Edited by David McKeehan. 1807. Reprint. Minneapolis: Ross and Haines, 1958.

Hawke, David Freeman. *Those Tremendous Mountains: The Story of the Lewis and Clark Expedition*. New York: W. W. Norton & Co., 1980.

Jackson, Donald, ed. *Letters of the Lewis and Clark Expedition with Related Documents, 1783–1854.* 2d ed. 2 vols. Urbana: University of Illinois Press, 1978.

———. *Thomas Jefferson and the Stony Mountains: Exploring the West from Monticello*. Urbana: University of Illinois Press, 1981.

Josephy, Alvin M., Jr. *The Nez Perce Indians and the Opening of the Northwest*. New Haven: Yale University Press, 1965.

———. *Chief Joseph's People and Their War*. Bozeman, Montana: Yellowstone Library and Museum Association and National Park Service, 1964.

Libby, O. G., ed. *The Arikara Narrative of the Campaign against the Hostile Dakotas, June 1876*. New York: Sol Lewis, 1973.

Matthiessen, Peter. *In the Spirit of Crazy Horse*. New York: Viking Press, 1980.

McHugh, Tom. *The Time of the Buffalo*. 1972. Reprint. Lincoln: University of Nebraska Press, 1979.

McNamee, Thomas. *The Grizzly Bear*. New York: Alfred A. Knopf, 1984.

Morris, Edmund. *The Rise of Theodore Roosevelt*. New York: Coward, McCann & Geoghegan, 1979.

Neihardt, John G. *The River and I*. 1910. Reprint. Lincoln: University of Nebraska Press, 1968.

Osgood, Ernest S., ed. *The Field Notes of Captain William Clark, 1803–1805*. New Haven: Yale University Press, 1964.

Porter, Joseph C. *Paper Medicine Man: John Gregory Bourke and his American West*. Norman: University of Oklahoma Press, 1986.

Quaife, Milo M., ed. *The Journals of Captain Meriwether Lewis and Sergeant John Ordway*. Madison: Historical Society of Wisconsin, 1916.

Ronda, James P. *Lewis and Clark Among the Indians*. Lincoln: University of Nebraska Press, 1984.

Roosevelt, Theodore. *The Winning of the West*. New York: G. P. Putnam's Sons, 1889.

Settle, William A., Jr. *Jesse James Was his Name: Or, Fact and Fiction Concerning the Careers of the Notorious James Brothers of Missouri.* 1966. Reprint. Lincoln: University of Nebraska Press, 1977.

Snyder, Gerald S. *In the Footsteps of Lewis and Clark.* Washington, D.C.: National Geographic Society, 1970.

Space, Ralph. *Lewis and Clark through Idaho.* Lewiston, Idaho: Tribune Publishing Co., 1964.

Steffen, Jerome O. *William Clark: Jeffersonian Man on the Frontier.* Norman: University of Oklahoma Press, 1977.

Sullivan, Walter. *Landprints: On the Magnificent American Landscape.* New York: Times Books, 1984.

Thwaites, Reuben G. ed. *The Original Journals of the Lewis and Clark Expedition.* 8 vols. New York: Dodd, Mead and Co., 1904–1905.

Toole, K. Ross. *Montana: An Uncommon Land.* Norman: University of Oklahoma Press, 1959.

Turner, Frederick. *The Frontier in American History.* New York: Holt and Co., 1921.

Vestal, Stanley. *The Missouri.* 1945. Reprint. Lincoln: University of Nebraska Press, 1964.

Webb, Walter Prescott. *The Great Plains.* 1931. Reprint. Lincoln: University of Nebraska Press, 1981.

Wheeler, Olin D. *The Trail of Lewis and Clark, 1804–1904.* 2 vols. New York: G. P. Putnam's Sons, 1904.

Index